Musical Constructions of Nationalism

Musical Constructions of Nationalism:
Essays on the History and Ideology of European Musical Culture 1800–1945

edited by
HARRY WHITE and
MICHAEL MURPHY

First published in 2001 by
Cork University Press
University College
Cork
Ireland

© the editors and contributors 2001

All rights reserved. No part of this book may be reprinted
or reproduced or utilized in any electronic, mechanical or other
means, now known or hereafter invented, including photocopying and
recording or otherwise, without either the prior written permission
of the Publishers or a licence permitting restricted copying in
Ireland issued by the Irish Copyright Licensing Agency Ltd,
The Irish Writers' Centre, 19 Parnell Square, Dublin 1.

British Library Cataloguing-in-Publication Data
Musical constructions of nationalism / edited by Harry White and Michael
Murphy
 p. cm.
 Includes biographical references and index.
 ISBN 1-85918-153-8 (alk. paper) – ISBN 1-85918-322-0 (pbk.: alk.
paper
 1. Music–Europe–19th century–History and criticism. 2.
Music–Europe–20th centuryHistory and criticism. 3. Nationalism in
Music.   I. White, Harry, 1958-   . II. Murphy, Michael, 1968-   .
 ML240.1.M86 2001
 781.5'5'99'09–dc21
                                00-065880

ISBN 1 85918 153 8 hardback
ISBN 1 85918 322 0 paperback

Typeset by Tower Books, Ballincollig, Co. Cork
Printed by MPG Books Ltd, Cornwall

Contents

Notes on Contributors — vii
Acknowledgments — xi

Introduction — 1
Michael Murphy

1. Béla Bartók and the Question of Race Purity in Music — 16
   David Cooper

2. Grove's Musical Dictionary: A National Document — 33
   Jeremy Dibble

3. Eros and Paneuropeanism: Szymanowski's Utopian Vision — 51
   Stephen Downes

4. Gendering the Nations: The Ideologies of French Discourse on Music (1870–1914) — 72
   Annegret Fauser

5. Against Germanic Reasoning: The Search for a Russian Style of Musical Argumentation — 104
   Marina Frolova-Walker

6. Horn Calls and Flattened Sevenths: Nielsen and Danish Musical Style — 123
   Daniel Grimley

7. Following Grieg: David Monrad Johansen's Musical Style in the Early Twenties, and His Concept of a National Music — 142
   Ståle Kleiberg

8. Moniuszko and Musical Nationalism in Poland — 163
   Michael Murphy

9. Music and Nationalism in Italy — 181
   John Rosselli

10. The Tone of Defiance — 197
    Joe Ryan

11. The Political Parlour: Identity and Ideology in Scottish
    National Song   212
    Steve Sweeney-Turner

12. Wagner's Children: Incest and *Bruderzwist*   239
    Robert Vilain

13. Nationalism, Colonialism and the Cultural Stasis of Music
    in Ireland   257
    Harry White

Bibliography   273
Index   275

Notes on Contributors

David Cooper

David Cooper is a Senior Lecturer in Music at the University of Leeds. He is the author of the *Cambridge Music Handbook* on Bartok's Concerto for orchestra, is a contributor to the forthcoming *Cambridge Companion to Bartok*, and the author of a number of articles and conference papers about the composer. His other interests include Irish music, and in particular, the collection of George Petrie, and Music and Technology. He is currently the director of a major British Academy funded project whose intended outcome is an optical recognition system of handwritten music manuscript.

Jeremy Dibble

Jeremy Dibble read music at Trinity College, Cambridge and the University of Southampton before being appointed Lecturer in Music at University College, Cork in 1987. While at Cork he published his first major book with Oxford University Press on the life and music of Sir Hubert Parry. In 1993 he joined the staff at the University of Durham where he is now Reader in Music and Head of Department. He has written widely on British and Irish music of the Victorian, Edwardian and Georgian eras, has written articles for numerous periodicals, journals and dictionaries (including the forthcoming, *The New Dictionary of National Biography*, and the revised *Oxford Companion to Music*), and has acted as editorial consultant on the music of Parry and Stanford for various recording companies. Recent publications include essays for Vaughan Williams in perspective (1998), *To Talent Alone: The Royal Irish Academy 1848–1998*, (1998), and *Music in Twentieth-Century Britain*. He is now finishing a major study on Sir Charles Villiers Stanford of Oxford University Press.

Stephen Downes

Stephen Downes is Lecturer in Music, at the University of Surrey. Since his PhD ('Szymanowski as Post-Wagnerian', published by Garland, 1994), he has published several articles and reviews on Szymanowski. He is a frequent visitor to Poland as teacher and public speaker. He won the 1988 Wilk Prize for Research in Polish Music and in 1999 was awarded the Karol Szymanowski Memorial Medal. His recent research has investigated the issue of music and eroticism in a range of 19th and

20th-century contexts, including Kierkegaard, Schumann, Bartok, Poulenc and Penderecki.

Annegret Fauser

Annegret Fauser studied musicology, art history and philosophy at the University of Bonn where she gained her PhD. She spent five years in Paris, first as a postgraduate student at the Ecole Normale Supérieure, and later as a post-doctoral fellow at the Maison des Sciences de l'Homme. From 1993 to 1995 she taught musicology at the Humboldt-Universität in Berlin. She is now lecturer in music at City University, London. She has published a book on french orchestral song 1870–1920, articles on 19th-century and early 20th-century music. She is currently editing Othmar Schoeck's opera Venus for the Othmar-Schoeck-Gesamtausgabe (Zurich) and writing a book about women and musical culture in *fin-de-siècle* Paris. She has also edited a collaborative volume on french orchestral song (Paris, 1999) and is co-editing a major publication on Wagnerism in French music and musical culture: Annegret Fauser & Manuela Schwartz, *von Wagner zum Wagnèrisme: Music, Literature, Kunst, Politik* (forthcoming Leipziger Universitätsverlag, 1999).

Marina Frolova-Walker

Dr Marina Frolova-Walker is University Lecturer in the Faculty of Music and Fellow of Clare College. Before coming to Cambridge, she taught at the Moscow Conservatoire College, the University of Ulster, Goldsmiths' College London and University of Southampton. Her principal fields of research are German Romanticism, Russian and Soviet music and nationalism in music. She has published articles in *The Cambridge Opera Journal* and the *Journal of the American Musicological Society*, as well as contributed some of the Russian entries in the *Revised New Grove*. She is currently writing *Russia: Music and Nation*, commissioned by the Yale University Press.

Daniel Grimley

Daniel Grimley completed his PhD (Nielsen, Nationalism and Danish Musical Style) at King's College, Cambridge in 1998, before taking up a Junior Research Fellowship at Selwyn College, Cambridge. From Autumn 2000 lecturer in music at the University of Surrey, Guildford.

Ståle Kleiberg

Ståle Kleiberg is a composer and musicologist, and is Associate Professor at the University of Trondheim. His major compositions include *The Rose Window, The Bell Reef,* Symphony No. 1, Chamber Symphony (Symphony No. 2) Dopo (cello and string orchestra), String Quartet, *Two Poems by Montale,* Sonanz and e cadenza. His publications include '*Grieg's Slatter op.*

72: Change of Musical Style or New Concept of Nationality' (JRMA, 1996); C.P.E. Bach and the individual expression (Oslo, 1989), *The Music of Hans Abrahamsen* (Oslo 1986), *Form in Impressionism* (Oslo, 1985).

Michael Murphy

Michael Murphy was awarded his PhD from the National University of Ireland in 1994 for his thesis on the music of the Polish composer Mieczsław Karłowicz. Until 1998 he lectured in the Music Department at University College Cork. Aside from his research activities in the area of Polish music he has also lectured and broadcast on the Irish music of Stanford. He is currently researching the role of Information and Communication Technologies in education in Trinity College Dublin, with reference to music in primary education.

John Rosselli

John Rosselli, until 1989 Reader in History in the University of Sussex, has worked for over twenty years on the social history of opera. He is the author of *The Opera Industry in Italy from Cimarosa to Verdi: the Role of the Impresario* (1984), *Singers of Italian Opera: the History of a Profession* (1992), *The Life of Bellini* (1996), and *The Life of Mozart* (1998), all published by Cambridge University Press.

Joseph J. Ryan

Commandant Joseph Ryan is the conductor of the Army No. 1 Band, the senior military band of the Irish Defence Forces. Dr. Ryan received his musical education in the College of Music and in the National University of Ireland. He was for sometime, prior to joining the Defence Forces, a head of Music Department in a Dublin secondary school and senior tutor in University College Dublin. Within the army he has served as instructional officer and as conductor of the Band of the Curragh Command prior to assuming his current appointment in 1990. A principal area of research has been the history of music in Ireland, and he has both written and broadcast extensively on this topic: his radio documentary *Writing Irishly* was RTE's prize-winning entry for the Fifth International Radio Competition held in Shanghai in 1995.

Steve Sweeney-Turner

Steve Sweeney-Turner lectures in popular musicology at the University of Leeds, and is editor of *Critical Musicology Journal* on the Internet. His research areas include not only Scottish popular-classical crossovers, but also post-structuralist philosophies, issues of ethnicity and post-colonial theory, and the avant-garde and its relation to theories of Modernism and postmodernism.

Robert Vilain

Robert Vilain is a Lecturer in German at Royal Holloway, University of London. He has published on Hugo von Hofmannsthal, Yvan and Claire Goll, Rilke and other aspects of late 19th- and early 20th-century German and Austrian literature, including its links with music. In collaboration with Geoffrey Chew he has published on Janáček and Kurt Weill. Forthcoming publications include a monograph on Hugo von Hofmannsthal's poetry, an edition of Giraud/Hartleben's 'Pierrot Lunaire', a bibliography and monograph on Yvan Goll.

Harry White

Harry White has been Professor of Music at University College Dublin since 1993. In 1996 he was Visiting Professor at the University of Western Ontario (Canada) and in 1999 he was Visiting Professor of Musicology at Ludwig-Maximilians-Universitaet, Munich. His books include *Johann Joseph Fux and the Music of the Austro-Italian Baroque* (editor) and *The Keeper's Recital: Music and Cultural History in Ireland, 1700–1970*. He is general editor of the series *Irish Musical Studies* and was a national advisory editor for the second edition of *The Grove Dictionary of Music and Musicians*. His *The History of a Baroque Oratorio* will be published by Ashgate in 2002.

Acknowledgements

The editors would like to express their gratitude to the contributors for their scholarship and patience in bringing this book to fruition.

We would also like to thank Claire O'Leary of Leading Note for typesetting the musical examples.

The original inspiration for this book came from the international activities of the TEMPUS project in the mid 1990s. In particular I would like to thank Geoffrey Chew of Royal Holloway Music Department for his discussions and encouragement in the early stages of this book.

Michael Murphy
April 2001

The publishers gratefully acknowledge the Bibliothèque National de France for permission to reproduce a contemporary poster advertising *Jeanne d'Arc* by Gaston Serpette (1871), and the National Museum of Stockholm for permission to reproduce *Landscape, Lejre* (1905) by Vilhelm Hammershzøi.

Introduction

MICHAEL MURPHY

Despite the familiarity of 'musical nationalism' in musicological literature, particularly in the study of nineteenth-century European musical culture, it is a subject that has received relatively little attention from musicologists for most of the twentieth century. While Joseph Kerman noted that after the Second World War 'the anti-Romantic reaction [in musicology] ... passed and musicologists ... moved back with confidence to the study of nineteenth-century music',[1] this renewed vigour did not include analysis of the political meaning of that repertoire with respect to nationalism. In short, that *The New Grove Dictionary of Music and Musicians* has not included an article on the subject is a measure of the bibliography on musical nationalism in Anglophone musicology to date.[2]

A number of phenomena have brought about a strong interest in the study of political nationalism in recent decades: the persistence of nationalism and ethnic conflict throughout the world, the perceived threat to national identity in the face of economic and political integration in Western Europe, and the emergence of over a dozen ethnically based states in the wake of the break-up of the Soviet Union.[3] In 1990 Eric Hobsbawm suggested that in the period between 1968 and 1988 there was a larger output of scholarship on the subject of nations and nationalism than in any prior period of twice that length.[4] More recently, John Hutchinson and Anthony Smith have contrasted the 'reserve' of Anglo-Saxon scholars during the greater part of the present century with the recent profusion of books, articles, journals, conferences, and university courses on ethnicity and nationalism, and they cite a substantial list of disciplines that have engaged with the subject.[5] It is only in the last decade that musicologists have begun to investigate the issue in light of new analytical approaches.[6]

The editors of *Musical Constructions of Nationalism* asked the contributors to consider how nationalist ideology was a vital factor in conditioning musical culture with respect to nationalism in Europe. This is a vague instruction, and no normative description of nationalism was offered by the editors. Thus this volume does not constitute a history of musical nationalism, nor is it primarily theoretical in its focus. Nevertheless, the editors intend that this volume should contribute to the general reorientation of perspective that is currently in train with regard to musical nationalism.

The balance of this introduction is divided into three sections: a survey of theories of nationalism, a survey of musicological scholarship on nationalism in the twentieth century and a review of the contents of the present volume.

Theories of nationalism

A survey of the theoretical literature shows that no normative definition of 'nation' or 'nationalism' is possible. This daunting situation reflects the fact that nationalism is not a single doctrine, that its origins are spurious and various and that its manifestations are moulded by circumstance. As Anthony Smith noted, an historian may be tempted to abandon the search for a 'unitary concept' of nationalism and opt instead for a 'contextualist' approach.[7] But such an approach presupposes a general idea of nationalism that the particular instances exemplify, thus allowing it to be compared or contrasted with other social, cultural and political movements.

The broadest sketch of nationalism shows that the nineteenth century took for granted that the world was divided naturally into nations, and that, in the modernist crisis between established ecclesiastical authority and secular state power, intellectuals, politicians and educated populations throughout Europe looked to the nation as the source of identity, education, state power, culture, history and destiny. Clearly, nineteenth-century nationalism must be viewed in the context of the modernisation of society: namely the change from feudalism to citizenship and social mobility, the move to industrialisation and capitalism, the nationalisation of previously 'regional' languages and the development of national education systems. Furthermore, we can trace a fundamental change in the dynamic of nationalism as the nineteenth century progressed. While the proclamation of the Second Republic in France in 1848 was seen across Europe as the fulfilment of the promise of 1789, and the consequent demise of the Holy Alliance saw the rise of popular parliament in the 'Spring of the Peoples', the course of nationalism changed throughout Europe in the second half of the nineteenth century as a consequence of its own assumptions and in response to historical developments. The initial universalism of nationalism that sought freedom for all nations was superseded by a narrower brand of nationalism based on historical rights, economic interests and policies of protectionism (e.g. *Machtpolitik* and *Realpolitik*).

But nationalism was not only a public political ideology and movement, it was registered also in the identification of the individual's fate with that of the nation. By the early decades of the nineteenth century Hegel was able to declare in his *Philosophy of World History* that

> Individuals withdraw into themselves and pursue their own ends, and this ... is the nation's undoing ... The worth of individuals is measured by the extent to which they reflect and represent the national spirit.[8]

The imperative status of 'national identity' proved to be a powerful agent in the emergence of nations in the nineteenth and twentieth centuries.

When we turn to the scholarship on nations and nationalism we are confronted with a plethora of theories, many of them oppositional, especially with regard to the vexed question of typology. At the risk of oversimplification we can see that nations fall into one of two categories: the cultural or the political. This division was famously formulated by Friedrich Meinecke in his *Weltbürgertum und Nationalstaat* (1907) and it has persisted in various forms ever since. Meinecke distinguished between 'nations that are primarily based on some jointly experienced cultural heritage [*Kulturnation*], and nations that are primarily based on the unifying force of a common political history and constitution [*Staatsnation*]'.[9] While the *Kulturnation* was defined in terms of common language, literature and religion, the *Staatsnation* was the product of political nationalism as defined by the spirit of the French Revolution with its ideas of self-determination and sovereignty.

Hans Kohn subsequently distinguished between Western and Eastern models of the nation. The Western model describes nation-formation in England, France, the Netherlands, Switzerland, the United States and the British Dominions where 'the rise of nationalism was a predominantly political occurrence; it was preceded by the formation of the future national state'.[10] In Eastern Europe (east of the Rhine) and Asia, nationalism was not only a later phenomenon but was characterised by its protest against and conflict with the existing state pattern.[11] Kohn identifies this Eastern nationalism as essentially cultural in nature due to the 'backward' state of political and social structures. In Kohn's formulation, German nationalism was non-Western in as much as it 'substituted for the legal and rational concept of "citizenship" the infinitely vaguer concept of "folk", which, first discovered by the German humanists, was later fully developed by Herder and the German romanticists'.[12]

Such rigid distinctions have been questioned in recent scholarship. Anthony Smith modified the inflexibility of Kohn's model by identifying a 'civic-territorial' model on the one hand and an 'ethnic-genealogical' model on the other.[13] This is a useful distinction that does not rest solely on geo-political criteria. Furthermore, it can be applied to conflicting versions of the nation *within* a single nation. For example, Heinrich August Winkler noted that the question 'What is the German Fatherland?' was one that 'the liberals of 1848 tended, in the main, to answer tactically'.[14] In this regard, Peter Alter analyses the fluctuating German claims for minority groups:

> before 1918 Germans emphasized subjective, political factors in the case of East Prussian Masurians who spoke a Polish dialect, and pointed to objective, cultural considerations [i.e. the German language] where Alsatians were concerned.[15]

Thus, when Renan stated that 'A nation's existence is, if you will pardon the metaphor, a daily plebiscite',[16] he was arguing against the theory of historical rights and ethnic solidarity that the Germans used to justify the annexation of Alsace-Lorraine in 1871 against the will of its population. At the same time, Renan's Republican patriotism was in opposition to conservative Catholic French nationalism.[17] As history clearly shows, nationalists were prone to adapt their dogma according to circumstance.

It is evident that theorists who rely on statist models of the nation have tended to devalue or ignore the cultural aspect of nationalism. John Hutchinson has challenged Kohn's failure to appreciate the modernising effect of cultural nationalism in non-Western countries. While carefully distinguishing between cultural and political nationalism, Hutchinson argues that cultural nationalism is itself a political movement that rejects the passive isolationism of traditionalism, and promotes the nation as a progressive and modern culture.[18] He sees cultural nationalists as 'moral innovators' who establish 'ideological movements at times of social crisis in order to transform the belief-systems of communities, and provide models of socio-political development that guide their modernizing strategies'.[19]

If theories of nationhood are contentious, so too is the question of the origins and development of nationalism. In recent years there has been a move away from the history of ideas to a broadly sociological approach. This may be represented by Ernest Gellner's uncompromising belief that to focus on the intellectual history of nationalism is to enter a state of false consciousness. In particular he rejects Elie Kedourie's 'perplexing and unfair inculpation' of Kant's philosophy of self-determination in the origins and development of nationalism.[20] Gellner argues that Kant was essentially concerned with the 'universal' in man', rather than 'the *culturally* specific'.[21]

Gellner's influential scholarship identifies the modernist character of nationalism. While nationalists propagated the myth that nations had existed from time immemorial and that nationalism, therefore, was the revival of nations from slumber, Gellner emphasises that we should not accept the 'sleeping-beauty' model of nationalism (e.g. *Risorgimento*); rather, we should regard nations as the crystallisations of new social units. Nationalism is 'in reality the consequence of a new form of social organization, based on deeply internalized, education-dependent high cultures, each protected by its own state'.²² We may represent Gellner's conclusion with the following powerful credo:

> The basic deception and self-deception practised by nationalism is this: nationalism is, essentially, the general imposition of a high culture on society, where previously low cultures had taken up the lives of the majority, and in some cases of the totality, of the population ... But this is the very opposite of what nationalism affirms and what nationalists fervently believe. Nationalism usually conquers in the name of a putative folk culture. Its symbolism is drawn from the healthy, pristine, vigorous life of the peasants, of the *Volk*, the *narod*.²³

We may contrast Gellner's model with that of another sociologist's, Anthony Smith. If we consider the relationship between state and nation we can see fundamental differences in Gellner's and Smith's conclusions. Gellner believes that nationalism was primarily a political principle which 'holds that they [nation and state] were destined for each other'²⁴ and that the nation cannot survive without its own 'political shell, the state'.²⁵ Smith, however, argues that 'nationalism is an ideology of the nation, not the state'.²⁶ On Smith's view, the concept of the nation-state was not the *raison d'être* of nationalism. As Smith argues, the acquisition of statehood was neither necessary nor universal in early theories of nationalism (e.g. Rousseau, Herder), and many nationalists (e.g. Scots, Flemish, Catalan) were more concerned with 'home rule and cultural parity in a multinational state than with outright independence'.²⁷ He continues: 'More than a style and doctrine of politics, nationalism is a *form of culture* – an ideology, a language, mythology, symbolism and consciousness'.²⁸ If nationalism is about the imposition of high culture, as Gellner argues, then nationalism has been conspicuously successful. But the fact that Poland and Ireland in the nineteenth century, for example, generated and sustained national cultures without a state apparatus, and indeed against a colonial state apparatus, demonstrates that nations are, in essence, independent of statehood.

A central feature of Smith's scholarship is his emphasis on the role which ethnicity has had in defining national identity. Ethnic distinctiveness, which he defines as 'shared ancestry myths, common historical memories, unique cultural markers, and a sense of difference, if not election' remains 'a *sine qua non* of the nation'.²⁹ For Smith, the potency of ethnic elements for national identity lies in the fact that the ethnic model of the nation was compatible with 'the pre-modern "demotic" kind of community' which remained widespread throughout the world in the modern era; in his phrase, 'the ethnic model was sociologically fertile'.³⁰ However, it is worth entering the caveat that the reputed 'ethnic distinctiveness' of a nation does not mean that it is ethnically homogenous; nations were typically formed around a dominant *ethnie*.

Smith also promotes the role of historicist intellectuals in generating the ideology of political nationalism and, at times, in leading it.[31] Smith argues for the importance of a sense of 'identity crisis' amongst intellectuals who found themselves in the midst of the demise of traditional religious forms of culture and society, and who were challenged by political revolution and emerging scientific states. The importance of the historicist myth for intellectuals was that it allowed for a world-view that was just as 'cosmic' as were the more traditional religions. In this new context, intellectuals did not create national(ist) cultures *ex nihilo* but from the models of collective identity that they inherited from late medieval and early modern Europe.

In the postmodern world, national identity is continually being explored and debated across the globe. Whether this signifies the demise of national identity in favour of regional identity or a resurgence of national identity in the face of perceived globalisation is impossible to predict.

With the continuous research into political and cultural nationalism across a wide range of disciplines there is little chance of finding a unitary model of nationalism and nationhood that musicologists can readily apply to the study of musical culture. In the following section we will see that the division between the history of ideas and the sociological method has come to dominate current debate on the musical nationalism.

The musicological study of nationalism in the twentieth century

The marginalisation of the study of musical nationalism in musicology during the twentieth century was a result of both musicological and political factors. In the early twentieth century Guido Adler assigned the investigation of the development of musical style to musicology.[32] Leo Treitler describes this methodology 'as an effort to "mediate between aesthetics and history," to write history without "doing violence to the aesthetic autonomy of works," to the "strong concept of art."'[33] In this regard, an overtly nationalist aesthetic fell short of the status of the great works of art of the Austro-German canon, the chief characteristic of which was autonomy.[34] Historical musicology assumed the presence of 'an "ideal object" whose continuity is followed in the narrative'.[35] Treitler states

> The correlate is a history of compositional technique, or of musical logic. That meant music history as a narrative of change, with the emphasis on novelty. What 'belongs to history' is what is new. The framework of continuity in such narrative was the biographical or organismal model.[36]

Clearly, musicological methodology was incompatible with the study of nationalism as an ideology, and focused by default on the questions of national style and national histories.

This marginalisation of musical nationalism in musicology is characterised by a number of familiar assumptions. The most characteristic of these is that nationalism in music is primarily a feature of 'the national schools'. This particular category sets these schools in opposition to the 'central' musical nations, an assumption which leads to the conclusion that, in Cecil Gray's words, 'National schools are invariably short-lived; they have no capacity for replenishment or renewal, but perish like mayflies after a short and brilliant career'.[37] To no small degree nationalism in music was perceived as a species of exoticism.

Of great significance was the methodological precedent set by Paul Henry Lang when he wrote his section on 'Nationalism in Music' under the rubric 'The Peripheries of Nineteenth-Century Music and Its Practice' in his influential *Music in Western Civilization*.[38] The continuity between Lang's treatment of musical nationalism in 1941 and that of many post-war writers is striking.[39] However, considering the hopes for a post-national polity in the aftermath of the Second World War, the reluctance to engage with nationalism in the historical and political sciences, to say nothing of musicology, is unsurprising.

We may register this sensitivity, from a musicological point of view, in the second edition of Warren Dwight Allen's *Philosophies of Music History: A Study of General Histories of Music 1600–1960*.[40] The central thesis of his survey of 317 music histories was that the idea of 'progress' in the history of music was an insufficient explanatory model when compared with the sociological method in the history of art and literature. While Allen had already made this point in the 1939 edition, in the 1962 edition he wedded it to a strident anti-nationalist stance which he adopted as a matter of American democratic duty. While he believed that 'doctrines of development and evolution' formed the basis for nationalistic music history, it is clear that his rejection of these models was more than a purely methodological concern.[41] In particular he stressed 'that the histories of national musical life and the music of one's own area have tended to become neglected in a democratic country like our own and overstressed under dictatorships'.[42] Clearly, Allen was reacting to certain trends in European musicology: he refers, *inter alia*, to a 'Nazi version' of Hugo Riemann's *Musiklexicon, Theorie und Geschichte der Musik*.[43]

In direct proportion to his disdain of nationalism in European musicology was his concern to keep musical scholarship in America free from nationalism. As he was well aware, the influx of European musicologists to America before and after the war had a profound effect on American musicology: in his 'Preface', for example, he singled out Paul Henry Lang for his seminal contribution to the 'great strides made in American musicology in the last twenty years'.[44] Another notable immigrant was Alfred Einstein, whose *Geschichte der Musik* (1922) Allen declared was 'free from the virus of nationalism'.[45] This contrasts with Pamela M. Potter's view that Einstein had no reason to abandon his Germanocentric view of music history.[46] She notes that Einstein's *Geschichte der Musik* promoted the idea of a resilient German musical spirit that overcame foreign domination and found its voice in Bach, Haydn and Weber.[47] There is evidence, however, that Einstein distanced himself from nationalism after he settled in America: most notably he prefaced his influential *Music in the Romantic Era* (1947) with a disclaimer against overt nationalism. After remarking that 'the emphasis laid on the national element is one of the essential marks of Romanticism', he continued:

> If in this book the presentation of the Romantic movement in Germany occupies a wide space, it might be remembered that it is, at least in the eyes of a later generation, perhaps not a matter of pride for any nation to have been the one most strongly affected by the Romantic virus.[48]

While *Music in the Romantic Era* lay outside the scope of Allen's survey of general histories of music, he could not have been unaware of its importance, nor of the significance of Einstein's disclaimer.

In his attempt to immunise his own readers from any potential nationalist virus, Allen conjured with the idea of America under a Fascist dictatorship where the jazz idiom would be banned 'on account of the Semitic influence' as would 'all subversive tendencies inherent in "inferior" Negro culture', and where the '"Stars and Stripes Forever" could thus be held up as the highest flower of American music evolution'.[49] Consequently, he devoted his volume to finding 'a pluralistic method by which we may deal in a scientific way with different arts of music in different areas, with different peoples made up of different individuals'.[50] In short, musicology remained in step behind the social, political and historical sciences, and declined to study the political meaning of nationalism in music.

It was not until Carl Dahlhaus's writings started to exert an influence on Anglo-American musicology that the subject benefited from a more rigorous intellectual approach. His scholarship on musical nationalism reflected the dichotomy between the history of ideas and the sociological approach that existed in the historical and social sciences. In particular he suggested that musical nationalism should be studied in the context of political nationalism so as to determine whether there were any correlations between the condition of political nationalism and musical culture in a given nation.[51] While this is now an obvious point, it represents a break from the reticence as expressed by Allen, for example. (Indeed, Dahlhaus's suggestion is the point of departure for the present volume.) However, recent studies of Dahlhaus's scholarship, in particular James Hepokoski's 'The Dahlhaus Project and Its Extra-Musicological Sources', demonstrate the need for contexualising such statements with particular regard to nationalism.[52] Thus, Dahlhaus's statement that 'the national side of music is to be found less in the music itself than in its political and sociopsychological function'[53] is a methodological dispensation that is resonant with ideological assumptions about the nature of nationalist music and its historiography. Hepokoski emphasises that Dahlhaus's primary concern was 'how to write an art *history* that is a history of *art*'.⁵⁴ To this end Dahlhaus rejected the idea of a 'metanarrative' of 'History', proposing instead 'empirical studies within a history of a "medium" order of magnitude'.⁵⁵ Hepokoski observes that the 'manifest plan of [Dahlhaus's] *Nineteenth-Century Music* is the study of differing, but contemporaneous, genres and categories, which we are apparently to understand as clusters of parallel but often conceptually separable *Geschichten*'.⁵⁶ However, he argues that Dahlhaus 'seems most centrally concerned with constructing the "History" of the Germanic institution of autonomous music'.⁵⁷ According to Hepokoski, Dahlhaus's emphasis on the immanent identity of the art work was a strategy to 'shelter the German Romantic canon from ideology critique'⁵⁸ in the atmosphere of late post-war divided Germany.

A more recent study of musical nationalism by Celia Applegate – 'How German is it? Nationalism and the Idea of Serious Music in the Early Nineteenth Century'⁵⁹ – has again highlighted the issue of ideological perspective. Her adoption of a sociological approach is specifically designed to deconstruct the edifice of German musical nationalism. In this regard, she challenges the conclusion, *pace* Rumph and Pederson, that the idea of aesthetic autonomy was the product of early nineteenth-century German nationalism.⁶⁰ In a revisionist style predicated on the model of Gellner as transmitted through James J. Sheehan,⁶¹ Applegate believes that authors such as Dahlhaus, Hepokoski and William Weber take German nationalism too much for granted. She states:

> In each case [Dahlhaus, Hepokoski, and Weber], German nationalism or national identity or indeed nationhood looms as an undifferentiated whole, lurching its monolithic way through the nineteenth century into the disastrous twentieth and contaminating musical culture along with everything else.⁶²

Likewise, she accuses Rumph and Pederson of exaggerating the nationalism of Hoffmann and Marx 'by simplifying the politics of the time, the significance of nationalism in Prussian Berlin and in these critics' imaginary [*sic*].'⁶³ Applegate is primarily concerned with distancing musicology from 'yesterday's models of German national development' where Hoffmann and A. B. Marx are aligned with the Luther-to-Bismarck-to-Hitler trajectory in a bid to insert music into intellectual and political history. In particular, she contrasts her own study of Zelter with Georg Schünemann's 'stridently nationalist portrait' in which Zelter, Stein and Hardener are implicated in preparing 'the ground for a destined unification of Germany under Prussia'.⁶⁴

To demonstrate the incoherence of nationalism in the early decades of nineteenth-century Germany she opts for a socio-cognitive model that is directed to a study of the music profession itself. She argues that the musicians who turned to a national discourse did so, not for political reasons, but rather for social mobility and ease of integration with the educated élite.[65] She repeatedly claims that musicians became the 'movers and doers' of society by developing the ideas and institutions that promoted music as 'serious' culture and, therefore, as 'German'.[66] In essence, the turn to nationalism by Zelter et al. can be understood in the context of the 'identity-crisis' amongst intellectuals in post-revolutionary Europe.

In a sense, Dahlhaus and Applegate represent the opposing perspectives of the history of ideas and the sociological approach. In the end, as Dahlhaus has suggested, most historians are eclectic in their approach. Equally, no one can be free from perspective. This volume represents a variety of approaches.

Review of the contents

As a whole, the essays in this volume explore many aspects of musical culture beyond the issue of national musical style. To take a few examples, Marina Frolova-Walker and John Rosselli consider the question of nationalist historiography; Jeremy Dibble focuses on nationalism in musicology; Robert Vilain explores the literary reception of music; Stephen Downes explores the relationship between sexuality, politics and music; Annegret Fauser considers the politics of gender in relation to music; while Daniel Grimley and Ståle Kleiberg consider in detail the question of musical style. At the risk of oversimplification, one can observe that the majority of essays focus on musical culture after 1870 (cf. Dibble, Fauser, Vilain, Kleiberg, Grimley, Cooper, Downes, Ryan), and the others are mostly concerned with musical nationalism in the mid-nineteenth century (cf. Murphy, Rosselli, White, Frolova-Walker, Sweeney-Turner). Not surprisingly, therefore, a theme that is common to all but the chapters on Ireland, Scotland and mid-nineteenth-century Poland is the attempt to find a national source of cultural authority as an alternative to Germanism after 1870 (Frolova-Walker examines this issue in the mid-to late-nineteenth century). This question, however, is a very complex one, and nationalists were adept at simultaneously repudiating and assimilating German influences (cf. Dibble and Frolova-Walker, for example). As a cursory glance at the chapters will show, the question of musical nationalism cannot be reduced to the anxiety of influence. Indeed, those who can be called 'musical nationalists' were typically engaged with generating a cosmopolitan musical culture, the authenticity of which was underscored by the national element.

Jeremy Dibble's main concern is with the need for late nineteenth-century English musicology to put itself on an equal footing with the German tradition of *Musikwissenschaft*. Ironically, despite the Anglocentric bias of Grove's *Dictionary*, this scholarship reflected the high status and formative influence of German musical culture in England.

In her comprehensive chapter, Annegret Fauser focuses on how the 'masculinising' of French art in the post-1870 era was a means of bestowing cultural identity and power on a defeated France. She theorises the gendering of nationhood in the context of a divided polity, and she extensively examines the intellectual discourses that dominated French scholarship and civic society, with particular reference to masculinised representations of Jeanne d'Arc.

The issue of international tension is further explored in Robert Vilain's examination of Wagner's reception in Germany and France. In particular he explores the complex relationship between the nationalistic and aesthetic elements in Thomas Mann's and Stéphane Mallarmé's reception of Wagner. The rivalry between Thomas Mann and his brother, Heinrich, is examined against the background of the political tensions within Wilhelm II's Germany.

The influence of German symphonicism on Russian orchestral music is analysed by Marina Frolova-Walker in her critique of the enduring mythology of 'Russianness' in music. She notes that Western critics were happy to reproduce the Russian nationalist mythologies according to their quasi-oriental view of Russia, an interpretation which she shows does not withstand the scrutiny of those 'Russian' symphonies.

The fate of the multi-ethnic Hungarian nation is central to David Cooper's chapter on Bartók. Cooper argues that the composer's rejection of Gypsy music in favour of peasant music represented a musical and political *volte-face*, the musical modernism of which challenged the conservative nationalism of the Hungarian state.

John Rosselli, in his chapter on music and nationalism in Italy, observes that it was only after political unification, and the resulting discontent that it engendered, that nationalist discourse came to engage seriously with music. Rosselli argues that the coming of Italian nationhood led to a loss of confidence in the primacy of Italian music, and this, coupled with the perceived threat of Germanism, acted as a spur to the more nationalistically minded critics and composers.

Stephen Downes's exploration of the erotic nature of Szymanowski's work goes to the core of the meaning of nationalism as an ideology. In essence, Downes argues that Szymanowski's liberation of Eros had the power to subvert and transcend the insidious divisions at the heart of political nationalism.

Ståle Kleiberg explores David Johansen's national style in the context of the polarised condition of Norwegian nationalism, i.e. between those who wanted to Norwegianise the Danish language on the one hand and those who wanted to formulate a 'New' Norwegian literate language on the other.

Daniel Grimley considers the marginalisation of Scandinavian music in musicological writing with particular reference to the issue of nationalism.

He draws on Hutchinson's model of cultural nationalism to explore the progressive nature of Nielsen's construction of 'northerness'.

If many European musical cultures needed to be 'liberated' from the hegemony of German music, Irish music needed to be liberated from itself. As Harry White argues, the concept of Irish music came to signify the 'soul of the nation' to the extent that the music itself became fixed in a metaphorical register and thereby all but ceased to exist as an independent art form. The legacy of this nationalism is explored by Joe Ryan, who pessimistically notes that, in the context of a largely musically illiterate nation, 'the few who seek to create through sound end up soliloquising or addressing a foreign audience'.

Steve Sweeney-Turner examines competing political interpretations of Burns's famous song, 'Bruce's Address to his Army' (also known as 'Scots Wha Hae wi' Wallace Bled'). In particular he explores how Burns was represented in the Scottish Radical tradition on the one hand, and British imperial culture on the other.

My own chapter considers Moniuszko's *Halka* in light of the conflicting theoretical debates that dominated Polish nationalism in the mid-nineteenth century. I focus on the genesis of the opera, with particular reference to the revolutionist conception of social equalisation.

There is no ready definition that describes the relationship between political nationalism and musical culture. The limit of Dahlhaus's claim that 'Nationalistic music, it seems, invariably emerges as an expression of a politically motivated need, which tends to appear when national independence is being sought, denied, or jeopardized rather than attained or consolidated'[67] is easily reached. It is clear from the contents of this volume that those who generated musical culture were deeply concerned with the survival of 'the nation' in modern Europe. However, their engagement with nationalism transcended the strictly political concerns of statehood and independence, and focused instead on the more fundamental questions of the composition of civil society and national culture. In other words, the question 'What is the nation?' drew a response from composers, musical theorists, scholars and critics. In this regard, many of the contributors examine nationalist musical cultures in the context of conflicting models of the nation and nationalism. Furthermore, that nationalism was a powerful force for social and cultural homogenisation is a central issue in understanding the nature of musical nationalism: the question of how musicians contributed to or reacted against such processes of homogenisation is a frequent theme in this volume. In short, the degree to which musical culture was more or less nationalist was contingent on circumstance, and this volume is dedicated to examining such concrete incidents.

The title of the present volume suggests that when musical culture engages with political and cultural nationalism it constructs its own unique musical terms of reference that are nevertheless inextricably linked to the wider world of nations. The plurality of musical culture disclosed in these essays confirms the plural condition of 'musical nationalism' itself. As a concept, as a term of reference which provides an interface (as it were) between art and ideology, 'nationalism in music' functions not as a peripheral or simplistic phenomenon. Rather it denotes a complex, multivarious and central manifestation of the often vexed relations between music, society and culture.

Notes and References

1 Joseph Kerman, *Musicology* (London, 1985), p. 38.
2 Stanley Sadie (ed.), *The New Grove Dictionary of Music and Musicians* (London, 1980). The seventh edition (forthcoming) will include an article on the subject.
3 For example, Benedict Anderson in his *Imagined Communities: Reflections on the Origin and Spread of Nationalism* (London, 1983), p. 12, states: '. . . since World War II every successful revolution has defined itself in *national* terms – the People's Republic of China, the Socialist Republic of Vietnam, and so forth – and, in so doing, has grounded itself firmly in a territorial and social space inherited from the prerevolutionary past'.
4 E. J. Hobsbawm, *Nations and Nationalism since 1780: Programme, Myth, Reality* (Cambridge, 1990), p. 5.
5 John Hutchinson and Anthony D. Smith (eds.), *Nationalism: A Reader* (Oxford, 1994), 'Preface'.
6 One important early study was the translation of Carl Dahlhaus's 'Nationalism and Music', in *Between Romanticism and Modernism: Four Studies in the Music of the Later Nineteenth Century*, trans. Mary Whittall (California, 1980). More recent studies are discussed in the course of this introduction.
7 See Anthony Smith, *National Identity*, (London, 1991), p. 79. For a comprehensive introduction to nationalism with source readings see Hutchinson and Smith (eds.), *Nationalism*.
8 G. W. F. Hegel, *The Philosophy of World History* (1823–1831), quoted in O. Dahbour and M. R. Ishay (eds.), *The Nationalism Reader* (New Jersey, 1995), pp. 79–84. This is not to say that Hegel was a nationalist: as a rationalist, his primary concern was with the State not the nation; see Elie Kedourie, *Nationalism* (London, 1960 [reprinted 1985]), p. 36.
9 F. Meinecke, *Weltbürgertum und Nationalstaat* (New Jersey, 1970), p. 10, quoted in Andrzej Walicki, *Philosophy and Romantic Nationalism: The Case of Poland* (Indiana, 1994 [1st edn., 1982]), p. 65.
10 Hans Kohn, *The Idea of Nationalism* (New York, 1945), quoted in Hutchinson and Smith (eds.), *Nationalism*, p. 164.
11 Ibid.
12 Ibid.
13 Smith, *National Identity*, pp. 11–12. For a further critique of Kohn see Walicki, *Philosophy and Romantic Nationalism*, pp. 66–9.
14 Heinrich August Winkler, 'Nationalism and nation-state in Germany', in Mikuláš Teich and Roy Porter (eds.), *The National Question in Europe in Historical Context* (Cambridge, 1993), p. 183.
15 Peter Alter, *Nationalism*, trans. Stuart McKinnon-Evans (London, 1989), p. 17.
16 Ernest Renan, 'Qu'est-ce qu'une nation?' (a lecture delivered at the Sorbonne in

1882), trans. and annotated by Martin Thom, 'Tribes Within Nations: The Ancient Germans and the History of Modern France', in Homi K. Bhabha (ed.), *Nation and Narration* (London, 1990), p. 19.
17 Thom argues, however, that Renan was not as committed to the 'voluntaristic' argument as his essay suggests: see Thom, 'Tribes Within Nations', in Bhabha (ed.), *Nation and Narration*, pp. 22–43.
18 Hutchinson, *The Dynamics of Cultural Nationalism* (London, 1987), quoted in Hutchinson and Smith (eds.), *Nationalism*, p. 131.
19 Ibid., p. 127.
20 See Ernest Gellner, *Nations and Nationalism* (Oxford, 1983), pp. 30ff., for his critique of Kedourie, and see also Kedourie, *Nationalism* [reprinted 1985], pp. 142ff. for his reply to Gellner.
21 Gellner, *Nations and Nationalism*, p. 131.
22 Ibid., p. 48.
23 Ibid., p. 57.
24 Ibid., p. 6.
25 Ibid., p. 143.
26 Smith, *National Identity*, p. 74.
27 Ibid., p. 74.
28 Ibid., p. 91.
29 Ibid., p. 70.
30 Ibid., p. 41.
31 Ibid., p. 93. It is worth noting that Smith distinguishes between the intellectuals who generate ideas and artistic works from the much wider stratum of the intelligentsia whose function as professionals it is to disseminate those ideas and creations.
32 Guido Adler, *Der Stil in der Musik* (Leipzig, 1911).
33 Leo Treitler, 'What Kind of Story Is History?', in *Music and the Historical Imagination* (Harvard, 1989), p. 170.
34 Two recent articles argue that this notion of 'autonomy' was the product of German nationalism: see Sanna Pederson, 'A. B. Marx, Berlin Concert Life, and German National Identity', *19th-Century Music* XVIII, 2 (California, 1994), pp. 87–107; Stephen Rumph, 'A Kingdom Not of This World: The Political Context of E. T. A. Hoffmann's Beethoven Criticism', *19th-Century Music* XIX, 1 (California, 1995), pp. 50–67.
35 Treitler, 'What Kind of Story Is History?', pp. 169–70.
36 Ibid.
37 Cecil Gray, *Predicaments. Or Music and the Future: An Essay in Constructive Criticism* (London, 1936), p. 136.
38 See Paul Henry Lang, *Music in Western Civilization* (New York, 1941), pp. 916ff.
39 See Donald J. Grout, *A History of Western Music* (London, 1962 [4th edn., 1988]); Alec Harman, Anthony Milner and Wilfrid Mellers, *Man and His Music: The Story of Musical Experience in the West* (London, 1962 [4th edn., 1971]); Ronald Stevenson, *Western Music: An Introduction* (London, 1971); Rey M. Longyear, *Nineteenth-Century Romanticism in Music* (New Jersey, 1973); Leon Plantinga, *Romantic Music. A History of Musical Style in Nineteenth-Century Europe* (New York & London, 1984).
40 Warren Dwight Allen, *Philosophies of Music History: A Study of General Histories of Music 1600–1960* (New York, 1962 [1st edn., 1939]).
41 Ibid., p. 152.
42 Ibid., p. xxi.
43 See Allen, 'Bibliography', in *Philosophies of Music History*, p. 351. The Nazi version of Hugo Riemann's *Musiklexicon, Theorie und Geschichte der Musik* was edited by Josef Müller-Blattau.

44 Allen, *Philosophies of Music History*, 'Preface', p. v.
45 Ibid., p. 133.
46 For the influence of German nationalism in American musicology see Pamela M. Potter, 'Musicology Under Hitler: New Sources In Context', *Journal of the American Musicological Society* XLIX, 1 (1996), pp. 70–113.
47 Alfred Einstein, *Geschichte der Musik* (Leipzig, 1922), quoted in Potter, 'Musicology Under Hitler', p. 106.
48 Alfred Einstein, *Music in the Romantic Era: A History of Musical Thought in the 19th Century* (New York and London, 1947), pp. xi–xii.
49 Allen, *Philosophies of Music History*, p. 170. Allen advises the reader that this was not in any sense derogatory of Sousa and his vital contribution to American music.
50 Ibid., p. xxvi.
51 Dahlhaus, 'Nationalism and Music', p. 89.
52 James Hepokoski, 'The Dahlhaus Project and Its Extra-Musicological Sources', *19th-Century Music*, XIV, 3 (1991), pp. 221–46.
53 Carl Dahlhaus, *Nineteenth-Century Music*, trans. J. B. Robinson (Berkeley, 1989), p. 217.
54 Dahlhaus, *Foundations of Music History*, trans. J. B. Robinson (Cambridge, 1983), p. 129.
55 Ibid., p. 52.
56 Hepokoski, 'The Dahlhaus Project', p. 235.
57 Ibid., p. 236.
58 Ibid., p. 225.
59 Celia Applegate, 'How German Is It? Nationalism and the Idea of Serious Music in the Early Nineteenth Century', *19th-Century Music* XXI, 3 (1998), pp. 274–96.
60 Ibid., pp. 277ff. See note 34 above re Rumph and Pederson.
61 See James J. Sheehan, *German History, 1700–1866* (Oxford, 1989), p. 372, for his debt to Gellner.
62 Applegate, 'How German is it?', p. 277
63 Ibid., p. 279.
64 Ibid., p. 294. The reference is to Georg Schünemann's *Carl Friedrich Zelter: Der Mensch und sein Werk* (Berlin, 1937).
65 Applegate, 'How German Is It?', p. 288.
66 Ibid., p. 295.
67 Dahlhaus, *Nineteenth-Century Music*, p. 38.

1.
Béla Bartók and the Question of Race Purity in Music

DAVID COOPER

Béla Bartók's rejection around 1905 of the conventions of what was until then regarded as 'genuine' Hungarian music, namely that composed in the main by dilettantes of the gentry class and disseminated by Gypsy musicians, and his adoption of a style inspired by the musical practices of the least educated and most conservative strand of peasant society, has been seen as a political and artistic transfiguration. His position as a nationalist composer is problematised, however, by the apparent diversity of his sources (Eastern and Western, high and low) and by what Adorno describes as his music's 'extra-territorial' quality.

The Hungary, or rather 'Transleithania', of the composer's early years was extraordinarily heterogeneous in terms of the racial origins of its inhabitants.[1] In 1890 the ethnic Hungarians, the Magyars, formed only 42.8 per cent of a population approaching twenty million people.[2] Romanians, Germans, Slovaks, Croats, Serbs, Ruthenians, Jews and Gypsies coexisted as the majority in a state which repressed and penalised them for their non-Magyar extraction. The policy of Magyarisation adopted after the *Ausgleich* (compromise) of 1867 effectively denied them citizenship, for 'only Hungarian citizens "of a separate mother tongue" were formally recognised and nominally accorded equal civic rights, the unrestricted use of their native language in the lower levels of the administration, the judicial system, and elementary and secondary schools'.[3] In order to promote political integration, the primary language to be taught in schools at every level was Hungarian, and schools serving the non-Magyar communities were required to demonstrate their ability to teach in Hungarian or face the threat of closure. Social and political advancement was thus dependent upon assimilation.

The process of assimilation appears to have been rather more spontaneous than some earlier historians have suggested. Jeszensky remarks that it was 'due to economic transformation, urbanization and "embourgeoisement"', resulting from 'the demands of society, the interests of the individual, and internal migration' rather than as a consequence of coercion.[4] For some parts of the populace assimilation seems to have been relatively unproblematic at first. In particular Jews, who had been emancipated in 1849 and 1867, rapidly adopted both the Magyar language and the national ideals of the gentry.[5] Many were soon absorbed into the developing urban middle classes as doctors, lawyers, bankers and merchants, and by 1910 they formed around 25 per cent of the population of Budapest.[6] Although the government policy was to actively encourage assimilation and oppose anti-Semitism, parts of the population openly exhibited anti-Jewish feeling. As Berend and Ránki note:

> on this fertile ground of the antithesis of agriculture and industry, of countryside and town, of rural and urban values, nationalism flourished. It fed on hatred of aliens, both insiders and outsiders, and was conjoined to a kind of conservative, romantic anti-capitalism.[7]

For other groups, particularly the Romanian peasantry of Transylvania, a region given to Hungary in 1867 as part of the *Ausgleich*, Magyarisation was apprehended as a much greater threat. Demands increased for the restoration of the autonomy of the Transylvanian principality, either as a constituent of a federal 'Greater Austria' or in union with the kingdom of Romania (which had been part of the Ottoman Empire until 1878), and these were fuelled in the first decade of the twentieth century by irredentist Romanian popular politicians who 'were openly proclaiming the annexation of Transylvania as the supreme object of the nation's policy'.[8]

The defeat of the Central Powers in 1918 resulted in a radical transformation of the geography and demography of Hungary. The Treaty of Trianon, signed in June 1920, transferred some five-sevenths of the former territory of Hungary to neighbouring powers in an attempt to solve the 'nationalities problem', and the population fell at a stroke from almost 21 million to less than 8 million. The land ceded to Romania alone (Transylvania, the eastern Banat, much of Körös, Tisza and the southern Máramaros) was greater than that remaining to the independent Kingdom of Hungary. The population was now largely, though not exclusively, autochthonous Hungarian, some 90 per cent having Magyar as their mother tongue.

Whilst anti-Semitism had, at least to some extent, been held in check before the First World War largely for economic reasons (Deák argues that 'there had existed, since the 1840s, a sort of silent contract between the Hungarian gentry and the Jewish social élite for a division of labour in modernizing Hungary'),[9] Admiral Miklós Horthy's period as Regent from 1920 to 1944 was imprinted from its inception by blatant anti-Semitic activity, which was in part driven by the public perception that the short-lived Bolshevik revolution of 1919 was Jewish-inspired. Discrimination took many forms, and included legislation to cap the number of university admissions (which had the effect of reducing the percentage of Jewish students from 34 per cent in 1917–18 to 8 per cent in 1935–6), restrictions on the trades Jews could perform and confiscation of their land.[10]

Issues of racial purity which had been set to one side in the earlier period of Magyarisation (the process of assimilation was clearly founded upon the premise that a non-Magyar could 'become' a Magyar if he or she were to adopt the Hungarian language and customs) came to the fore in ways that paralleled developments in Nazi Germany all too closely. Prime Minister Bethlen's resignation in 1931, and his replacement by the pro-fascist demagogue Gyula Gömbös, marked a turn to the far right for a substantial part of the governing party, and the period from 1931 to 1944 was conspicuous for its oscillation between the moderate and extreme right.[11] The National Socialist Hungarian Workers' Party, founded in 1931, demanded the 'exclusion of all "non-turanic-aryan elements" from important posts',[12] and the Arrow-Cross Party formed by Ferenc Szálasi, which became an umbrella organisation for many of the fascist parties, modelled itself closely on Hitler's Nazi movement. In 1938 Hungary became Germany's first successor in the introduction of anti-Jewish laws to protect 'racial purity'.[13] This initial law, which restricted the number of Jews in 'free professions' and clerical positions to a maximum of 20 per cent, was met with some opposition from the moderate wing in parliament, and Bartók, Kodály and a number of other artists and intellectuals responded by signing a public declaration of protest.

> A real Hungarian music can originate only if there is a real *Hungarian* gentry. This is why the Budapest public is so absolutely hopeless. The place has attracted a haphazardly heterogeneous, rootless group of Germans and Jews; they make up the majority of Budapest's population. It's a waste of time trying to educate them in a national spirit. Much better to educate the (Hungarian) provinces.[14]

The 24-year-old Bartók had made his first discovery of an 'authentic' strand of Hungarian music only a matter of months before writing these words to Irmy Jurkovics. The few songs he had heard the Transylvanian servant girl Lidi Dósa sing in late 1904 were not, as he was to find later, representative of the oldest peasant melodies, but they were clearly different in character to the Gypsy music (cigányzene) which he had hitherto regarded as Magyar folk music. These first intimations of another (or perhaps an 'other') national music were consolidated through the influence of Zoltán Kodály from around 1905. There can be little doubt that the original stimulus for Bartók's folk music research was the chauvinistic nationalism he had begun to cultivate in his early twenties. He had at first adopted the *style hongrois* mannerisms that were commonly held to represent the Hungarian national spirit, most clearly in the symphonic poem *Kossuth* (1903), the Rhapsody Op.1 and the Scherzo Op.2. However, he soon became dissatisfied with the style of the Gypsy-disseminated music upon which it was founded, as much for its racial impurity as its perceived musical failings. In 1911 he noted that 'its main characteristics are the melodic distortions of an immigrant nation, the gipsies' [sic], and that even those songs which originally derived from peasant music were to be regarded as being 'unimaginably marred almost past recognition by their oriental fantasy'.[15] The peasant music offered him an alternative – an autochthonous national music which would allow the expression of difference from Germanic cultural hegemony as a replacement for a 'corrupt' non-Magyar-influenced one.

This 'discovery' of an aboriginal music involved considerable scientific effort on the part of Bartók and his fellow researchers, as much in the development of a coherent strategy for the codification and interpretation of the material as in its collection.[16] The Hungary of Bartók's formative years provided the perfect laboratory for the collection of data and testing of hypotheses, for, as explained above, in the pre-Trianon period it was a racial melting-pot in which the peasant classes, despite Magyarisation, retained many of their own national cultural practices. Within the same territory the student of folk music could hear Magyar, Romanian, Slovakian, Ruthenian, Croatian, Serbian, Gypsy, German and Jewish songs and dance music, without the complexities of organising complex travel documentation or risking the displeasure of unfriendly government agencies either at home or abroad.[17]

The attempt to reconstruct a national style using this peasant music found little favour with the nobility. They were indifferent to the provenance of the Gypsy music they relished, reacting with 'compulsory national enthusiasm' to songs which were in fact of Slavonic origin, yet unable to respond to what Bartók felt to be the beauties of the 'recently discovered and very valuable ancient Hungarian melodies of Transylvania, which are unlike any folk melodies they have heard before'.[18] As late as 1934 we still find Bartók reporting to a correspondent that '80 or perhaps 90 per cent of the Hungarian upper classes even now look on me and my colleagues as traitors, simply because I study and propagate the music of the Hungarian village (instead of the art-music called "Magyar songs"!)'.[19] His gradual disillusionment with conventional nationalism was probably partly due to this lack of engagement on the part of the establishment, partly to his discovery of the music of the peasantry of the national minorities within Hungary and of neighbouring states (in particular Romania), and partly to a growing social awareness. In a letter to his Romanian friend and companion on some of his folk song collecting trips, János Buşiţia, he draws his attention to the text of the first of a set of poems by Endre Ady which are enclosed with the letter:

> The first one says that Hungarians, Rumanians and Slavs in this country should all be united, since they are kindred in misery. We never had a poet who would dare to write such things.[20]

The move from Gypsy to peasant music marked both a musical and political *volte-face*, for as Judit Frigyesi has argued, the former was intimately associated with the aristocracy and gentry.[21] Bartók made the link explicit in his 1931 essay 'Gipsy Music or Hungarian Music'.[22] Contradicting Liszt's misconstruction of Gypsy music, Bartók explained that this music was indeed Hungarian in origin, but was a 'fairly recent type of Hungarian popular art-music composed, practically without exception, by Hungarians of the upper middle class', whose social status precluded them from performing it themselves 'for money'.[23] Ironically the gentry relied on the services of socially and economically inferior non-Magyars to validate their Hungarian identity, to play the music of their 'soul'. Gypsy performance of this repertoire was instrumental rather than vocal, the members of the Gypsy bands mutely performing their material, like eunuchs in the gentry's harem, guarding the beauties but not corrupting them with their foreign vocal patterns. They could articulate the bipolar shifts between lamentation and joy so beloved by their employers with tremendous virtuosity and pathos, in a musical dialect which was exotic without being intimidating. While the financial success of bourgeois Jews presented an explicit threat to the gentry, the Gypsies (or at least the Gypsy musicians) were more innocuous, and were tolerated as entertainers if not as full and equal citizens.

Liszt's construction of the Gypsy in the essentialist and often grotesque *The Gipsy in Music* was of the 'special votary of nature':

> Can it be that the Gipsy race is more susceptible than others to the sensations, as exquisite as they are intense, produced by Nature's marvels? One is almost tempted to think so, seeing it stand so completely alone in rejecting with utter pertinacity everything which might in the least degree tend to imperil the satisfaction of that one excessive passion.[24]

Music, in Liszt's Schopenhauerian reading, required no mediation by thought or idea to 'directly awaken emotion by sensation',[25] and instrumental music in particular allowed the passions which were 'depicted in their glow of virtual strength' to be 'enjoyed in their purest essence'.[26] The guileless, uneducated child of nature, the Gypsy, was thus the most 'natural' musician. His art was doomed to inferiority, however, for although he had 'instinctively discovered the secrets of how to render in art the mode and intensity of his deepest feelings', he was unable to transfer them to the realm of action, to 'the *good*'.[27] Despite this imperfection in the performer (shared, as far as Liszt was concerned, by much of mankind), the Gypsy (or 'Bohemian') melodies formed a Hungarian national music equal in quality to any other art. That of the peasantry, both vocal and instrumental was, however, 'too poor and incomplete to produce any new artistic result' and could not yet 'even pretend to the honour of being universally appreciated; yet still less to that of being ranked with lyrical works which have already attained to a high degree of repute'.[28] Strangely, Liszt (or rather Princess Carolyne von Sayn-Wittgenstein, who was responsible for 'correcting' the proofs for the revised edition of 1881, and in so doing adding much of the anti-Semitic material)[29] stresses the Gypsy's racial purity in a section titled *Contrast with the Jews*, noting that they had resisted the 'weakness of allowing a drop of foreign blood to mingle with their race', and remarking that women who had been 'contaminated' by liaisons with non-Gypsies were normally ostracised by the rest of the community.[30]

Bartók's position *vis-à-vis* peasant music presents an almost Derridean deconstruction of that of Liszt. The 'pure' folk music of the peasantry, 'a natural phenomenon',[31] is now prioritised at the expense of the 'professional' Gypsy music, a primarily *urban* and composed art music which is performed for profit.[32] Whilst, for Liszt, peasant music was in large part a corruption of the Gypsy music to which Hungarian lyrics had been added by the musically illiterate rustic,[33] for Bartók, Gypsy music is not composed or improvised by its executants, but is borrowed and adapted from material produced by Magyars (for the most part the gentry, though a number of Gypsy melodies can be regarded as garbled versions of peasant songs). Bartók's only concession is to grant that, despite the poverty-stricken and factory-produced nature of the Gypsy repertoire, it is nonetheless Hungarian in origin, and thus superior to that of the 'jazz and salon orchestras' with their 'admixture of waltzes, song hits, jazz elements, and what not'.[34]

What remains invariant in Bartók's reversal of the *status quo* is the 'natural' basis for the music, now transferred from Gypsy to peasant. The most ancient strand of rural folk music, sung and performed by some elements of the peasantry (generally the poorest and least educated), is as much a manifestation of 'nature' as the plants and animals he or she tends.[35] Although individual peasants are not to be invested with agency as composers of the material they reproduce, they are granted (by Bartók) the innate, untutored ability to transform it, in much the same way that environmental factors influence the development of a living organism. Such a view appears to be founded upon a constrained and idealised notion of 'pure' nature separate from more or less 'impure' humanity, for we are faced with the clear implication that the popular art music of the city (despite being composed and performed by people who are as much an element of the 'natural' world as any other) is both 'artificial', impotent and *vulgar*. In his essay of 1921, 'The Relation of Folk Song to the Development of the Art Music of Our Time', Bartók clearly articulates his philosophy of aesthetic value:

> At all events it is a noteworthy fact that artistic perfection can only be achieved by one of the two extremes: on the one hand by peasant folk in the mass, completely devoid of the culture of the town-dweller, on the other by creative power of an individual genius. The creative power of anyone who has the misfortune to be born between these two extremes

leads only to barren, pointless and misshapen works. When peasants or the peasant classes lose their naïvety and their artless ignorance, as a result of the conventional culture, or more accurately half-culture, of the town-dwelling folk, they lose at the same time all their artistic transforming power.[36]

It is tempting, perhaps, to see a socialist programme underlying Bartók's espousal of the peasant music, particularly considering his involvement in 1919 in the short-lived communist government of Béla Kun, as a member, along with Dohnányi and Kodály, of the Musical Directorate of the Commune, to whose care was consigned 'the guidance of the entire musical life'.[37] These artists apparently offered their services for two primary reasons, one positive and one negative: firstly, they hoped that social and economic conditions might see some improvement under the communist regime; and secondly, they wished to prevent any mishaps befalling Hungarian musical life, and to cut 'the ground from under the feet of ungifted musical parvenus'.[38] The soviet-style dictatorship lasted a mere 133 days, however, and the three musicians were left in the embarrassing position of having publicly supported the 'wrong' faction, creating considerable discomfort for them in the ensuing period of counter-revolution.

The political climate in Horthy's Hungary would certainly have made any open support for socialist policies potentially dangerous for Bartók, but there seems to be relatively little biographical information, which suggests that his inclinations were particularly radical. The Marxist critic Béla Balázs, librettist of *Duke Bluebeard's Castle* and author of the scenario for *The Wooden Prince*, proposes that the composer's 'love of the people' exemplified in his dissemination of their music was indicative of a 'class-based attitude'.[39] Gillies, less idealistically, submits that the composer was inclined to offer his support to the underdog,[40] a perverse tendency which could have been a minor variable in his reorientation of 'authentic' Hungarian folk music from the Gypsy to the peasant. The composer was certainly damning in his assessment of the period of socialist control, particularly in consideration of its handling of musical matters, noting that 'the Trades Union of Musicians (artists) and Musical Craftsmen (both classes were coupled together in one union!) stubbornly – albeit unsuccessfully – attempted, with the backing of the proletariat, to launch its most untalented but noisiest claimants for fame into leading positions'.[41]

Although their social and political conditions saw little improvement in the Horthy period, the lifestyle of the 'sturdy and healthy' Hungarian peasants was increasingly commended in crude blood-and-soil ideology by the ruling élite, while that of the urban proletariat and (in particular the Jewish) bourgeoisie was presented as dubious or even disreputable.[42] It is perhaps ironic that this standpoint (including to some extent, as Frigyesi's research has shown, the anti-Semitic element)[43] should be disconcertingly close to that of Bartók, as expressed in his writings and implied in some of his musical works (for instance, the pantomime *The Miraculous Mandarin*).[44] It is also notable that, despite any contempt he may have felt for Horthy and his cronies and their racial policies, Bartók chose to remain in Hungary for twenty years of his reactionary regime.

Given that Arnold Schoenberg and many other Jewish composers and artists who were vilified by the Nazis as degenerates were taking refuge in America at the same time as Bartók, one might have expected an essay entitled 'Race Purity in Music', published in the United States in 1942, to have contained an unambiguous response to the Nazi treatment of Jews and Jewish music in particular. Rather curiously, he side-steps the issue in his opening paragraph:

> There is much talk these days, mostly for political reasons, about the purity and impurity of the human race, the usual implication being that purity of race should be preserved, even by means of prohibitive laws. Those who champion this or that issue of the question have probably studied the subject thoroughly (at least they should have done so) spending many years examining the available published material or gathering data by personal investigation. Not having done that, perhaps I cannot support either side, and may even lack the right to do so.[45]

János Breuer has chronicled Bartók's dealings with the Third Reich, and notes that only four of the published letters written before 1938 make any reference to Nazism. In 1934, in order to squash rumours that Bartók was Jewish, Universal Edition suggested that he send documentation to prove his Christian parentage to the Nazi authorities, and this was met with his blunt refusal.[46] From 1935 to 1938 a number of concerts and lectures by Bartók were scheduled in the Third Reich (in Berlin, Frankfurt and Wiesbaden among others), though, for one reason or another, none took place.[47] According to Breuer's research, however, there were at least 47 performances of Bartók's works in Nazi Germany between 1933 and 1942 (as reported in German musical periodicals of the time), including a minimum of twelve of *Music for Strings, Percussion and Celesta*.[48] It seems that these concerts occurred, despite the antipathy of Nazi music critics, largely because of the Reich's policy of encouraging works by artists in countries which were supportive of the Nazi regime, which clearly would have included Horthy's Hungary.[49]

If Bartók is less than willing to clarify his position on the Nazi doctrine of race purity in his essay, he shows no such disinclination to assert the importance of impurity in the development of a national folk music. The intermingling of races brought about by war, famine or economic necessity has had two major impacts on folk music, he argues: in the first case it has provided for the transfer of melodies from one race to another (melodies sometimes 'crossing and recrossing' between them);[50] and in the second it has encouraged new hybrid styles to be formed, which, despite their assimilation of many and varied national elements, are adapted to the 'spirit' of the indigenous culture and exhibit a 'perfect purity of style'.[51]

At the heart of the 1942 essay lies a curious paradox, for, while Bartók regards internationalisation as detrimental to the development and continuation of peasant music, he believes that the best means of circumventing it is by allowing peasant musics from different cultures to interact, for by doing so the 'material of each, however heterogeneous in origin, receives its marked individuality'.[52] The preservation of a culture by artificially segregating it from alien influences restricts the potential gene pool, resulting in a poverty-stricken and stagnant music.[53] Bartók likens the changes that affect folk material when it is transferred from one race to another, and sometimes back again, to those which influence linguistic developments in similar circumstances, pointing as an example to the relative impurity of the English language, whose vocabulary is only around sixty per cent Anglo-Saxon, yet which has 'developed incomparable strength of expression and individuality of spirit'.[54]

Bartók implies that the greatest threat to peasant music is from the culture of the city, a point on which he is most pessimistic, noting that 'any hope for the survival of folk music in the near or distant future' is 'rather doubtful considering the intrusion of higher civilisation into the more remote parts of the world'.[55] Sympathetic as he was to the plight of the peasantry, one must remember that the very existence of their music was founded upon abject poverty: some 40 per cent of them, over 30 per cent of the total population of Hungary, were landless agricultural labourers who subsisted on around 100 days of work per year.[56] A jaundiced peasant might have suggested that it was all very well for the sophisticated middle-class composer and ethnomusicologist to lament the decline of a music founded upon poor dietary and sanitary conditions, lack of education, disease, inadequate housing and short lifespan, but that social advances and improvements in living standards were of more moment than the retention of ancient cultural practices.

What then was Bartók's construction of musical nationalism? He believed that nineteenth-century nationalists such as Dvořák and Grieg had 'embedded' musical elements from rural (or more often semi-rural) folk materials within a style which, by and large, retained the conventions of common-practice melody, harmony, orchestration and form.[57] The failure to fully synthesise implied by the term 'embed' was the result of a stylistic mismatch, the implication being that a successful national style should be syncretic, 'high' and 'low' elements being absorbed within each other, neither dominating. To compose such a music (and Bartók believed that he and Kodály had at least attempted, if not fully succeeded, in what was an almost religious mission) one had to be fully attentive to every detail and nuance of the folk material.

As he discovered when making notations of autochthonous folk music during his collecting trips, transcription of the often elaborately decorated tunes using the tools of 'high-art' music (an approach which contemporary ethnomusicologists describe as etic) can constrain the metrical and rhythmic patterns of the music to fit the conventions which the method of notation has evolved or been designed to visually display. Bartók's concern for accuracy of representation led him to notate his transcriptions with extraordinary detail, especially the parameters of pitch and duration. Whilst this may appear counterproductive from the performer's point of view (the scores are often virtually unreadable and freedom of interpretation is almost entirely excluded), it has the positive effect of compelling the composer to be aware of the danger of normalising his or her sources by flattening their contours. The dirt and grime of the peasant performance is thus not simply brushed off, but is allowed to permeate both the transcription and the compositional style derived from it.[58]

Adorno observed, in consideration of the music of Bartók and Janáček, that, 'in contrast to the blood-and-soil ideology – a party-line tenet of National Socialism – truly extra-territorial music . . . has a power of alienation which places it in the company of the avant-garde and not that of nationalistic reaction'.[59] For Bartók, an essential feature of all the peasant music he studied was its 'complete absence of sentimentality or exaggeration of expression',[60] a characteristic which placed it in stark relief to both the pathos-laden gentry-authored pseudo-folk music in particular and 'popular' music in general, and which informed his own compositional and performance styles. One might argue that Bartók defused the orthodoxy of nationalism by so tightly weaving the 'objective' peasant materials from eastern Europe, the Balkans and north Africa (including their roughness and grit), using the techniques of occidental art music, that the tensions between the competing 'high' and 'low' styles dissipated themselves. Indeed, many Bartók scholars have suggested that he seamlessly integrated his sources in a supra-national or universal idiom which reflected his belief in a 'brotherhood of peoples'.[61] This may represent an idealistic view of his success in combining his multifarious influences, for listeners with some knowledge of both east-central European folk and Western 'high-art' music will probably be aware of some friction between the different elements. What may be accepted by most people is the absence of triumphalism or 'musical jingoism' in the mature style (perhaps the Finale of the Concerto for Orchestra is closest to an exception, though many of its sources are actually Romanian rather than Hungarian). It is certainly difficult to imagine brass or wind band arrangements of many of Bartók's mature compositions being used to accompany military reviews or nationalist celebrations in the way that Tchaikovsky's or Smetana's are.

Bartók, like Schoenberg, asserted the importance of musical tradition, and a belief in evolutionary rather than revolutionary processes in the development of a musical 'language'.[62] In the series of lectures delivered at Harvard University in 1943 (which had to be truncated because of the composer's ill health), he showed disdain for the experimental compositions of composers such as the Czech Alois Hába and his own former piano student Imre Weisshaus, as well as equivalent works of literature and art (in particular those of Piet Mondrian);[63] Schoenberg and Stravinsky were both, however, to be seen as inheritors of conventions – that of Austro-German romanticism in the former case and Russian 'high-art' and peasant music in the latter.[64] Having dismissed the music traditionally considered to be Hungarian, namely that performed by the Gypsies, as inauthentic (and in a sense 'unnatural'), Bartók required another 'style and means' which could offer the potential for evolutionary development to act as a source for his music. This wellspring was, of course, peasant music, the 'national style' he adopted, owing its inception not to the nobility, the hereditary guardians of national identity, nor the bourgeoisie, the ascendant social class, nor the urban proletariat on whose labour was largely built the nation's wealth and prestige, but to the lowest strand of the rural peasantry, the part of the community which had the least direct influence on the formation of an ideology of nationhood, and, given that many peasants were struggling even to survive, probably the least interest in one.

Bartók's musical 'nationalism' would thus appear to be founded both on social divisiveness in its delegitimation of a widely accepted popular national style, and on assimilation in its integration of non-Hungarian influences. Although his music was written for a largely bourgeois audience (the concert-going public), it prioritised musical material (that of the peasantry) which was in the main antipathetic to their sensibilities. The extent to which it could antagonise some early critics because of its putative disorder is evinced in a review in the *Cincinnati Enquirer* of 26 February 1928 of a performance by the composer of his First Piano Concerto:

> It has been said that the Concerto is based on folk tunes. They have been successfully concealed. Only tonal chaos arises from the diabolical employment of unrelated keys simultaneously. It is like a mystic maze. The guide alone knows the way out.[65]

The type of folk music that the anonymous reviewer was probably expecting was the domesticated sort: the sentimentalised, metrically regular, urban view of the pastoral, which, like the well-tended suburban garden, provides an illusion of nature whilst denying its entropic tendencies. The town garden symbolises control rather than freedom: lawns which are not mown and weeded, and are allowed to go to seed, are usually seen to be symptomatic of social disorder and urban decay. Rural 'nature' is both enchanting and threatening, however, for both growth and decay, which the city attempts to veil, are ever-present, reminding us of both our mortality and our social fragility. This warning must have been particularly clear to the urban Hungarian gentry, for they could discern in their impoverished lower brethren, who were living in the country often in worse economic conditions than the wealthier peasantry, the possibility of their own decline and fall.

Ironically, particularly given the composer's disdain for 'experimental' art, Bartók's works, which were composed under the influence of the 'music of Nature' and which involved the application of techniques derived from the detailed study of peasant music, have often been perceived as cerebral or 'mathematical', epithets commonly associated with formalism. For some listeners, his music would appear to exemplify two of the basic anxieties of bourgeois society with regard to musical modernism: anarchy and intellectualism, or in the words of the anonymous critic cited above 'tonal chaos' and the 'mystic maze'. As another American reviewer put it in 1928, 'he has achieved one of the great desires of the modernists, in turning things upside down'.[66] Bartók indicated in his writings the extent to which peasant influences had resulted in harmonic and melodic structures which appeared superficially similar to those used by modernist composers such as Schoenberg, and this tendency, and his penchant for 'scientific' data-handling techniques and structural analysis, seem to place him securely in the camp of modernism.[67]

Botstein has noted in a recent essay that 'a modernist synthesis between the Hungarian and the European could demonstrate how the preindustrial world and its protagonist, the peasant . . . functioned as a source of modernism independent of the nineteenth century'.[68] As Ashcroft et al. point out, much of the impetus for the development of modernism in arts other than music actually came from the European discovery of 'primitive' (in particular African) art forms which exhibited very different modes of expression from accepted European norms.[69] The influence of the 'primitive' on European art took two primary forms: as the 'negative of the positive concept of the civilized, the black Other to the white norm . . . Or, in what is really only a false converse to the same Eurocentric viewpoint . . . as the liberating Dionysiac force which could shatter the Apollonian certainty of nineteenth-century bourgeois society'.[70] For many of Bartók's critics, the peasant music which he studied and absorbed represented, in its most elemental form, the 'East', or, using Lendvai's term, the Orient,[71] although in reality most of it came from east-central Europe, and relatively little from what are now described as the Middle or Far East.[72] Certainly, what initially fascinated Bartók about it was its *difference*: its temporal and spiritual detachment from popular art music, which, he believed, gave it the possibility of both revitalising 'high-art' music and making it relevant to a fully independent Hungary.

Ashcroft et al. remark that 'the crucial function of language as a medium of power demands that post-colonial writing define itself by seizing the language of the centre and re-placing itself in a discourse fully adapted to the colonized place'.⁷³ If 'music' is substituted for 'language' in this formulation, and the music of the centre is taken to be that of the Austro-German 'high-art' tradition,⁷⁴ exemplified at the end of the nineteenth century by figures such as Wagner, Brahms and Strauss, could Bartók's rejection of the hegemonic style for one more clearly influenced by the Hungarian composer Liszt around 1904 not be considered as an act of abrogation,⁷⁵ 'a refusal of the categories of the imperial culture, its aesthetic, its illusory standard of normative or "correct" usage, and its assumption of a traditional and fixed meaning'?⁷⁶ This first stage of transformation of his style from that of the 'centre', Vienna, to that of the 'periphery', Budapest, was followed by a second and more important one from urban to rural which came with his integration of peasant-influenced material in a syncretic musical idiom, which might, perhaps, be seen in post-colonial terms as an act of appropriation ('the process by which the language is taken and made to "bear the burden" of one's own cultural experience').⁷⁷

If Bartók's music is to be regarded as post-colonial rather than nationalist and modernist, it must be expected to exhibit a transformation of the terms of the musical discourse instead of a mere repudiation of Austro-German musical hegemony. It could be argued that Bartók's 'language', in which both large-scale structure and local detail are fundamentally affected by the folk music, manifests just such a shift in the discourse. The peasant music represented for him the literal roots of his identity, and he immersed himself within the culture it issued from to the extent that it became his vernacular, his 'mother tongue', and no longer the exotic 'other' to be invoked using the codes of orientalism. As a result of this musical rebirth, his large-scale works were increasingly composed 'outwards' from the peasant music, rather than inwards from the European frame, producing 'a musical style imbued even to the slightest details with emanations from this virgin source'.⁷⁸ An effect of this reorientation of foreground detail and global structure is an apparent fracturing of the musical fabric, for, whilst a fundamental feature of eighteenth- and nineteenth-century Austro-German music is the carefully wrought illusion of wholeness and smoothness in which irregularity, particularly of phrase length, is ingeniously concealed, the surface of Bartók's music often seems to be more deliberately fragmented, despite its formal integrity, a dynamic tension being established between structure and content. It is this tension which seems to place the music 'within and between' the two worlds of colony and independent state (although the former term is complicated by Hungary's position as junior partner in the Habsburg Empire, which was similar in some respects to that of Scotland in Great Britain after Union), and not as a simply 'affirmative' form of nationalism.

Although in retrospect it is possible to view Bartók's output as an example of a 'counter-discursive practice' which subverts and interrogates the tenets of the Austro-German tradition, it is fairly clear that the composer himself was more concerned about the development of a 'homologous practice', the formation of an 'authentic' Hungarian music.[79] In the conclusion to his essay on race purity in music, he draws the reader's attention to the musical sources of the patriotic Hungarian melody, the *Rákóczi March*:

> elements originating from the Arabic-Persian 'long melody', Eastern European-Hungarian elements, and ornamental motives of Central European art music: quite a collection of the most heterogeneous elements! Nevertheless, the way they are transformed, melted, and unified presents as a final result a masterpiece of music whose spirit and characteristics are incontestably Hungarian.[80]

Bartók's own compositions reconstruct Hungarian nationalism by accepting the importance of racial impurity and hybridisation in the art work, and by allowing that identity, whether individual or societal, is not static, but subject to the changes brought about by continual 'crossing and re-crossing' between national, social or musical boundaries.

Notes and References

1. The name Transleithania ('across the Leitha', a river running to the south and east of Vienna roughly parallel to the Danube), given to Hungary in the Dual-Monarchy period (1867–1918), neatly underlines the relationship between the two states, for the perspective is that of Austria (in Cisleithania or 'this side of the Leitha').
2. R. Pearson, *The Longman Companion to European Nationalism* (Harlow, 1994), p. 239.
3. J. K. Hoensch, *A History of Modern Hungary* (Harlow, 1984), pp. 28–9. The compromise gave a degree of autonomy to Hungary, though the Imperial Habsburg dynasty retained control over all military and diplomatic matters.
4. G. Jeszensky, 'Hungary Through World War I and the End of the Dual Monarchy', in P.F. Sugar, P. Hanák and T. Frank (eds.), *A History of Hungary* (London, 1990), p. 274.
5. Hoensch, *A History of Modern Hungary*, p. 32. By 1910 the first language of 75 per cent of the Jews was Hungarian.
6. I. T. Berend and G. Ránki, *East Central Europe in the 19th and 20th Centuries* (Budapest, 1977), p. 33 indicate that nearly half of all doctors and lawyers were Jewish by extraction.
7. Ibid., p. 33.
8. C. A. McCartney, *Hungary: A Short History* (Edinburgh, 1962), p. 202.
9. I. Deák, 'Admiral and Regent Miklós Horthy', *The Hungarian Quarterly*, 37, 143 (1996), p. 82.
10. Hoensch, *A History of Modern Hungary*, p. 106. Deák notes that during the ten years of Count István Bethlen's period as Prime Minister the practices of pre-war Hungary were largely reinstated, and the law which limited Jewish access to universities was generally ignored; see Deák, 'Admiral and Regent Miklós Horthy', p. 83. During the interwar years Jews formed around 5 per cent of the population.
11. According to Deák the moderate right contained 'Social democrats, peasant politicians, anti-conservative monarchists, rich Jewish liberals, mildly anti-Semitic counter-revolutionary politicians, and such Hungarian racists for whom the German minority represented more of a threat than the Jews. In the other camp

were pro-German counter-revolutionary politicians, most army officers, fascist ideologues, rabid anti-Semites, much of the non-Jewish middle class and petite bourgeoisie, and masses of poor people for whom National Socialism promised salvation from oppression by Jewish capitalists and aristocratic landowners' ('Admiral and Regent Miklós Horthy', p. 84).

12 Hoensch, *A History of Modern Hungary*, p. 128.
13 Deák argues that the effects of the anti-Jewish laws were moderate compared to those of other states, to the extent that, by 1944, 95 per cent of the Hungarian Jewish population was still alive, and that Horthy persuaded Hitler that the war industry was dependent upon Jewish workers ('Admiral and Regent Miklós Horthy', p. 85–6). However Berend and Ránki note that almost 500,000 people were murdered in Hungary before the end of the war (*East Central Europe in the 19th and 20th Centuries*, p. 154). This may well be a conservative estimate.
14 Letter to Irmy Jurkovics, 15 August 1905, in J. Demén (ed.), *Béla Bartók Letters* (Budapest, 1971), [26] p. 50.
15 Bartók, 'On Hungarian Music' (1911), in B. Suchoff (ed.), *Béla Bartók Essays* (Lincoln Y, London, 1976), [38] p. 301.
16 The term 'ethnomusicology' was not coined until the decade after Bartók's death.
17 Bartók apparently showed no inclination to collect from the latter two ethnic groups. He did, however, collect examples of 'peasant' Gypsy music, especially in Transylvania.
18 *Béla Bartók Essays* [38] 'On Hungarian Music' (1911), p. 302.
19 *Béla Bartók Letters* [175] to Vinko Žganec, 27 October, 1934, p. 229.
20 *Béla Bartók Letters* [81] to János Buşiţia, January 1912, p. 113.
21 J. Frigyesi, 'Béla Bartók and the Concept of Nation and Volk in Modern Hungary', *The Musical Quarterly*, 78, 2 (1994), pp. 255–87.
22 *Béla Bartók Essays* [29] 'Gipsy Music or Hungarian Music' (1931), p. 206. A damning review of the fourteenth volume of Heinrich Möller's *Das Lied der Vlker*, dedicated to Hungarian folk music.
23 In *Béla Bartók Essays* [39] 'Hungarian Peasant Music' (1920), he uses the term 'upper classes' rather than upper middle class. He is clearly referring to the lower strand of the nobility or gentry, the majority of whom lost their land in the latter part of the nineteenth century, and who formed a large part of the civil service.
24 Liszt, *The Gipsy in Music (Des Bohémiens et leur Musique en Hongrie)* trans. E. Evans (London, 1926), p. 84.
25 Ibid., p. 91. See, for instance, Schopenhauer, *The World as Will and Idea*, trans. R. B. Haldane and J. Kemp (London, 1891), Book 3, p. 232: 'That music acts directly upon the will, *i.e.*, the feelings, passions, and emotions of the hearer, so that it quickly raises them or changes them, may be explained from the fact that, unlike all the other arts, it does not express the Ideas, or grades of the objectification of the will, but directly the *will itself.*'
26 Liszt, *The Gipsy in Music*, p. 13.
27 Ibid., p. 92.
28 Ibid., p. 296.
29 See A. Walker, *Franz Liszt: The Weimar Years* (London, 1989), pp. 388–90. Although Walker suggests that it was common knowledge in Liszt's circle that Princess Carolyne was the author of the material concerning Jews, Liszt does not seem to have made any attempt to suppress it from the revised version, though he was unaware of the major changes she had made to this section until the book appeared. He made no public comment about the authorship of it, probably to spare Carolyne any embarrassment.
30 See Walker, *Franz Liszt: The Weimar Years*, p. 18.

31 *Béla Bartók Essays* [41] 'The Relation of Folk Song to the Development of the Art Music of Our Time' (1921), p. 321.
32 In his later writings Bartók was to acknowledge a distinction in performance style between the urban Gypsies and those who inhabited the most remote regions of Hungary and who lived in the closest proximity to the peasantry. In *Béla Bartók Essays* [29] 'Gipsy Music or Hungarian Music' (1931), p. 222, he notes the following: 'The simple rural gipsy plays in a manner entirely different to his urban cousins ... in the poor Rumanian villages of the County of Maramure music has passed from the hands of the native peasant bagpipers into those of the gipsies. Most of these gipsies fiddle the repertory they inherited from the pipers in a genuine peasant style.'
33 The peasant's 'inferior musical organisation would render him less conscious of the imperfections of his singing' (Liszt, *The Gipsy in Music*, p. 295).
34 *Béla Bartók Essays* [29] 'Gipsy Music or Hungarian Music' (1931), p. 207.
35 'We created through Nature, for: the peasant's art is a phenomenon of Nature', *Béla Bartók Essays* [42] 'The Folk Songs of Hungary' (1928), p. 338.
36 *Béla Bartók Essays* [41] 'The Relation of Folk Song to the Development of the Art Music of Our Time' (1921), p. 322.
37 *Béla Bartók Essays* [69] 'Post-war Musical Life in Budapest to February, 1920' (1920), p. 462.
38 Ibid. p. 462.
39 B. Balázs, 'From a Distant Land to a Distant Land: On the Occasion of Béla Bartók's Sixtieth Birthday', trans. D. Balázs, in P. Laki (ed.), *Bartók and His World* (Princeton, 1995), p. 266.
40 M. Gillies (ed.), *The Bartók Companion* (London, 1993), p. 11.
41 *Béla Bartók Essays* [69] 'Post-war Musical Life in Budapest to February, 1920' (1920), p. 462. He also strongly attacks the practice of singing the 'outrageous' *Liedertafel* melody of the *Internationale*, utterly devoid of both harmony and mentality', before performances at the Opera.
42 See Deák, 'Admiral and Regent Miklós Horthy', p. 82. Balázs writes in 1941 'the bourgeois demagogy has come to require the slogan of the "folk" to take in the folk. But then, it costs less to propagate the peasants' art than to distribute the land' ('From a Distant Land to a Distant Land: On the Occasion of Béla Bartók's Sixtieth Birthday', p. 272).
43 J. Frigyesi, 'Béla Bartók and Hungarian Nationalism: The Development of Bartók's Social and Political Ideas at the Turn of the Century (1899–1903)' (PhD diss., University of Pennsylvania, 1989).
44 Lawrence Kramer, in *Classical Music and Postmodern Knowledge* (Berkeley, 1995), remarks that both *The Miraculous Mandarin* and Stravinsky's *Rite of Spring* manifest 'a volatile mixture of fear and desire of the other'. This could be taken as a perceptive summary of the relationship between the sophisticated composer and the peasantry in general.
45 *Béla Bartók Essays* [5] 'Race Purity in Music' (1942), p. 29.
46 J. Breuer, 'Bartók and the Third Reich', *The Hungarian Quarterly*, 36, 140 (1995), p. 135.
47 Ibid., p. 135–6.
48 Ibid., p. 137–8.
49 Ibid., p. 137.
50 *Béla Bartók Essays* [5] 'Race Purity in Music' (1942), p. 30.
51 *Béla Bartók Essays* [11] 'Hungarian Folk Music' (1921), p. 59.
52 *Béla Bartók Essays* [5] 'Race Purity in Music' (1942), p. 30.
53 A distinction must be made between the artificial isolation of a culture and the 'natural' state of such regions as the Arab areas of North Africa, which, Bartók

hypothesises, have seen few migrations or intermarriages with other races. *Béla Bartók Essays* [5], p. 31.
54 Ibid.
55 Ibid. He remarks in *Béla Bartók Essays* [13] 'Hungarian Peasant Music' (1933) p. 83, that when art music compositions in folk style pass to the peasantry 'their form usually perfects itself during this process!'.
56 See Berend and Ránki, *East Central Europe in the 19th and 20th Centuries*, p. 118.
57 See *Béla Bartók Essays* [47] 'Hungarian Music' (1944), p. 393.
58 It should be noted that Bartók rarely quotes from actual folk music in his large-scale works.
59 T. W. Adorno, *Philosophy of New Music* (New York, 1980), pp. 35–6.
60 *Béla Bartók Essays* [47] 'Hungarian Music' (1944), p. 395.
61 *Béla Bartók Letters* [152], to Octavian Beu, 10 January 1931, p. 201. Bartk's librettist Béla Balázs encapsulates this latter point in his panegyric 'From a Distant Land to a Distant Land: On the Occasion of Béla Bartók's Sixtieth Birthday': 'Because for you, as for Herder in his own time, it was not chauvinism, but a deeply understood internationalism that made it possible for you to hear and understand "die Stimme der Vólke."' (in Laki [ed.], *Bartók and His World*, pp. 266–7).
62 See for instance Schoenberg's statement about the move to atonality in his essay 'How One Becomes Lonely' (1937): 'it called into existence a change of such an extent that many people, instead of realizing its evolutionary element, called it a revolution . . . I always insisted that the new music was merely a logical development of musical resources' (in L. Stein [ed.], *Style and Idea* [London, 1975]).
63 *Béla Bartók Essays* [46] 'Harvard Lectures' (1943), pp. 355–8.
64 Bartók's position with regard to Stravinsky is not entirely consistent. In a draft of a pre-concert talk of 1928 or 1929 he describes him as a revolutionary! See D. Schneider, 'Bartók and Stravinsky: Respect, Competition, Influence, and the Hungarian Reaction to Modernism in the 1920s' in Laki (ed.), *Bartók and His World*, p. 183.
65 Quoted in N. Slonimsky, *Lexicon of Musical Invective*, 2nd edn. (Seattle and London, 1953/1965), p. 41.
66 Ibid., p. 40 (*Christian Science Monitor*, Boston, 16 February 1928).
67 See, for example, *Béla Bartók Essays* [42] 'The Folk Songs of Hungary' (1928), pp. 331–9.
68 L. Botstein, 'Out of Hungary: Bartók, Modernism, and the Cultural Politics of Twentieth-Century Music', in Laki (ed.), *Bartók and His World*, p. 50.
69 B. Ashcroft, G. Griffiths and H. Tiffin, *The Empire Writes Back* (London, 1989), p. 156.
70 Ibid., p. 159.
71 See E. Lendvai, *The Workshop of Bartók and Kodály* (Budapest, 1983), p. 9.
72 See Said's discussion of the construction of the Orient in *Orientalism* (London, 1995). As this essay is being written (February 1997), television journalists are discussing Bulgaria's 'second chance to *rejoin* Europe'!
73 Ashcroft et al., *The Empire Writes Back*, p. 38.
74 One could argue that 'German' music held an equivalent position to that held by the English language for post-colonial literature.
75 See *Béla Bartók Essays* [52] 'Autobiography' (1921), p. 408.
76 Ashcroft et al., *The Empire Writes Back*, p. 38.
77 Ibid.
78 *Béla Bartók Essays* [47], p. 393.
79 See Ashcroft et al., *The Empire Writes Back*, p. 196.
80 *Béla Bartók Essays* [5], p. 32.

2.
Grove's Musical Dictionary: A National Document

JEREMY DIBBLE

The popular perception of British musical nationalism as a construction is one that attempts to define an emancipation from the cultural hegemony of Teutonicism. While such a sentiment may have been latent at the end of the nineteenth century, it veritably erupted in the years leading up to the First World War as Germany's industrial strength, personified by the arms race, surged ahead of Britain's. Perhaps the most vivid, not to say pugnacious, exposition of anti-German feeling is articulated in the writings of Cecil Forsyth, best known nowadays for his treatise, *Orchestration*. As Stradling and Hughes have identified, Forsyth adopted the manner of a politician in a blistering attack of national chauvinism against the immigrant musician:

> How long will it be before we realise the fact that where the foreign musician is there is the enemy? He may come to this island in shoals, but he comes for one purpose only – the money he can take back across the water, and he well knows that the surest way to make his position firm here is to denationalise our music.[1]

Forsyth's venom, fuelled by the jingoism of the time, was principally aimed at a bourgeoisie who still preferred to consider music as a foreign commodity. Opera, that most national of musico-dramatic vehicles, had, so Forsyth irascibly proclaimed, not been able to take root in British society, in spite of various attempts to establish it by Balfe, Pyne and Harrison, Mapleson, Rosa, D'Oyley Carte and Stanford. Stanford's attempts to persuade the London County Council to invest public money in a national opera venture had come to nought, even after the debate had reached the floor of the House of Commons in April 1903.[2] His solution to the problem was the creation of a national operatic institution that would be purely indigenous in its choice of singers, composers, conductors, players and designers, supported through unabashed patriotic fervour and by government subsidy. Immigrant musicians were to play no part in the process or performance, thereby assuring a potent ethnocentric base for the development of a genuine national voice. It was a recipe for cultural protectionism.

Though extreme in their polemicism, Forsyth's views represented a standpoint from which composers took a lead, particularly after 1918. Fuelled by motives of recrimination and chastisement, the need to free British music from German domination became an imperative for composers and critics alike. To be nationalist, or more precisely to be 'English', became the watchword in the 1920s, and found its natural home in the appropriation of folksong, a nostalgia for a lost pastoral Arcadia and the belief in a spiritual link with the Tudor period. This was the preserve of the younger generation who had turned their back on pre-war values and, more specifically, on the overtly pro-German eclecticism of their forebears. Stanford, perhaps more than any of his older contemporaries, rudely witnessed the sea-change as publishers refused to take any of his late instrumental works,[3] but there is no doubt that others such as Mackenzie, Elgar and Cowen were aware that the new age did not belong to them.

It is necessary to underscore this twentieth-century construction of nationalism in Britain in order to provide a means of comparison with developments in the later nineteenth century when a different set of criteria held sway. One of the most important of these criteria was the acceptance of music as essentially a foreign commodity. Continental conductors, singers, instrumentalists and composers successfully colonised Britain's major cities and indulged in an art form that ran counter to the public utilitarian ideals of Bentham and John Stuart Mill. Attitudes began to change in the 1850s, largely at the behest of the Prince Consort. After the international success of the Great Exhibition in 1851, which served to heighten awareness of the nation's scientific and artistic potential, music was given royal endorsement as a focus for national improvement. Energies were devoted to the foundation of a conservatory actively supported by members of the royal family and politicians.[4] The ancient universities instituted reforms to their degrees while elementary schools were directed to include the teaching of music as part of the Education Act of 1870. Yet, while these initiatives gathered momentum, Britain began to realise that, while it could boast great traditions of international repute in literature and the visual arts, there was no natural infrastructure for the serious cultivation of music that could rival its continental counterparts. Moreover, to compound this sense of inadequacy, Britain could not but be aware that Europe itself was undergoing significant changes, the most potent of which was Germany's unification and subsequent rise to power. More than any other country, Germany had been perceived by Britain as the principal repository of musical values. She had produced Handel and Mendelssohn, as well as Leipzig, the mecca for compositional instruction for most British composers travelling abroad. Moreover, Germany's aesthetic sensibility was shored up by the significant population of Austro-German musicians who settled in Britain's major cities. One thinks of August Manns, Ludwig Strauß, Charles Hallé, Otto Goldschmidt, Ernst Pauer, Edward Dannreuther, Oscar Beringer, Carl Engel and Hans Richter, and also those who came for a limited period, such as Max Bruch, and frequent visitors, such as Joseph Joachim. And there were of course many minor figures such as Otto Beyschlag (the conductor of the Leeds Philharmonic Choir) and Augustus Jaeger. Britain's musical environment was therefore strongly coloured by the stylistic imperatives of German music, performance-practice and organisation. It naturally followed that what Britain aspired to was equality with, rather than differentiation from, Germany. Recognition by Germany, whether from a publisher, a conductor or the press, was considered a major artistic *coup* for the composer or performer, and it was this essential desire, fed by the anxiety of inferiority, that fuelled a sense of musical purpose in Britain. Such a feeling was especially prevalent in the 1870s.

Besides the urgency to ameliorate standards of composition, orchestral playing, national teaching institutions and, most importantly, social access, there was one vital area of British musical life that lacked proper credence or definition: this was musicology. As a focus of scholarship, which elevated music to the level of a science, musicology (*Musikwissenschaft*) was effectively a Teutonic invention and one in which the German-speaking nations of Europe led the way unassailably. In Britain, however, the establishment of any kind of musicological tradition had laboured under the yoke of utility. Thinking about music was limited essentially to the 'practical' and 'useful', an attitude powerfully illustrated by the preoccupation of the ancient universities with contrapuntal stringency of the 'exercise', and one confirmed by the examination papers introduced by Sterndale Bennett in Cambridge (1855) and Ouseley in Oxford (1861). Such training as these degrees furnished was not designed to broaden the intellect of the supplicant; instead it acted essentially as a technical preparation for the cathedral organist, or more essentially the church musician.[5] This utilitarian attitude was underlined by the very status of the degree itself, which was non-resident and therefore possessed no programme of lectures or tutorials. As a result, music as an academic discipline, was relegated to the status of a 'second-class' subject, in spite of its ancient contribution to the universities' *quadrivium*. Only in 1893 did music finally gain this status in Cambridge with Stanford's radical reform; Oxford, much to Parry's chagrin, had to wait far longer.

By the early 1870s the need for change could be sensed in various quarters. As identified by Stradling and Hughes,[6] Pater's influential *The Renaissance* called for a new artistic philosophy:

> For us the Renaissance is the name of a many-sided but yet united movement, in which the love of the things of the intellect and the imagination for their own sake, the desire for a more liberal and comely way of conceiving life, make themselves felt, urging those who experience this desire to search out first one and then another means of intellectual

or imaginative enjoyment, and then directing them not only to discovery of old and forgotten sources of this enjoyment, but to the divination of fresh sources thereof – new experiences, new subjects of poetry, new forms of art. Of such feeling there was a great outbreak in the end of the twelfth and the beginning of the following century. Here and there, under rarer and happy conditions, in pointed architecture, in the doctrines of romantic love, in the poetry of Provence, the rude strength of the middle ages turns to sweetness; and the taste for sweetness generated there becomes the seed of the classical revival in it, prompting it constantly to seek after the springs of perfect sweetness in the Hellenic world. And coming after a long period in which so many sources of intellectual and imaginative enjoyment had actually disappeared, this outbreak is rightly called a Renaissance, a revival.[7]

The passion of Pater's book, with its evocative, often imprecise language, presaged a new form of criticism and reception which challenged the moral aesthetics of Ruskin while at the same time attempting to build more radically on the ideas of Matthew Arnold.[8] The imperative of 'the desire of beauty [and] art for its own sake'[9] seemed to represent a watershed in which the old 'Hebraism', with its stultifying puritanism, was rejected in favour of a new, sensuous aesthetic world. By the same token attitudes to music, and more particularly to the cultivation of musicology as an intellectual stimulus within the spheres of science, literature and history, were awakened with considerable alacrity.

It is surely significant that one of Britain's most accomplished immigrant musicologists, the now largely neglected Carl Engel, should have pointed out the pressing need for a musical library where all aspects of its study – primary sources, scores, books, treatises, theoretical works, histories, journals, dictionaries and catalogues – should be available in the one place. 'There is no necessity for extending this list any further,' Engel exclaimed, 'as it will suffice to indicate the plan which, in my opinion, ought to be pursued in the formation of a national musical library.'[10] Engel's vision was keenly informed by his holistic German heritage and it was one that he wished to see complement the 'extraordinary progress which, during [the last 20 or 30 years], has been made in the diffusion of musical knowledge'.[11] In urging the Musical Library of the British Museum to reconstitute itself into a serious repository of musical sources, Engel touched on a detail which struck at the very heart of Britain's neglect of music as a legitimate, professional field of study:

> The English language possesses no musical dictionary, technical, biographical, or bibliographical, similar to the French and German works by Fétis, Schilling, Gerber, Koch, Rousseau, and others, which are indispensable for the library. With these may be classed the useful works on the Literature of Music compiled by Forkel, Lichtental, and Becker, as well as Hofmeister's comprehensive 'Handbuch der musikalischen Literatur.'[12]

The publication of Engel's essay, 'A Musical Library', appeared in the first volume of essays, *Musical Myths and Facts*, in 1876, a timely moment, in that, only two years before, the prospectus of Britain's first major musical lexicon, *A Dictionary of Music and Musicians (1450–1880) by Eminent Writers, English and Foreign, with Illustrations and Woodcuts* edited by George Grove, was published by Macmillan. Its tone pre-echoed Engel's aspirations:

> The want of English works on the history, theory, or practice of Music, or the biographies of musicians accessible to the non-professional reader, has long been a subject of remark. The 'Biographical Dictionary of Musicians', the latest English book of the kind, was published in 1827, and even for that date is very incomplete. Dr Callcott's 'Grammar of Music', though issued in 1817 [sic.], is the latest attempt to give a general account of the form and terms of the art in a popular style. But to Dr Callcott modern instrumental music was (naturally) a *terra incognita* – the name of Beethoven occurs only once in the entire volume.[13]

Attempts to produce dictionaries much earlier in the nineteenth century had largely come to nought. Callcott, referred to in the *Grove* prospectus, had produced a slight but not insignificant publication, *An Explanation of the Notes, Marks, Words, &c. used in Music* in 1793 and *A Musical Grammar* in 1806. A much more ambitious dictionary was proposed in *A Plan of Practical Dictionary of Music*, published in 1799, but the grand scheme never reached fruition.[14] Others such as the critics William Ayrton and Richard Bacon entertained similar ideas, but it was not until Sainsbury's *Dictionary of Musicians* appeared in its first edition of 1824 that Britain could boast of a biographical dictionary in English. Sainsbury's *Dictionary* was modelled essentially on the biographical model of Choron and Fayelle's *Dictionnaire historique des musiciens*, published in Paris (1810–11), and was heavily dependent on its information (indeed Sainsbury's preface went so far as to be a translation of its French predecessor). Other British musical publications of the first half of the nineteenth century concerned themselves with matters terminological. Various dictionaries of musical terms appeared between 1803, with Thompson's *A Dictionary of Music*, and 1834, with J. A. Hamilton's *A Dictionary of 1,000 Musical Terms*, though both were superseded by Stainer and Barrett's *A Dictionary of Musical Terms* (1876), which became widely used as a student primer. However, there had been no attempt in Britain to publish an encyclopaedic work bringing together elements of musical science with terminology, biography, bibliography and history. It was precisely to this lacuna that Engel referred and that Grove, seizing the opportunity, wished to remedy.[15]

Grove's energy, experience and skill were highly suited to the production of a musical encyclopaedia. Though he remained, in essence, an amateur in the musical profession – he was trained as an engineer – he nevertheless gained immense knowledge of music (and other subjects) as an administrator and facilitator. Perhaps the most important catalyst in this respect was his acquaintance with J. S. Russell (also a civil engineer), who was secretary to the Royal Society of Arts. Grove became assistant secretary to the RSA and succeeded Russell in 1850. This brought Grove directly into contact with the Great Exhibition, with Henry Cole (the force behind the establishing of the National Training School), and to the secretaryship of the Crystal Palace. During the late 1850s and 1860s his interests in biblical research brought him into contact with William Smith and the production of *The Dictionary of the Bible*, an ambitious project which involved two visits to the Holy Land in 1858 and 1861. He also formed a close friendship with Dean Stanley, and was involved in the establishment of the Palestine Exploration Fund. During this time Grove was able to develop his musical study, first as the organiser of the Crystal Palace Concerts (for which he provided analytical essays for the programmes), and second by acquaintance with a wide circle of musicians, both in Britain and on the continent. Friendships with Sullivan, Clara Schumann, Alexander Thayer (the biographer of Beethoven), A. Maczewski (Concert Director of the *Kaiserslautern*) and M. Gustave Chouquet (keeper of the museum of the Conservatoire de Musique in Paris) were cemented and his famous journey to Vienna in 1867, which led to the discovery of the partbooks of Schubert's *Rosamunde*, established a close relationship with C. F. Pohl, the librarian of the *Gesellschaft de Musikfreunde*. To this diverse field of experience Grove added the editorship of *Macmillan's Magazine* in 1868 (a job he retained until 1883); the association with Macmillan, a major publisher in London, would prove crucial to his plans for a musical dictionary.

The opportunity to edit a major musical publication along the lines of an encyclopaedia provided Grove with the chance to execute a project that would not only do much to promote music at a time when national perceptions of the art were noticeably ameliorating (*teste* Grove, Macmillan and Engel) but which would also bolster nationalist perceptions of Britain as a musical nation emerging with a new confidence in all areas of the subject.[16] The proposed dictionary could enshrine the awakening of national talent in composition; it could point to national scholars in the areas of history, organology, and theory; it could shed light on the nation's own genuine musical past, and confirm the nation's own sense of renaissance. In fact, it could act as a galvanising manifesto for British music,[17] whether in education, libraries, choral societies, festivals, scholarship and composition and in the formation of national musical standards and tastes. Most importantly, the dictionary could stand as a national monument, which, as evidence of British musical earnestness and scholarly credentials, could be observed from the outside, not least by the Austro-German axis, with admiration and respect.

In the preface to Volume I of his dictionary, Grove was uninhibited in stating his intention to emphasise the existence (and value) of his country's past musical heritage: 'In an English dictionary it has been thought right to treat English music and musicians with special care, and to give their biographies and achievements with some minuteness of detail.' In addition it was necessary to pursue this goal using native writers of national stature; 'their names', Grove affirmed, 'are in themselves a guarantee for the value of their contributions.' Obvious choices were Edward Francis Rimbault and William Chappell, who together formed the Musical Antiquarian Society in 1840, which itself had produced nineteen folio volumes of transcriptions of English sixteenth- and seventeenth-century music. Indeed Rimbault's work for the Musical Antiquarian Society was hugely influential, for his editions of Byrd, Bateson, Gibbons, Morley and Purcell brought such music before a public largely unfamiliar with England's past. He also took an active interest in Britain's eighteenth-century musical heritage, notably the cathedral music of Samuel Arnold. Rimbault, an inveterate collector of manuscripts and old editions, was the author of numerous articles and might have produced many more had he not died in 1876 as the dictionary was getting under way. Reflecting his scholarly interests, he produced articles on 'Byrd', 'Samuel Arnold' and 'William Boyce' as well as a number of brief accounts of minor personalities such the seventeenth-century composer 'John Attey' and 'Robert Bremnor', the eighteenth-century Scottish singer and teacher who authored *Rudiments of Music, with Psalmody* and arranged Scottish songs for voice and harpsichord. But far more prolific than Rimbault was William Husk, the librarian to the Sacred Harmonic Society. In asking Husk to provide a substantial number of articles on English musicians of the sixteenth and seventeenth centuries, Grove was effectively recognising and highlighting the significance of the Sacred Harmonic Society as a major British choral institution, as well as the Society's extensive library, the first catalogue of which (by Husk) was published in 1862. Husk applied himself to the task with assiduousness, providing articles on English Renaissance masters such as 'Tye', 'Tallys [sic]', 'Orlando Gibbons', 'Christopher Gibbons', 'Farrant' and 'Ferrabosco', 'Purcell', 'Locke', 'Blow', eighteenth-century composers such as 'Arne' and 'Boyce', and well-known names of the nineteenth century such as 'H. J. Gauntlett' who died only three years before the publication of Volume I of the *Dictionary*. But there is a profusion of short items in a similar vein to those by Rimbault (whose article Husk also provided) such as entries on 'Luffman Atterbury', 'Richard Bellamy', 'George Farquhar Graham' and 'William Tans'ur' all of which were designed to accentuate the variety and abundance of indigenous music-making.[18] In accordance with Grove's national stratagem, Husk also attempted to define the characteristics of 'English Opera' and its chequered history of false dawns and failures, though he was not in time to document the enormous success of Gilbert and Sullivan,[19] nor of Carl Rosa's commissioning of British operas between 1883 and 1887.

In addition to biographies, Grove took care to draw attention to the range of musical institutions in Britain, particularly those with a history.

William Chappell provided such articles as the 'Musical Antiquarian Society' and the 'Musician's Company of the City of London' established during the reign of Edward IV – a strategic example of ancient pedigree – as well as one on the family firm ('Chappell & Co.'). But there were many contemporary organisations which lent weight to Grove's portrayal of a musical Britain. Fuller Maitland provided an article on the 'Musical Society of London', his brother-in-law William Barclay Squire wrote one on the 'Musical Union', while Charles Mackeson, a surgeon by profession, supplied pieces on concert life, including the 'Academy of Antient Music', 'British Concerts', 'Eisteddfod' and 'Festivals', as well as those on active societies, namely the 'Bach Society', the 'Madrigal Society', the 'Society of British and Foreign Musicians', the 'Society of British Musicians' and, of recent vintage, the 'Musical Association'. William Cummings also produced accounts of the 'Royal Society of Musicians of Great Britain' and the 'Royal Society of Female Musicians', which became affiliated to the former institution in 1866. Other major concert venues, such as the 'St James's Hall', the 'Philharmonic Society' and 'National Concerts', were contributed by William Chappell, Stanley Lucas and Fuller Maitland respectively, while Grove, not surprisingly, wrote the article on the 'Crystal Palace Saturday Concerts'. Alongside this 'corroboration' of Britain's active musical past was the more optimistic statement of the country's present in terms of its institutions.[20] At the time of the *Dictionary*'s conception, the possibility of a national conservatory of music was the subject of hot debate. Barclay Squire produced a tactful article on the 'Royal Academy of Music', which had once been the target of Henry Cole's aspirations for a new, enlarged national institution. But after the plan was rejected by Sterndale Bennett, who wanted the RAM to remain independent, Cole decided to push ahead with his own plans for a National Training School of Music (NTSM) with royal support. Fuller Maitland's equally tactful article on the NTSM, which conspicuously avoided all mention of the original contention over the RAM, appeared in Volume II of the *Dictionary*, only two years before the NTSM was closed, making way for the Royal College of Music with Grove at its helm. By the time Volume III was published in July 1883, Fuller Maitland's article (the 'National Training School for Music') had been superseded by Grove's ('[National] Training School for Music) which, in announcing the closure of the NTSM ushered in the RCM as a subsidiary article, proudly listing its staff, its newly gained library holdings of the Sacred Harmonic Society, and even its first examiners.[21] The grand national plan was gaining momentum![22]

Biography and infrastructural history were important to Grove's Anglocentric agenda, but other components were equally vital. His reliance on British scholarship (or on those immigrant scholars who had made Britain their home) for all aspects of theory, acoustics, genre, terminology, organology, libraries and manuscript sources had the effect of lending integrity to the nation's musicological aspirations. Heads of prominent academic establishments were approached, namely Ouseley (Oxford), his successor Stainer, Macfarren (Cambridge), Oakeley (Edinburgh), Robert Prescott Stewart (Dublin) and Sullivan (National Training School), which lent a degree of prestige.[23] The revival of plainchant and parochial music in the Anglican tradition, spearheaded by St Mark's College, Chelsea, was acknowledged by the inclusion of articles on 'Chant', 'Fauxbourden' and 'Gregorian modes' by Thomas Helmore, regarded by all in the 1860s and 1870s as the authority on plainsong.[24] Helmore retired from St Mark's in 1877 during the compilation of Volume I of the *Dictionary*, though he retained his post as Master of the Children of the Chapel's Royal, a position of kudos acknowledged by Grove in the 'List of Contributors'. The article on 'Plainsong' which appeared in Volume II was contributed by William Rockstro, who, by the 1880s, was regarded as Britain's leading authority on early music. Rockstro, a Leipzig student and a pupil of Mendelssohn, was highly regarded as a piano teacher, but he was to become better known as a scholar, first and foremost in the areas of modes and notation; he was also recognised as an historian. Rockstro contributed prolifically to Volumes II, III and IV, notably in the discussion of early musical subjects, whether of a technical ('Gradual', 'Hymn', 'Hexachord', 'Hidden Fifths and Octaves', 'Notation', 'Plagal Modes', 'Tablature'), generic ('Litany', 'Mass', Motet', 'Passion Music') or biographical nature ('Monteverde', 'Peri'). He also contributed numerous extended essays, notably 'Opera', 'Oratorio', 'Orchestra' and 'Orchestration'. These four articles form a conspicuous portion of Volume II, which suggests that, as the *Dictionary* began to expand, Grove became increasingly dependent on Rockstro's musicological expertise. Other regular contributors with reputations as national authorities were enlisted. On matters to do with singing ('Grand Opera', 'Bass', 'Contralto', 'Falsetto', 'Mezzo'), the services of John Hullah, the renowned educationist and author of musical primers, were secured.[25] Prout contributed a moderately large article on 'Concertante' and 'Concerto' but fell out of favour with Grove over an article on 'Dance'.[26] Scientific and acoustical articles ('Analysis', 'Acuteness', 'Pitch') were assigned to William Pole, civil engineer, musician and examiner for music degrees at the University of London. Pole's article on 'Pitch' is very much a summary of the work in which he, together with A. J. Ellis and A. J. Hipkins, was heavily engaged to lower the high English concert pitch to that adopted by the French in 1859, as well as a means of proselytising his convictions.[27] Hipkins, of his time the authority on keyboard instruments, was the author of major articles on the 'Clavichord', 'Harpsichord', 'Spinet', 'Virginal' and 'Piano' as well as smaller essays such as 'Action', 'Keys' and one on his former employer 'Broadwood'. Other members of Grove's network were James R. Sterndale Bennett (the son of William Sterndale Bennett), the author of a number of pieces on Flemish Renaissance composers (e.g. 'Claude le Jeune', 'Brumel') as well as an extended article on 'Lassus'; Franklin Taylor, who contributed numerous short technical articles (e.g. 'Appoggiatura', 'Arpeggio', 'Bar'); C. A. Fyffe, the historian, who provided accounts of university degrees ('Degree', 'Bachelor of Music', 'Doctor of Music'); Edward John Hopkins, the organist of the Temple Church, who produced a lengthy article on the 'Organ'; William Stone, a physician at St Thomas's Hospital and a renowned expert on wind instruments; William Barclay Squire; and J. A. Fuller Maitland. Squire and Fuller Maitland, both Cambridge men, were introduced to Grove in 1877 during the production of Volume I of the *Dictionary*, though neither of them began to contribute until Volume II was under way. Both came with Stanford's fullest recommendations and immediately became part of Grove's inner circle. Grove gave Fuller Maitland an introduction to John Morley, the editor of the *Pall Mall Gazette*, in 1882 and assisted again when Fuller Maitland moved from the *Guardian* to *The Times* in 1889;[28] similarly Squire's appointment as an assistant in the printed music section of the British Museum was supported by a testimonial from Grove (along with Arthur Duke Coleridge, Husk, Rockstro, J. Frederick Bridge and Leslie Stephen). Both men, in their different ways, were to aid Grove. Fuller Maitland provided many short biographical articles and, with his knowledge of musical journalism, an important contribution on 'Musical Periodicals'. His interest in early music, fortified through his friendship with Rockstro, also proved useful to the *Dictionary*'s furtherance of that field of research. Squire, who was asked to contribute to the *Dictionary* while still an undergraduate, possessed similar interests, but his bent was for manuscript sources, music printing, musical libraries and the establishment of professionally constructed catalogues. Grove saw in Squire the potential of a major 'national' librarian to match that of Gustave Chouquet at the Museum of the Paris Conservatoire of Music and Ferdinand Pohl at the Gesellschaft der Musikfreunde in Vienna. Tireless in his enthusiasm, Squire more than lived up to Grove's expectations, expanding the British Museum's collections of manuscripts and printed music and improving the catalogue. This side of Squire's ability is reflected in his contribution to 'Musical Libraries' in Volume II (and assiduously amplified in the Appendix of Volume IV), which functioned as a powerful advertisement for Britain's rich store of manuscripts and printed musical material. Squire's abilities as a scholar are also demonstrated in 'Virginal Music', an article focusing exclusively on English collections of virginal music (influenced by his editorial work with Fuller Maitland on *The Fitzwilliam Virginal Book*, begun in 1879 and later published in 1894),[29] and in 'Byrd' and 'Dunstable' (who did not figure in Volume I) in the Appendix.[30]

Yet perhaps the most historiographically discursive contribution to the *Dictionary* was made by Hubert Parry. Grove was introduced to Parry as early as 1868, but it was not until 1875 that their friendship became closer.[31]

At the end of that year Grove became so overwhelmed with work for the *Dictionary* that he asked Parry to take on the role of sub-editor.[32]

As a contributor to the *Dictionary*, Parry brought an important set of indigenous philosophical and aesthetic values to bear on musical historiography that were highly influenced by current modes of British thought. At Oxford he had been affected by Ruskin's lectures on art (and particularly by views elucidated in Ruskin's *The Queen of the Air*, published in 1869) and Ruskin's dictum that 'every work of art has a tendency to reproduce the ethical state which first developed it'.[33] This ethical factor imbued all of Parry's later writings on music history, but even more significant was his adoption of British empiricist thinking, notably the utilitarian rationalism of John Stuart Mill (whom Parry read in abundance in the 1870s) and, crucially, the ideas of 'social Darwinism' central to the synthetic philosophy of Herbert Spencer. Parry, inspired by Darwin's concept of natural selection, sought to parallel human social and intellectual history (in turn a parallel of man's biological past) with that of music, and took the opportunity on several occasions to explicate the relation between music history and Spencer's evolutionary theory – 'the change from indefinite incoherent homogeneity to a definite coherent heterogeneity' – in articles and lectures.[34] Parry's interests in philosophical and aesthetic issues, and to the whole subject of historiography, suited him primarily to writing articles of a terminological and generic nature. Many of the short articles provide an illuminating explanation of musical terms and expressions (e.g. 'Basso Continuo', 'Consecutive', 'Countersubject', 'Dominant', 'Interval'), but it is for the longer, discursive articles ('Form', 'Harmony', 'Sonata', 'Symphony', 'Variations', 'Working-out') that Parry reserved his most searching and original arguments. From his evolutionary ruminations Parry concluded that the organic imperative of German music represented the highest stage of musical development and that this was embodied in pure instrumental music, abstract instrumental forms (particularly those of Bach, Beethoven and Brahms), and in the elevation of intellectualism as an ideal. Inherent in Parry's theory of progress was the acceptance of inherited values, techniques and tradition, a view that militated against iconoclasm and experimentation, which were relegated to 'by-ways'. Such a theory also carried with it a strongly held belief in ethnocentrism and the exclusivity of national schools, a perspective which tended to venerate German ideals to the detriment of French, Italian and Russian repertoire. The dominance of German works is particularly conspicuous in 'Sonata', 'Symphony' and 'Variations', where Parry clearly reveals his deference to Beethoven (whom he sees as superior to Mozart and Haydn) as the paragon of sophistication.

While we may now view Parry's evolutionary convictions as a weakness in terms of his historiographical method, there can be no doubt that his articles for the *Dictionary* were hugely important. For Parry himself they were critical as preliminary explorations for his later, seminal publication,

The Art of Music (1893, revised 1896), where his theories and conclusions were more thoroughly worked out. Moreover, the articles provide us with a telling 'policy statement' which was to colour the entire educational ambience of the RCM and other English academic establishments for years to come. As the first Professor of Musical History at the RCM, Parry was to bring his evolutionary vision to generations of students (while he and Stanford together would act as fervent apologists for the German *Weltanschauung* in the field of composition). One cannot also underestimate the far-reaching influence of Parry's historiographical outlook initiated in his *Dictionary* articles. We know, for example, that the young Elgar regarded Parry's articles as a major pedagogical source,[35] and Vaughan Williams evidently considered Parry's writings as complementary to his own historical outlook.[36] That *The Art of Music* reached its tenth edition in 1931 bears witness to its longevity and to the fact that evolutionary theories of music still persisted in Britain well after the First World War. This is also borne out by Colles's decision, in editing the third edition of the *Dictionary* in 1927, to retain Parry's articles with supplementary material of his own. Furthermore, Colles's retention of Parry's articles acted as a powerful endorsement of the evolutionary theory as a 'national' method, distinct from the Hegelian and Herbartian mindsets of Austro-German musicology.

To balance the assemblage of indigenous authors, Grove determined that the *Dictionary* should also have a continental dimension. From his Viennese friend, Ferdinand Pohl, he commissioned major articles on 'Mozart' and 'Haydn' as well as many shorter pieces relating to Austro-German music of the eighteenth and early nineteenth century. From A. Maczewski came articles on the entire Bach family, 'Cornelius', 'Hiller', 'Brahms', 'Brendel' and numerous other German musicians,[37] while Philip Spitta, renowned for his epoch-making study of Bach (published in 1873), wrote substantial pieces on 'Weber', 'Spontini' and 'Schumann'. The vast majority of articles on French music were commissioned from Gustave Chouquet, who was pre-eminent enough to merit his own article in the *Dictionary*,[38] and those on major contemporary Italian figures (e.g. 'Verdi') were contributed by Gian Andrea Mazzucato,[39] a former professor of aesthetics at the Milan Conservatory who moved to London in 1880 to become a critic, teacher of singing and translator of Italian. Articles on seventeenth- and eighteenth-century Italian musicians, however, came from a mixture of non-Italian sources including Ferdinand Pohl (e.g. 'Caldara', 'Cavalieri', 'Carissimi'), Franz Gehring ('Basili', 'Lotti') and J. P. Paul David ('Corelli', 'Geminiani', 'Locatelli'), the son of Ferdinand David, the most influential of violin teachers in Germany.[40]

Although commissioning articles from continental scholars was an important feature of Grove's scheme, he clearly recognised that inviting contributions from immigrant musicologists, such as Mazzucato, David and Ernst Pauer, was a way of enhancing Britain's reputation, and particularly of London's standing as a musical capital.[41] Perhaps even more significant though was Grove's employment of the critics Francis Hueffer, who wrote for the *North British* Review, the *Fortnightly*, the *Academy* and later for *The Times*, and Edward Dannreuther, the Alsatian piano virtuoso, concert promoter and champion of new music. Both men were well known as progressives and especially for their support of Wagner and Liszt. Hueffer was called upon to write several articles on early nineteenth-century French opera ('Auber', 'Boieldieu', 'Félicien David') as well as an article on 'Libretto' (foreshadowing his own production of libretti for Mackenzie and Cowen), but his most significant article was on 'Liszt'. Dannreuther's contributions were characteristically more catholic. Dannreuther became a celebrity virtuoso during the 1870s for the first performances in England of Grieg's Piano Concerto (18 April 1874), Liszt's Piano Concerto in A (21 November 1874) and Tchaikovsky's Piano Concerto in B flat minor (11 March 1876). Moreover, the semi-private chamber concerts of instrumental music and songs which he held at his home at 12 Orme Square, Bayswater, were renowned for their radically contemporary programmes. Furthermore, as the founder of the London Wagner Society in 1872 and the promoter of Wagner concerts in 1872 and 1873, Dannreuther became inextricably linked with Wagner's music in England, a reputation that was reinforced first by his writings on Wagner's concept of music drama and, secondly, by the Wagner Festival in London in 1877 when Wagner himself visited London and stayed at Orme Square as the guest of the Dannreuther family. The articles for the *Dictionary* are therefore representative of Dannreuther's varied musical interests. To the subject of the virtuoso piano repertoire ('Alkan', 'Chopin', 'Clementi', 'Cramer', 'Field', 'Henselt', 'Hummel', 'Kalkbrenner', 'Moscheles' and 'Tausig') he brought the perspective of a brilliant performer, and his close friendship with Bronsart, Bülow and Klindworth provide useful insights into three of the most important executors of the time. But it is Dannreuther's enthusiasm for the new which led to articles on 'Berlioz', 'Franz', 'Glinka', 'Grieg', 'Tchaikovsky', and most of all, 'Wagner'. Indeed the 29-page article on Wagner, a pioneering model for its time, is a remarkable achievement. Dannreuther's article, replete with copious footnotes, is a valuable exposé from someone who was close to Wagner in the years leading up to the first complete performance of *Der Ring des Nibelungen* at Bayreuth in 1876, Wagner's visit to London (which included the first reading of the poem to *Parsifal* at Orme Square) and the first performances of *Parsifal* in 1882 (which Dannreuther attended with Parry). Not only was Dannreuther familiar with Wagner as man and composer, but he was a perceptive and investigative writer on Wagner's dramatic philosophy. The second part of Dannreuther's article deals explicitly with Wagner's reform of opera (drawing on the author's two books, *Richard Wagner: His Tendencies and Theories* and *Richard Wagner and the Reform of the Opera*, published in 1873. This section is based largely on a discussion of Wagner's principal essays, 'Die Kunst und die Revolution', 'Das Kunstwerk der Zukunft' (translated by Dannreuther in 1873) and 'Oper und Drama', finishing up, not surprisingly, with mention of Wagner's two essays, 'Beethoven' and 'Über das Dirigiren', which Dannreuther translated in 1880 and 1887 respectively. Part three seeks, with a sense of missionary zeal, to assess Wagner in a nineteenth-century historical context, and again there is much of value in Dannreuther's appraisal of Wagner's harmonic language (using appropriate cross-references with Parry's 'Harmony' article) and the legacy of Beethoven.

The length accorded to Dannreuther's article on Wagner is indicative of Grove's general endorsement of Germanic music and Germanic composers as the accepted canon. In fact it would be no exaggeration to suggest that Grove wished to act as a major arbiter of national taste in the way he was prepared to give priority to the music of northern Europe over that of France, Italy and Russia. This is borne out by the largest articles in the *Dictionary* – Pohl's extensive essays on 'Haydn' (21 pages) and 'Mozart' (28 pages), Spitta's articles on 'Schumann' (38 pages) and 'Weber' (33 pages), and Parry's discursive expositions on 'Symphony', 'Sonata', 'Suite' and 'Variations' central to the Teutonic aesthetic – but it is sealed by Grove's own centrepieces on 'Beethoven' (37 pages), 'Mendelssohn' (58 pages) and, as a public attestation of his scholarly industry, 'Schubert' (64 pages), who receives the most protracted consideration. But, most of all, Grove's German bias is affirmed by Rockstro's extensive article (divided into 25 sections) on 'Schools of Composition', which reifies nineteenth-century Teutonic values. Rockstro's national divisions and hierarchies also provided a pretext for the definition (and reclamation) of an 'English School' (stretching back to the thirteenth century) that could stand proudly, shoulder to shoulder, with its European neighbours, not least with Germany its emerging rival. It was an ideal construction, for not only did it affirm Britain's distinguished and ancient musical lineage, but it also legitimated the present younger generation of Sullivan, Parry, Stanford, Corder, Mackenzie, Cowen, Swinnerton Heap and others (faithfully included in the *Dictionary* by Grove) in whom the nation's creative hopes now resided. As Rockstro confidently asserted:

> We have proved that its [i.e. the English School's] descent is as pure as that of any other School in Europe; that we can trace back its pedigree, link by link, from its living representatives ... We have shown – and shall presently show more plainly still – that, at the present moment, it is more active than it has ever been before; doing excellent work; and giving rich promise for the future. There has never been a time at which English Composers have more faithfully fulfilled the trust committed to them now. They have conducted us, step by step, to a very high position indeed. We shall be cowards, if we recede from it. In order to prevent such a disaster, we have only to bear the work of our forefathers in mind;

and, so long as this is healthily remembered, we need entertain but little dread of retrogression.

Here, perhaps more than anywhere else in the *Dictionary*, was Grove's national aspiration made plain. What is more, Rockstro's didactic words confirm the presence of a significant political agenda which was to remain at the forefront of Fuller Maitland's second edition of 1902, and even more so in Colles's nationalistically self-conscious third edition, published in 1927.

Notes and References

1. Cecil Forsyth, *Music and Nationalism* (London, 1911), p. 260, quoted in R. Stradling and M. Hughes, *The English Musical Renaissance 1860–1940: Construction and Deconstruction* (London, 1993), p. 99.
2. The motion, to agitate for state subsidy for a national opera, in the House of Commons was moved by Galloway (MP for Manchester SW) and Hay (MP for Shoreditch and Hoxton) and took place on 7 April 1903. Stanford attended the debate. Galloway and Hay were informed that the government were preparing a White Paper on the matter, so the motion was withdrawn. The White Paper was published at the end of 1903 (see House of Commons, *Command Paper Miscellaneous No. 6*, 1903).
3. Stanford's Concert Piece for organ and orchestra (1921) was turned down by a series of London publishers, but there were other works, *A Song of Agincourt*, the Fifth and Sixth Irish Rhapsodies and the Piano Concerto No. 3, that had no chance of getting into print.
4. After some difficulties, including the ruling out of an expansion of the Royal Academy of Music into a much larger national institution, the National Training School for Music was opened in 1876. Lasting only six years, it effectively functioned as a preparation for a more ambitious project, the Royal College of Music, spearheaded by Sir George Grove. The RCM opened its doors in 1883.
5. Parry's account of his supplication for the B.Mus. at Oxford in 1866 provides a useful perspective on the nature of the expectations of the musical degree. See Jeremy Dibble, *C. Hubert H. Parry: His Life and Music* (Oxford, 1992, rev. 1998), pp. 41–8.
6. R. Stradling and M. Hughes, *The English Musical Renaissance 1860–1940: Construction and Deconstruction* (London, 1993), p. 18.
7. Walter Pater, 'Two Early French Stories', *The Renaissance: Studies in Art and Poetry* (London, 1873), ed. Adam Phillips (Oxford, 1986), pp. 1–2.
8. See in particular Arnold's *Culture and Anarchy* and *Essays in Criticism*.
9. Pater, 'Conclusion', *The Renaissance*, p. 153.
10. Carl Engel, 'A Musical Library', *Musical Myths and Facts*, Vol. 1 (London , 1876), pp. 5–6.
11. Ibid., p. 1.
12. Ibid., p. 5.
13. Prospectus for *A Dictionary of Music and Musicians (1450–1880) by Eminent Writers, English and Foreign, with Illustrations and Woodcuts*; also quoted in P.M.Young, *George Grove 1820–1900: A New Biography* (London, 1980), p. 127n.
14. Although Callcott did not finish his dictionary, he nevertheless left behind 36 volumes of manuscript material (collected between 1797 and 1802) and the manuscript of his dictionary in two manuscript volumes (now housed in the British Library).

15 Gustave Chouquet's article 'Dictionaries of Music' in Grove's *Dictionary* provides an interesting contextual commentary, not only because of its historical exposition of the principle continental works, but also because of its evaluation of English works. It is perhaps significant that Chouquet notes Stainer and Barrett's *Dictionary of Musical Terms* as 'a great advance' which yet 'leaves something to be desired'.

16 The fact that Grove's *Dictionary* fulfilled this national need is confirmed by the expansion of the two-volume plan (evident from the title page of Volume I of 1879) to three volumes (on the title page of Volume II of 1880) and finally to four volumes (published in 1883 and 1889).

17 See Stradling and Hughes, *The English Musical Renaissance*, p. 20.

18 Perhaps the most blatant example of constructing England's musical history is the inclusion of Rockstro's article 'Sumer is icumen in' (straddling Volumes III and IV) which stands as a national symbol of creative flair and distinction. It is also significant that a cross-reference is made to Rockstro's 'Schools of Composition', where considerable emphasis is placed on the existence of English schools throughout the centuries. Such was the importance of this piece that it was reproduced complete both in facsimile and full score.

19 Husk only cites Sullivan's *Cox and Box* (1867), *Trial by Jury* (1875) and *The Sorcerer* (1877), in marked contrast to Grove's article on Sullivan in Volume III which cites *HMS Pinafore, The Pirates of Penzance, Patience* and *Iolanthe,* performed between 1878 and 1882.

20 In order to provide a credible context for Britain's teaching institutions, Grove took care to include articles on 'Leipzig' (by Grove), the 'Academie de Musique' (Hullah), the 'Conservatoire de Musique' (Chouquet) and the 'Musik, Hochschule für' (Barclay Squire).

21 A supplement to Grove's article on the RCM appeared in the *Dictionary*'s appendix. Fuller Maitland's article, which updates information about the staff, the proliferation of scholarships, the increase in student numbers and the opening of Alexandra House, could almost be read as an advertisement.

22 In addition to the articles on London's musical conservatories, Grove was similarly eager to enhance his propaganda with a piece on 'Kneller Hall', founded in 1857, noting that 'England is as yet the only country which has adopted a systematic method of educating bandsmen and bandmasters, and the great improvement both in the moral conduct and the efficiency of the men which has taken place since the foundation of Kneller Hall cannot be too warmly welcomed.'

23 Grove clearly regarded Ouseley, the author of *A Treatise on Counterpoint, Canon, and Fugue, based on Cherubini* (published in 1869), as the authority on counterpoint and contrapuntal techniques. Consequently Ouseley contributed articles such as 'Augmentation', 'Arsis et Thesin', 'Cancrizans', 'Canon', 'Counterpoint', 'Fugue' and 'Imitation' to Volume I. 'Inversion' for Volume II was shared with Rockstro. Oakeley, whose contribution is by no means extensive, provided articles on 'Ouseley' and the 'Niederrheinische Musikfeste'. Macfarren, who succeeded Sterndale Bennett at Cambridge in 1875, contributed only after the publication of Volumes I and II. Stanford, who succeeded Macfarren in 1887, assisted Grove with his Schubert research in Vienna in the early 1880s, but, perhaps surprisingly, he did not contribute to the *Dictionary*. Stewart contributed a number of articles including 'Irish Music'. Sullivan wrote only two articles for the *Dictionary*: one on Louis Plaidy, his piano teacher at the Leipzig Conservatory, and the other on Frederic Clay, a contemporary rival in the province of light opera.

24 See Bernarr Rainbow, *The Choral Revival in the Anglican Church 1839–72* (London, 1970).

25 Hullah died in 1884 and so did not contribute the later articles, 'Tenor' and 'Soprano'. 'Tonic Sol-Fa', the system which Hullah had done much to initiate but which had been superseded by Curwen's 'moveable do', was written for Volume IV by R. B. Litchfield (as was 'Tonic Sol-Fa College'). Later articles on vocal topics were written by Harry Collings Deacon, who became Professor of Singing at the RCM.
26 See Young, *George Grove*, p. 150. Prout produced other smaller articles on dances such as 'Bourée', 'Branle', 'Entrée', 'Fandango', 'Gavotte', 'Minuet' which appear in Volumes I and II, but he is conspicuously absent from Volumes III and IV.
27 It is significant that, in discussing the predicament of English pitch at the time of the *Dictionary*'s publication, Pole chose to vent his indignation at the confusion between orchestral pitch and that preferred by singers. 'Hence all uniformity', he wrote, 'in the practical interpretation of music becomes out of the question; – a state of things most deplorable, and a disgrace to the musical education of the country.'
28 J. A. Fuller Maitland, *A Door-keeper of Music* (London, 1929), pp. 88 and 124.
29 Interest in the value and significance of the Fitzwilliam Museum's collections was signalled by Grove's article in Volume I, a catalogue of whose holdings, completed by Fuller Maitland in 1879 (though not published until 1893), was acknowledged in Squire's article.
30 The intention of Squire's article on Byrd was to replace that by Rimbault in Volume I, on account of all the available new research, much of which was published in Squire's article for the *Musical Review*, 1881, Nos. 19–21.
31 From 1868 Parry saw Grove intermittently at the Crystal Palace, at the home of his friends the von Glehns, and at Dannreuther's studio at Orme Square, Bayswater. Parry's poems, *A Sequence of Analogies*, was also published by *Macmillan's Magazine* in May 1875. The invitation to contribute to the *Dictionary* occurred in July 1875 (see Dibble, *C. Hubert H. Parry*, p. 127). His first article was 'Arrangement'. Grove also admitted years later that Parry was 'one of the first persons I asked to help me when I first began the Dictionary' (letter to F. G. Edwards, 4 June 1898, *Lbm*.Eg.MS.3091.f.237).
32 Dibble, *C. Hubert H. Parry*, p. 128.
33 John Ruskin, *The Queen of the Air* (London, 1869), p. 59.
34 The most significant of these papers and lectures were a paper, 'Some Bearings of the Historical Method upon Music', for the Musical Association (*Proceedings of the Musical Association* xi [1884–85], pp. 1–9) and a lecture, 'Evolution in Music', for the Royal Institution in 1890.
35 See *The Strand Magazine*, May 1904, p. 539; see also J. Northrop Moore, *Edward Elgar: A Creative Life* (Oxford, 1984), p. 85.
36 See Jeremy Dibble, 'Parry, Stanford and Vaughan Williams: The Creation of Tradition', in L. Foreman (ed.), *Vaughan Williams in Perspective* (London, 1998).
37 Maczewski's article is perhaps surprisingly short (less than three columns), but one should remember that, when the article was written in the mid-1870s, Brahms's reputation in England was only just gaining momentum. The supplement for the Appendix was written by the up-and-coming Rosa Newmarch, yet to establish herself in the field of Russian music. It is also significant that Maczewski (rather than Chouquet) authored the article on 'Cherubini', who is regarded as having greater affinity with German Romanticism.
38 Numerous articles for the Appendix, such as those on 'Fauré', came from Adolphe Jullien, the major French critic and writer who produced substantial works on Berlioz and Wagner during the 1880s.
39 It should be noted, however, that the article on Rossini came from Gustave Chouquet, while 'Donizetti' was written by H. Sutherland Edwards.

40 Paul David was leader of the orchestra at Carlsruhe between 1862 and 1865. He came to England in or around 1865, after which he became music master at Uppingham School. His articles on the Italian violin masters naturally reflect his own bias as a violinist.
41 A surprising omission in the list of contributors is Carl Engel, although an article on him is included in Fuller Maitland's Appendix.

3.
Eros and Paneuropeanism: Szymanowski's Utopian Vision

STEPHEN DOWNES

The rebirth of the Polish nation in the aftermath of the First World War was slow, painful and bloody.[1] In particular, there were prolonged difficulties in establishing a border in the east. The Treaty of Versailles (June 1919) managed only to secure Poland's western boundary with Germany – the eastern borderlands lying between the Baltic and the Black Sea were, in effect, left to be fought over. The turbulence and unrest experienced by those who lived in the Ukraine at this time was particularly acute, vulnerable as they were to invasion from all directions. The Russian revolutions of March and November 1917 had compounded the instability of the final phase of the war. In the winter of 1917–18 the Ukrainians resisted Bolshevik aggression and in February 1918 a Ukrainian Central Council was established with German co-operation. When the Germans left in defeat in November 1918, however, the Council was succeeded by a communist leadership, independent of Moscow.

After the 'peace' of 11 November 1918, Józef Piłsudski – leader of the Polish Socialists – returned to Warsaw from German captivity eager to begin the task of rebuilding his nation. The fledgling Ukrainian People's Republic was overturned by the Polish army but within three months the Russians had invaded the Ukraine and occupied Kiev. In July 1920 they attacked Poland to the north, reaching the outskirts of Warsaw by August. In one of the most celebrated events of Polish military history, the Red Army was defeated. The Riga Treaty of March 1921 drew up fresh boundaries, but the borderlands remained problematic and unstable, with many non-Poles finding themselves within Polish borders. Between 1922 and 1924 armed Belorussian and Ukrainian elements continued to trouble the new Polish nation.

During these torrid years Polish politics were marked by continuous disagreements between Piłsudski's Socialist 'left' and Roman Dmowski's National Democrat 'right' over how to assure the future of the Polish nation. The problem of the eastern borderlands highlighted their divergent visions yet common prejudices, in particular concerning the vexed question of security between Poland and the Russian Bolsheviks. Dmowski, who during the First World War viewed allegiance with Britain and Russia as a necessary step to Poland's independence, was suspicious of Ukrainian and Baltic national aspirations. Piłsudski, who had thought a German victory would be more likely to establish Polish freedom, envisaged a 'federation' running from the Baltic to the Caucasus as a buffer against any Russian expansionist aggression but was as dismissive as Dmowski about the possibility of independence for borderland peoples. Faced by its perennially problematic geographical position between 'east' and 'west', Polish politics became deeply factionalised. As the debate on the form and outlook of the new nation continued, so did the social upheaval and the killing.[2]

Continuous, vigilant self-defence was essential for anyone living in the Poland–Ukraine–Russia borderlands at this time. For Szymanowski, an artist living in the Ukraine who had enjoyed the privileges of minor Polish nobility, the change in circumstances was a terrible shock. Recalling the horrors of the winter of 1917–18, he wrote:

> You have no idea what we went through during the winter (although it cannot be compared with Kiev, for example, or Moscow). Just imagine such a *'petit maitre'* like me keeping watch whole nights at a time with rifle and revolver, coming up against everything which before would have made me faint at the very least – corpses, the wounded, terrible bands of robbers, etc . . . I suppose it's a marvel that we all emerged from this enterprise in one piece! And just imagine – it turned out that I am not a coward at all, as incidentally, I had rather expected I would be.[3]

The Szymanowski family had been forced to leave their idyllic Ukrainian estate at Tymoszowka in October 1917 and take residence in a house in Elisavetgrad, a town to the south-east of Kiev. During the life-threatening unrest of the following winter, Szymanowski felt unable to compose and his thoughts turned to literary work – 'simply', he said, 'to get things off my chest'.[4] In the next two years, trapped by the armed struggles which surrounded him, he wrote 'Efebos' – an extraordinary outpouring of personal views on art, sexuality and politics. Only parts of the work survive, but it is clear that the idea which underlies the discussion of its three main topics is 'freedom' guaranteed by 'love'. As Szymanowski writes in the Introduction:

> it was the inner story of [a man's] soul, proceeding step by step towards a wider understanding of life, its duties and its deep significance – the history of a gradual liberation from various types of traditional, inherited slavery by an increasingly clear mirage of the true freedom of the soul, springing from love and an independence, formulated not from the point of view of this or that social, religious or moral doctrine, but flowering as if by itself from the fertile soil of the human soul's deepest layers and most intimate relationship with its own life.[5]

This freedom, urges Szymanowski, should inform the artist's inspiration, the individual's erotic life, and the relationships between nations.

A substantial part of the work consists of a discussion of Eros, the post-Platonic agenda of which is signalled by its very title, 'Sympozjon (Uczta)' (Symposium [the Feast]). Ideas drawn from Plato's *Symposium* and *Phaedrus* inform a dialogue between 'highly cultured representatives of different nations' which explores the workings of the erotic in the artist's creative inspiration and personal relationships. These thoughts were written after a crucial period in the composer's life in which his sexual preferences were clarified. It seems that trips to Italy and North Africa with Stefan Spiess in 1911 and 1914 were defining moments, when Szymanowski's homosexuality was confirmed. Memories of these trips continued to resonate powerfully in his mind during the enforced isolation in war-torn Ukraine. Italy, 'the homeland of all dreamers about a heightened sense of living', provided the natural setting for the dialogue.[6] Halfway through the dialogue, a definition of 'true human love' is proposed:

> [it] is boundless/sinless in its freedom, its freedom of choice, based entirely on the subjective, individual, psychic and physical properties of man. And nothing or no-one, not even 'public opinion', has the courage to limit this freedom. Its only controls are a man's innate instinct and his convictions of truth, goodness and beauty – as Socrates himself might have said.[7]

By turning to the erotic, Szymanowski continues a long legacy in Polish letters – a century earlier the great Polish Romantic poet Adam Mickiewicz imagined an 'erometer' to 'measure' sexual content – and, in particular, reflects the interests of many influential figures in early Polish modernism. For example, Stanisław Witkiewicz (one of the leading artists and playwrights of the time, with whom Szymanowski had a notably turbulent relationship) employed overt erotic imagery to describe aspects of art and politics. Similarly, the works of Witkiewicz's long-standing friend and sometime travelling companion, the anthropologist Bronisław Malinowski, attached great importance to the role of sex in the development of human culture.[8]

Witkiewicz underwent Freudian psychoanalysis in 1912, and in 1936, three years before he committed suicide, he wrote, in his *Unwashed Souls: A Psychological study of the Inferiority Complex carried out according to Freud's system with special emphasis to Polish Problems*,

> Laymen who understand nothing about psychoanalysis accuse Freud of psychological erotomania and of reducing everything to the erotic, and even of wallowing in filth for its own sake and psychocoprophalia or something of the sort. I maintain that the charge is false. Freud devotes exactly as much attention to the erotic as it deserves . . .
>
> Quite justifiably, Karol Szymanowski used to say in his unforgettable little voice, as subtle as that of the metaphysical ruler of a land of hyper-

ephebi out of this world: "You know, for me the erotic is something so diabolical that, you know, it is simply shocking."[9]

Witkiewicz's calling up of Szymanowski in support of Freud is appropriate, for their writings on Eros share important features. (Szymanowski's psychological insight is confirmed by one of the 'Scraps' appended to the incomplete 'Efebos': 'Exactly in "understanding": in transferring some truths from the sphere of instincts into the sphere of intellectual awareness the greatest terror resides.'[10]) In particular, both Szymanowski and Freud acknowledged the continuing relevance of Plato. In *Beyond the Pleasure Principle* (1920) Freud refers to the 'myth' of primordial unity described in Plato's *Symposium*: 'in the first place, the sexes were originally three in number, not two as they are now; there was man, woman, and the union of the two'. Subsequently divided by an angry Zeus, 'the two parts of man, each desiring his other half, came together, and threw their arms about one another eager to grow into one'. Freud's view is that the sexual instinct arises from a desire to restore 'original' unity.[11] A year later, in *Group Psychology and the Analysis of the Ego* he writes: 'In its origin, function and relation to sexual love, the "Eros" of the philosopher Plato coincides exactly with the love-force, the libido of psychoanalysis.' He then speculates on the binding force of Eros:

> We will try our fortune, then, with the supposition that love relationships . . . also constitute the essence of the group mind . . . Our hypothesis finds support in the first instance from two passing thoughts. First, that a group is held together by a power of some kind: and to what power could this feat be better ascribed than to Eros, which holds together everything in the world? Secondly, that if an individual gives up his distinctiveness in a group and lets its other members influence him by suggestion, it gives one the impression that he does it because he feels the need of being in harmony with them rather than in opposition to them – so that perhaps after all he does it '*ihnen zu Liebe*'.[12]

As is well known, Freud then posits that this preserving, uniting instinct coexists with a destructive, death instinct and that it is the struggle between the two which underlies the development of civilisation:

> I may now add that civilisation is a process in the service of Eros, whose purpose is to combine single human individuals, and after that families, then races, peoples and nations, into one great unity, the unity of mankind. Why this has to happen, we do not know; the work of Eros is precisely this. These collections of men are to be libidinally bound to one another. Necessity alone, the advantages of work in common will not hold them together. But man's natural aggressive instinct, the hostility of each against all and against each, opposes this programme of civilisation.[13]

I will return to the destructive instincts later, but the similarities between Freud's and Szymanowski's post-Platonic Eros are striking. This is particularly so when, at the climax of Szymanowski's 'Symposium', the composer Korab recognises the unity of Christ and Eros and, in this God of Love, the truth that Eros is the unifying factor in mankind's existence. Korab, for whom the Christian church meant nothing, relates how the figure on the crucifix in St Mary's, Kraków, 'ordered me to go into retreat and love God above all, and my neighbour as myself. I did not know what I should do, and in despair thought I was condemned to eternal torment from the Devil. For at that time I always pictured my "neighbour" as some alien, anonymous man in grey and how could I possibly love?' Korab continues that it was only when in Italy years later, on seeing Leonardo's image of Christ, 'did I grasp who He really was! He – Christ – Eros! . . . one who loved, born in boundless freedom, in an insatiable, deep desire for Eternity. And he loved his neighbour with the mysterious, burning ardour of existence, the insatiable desire to associate with the eternal, creative essence of the world.'[14] For Szymanowski, this Eros formed the basis for a union of individuals very different from what he observed in the 'mob' or 'rabble' – those, indeed, who crucified (and have ever since misunderstood) this God of Love. 'It is', he writes, 'not necessary to be a Gustave le Bon to be persuaded of the . . . unbelievable primitivism of the psychology of the mob.'[15] It was le Bon who provided a major point of departure from Freud's 'Group Psychology'. Freud quotes frequently and substantially from le Bon's *Psychologie des foules* (1895), including the following passage:

> by the mere fact that he forms part of an organised group, a man descends several rungs in the ladder of civilisation. Isolated, he may be a cultivated individual; in a crowd, he is a barbarian – that is, a creature acting by instinct.[16]

Szymanowski argues that 'the most elevated of attempts' is, by contrast with the psychology of the mob:

> complete liberation from the chains of instinct. Only then could the first law of love in nature – the difference of the sexes – give way to the most hotly contested right of the individual – the right of choice. Does it matter if it be male or female if as a human the choice satisfies our elevated concept of what is beautiful and of value?[17]

Under the rule of the mob, 'common sense' – the 'mass of "public opinion"' – has decreed what is 'normal' and 'abnormal'. This, Szymanowski argues, was the situation which led to the tragedy of Oscar Wilde: 'that beautiful, fragile, God-given being, akin to the divine Benvenuto [Cellini], broken, disfigured, thrown out with a brutal leer!'[18] Only when the ancient Greek concept of Eros is restored will these primitive judgements be discarded and man begin to enjoy absolute freedom. Szymanowski believes this possibility lies, undeveloped, in the whole of mankind:

> Eros was ... an elevated symbol of the capacity of the human heart for love in general ... How amazing it is that these most subtle ideas are characteristic not just of exceptional, talented people, but are embedded in the womb, the soul of a whole nation, existing, if I may put it this way, *in potentia*.[19]

It is striking that Szymanowski, despite being surrounded by (and compositionally silenced by) the political turmoil and sheer destructiveness of war, which could only confirm for him the barbarity of 'mob' psychology, should make such fundamentally optimistic, Utopian statements. He sees a potential union of mankind very different from what he calls the 'narrow-minded and egoistic nationalism which has been intensified by the political liberation of a whole series of young national entities'. Instead, he maintains his 'daydream' of 'paneuropeanism' – 'the gathering together of the best individuals around the greatest conquests of a distinctive, spiritual culture'.[20] Ultimately, Szymanowski is urging humanity to allow the higher power of Eros to dissolve primitive boundaries across all aspects of individual and group psychology – those constructed between sexual 'normality' and 'abnormality' and those between bigoted groups, national or otherwise. By this he is able to link his experiences as a homosexual and as a victim of brutality in the name of national 'freedom', both spheres in which inhumanity is perpetrated in the name of 'cleansing'. Jonathan Dollimore has recently written:

> The mythology which ... connects sexual deviation and political subversion is very old. It is typically inflected by other kinds of fear, especially religious and racial ones. A case in point is those forms of nationalism committed to policing not only geographical borders and literal or legally defined aliens, but symbolic and ideological boundaries (both internal and external) between the normal and the abnormal, the healthy and the sick, the conforming and the deviant.[21]

This is certainly true, but by juxtaposing erotic and national 'battlegrounds' Szymanowski reveals himself to be a child of his cultural time and place. The onset of war in the name of 'freedom' so soon after the personal discovery, or release, of his sexual preferences was a tragic coincidence which spurred him to seek a grand solution, which reveals the enduring legacy of both his artistic roots in the *fin de siècle* and his geographic roots in the unique 'borderlands' of the far south-eastern corner of Europe.

Anxiety over the perceived breakdown of boundaries which were believed to define identity was one of the principal features of the *fin de siècle*. One reaction to this was an attempt to bolster or protect these lines of demarcation. As Elaine Showalter puts it, 'in periods of cultural insecurity, when there are fears of regression and degeneration, the longing for strict border controls around the definition of gender, as well as race, class, and nationality, becomes especially intense'.²² Definitions of gender and of normal/abnormal behaviour were central concerns in the rising 'science' of sex. In particular, developments in the 'understanding' of homosexuality in the late nineteenth century led to renewed attempts to draw the 'map' of sexuality and to 'police' its frontiers. For many (perhaps today most familiarly Richard von Krafft-Ebing in his *Psychopathia sexualis* of 1886), as George L. Mosse says, 'the medical analysis of homosexuality during the nineteenth century helped demarcate a clear boundary between normal and abnormal sexuality'.²³ For others, however, the old distinctions were no longer tenable – in his book *Psychology of Sex* Havelock Ellis wrote, 'we may not know exactly what sex is . . . we do know that it is mutable, with the possibility of one sex being changed into the other sex, that its frontiers are often mutable'²⁴ – and this was something to celebrate. To bring the context back to Polish early modernism, for Stanisław Przybyszewski sex, which he celebrated as the vital and fundamentally 'creative' instinct, is worshipped as a deity which fuses male and female:

> In the beginning was sex . . . Sex longs for godliness! . . . And so sex is the androgynous 'Father and Mother' of all that is, that was, and that will be.²⁵

The pervasively erotic nature of Szymanowski's work must be seen against this background. However, it gains a wider, political and geographical significance when it is also viewed as a product of his birthplace. (Here, perhaps, I approach what Claude Lévi-Strauss identified as 'the borderline between anthropology and psychology' which 'demonstrates that it is possible to compare data from different areas without succumbing to the facile solutions of filling the gaps in each one with explanations borrowed from the other'.)²⁶ The Szymanowski estate lay in south-east Ukraine, not far from the Black Sea. These are the 'borderlands' where delight in erotic 'transgression' went hand in hand with a powerful mingling of the West and East in which the boundary between subject and 'other' – the very essence of exoticism – was broken down.²⁷ The Russian historian Mikhail Rostovtzeff, writing in the early 1920s, described the potent mix:

> I take as my starting-point the unity of the region which we call South Russia: the intersection of influences in that vast tract of country - Oriental and southern influences spreading along the sea routes, and Western influences passing down the great Danubian route; and the consequent formation, from time to time, of mixed civilisations, very curious and very interesting.²⁸

This is a region in whose history notions of 'civilised centre' and 'barbaric periphery', the power relations of 'West' and 'East', and binary oppositions of gender are all continually subverted.²⁹ In consequence artists from both

Poland and Russia – whose territories run into this region – are presented with rather special challenges. For Russians the question of whether they 'belong' to Europe or Asia is focused on this region, a piece of the empire which evoked ambivalent feelings of 'original' and yet 'distant' vitality (Russia's 'Freudian frontier' as one commentator has put it).[30] Poland has periodically looked to the West for its spiritual home, but the history of the Polish *szlachta*'s belief in its unique eastern ancestry is well known, largely through the adoption in the eighteenth century of supposedly 'Sarmartian' traditional costume (the Sarmartians were one of many ancient nomadic peoples to occupy the lands around the Black Sea).[31] For Szymanowski, though, the fascination with the diverse, boundary-breaking culture of this region went deeper than his aristocratic predecessors' *faux* affectations of dress. If, as Richard Taruskin has said, for Russian composers 'the eastward gaze is simultaneously a look in the mirror' ('oriental coloration . . . was simultaneously and ambiguously a self-constructing and an other-constructing trait'),[32] then, similarly, for Szymanowski the 'distance' between East and West was closed and the boundaries between self and other opened.[33]

Szymanowski's compositional silence was broken by one of his most overtly erotic and 'oriental' scores, the *Songs of a Mad Muezzin* Op.42. These settings of poetry by his cousin Jarosław Iwaszkiewicz were written in the autumn of 1918, when Szymanowski was finally able to get away from embattled Elisavetgrad and spend some time on the Black Sea coast at Odessa.[34] These songs continue to explore sensual worlds typical of his works from the earlier war years. When, in 1920, Szymanowski set a pseudo-archaic Polish text by Julian Tuwim (with the untranslatable title *Słopiewnie*), he was keen to emphasise that his use of Polish folk idiom represented a crucial 'turning point' in his compositional development. Iwaszkiewicz, who was at this time collaborating (on and off) on Szymanowski's emerging *magnum opus*, the opera *King Roger*, was, however, particularly perceptive in his review of a performance of this new cycle. After acknowledging that 'another period started with *Słopiewnie*', he then continued:

> Szymanowski set himself an immense goal: to reveal the mystical, Dionysian and Sufistic factors in the Slavonic. This is the highest goal a Polish composer could set himself. Let us hope that the achievement will be a revelation.[35]

This task was also attempted in the final act of *King Roger* (completed in 1924) – a work which is heavily indebted to the ideas contained in 'Efebos' – where melodies derived from the Polish highland folk idiom are introduced into a scene set in an ancient Greek amphitheatre in Sicily and coexist with material which recalls 'Oriental' music from the second act. The resulting musical and geographical *mélange*, in which an erotic–exotic idiom typical of the Muezzin songs coexists with archaic-slavic materials similar to those in *Słopiewnie*, is typical 'boundary-breaking' from Szymanowski and also, perhaps, curiously 'Polish'. (Czesław Miłosz has, for example, pointed to a frequent tendency for Polish thinkers to equate the 'pastoral civilisation of the Carpathians' with ancient Greece.)[36] Szymanowski appears to be asserting that, if one digs deep enough, apparently different 'national roots' are found to be intertwined and that imposing boundaries cuts off essential sources of inspiration and limits the freedom of the artist. It is an artistic standpoint which is proudly eclectic. In reply to those critics who accused him of betraying his national origins he wrote:

> should we not examine as carefully as possible and as objectively as possible the paths leading to liberation which have been trodden by others – paths which we also ought, indeed have to, tread? Has the independence of Polish music really to be defended from harmful influences by a police state and a protective tariff? Are we really afraid of these foreign influences? Are we as weak as all that?[37]

King Roger, like 'Efebos', is also about the frisson created by the acknowledgment that erotic attractions cross all gender boundaries, that ultimately no sexual preference is 'abnormal'. The moral social order of the King's court and church is thrown into disarray by the arrival of a beautiful young shepherd – an ephebe – proclaiming a religion of love. The boy's attractions prove irresistible to Roger's queen and subjects. The symbolism of the King's unsuccessful attempt to capture the Shepherd is clear: love must be released and people granted freedom to follow the call of Eros. When the Shepherd sings to the Polish folk melody it is as though Szymanowski is confirming that homoeroticism has 'come home' – it is no longer a characteristic assigned to distant others:[38] the sexual agenda of Orientalism and the political agenda of nationalism, both based on insidious divisions, have been discarded in the search for a new unity based upon the liberation of Eros. In the end, though, Roger – having acknowledged the power of Eros, resists the shepherd's call to follow him into the darkness of night and offers a hymn to the rising sun. Through the experience of his encounter with the ephebe, however, he is reborn – a new kind of man, a new kind of hero.[39]

It is crucial to establish what kind of figure is Szymanowski's paneuropean-erotic hero, and how this figure differs from the national-heroic archetype. King Roger's heroism is based upon the dawn of a psychological realisation that his erotic attraction to the beautiful young boy need not lead to renunciation of life but, rather, a wider embracing of the world; that acknowledgment of homoerotic tendencies can lead to a position of greater strength rather than one of 'diseased' weakness. In Plato's *Symposium*, Aristophanes, after explaining the cutting in two of man's originally unified body (which, as we have seen, Freud used to illustrate the reunifying power of Eros), goes on to describe the characteristics of the homosexual in markedly heroic terms:

> those who are halves of a male whole pursue males, and being slices, so to speak, of the male, love men throughout their boyhood, and take pleasure in physical contact with men. Such boys and lads are the best of their generation, because they are the most manly. Some people say that they are shameless, but they are wrong. It is not shamelessness which inspires their behaviour, but high spirit and manliness and virility, which lead them to welcome the society of their own kind. A striking proof of this is that such boys alone, when they reach maturity, engage in public life.[40]

This offers not only a direct contrast to the diseased and banished 'effeminate' homosexual of conventional, prejudiced, stereotyping but also a challenge to the role and character typically assigned to masculinity by modern nationalism. Mosse explains how, in the nineteenth century:

> the appearance and character of each individual was classified as normal or abnormal: nervousness was supposedly induced by the practice of vice, while virility and manly bearing were signs of virtue. Nationalism adopted this ideal of manliness and built national stereotypes around it.[41]

Mosse notes the delicious irony in the fact that this ideal of national manliness was in part based upon renewed interest in the descriptions of the beauty, youth and strength of ancient Greek male statues found in the writings of the homosexual Winckelmann. In the words of Walter Pater's famous commentary:

> The beauty of the Greek statues was a sexless beauty: the statues of the gods had the least traces of sex. Here there is a moral sexlessness, a kind of ineffectual wholeness of nature, yet with a true beauty and significance of its own. One result of this temperament is a serenity – *Heiterkeit* – which characterises Winckelmann's handling of the sensuous side of Greek art.[42]

Mosse points out that, despite Pater's insistence on the 'sexlessness' of these figures, 'the nakedness of Greek male sculpture as part of national self-representation did not cease to be troubling ... he was potentially a homoerotic symbol ... nationalism tried to exorcise homoeroticism from masculine beauty'.[43] This, to some extent, is what King Roger initially tries to do by ordering his guards to capture or banish the beautiful young shepherd, whose eroticism was undermining the control exercised by his court and church. Roger Scruton has called the church choruses of *King Roger* 'the voice of community.'[44] If it is, then this is a community based upon repression of the erotic and the erection of rigid boundaries between 'normal' and 'abnormal'. In the cosmopolitan 'East-West' mix of Sicily (which surely attracted Szymanowski because of its similarity in this respect to the Black Sea borderlands of the Ukraine), this retreat behind policed frontiers cannot last. Furthermore, a retreat from the glare and struggles of life into the secretive, furtive shadows of night is equally inadequate. As King Roger realises, a different response to the challenge of Eros is required if true 'freedom' is to be achieved. Once gained, this freedom requires a new, potentially greater, heroism in using this to promote the deeper unity of mankind.

Again, Szymanowski's response to the *fin-de-siècle* engagement with ancient Greek 'erotics' is important. In Xenophon's *Memorabilia*, part of the dialogue reads:

> 'Tell me, Euthydemus, do you think that freedom is a noble and splendid possession both for individuals and for communities?' 'Yes, I think it is, in the highest degree.' 'Then do you think that the man is free who is ruled by bodily pleasures and is unable to do what is best because of them?' 'By no means.'[45]

As Foucault explains, 'moderation' (*sophrosyne*) was characterised as freedom from slavery to desire through self-mastery; 'what was affirmed through this conception of mastery as active freedom was the "virile" character of moderation'.[46] In *The Republic* Plato states that 'true love' can have no contact with the 'frenzy' or 'excess' of sex, that 'to love rightly is to love what is orderly and beautiful in an educated and disciplined way' and this is revealed by the harmonious beauty of a man's soul and body.[47] As is well known, Plato argued that music and the arts should be carefully regulated, to avoid a demoralising, destructive effect. Pater, lover of Winckelmann's sexless Greek beauties, agreed with Plato's equation of artistic, individual and social harmony. Pater, too, advocates control – again, by way of virile, 'manly' imagery:

> Bravery ... manliness and temperance ... were the characteristics of that old pagan world; and in art they certainly seem to be involved with one another. Manliness in art, what can it be ... what but a full consciousness of what one does, of art itself in the world of art, tenacity of intuition, and of consequent purpose, the spirit of construction as opposed to what is literally incoherent or ready to fall into pieces, and, in opposition to what is hysteric or works at random, the maintenance of a standard ... Platonic aesthetics, remember! as such we are ever in closer connection with Plato's ethics. It is life itself, action and character, he proposes to colour; to get something of that irrepressible conscience of art, that spirit of control, into the general course of life.[48]

Szymanowski, who greatly admired much of Pater's work, tackled two issues emerging from this reading of Plato: the relationship of 'virility' and 'control', and the question of the individual artist's position in the community. In the search for a new 'heroic' answer to both questions, a central spur was his enduring, if necessarily ambivalent, fascination with Nietzsche.[49] Szymanowski's understanding of the coexistence of formal control and apparently 'incoherent' frenzy is fundamentally indebted to Nietzsche's familiar Apollonian–Dionysian dichotomy. The rehabilitation of the Dionysian is central to Szymanowski's ecstatic creations, where immersion in erotic desires is primarily viewed not as an enslavement but as a liberation. Furthermore, in the folk culture of the Polish Highlanders (for which he developed an enormous enthusiasm in the early 1920s), Szymanowski thought he perceived a particularly powerful union of raw energy and formal beauty which could serve as an inspirational model for a reinvigorated 'Polish' art of 'paneuropean' significance.[50]

The second problem concerns the relationship of the individual with the collective. Pater emphasised the importance of artistic development of an 'individual' language. Szymanowski dedicated 'Efebos', to those 'brooding solitary in high, impregnable towers on the mystery of love'[51] and many of Szymanowski's other writings from this time speak of retreat into caves and ascents to mountain tops, places distanced from the masses, where the artist may encounter deep truths (the cave is where the beautiful youth Eros/Dionysius sleeps).[52] However, just as Roger decides not to follow the shepherd into the darkness of the rocks but turns instead to the sun (potent symbol of the nation and collective will) and the sea (symbol of rebirth and voyages of discovery) so Szymanowski, once the political situation allowed, yearned to move out of his 'interior landscape' to the new post-war society of the reborn Poland.[53] He felt compelled to 'leave his rocky entrenchment' and speak his new-found truths to the world. The parallels with Nietzsche's Zarathustra are hard to resist,[54] particularly since both Szymanowski and Zarathustra discover that their message meets with misunderstanding and rejection. Szymanowski's first concert on his return to Warsaw (29 January 1920) drew a poor audience and critical censure. His initial reaction was to doubt whether he belonged to the 'new' Poland:

> I noted again the same state of things which compelled me to leave Warsaw seven years ago, namely there is no real contact between myself and the Polish (or at any rate Warsaw) public, I seem strange, incomprehensible to them . . . The European climate of my art does not suit this local provincialism . . . at the first opportunity I will leave Warsaw again and go west or south (to Italy).[55]

In October of that year he resumed the life of a cosmopolitan artist, visiting Paris, London and New York. In 1921, however, he wrote

> I feel I must return to the homeland, albeit for a few months! It is absolutely essential for my spiritual well-being, even though such a 'return' always ends – alas – in some sort of personal bitterness and a sense of isolation from society – precisely in the artistic field![56]

Thus he returned to Poland determined to promulgate his vision of a modern musical culture that was not provincial or national, but paneuropean. Again, there are parallels with Nietzsche, who looked for a similar, 'supra-European' music of the future in reaction to his despair at the state of German art:

> a deeper, mightier, perhaps wickeder and more mysterious music, a supra-German music which does not fade, turn yellow, turn pale at the sight of the blue voluptuous sea and the luminous sky of the Mediterranean, as all German music does; a supra-European music which holds its own even before the brown sunsets of the desert, whose soul is kindred to the palm-tree and knows how to roam and be at home amongst great beautiful solitary beasts of prey.[57]

Substitution of 'Polish' for 'German' in this text will reveal the similarity to aspects of Szymanowski's position – in particular the images of the sensuous Mediterranean and the call for the opening of cultural boundaries in the artistic imagination. Szymanowski argued that, to avoid the limitations of provincialism, artists needed to seek inspiration and forms which transcended parochial characteristics and experiences. In this regard he saw Chopin as the shining example of how a Polish artist could become paneuropean yet retain his national qualities. In 1923 he wrote:

> The 'Polish character' of Chopin's work is unquestionable; not because he also wrote polonaises and mazurkas . . . which forms . . . were often stuffed with alien ideological and literary contents *from the outside*. Through the absolute 'musicality' of his works he loomed large above his period in two ways: as an artist he looked for forms that stood apart from the literary-dramatic character of music which was a feature of Romanticism, as a Pole he reflected in his work the very essence of the tragic break in the *history of the people* and instinctively aspired to give the deepest expression of his nation that *transcended* history. For he understood that he could invest his music with the most enduring and truly Polish qualities only by liberating art from the confines of dramatic historical contents. This attitude toward the question of 'national music' – an inspired solution to his art – was the reason why Chopin's works have come to be understood everywhere outside of Poland . . . and were raised to the pinnacle of all human art. Therein lies the strange riddle of his eternal vigour.[58]

The anti-Romantic tone here (typical of much of Szymanowski's writing from the 1920s) is revealed in his belief that it was Chopin's ability to extract music from its disentanglement with tragic history, through the restoration of a degree of autonomy, that broke the 'barriers' to his universal (paneuropean) appreciation and assured the 'vigour' of his work.

Chopin, as an archetype of the *émigré* artist, is somehow both free of national boundaries and yet symbolic of the lost home. For much of his career Szymanowski was torn between nomadism (sometimes imposed, sometimes willed) and a yearning for his roots. As Salman Rushdie has recently put it:

> If writing turns repeatedly towards nation, it just as repeatedly turns away. The deliberately uprooted intellectual . . . views the world as only a free intelligence can, going where the action is and offering reports. The intellectual uprooted against his will . . . rejects, too, the narrow enclosures that have rejected him. There is a great loss, and much yearning, in such rootlessness. But there is also gain. The frontierless nation is not a fantasy.[59]

Rushdie also writes: 'nationalism is that "revolt against history" which seeks to close what cannot any longer be closed. To fence in what should be frontierless. Good writing assumes a frontierless nation. Writers who serve frontiers have become border guards.' The imagery is one Szymanowski would have appreciated. Like Rushdie, he understood that, once breached, the boundaries of nation, like those of culture, gender and sexuality, cannot be reconstructed.

As part of his vision of a Polish culture that would contribute to the 'paneuropean' scene, Szymanowski later drew up an elaborate philosophy of society and the role of education – one based on the evolution of a 'democratic' community of cultured individuals.[60] Aspects of this are prefigured in 'Efebos':

> Paneuropeanism is an evolutionary symptom: unheard of refinement of the culture of some individuals, increasing sensitivity on the one hand and intellectual on the other, encompassing more and more wider horizons of a mutual past (historical), and as a result it erases and minimises the present differences, bringing them down to 'provincialism'. This increased feeling of a common crib – due to the unravelling 'historical thinking' – must in the end lead to a single denominator of all cultured individuals and find a common tongue for communication.[61]

Unsurprisingly, music has special power in Szymanowski's vision ('music is a powerful weapon in the war against the obscurantism and barbarism of the masses . . . in the life of present-day society, music is a mighty, constantly active force, something which is simply essential'), but Szymanowski warns that 'this force can, however, act in two diametrically opposed directions: it can be a destructive element which annihilates instinctive susceptibilities, or else it can be constructve'.[62] This begins to resemble Freud's idea, elaborated in 'Civilisation and Its Discontents' and elsewhere, of the coexistence of constructive Eros with destructive Thanatos. As Chylińska says, however, Szymanowski's 'destructive' force lies in the abuse of music as a 'narcotic', as an 'art substitute for the masses', as exemplified by the propaganda culture typical of repressive political regimes.[63] Szymanowski argues that the constructive power of music lies in its 'special pathos, influences for the . . . process of refining and broadening human sensibilities, making possible a more profound awareness of the ethical essence of life'.[64] Through releasing this power a unified culture can be created across national boundaries. Furthermore, he believed that this synthesis might lead, eventually, to the evolution of a universal musical language. In 1933 Szymanowski wrote:

> It seems to me without doubt that if one descends towards the deepest levels of human conscience, in spite of all appearance to the contrary, one can establish already that we are on the path of great synthesis . . .
>
> Music, universally understandable language, has allowed us to descend to the very springs of the sensibility of no matter which nation whose spoken or written language would never entrust its true secrets to us. From the variety and indeed the richness of styles and means of expression due to the awakening of the consciousness of race, there was born a need for acquaintance and mutual drawing together . . .
>
> Could there come to life from these trends a new 'universalism', a certain unification of musical language, a sort of esperanto without colour or character which future generations of composers will make use of – this does not seems to me to be something to fear. It appears evident to us today that the ideal of human understanding does not consist of erasing the natural frontiers imposed by the distinctive characteristics of situation and race, but it is a question of getting rid of the 'spiritual customs posts' which, born of a false idea of national interest, are set against the mutual understanding of peoples.[65]

These words come from an address Szymanowski gave at the Madrid conference of the International Institute of Intellectual Co-operation. This body, under directions from the League of Nations, had previously initiated an exchange of letters between intellectuals on topics of international concern. Amongst early participants were Albert Einstein and, at Einstein's suggestion, Freud. Einstein's open letter to Freud asked the question 'Why War?'. Freud responded by reiterating his theory of the coexistence of constructive 'Eros' (again citing Plato) and destructive instincts:

> According to our hypothesis human instincts are of only two kinds: those which seek to preserve and unite – and which we call 'erotic', exactly as in the sense in which Plato uses the word 'Eros' in his *Symposium*, or 'sexual', with a deliberate extension of the popular conception of 'sexuality' – and those which seek to destroy and kill and which we group together as the aggressive or destructive instinct . . . Now it seems as though an instinct of the one sort can scarcely ever operate in isolation; it is always accompanied – or, as we say, alloyed – with a certain quota from the other side . . . Thus, for instance, the instinct of self-preservation is certainly of an erotic kind, but it must nevertheless have aggressiveness at its disposal if it is to fulfil its purpose. So, too, the instinct of love, when it is directed towards an object, stands in need of that object.[66]

Szymanowski's answer to the question 'why war?' would have been to point to the 'internationalism of the proletariat masses which is destructive in the very assumptions which underlie it' and to 'narrow-minded and egoistic nationalism' as examples of the 'primitivism of the psychology of the mob', but then to go on to propose a unifying alternative based, in contrast to Freud, on a conception of Eros as an unequivocally positive, emancipating force. Aggressive self-preservation held no place in his vision for the future of culture and society ('it is the absence of any selfish interest that is the cardinal condition, the only psychological basis upon which it is possible to found the astonishing phenomenon that is art in the spiritual life of man')[67] but neither is there a call for the erotic subject to be sacrificed to the collective. This is why Szymanowski was able to move out from an initial 'secret conspiracy of solitary men'[68] to a broad, encompassing vision of paneuropean culture.[69] It is a radical, optimistic alternative to Witkiewicz's pessimistic, ultimately catastrophic view of the power of the erotic and, indeed, seems to share something of Malinowski's hopes for international co-operation.[70] It is, of course, a Utopian vision. If Szymanowski had lived but two more years he would have seen war return to Europe and Poland brutally invaded yet again. This precipitated Witkiewicz's suicide. We can, of course, only speculate on how Szymanowski might have reacted. In 'Efebos', *King Roger* and other works conceived in the war-torn years of 1917–1921, however, we have a body of work representing a dazzling personal synthesis of cultural references, crossing the boundaries of nation, race and gender to form an affirmative belief in an international society of the future based upon the artistic freedoms granted by Eros.

Notes and References

1   Only a brief overview of these events is necessary here. For more details see Norman Davies, *Heart of Europe: A Short History of Poland* (Oxford, 1986), pp. 109–23 (on the problem of borders) and pp. 129–48 (on the Piłsudski/Dmowski 'duel'). See also Jerzy Tomaszewski, 'The National Question in Poland in the Twentieth Century', in Mikuláš Teich and Roy Porter (eds.), *The National Question in Europe in Historical Context* (Cambridge, 1993), pp. 293–316, and Peter Brock, 'Polish Nationalism', in Peter Sugar and Ivo Lederer (eds.), *Nationalism in Eastern Europe* (Seattle and London, 1969), pp. 311–67.

2   In 1922 the newly elected President, Gabriel Narutowicz, was murdered by a National Democrat extremist.

3   Letter to Zdzisław Jachimecki. It is undated but was written sometime before mid-June 1918; Karol Szymanowski, *Korespondencja Tom. 1: 1903–1919*, ed. Teresa Chylińska (Kraków, 1982), p. 531. This translation from Teresa Chylińska, *Karol Szymanowski: His Life and Works* (Los Angeles, 1993), pp. 128–9.

4   Letter to Jarosław Iwaszkiewicz, January 1918; *Korespondencja, Tom. 1*, p. 523.

5   Szymanowski, 'Efebos', in *Pisma Tom. 2: Pisma literackie* ed. Teresa Chylińska (Kraków, 1989), p. 126. This translation from Chylińska, *Karol Szymanowski*, p. 131.

6   Szymanowski, 'Efebos', *Pisma Tom. 2*, p. 126. In the eighteenth century the 'Grand Tour', and in particular travel to Italy, frequently provided opportunity for homoerotic discovery; see Gary C. Thomas, 'Was George Frederic Handel Gay?', in Philip Brett, Elizabeth Wood and Gary C. Thomas (eds.), *Queering the Pitch: The New Gay and Lesbian Musicology* (New York and London, 1994), pp. 155–203. Arthur Rubinstein recalled meeting Szymanowski for the first time since the war: 'Karol had changed; I had already begun to be aware of it before the war when a wealthy friend and admirer of his [Spiess] had invited him twice to visit Italy. After his return he raved about Sicily, especially Taormina. "There," he said, "I saw a few young men bathing who could be models for Antinous. I couldn't take my eyes off them." Now he was a confirmed homosexual, he told me all this with burning eyes' (Arthur Rubinstein, *My Many Years* [London, 1980], p. 103). The one surviving copy of Szymanowski's 'Uczta' is a Russian translation which the composer gave as a token of love to the young Boris Kochno (later to be an assistant to Diaghilev) in 1918.

7   Szymanowski, 'Efebos', *Pisma Tom. 2*, pp. 152–3. Translation by Alistair Wightman. I am grateful to Dr Wightman for sending me his translations of many of Szymanowski's writings. All subsequent translations from the Uczta chapter of 'Efebos' are Wightman's.

8   On Malinowski's intellectual background, see Jan Jerschina, 'Polish Culture of Modernism and Malinowski's Personality', in Roy Ellen (ed.), *Malinowski Between Two Worlds* (Cambridge, 1988), pp. 128–47. On Witkiewicz and his relationship with Malinowski, see Daniel Gerould (ed.), *The Witkiewicz Reader* (London, 1993), which, amongst much else of interest, contains a useful introduction by the editor and a fascinating selection of letters. In February 1914 Witkiewicz's fiancée, Jadwiga Janczewska, shot herself after severe difficulties in their relationship, a tragedy which he blamed partly on Szymanowski: in June, whilst accompanying Malinowski on a voyage to Australia, he wrote, 'Karol is a born scoundrel, and I feel less resentment against him than against myself for believing him' (Gerould, *The Witkiewicz Reader*, p. 86).

9   Ibid., p. 313. Witkiewicz met Szymanowski in Kiev in the spring of 1917 and they met frequently in the 1920s. Witkiewicz was extremely depressed at Szymanowski's death in March 1937, writing 'that scoundrel Szymanowski is calling me from the other side of the line' (but then Witkiewicz's innate pessimism had often made him contemplate suicide before the Nazi invasion of Poland in September 1939 actually drove him to follow it through).

10 Szymanowski, 'Efebos', *Pisma Tom. 2*, p. 197. Translation from Chylińska, *Karol Szymanowski*, p. 136.

11 Sigmund Freud, 'Beyond the Pleasure Principle' (1920), in *Standard Edition of the Complete Psychological Works of Sigmund Freud: Vol. 18 (1920–1922)*, trans. and ed. by James Strachey (London, 1955), pp. 57–8.

12 Freud, 'Group Psychology and the Analysis of the Ego' (1921), *Standard Edition: Vol. 18*, pp. 91–2.

13 Freud, 'Civilisation and Its Discontents' (1930), *Standard Edition: Vol. 22 (1927–1931)* (London, 1961), p. 122.

14 Szymanowski, 'Efebos', *Pisma Tom. 2*, pp. 166–7.
15 Ibid., p. 149.
16 Gustave le Bon, *Psychologie des foules* (1895); quoted in Freud, 'Group Psychology and the Analysis of the Ego', *Standard Edition: Vol. 18*, p. 77.
17 Szymanowski, 'Efebos', *Pisma Tom. 2*, p. 155.
18 Ibid., p. 150.
19 Ibid., pp. 161–2.
20 Ibid., p. 128.

21 Jonathan Dollimore, *Sexual Dissidence: Augustine to Wilde, Freud to Foucault* (Oxford, 1991), p. 236.
22 Elaine Showalter, *Sexual Anarchy: Gender and Culture at the Fin de Siècle* (London, 1991), p. 4.
23 George L. Mosse, *Nationalism and Sexuality* (Madison, 1985), p. 27. On Krafft-Ebing, see Renate Hauser, 'Krafft-Ebing's Psychological Understanding of Sexual Behaviour', in Roy Porter and Mikuláš Teich (eds.), *Sexual Knowledge, Sexual Science: The History of Attitudes to Sexuality* (Cambridge, 1994), pp. 210–27.
24 Quoted in Showalter, *Sexual Anarchy*, p. 9. On Freud's uncertainty with the blurring of the distinction between 'normal' and 'pathological' sexual behaviour, see Arnold I. Davidson, 'How to Do the History of Psychoanalysis: A Reading of Freud's *Three Essays on the Theory of Sexuality*', *Critical Inquiry*, 13 (1987), pp. 252–77.
25 Stanisław Przybyszewski, 'Sex' (1910); this translation from Donald E. Gordon, *Expressionism: Art and Idea* (New Haven, 1987), pp. 36–7.
26 Claude Lévi-Strauss, 'Cosmopolitanism and Schizophrenia', in *The View from Afar*, trans. by Joachim Neugroschel and Phoebe Hoss (London, 1987), p.179. Lévi-Strauss goes on to quote Roger Bastide: 'Analogy is not a reduction of a social structure to a different, mental structure; the analogy sheds light on differences as well as similarities. It is located between the categories of "same" and "the other".'
27 On Szymanowski's 'borderland soul', see Chylińska's introduction to Szymanowski, *Korespondecja Tom. 1*, p. 38.
28 Mikhail Rostovtzeff, *Iranians and Greeks in South Russia* (Oxford, 1922); quoted by Neal Ascherson, *Black Sea: The Birthplace of Civilisation and Barbarism* (London, 1996), p. 8.
29 A literary expression of the latter might be seen in the Transylvania of Bram Stoker's *Dracula* (1897), which Showalter characterises as the setting for exploring 'the thrills and terrors of blurred sexual, psychological, and scientific boundaries', a location 'on the "borders of three states" [Stoker] which we might read as the states of living, dead, and undead, or of masculinity, femininity, and bisexuality' (*Sexual Anarchy*, p. 179). Of course, the difference between Stoker and Szymanowski is that the former is constructing an image of eastern Europe from 'outside'. His first idea was to set the tale in Austria, but, as Christopher Frayling says, 'reading fashionable romantic travellers' tales and collections of folklore about eastern Europe ... persuaded him to change his mind and push the location further east'. In Emily Gerard's *The Land Beyond the Forest*, for example, Stoker read this description of Transylvania: 'it would almost seem as though the whole species of demons, pixies, witches, and hobgoblins, driven from the rest of Europe by the wand of Science, had taken refuge within this mountainous rampart' (Christopher Frayling, *Nightmare: The Birth of Horror* [London, 1996], pp. 97–8).
30 Geoffrey Hosking, 'The Freudian Frontier: Review of Susan Layton, *Russian Literature and Empire: The Conquest of the Caucasus from Pushkin to Tolstoy*', *Times Literary Supplement* (10 March 1995) p. 27. On the problem of mapping the boundary between Europe and Asia see Mark Bassin, 'Russia between Europe and Asia: The Ideological Construction of Geographical Space', *Slavic Review*, 50 (1991), pp. 1–17.
31 As David Crowley says, 'Some Polish artists and designers, fighting the absorption of Polish culture into those of the partitioning powers, found Polish echoes in the cultures of distant peoples ... Polish patriotism had periodically turned eastwards' (*National Style and Nation-state: Design in Poland from the Vernacular Revival to the International Style* [Manchester, 1992], p. 7). This should be contrasted with the following from Maryan Wawrzeniecki (in 1912): 'Throughout our country, now but a remnant of the once powerful Polish state, we are, as we have always been, the offspring of Western civilisation. Such was the fate alloted to us. This influence and

connection, which we shall uphold with pride, is confirmed alike by the art of our enlightened classes and by the art of our common people, and we intend to maintain it in the future' (quoted in Crowley, *National Style*, p. 1).

32 Richard Taruskin, *Defining Russia Musically* (Princeton, 1997), p. 185 and footnote on p. 158.

33 The Persian composer Kaikhosru Sorabji wrote of Szymanowski: 'here is no European in Eastern fancy dress, but one who, by . . . an astonishing kinship of spirit, succeeds in giving us in musical terms what we instinctively know and recognise as the essence of Persian art' (*Mi Contra Fa: The Immoralisings of a Machiavellian Musician* [London, 1948], p. 184).

34 The usual English title for this work is *Songs of the Infatuated Muezzin*, but the Polish *szalonego* is closer to 'mad' and, as I have argued elsewhere, an exploration of the 'boundary' between eroticism and 'madness' is an essential aspect of the work; see 'Madness in Music: Szymanowski's Op.42', paper delivered at the International Symposium on 19th and 20th-century Song, Kraków, October 1997

35 Jarosław Iwaszkiewicz, in *Wiadomości Literackie*, 27 April 1924. Reprinted in Karol Szymanowski, *Korespondencja Tom. 2 (1920–1926):**, od 1924*, ed. Teresa Chylińska (Kraków, 1994), p. 82 (my translation). The text of Szymanowski's Third Symphony ('The Song of the Night'), which he completed in the summer of 1916, is a translation of lines by the thirteenth-century Sufi mystic Jalal-al-din Rumi.

36 Czesław Miłosz, *Beginning with my Streets: Baltic Reflections*, trans. by Madeline G. Levine (London, 1992), p. 64.

37 Szymanowski,'Zagadnienie"Ludowoci"w stasunku do Muzyki Wspóczesnej' ('The Question of "Folk" with reference to Contemporary Music'), 1925, in *Pisma Tom. 1: Pisma muzyczne*, ed. Kornel Michałowski (Kraków, 1984), p. 170; trans. from Zdzisław Sierpiński (ed.), *Karol Szymanowski: An Anthology*, trans. by Emma Harris (Warsaw, 1986), pp. 181–2. Szymanowski characterised his article 'Drogi i bezdroża Muzyki Współczesnej' ('The Highroads and Byroads of Contemporary Music'), also written in 1925, as 'the improvisation of a wanderer who is always pressing on ahead towards new shores and new lands, an attempt to formulate all the factors affecting contemporary music from the standpoint of its inner dynamics . . . These are letters from a traveller in a strange country, written to those who – while remaining cowards on the shores already known to them – are trying, on the evidence of their own poor experience, to paint landscapes of the far-off and unattainable future' (*Pisma Tom. 1*, p. 185, trans. from Sierpiński, *Karol Szymanowski*, p. 149).

38 On the 'mapping of homosexual vice', see Rudi C. Bleys, *The Geography of Perversion: Male-to-male Sexual Behaviour outside the West and the Ethnographic Imagination 1750–1918* (London, 1996), pp. 145–206.

39 For a more extensive discussion of Eros in *King Roger* see my 'Themes of Duality and Transformation in Szymanowski's *King Roger*', *Music Analysis*, 14 (1995), pp. 257–91.

40 Plato, *The Symposium*, trans. by Walter Hamilton (Harmondsworth, 1951), pp. 62–3.

41 Mosse, *Nationalism and Sexuality*, p. 10.

42 Walter Pater, *The Renaissance*, ed. with an introduction by Adam Phillips (Oxford, 1986), p. 142.

43 Mosse, *Nationalism and Sexuality*, p. 16. See also Mosse's 'Masculinity and the Decadence', in Porter and Teich (eds.), *Sexual Knowledge, Sexual Science*, pp. 251–66.

44 Roger Scruton,'Between Decadence and Barbarism: The Music of Szymanowski', in Michał Bristiger (ed.), *Szymanowski in Seiner Zeit* (Munich, 1984), p. 167.

45 Quoted in Michel Foucault, *The History of Sexuality, Vol. 2: The Use of Pleasure*, trans. by Robert Hurley (Harmondsworth, 1985), p. 78.

46 Ibid., p. 82.

47 Plato, *The Republic*, trans. with an introduction by Desmond Lee (Harmonsworth, 1955), p. 105.
48 Pater, *Plato and Platonism* (1893); quoted, and discussed, in I. C. Small, 'Plato and Pater: *Fin-de-Siècle* Aesthetics', *British Journal of Aesthetics*, 12 (1972), pp. 376–7. This passage is also cited by Elaine Showalter in her discussion of 'Hysterical Narratives' in *Hystories: Hysterical Epidemics and Modern Culture* (London, 1997), pp. 81–99 (especially pp. 82–3).
49 According to Iwaszkiewicz, Szymanowski considered Nietzsche's *The Birth of Tragedy* to be one of the 'most beautiful books in the world'; Iwaszkiewicz, *Spotkania z Szymanowskim* (Kraków, 1986), p. 29. On Nietzschean and other aspects of *King Roger*, see Paolo Emilio Carapezza, 'Król Roger między Dionizosem i Apollinem', *Res Facta*, 9 (1982), pp. 50–61.
50 See Jim Samson, 'Szymanowski and Polish Nationalism', *Musical Times*, 131 (1990), pp. 135–7. Szymanowski was introduced to the Polish Highlanders' music by the musicologist Adolf Chybiński (they met in March 1920). Szymanowski was particularly delighted with Chybiński's speculative idea that a characteristic melodic element of this folk style (the Sabała descent) might also have been a feature of ancient Greek music; see Chybiński, *Szymanowski a Podhale* (Kraków, 1977). For this point I am grateful to Prof. Zofia Helman.
51 Szymanowski, 'Efebos', *Pisma Tom. 2*, p. 124.
52 In the draft version of *King Roger*, 'Sketch of a Sicilian Drama' – Iwaszkiewicz describes the beautiful youth as living in a cave. Roger's attempts to imprison him are, therefore, nothing more than an attempt to send him back from whence he came. In 'Opowieść o włóczvędze-kuglarzu i o siedmiu gwiazdach' ('The Tale of a Wandering Juggler and the Seven Stars'), a short story which Szymanowski wrote in 1921, an aged sage leads a young artist to a solitary cave in the hills where there is a statue of the God of Love. The artist returns to his public work to paint an image of this new God, which the masses find blasphemous; *Pisma Tom. 2*, pp. 312–17.
53 Roger's re-embracing of the world was Szymanowski's idea: Iwaszkiewicz's original scenario had the King follow the Shepherd into the darkness. On this alteration of the ending of the opera see Karol Berger, 'King Roger's *Liebesleben*', in Bristiger, *Szymanowski in Seiner Zeit*, pp. 21–8. The term 'interior landscape' is Jim Samson's; see his 'Szymanowski – an Interior Landscape', *Proceedings of the Royal Musical Association*, 106 (1979–80), pp. 70–6.
54 'When Zarathustra was thirty years old, he left his home and the lake of his home and went into the mountains. Here he had the enjoyment of his spirit and his solitude and he did not weary of it for ten years. But at last his heart turned – and one morning he rose with the dawn, stepped before the sun and spoke to it thus . . .', Nietzsche, *Thus Spoke Zarathustra*, trans. R. J. Hollingdale (Harmondsworth, 1969), p. 39. The parodies of Christ in the life of Zarathustra are obvious. Nietzsche also parodies Plato's *Symposium* and myth of the cave; see Kathleen Higgins, 'Reading Zarathustra', in Robert C. Solomon and Kathleen M. Higgins (eds.), *Reading Nietzsche* (Oxford, 1990), pp. 132–51. It should be clear that Szymanowski, too, held productive love-hate relationships with these two figures. In particular, Nietzsche and Szymanowski both believed that the Christian church had misrepresented Christ and that Plato/Socrates held misplaced faith in the control of reason. 'I will leave my rocky entrenchment . . .' was the title of an article Szymanowski published in 1923 ('Opuszczvę skalny mój szaniec . . .'), *Pisma Tom. 1*, pp. 80–8.
55 Letter of 29 January 1920 to Jachimecki; Szymanowski, *Korespondencja Tom. 2**, p. 46. Translation from Teresa Chylińska, *Szymanowski*, trans. by A. T. Jordon (Kraków, 1981), p. 101.
56 Translation from Chylińska, *Karol Szymanowski*, p. 174.

57 Nietzsche, *Beyond Good and Evil: Prelude to a Philosophy of the Future*, trans. by R.J. Hollingdale (Harmondsworth, 1990), p. 188.
58 Szymanowski, 'Fryderyk Chopin' (1923), in *Pisma Tom. 1*, p. 97–8. Translation from *Polish Music*, 1977 No. 3, p. 7.
59 Salman Rushdie, 'Writers and Nations', *Guardian*, 14 June 1997.
60 'Wychowawcza rola kultury muzycznej w społeczeństwie' ('The Educational Role of Musical Culture in the Social Order'), 1930: *Pisma Tom. 1*, pp. 264–92.
61 Szymanowski, 'Efebos', *Pisma Tom. 2*, p. 193. Translation from Chylińska, *Karol Szymanowski*, p. 135.
62 Szymanowski, 'Wychowawcza rola...', *Pisma Tom. 1*, p. 269. Translation from Chylińska, *Karol Szymanowski*, p. 224.
63 Chylińska, *Karol Szymanowski*, p. 225.
64 Szymanowski, 'Wychowawcza rola...', *Pisma Tom. 1*, p. 273. Translation from Chylińska, *Karol Szymanowski*, p. 255.
65 Szymanowski, 'L'avenir de la culture' (1933), *Pisma Tom. 1*, pp. 340–2. I am grateful to Heather Marsh for translating this article from the French.
66 Freud, 'Why War?', a response to Albert Einstein, September 1932, *Standard Edition: Vol. 22 (1932–1936)* (London, 1964), p. 209. Einstein's letter is also published in this volume, pp. 199–202.
67 Szymanowski, 'Wychowawcza rola...', *Pisma Tom. 1*, p .280. Translation from Chylińska, *Karol Szymanowski*, p.226.
68 Szymanowski, 'Efebos', *Pisma Tom. 2*, p. 129.
69 I have argued elsewhere that in Szymanowski's music of the 1920s the erotically charged, post-Wagnerian melodic process remains a defining stylistic element ('Szymanowski's Melodic Crisis', paper delivered at the International Szymanowski Symposium, Zakopane, March 1997 – proceedings forthcoming). This is a feature which distinguishes Szymanowski's style from that of Stravinsky's music of the same period. Both Theodor Adorno and Hans Keller (arguing from very different positions) characterised Stravinsky's music as 'sado-masochistic'. Keller, for example, writes – 'In terms of the later Freudian instinct theory, Stravinsky wages war against the musical expression of "Eros", which is what leads to "expressionism", by employing this instinct's own aim, the satisfaction through rhythm, in the service of "Thanatos".' ('Rhythm: Gershwin and Stravinsky', *The Score*, 20 (June 1957), p. 28; reprinted in Hans Keller, *Essays on Music*, ed. Christopher Wintle (Cambridge, 1994), p. 209.
70 On Malinowski's 'League of Nations idealism', see Gellner, 'A Non-nationalist Pole', in his *Encounters with Nationalism* (Oxford, 1994), pp. 74–80. Szymanowski's ideas of liberated Eros share some similarities with the post-Freudian vision which Herbert Marcuse expounded in a series of lectures in 1950–51 and published as *Eros and Civilisation* (London, 1969). Recently there has been something of a revival of interest in Marcuse's work: see, for example, Jeffrey Weeks, *Sexuality and Its Discontents: Meanings, Myths and Modern Sexualities* (London, 1985), pp. 165–70, and Anthony Giddens, *The Transformation of Intimacy: Sexuality, Love and Eroticism in Modern Societies* (Cambridge, 1992), pp. 164–8.

4.
Gendering the Nations: The Ideologies of French Discourse on Music (1870–1914)[1]

ANNEGRET FAUSER

When, on 7 December 1871, Ferdinand Hérold and Eugène de Planard's *opéra comique, Le Pré aux Clercs*, was performed for the thousandth time,[2] Gustave Bertrand, one of the music critics for *Le Ménestrel*, took advantage of this celebration – so close to the French defeat in the Franco-Prussian war – to make the following remarks:

> Finally we claim, and this is what we want to insist on most, that the thousandth performance of *Le Pré aux Clercs* is a celebration for the French school. At this moment more than ever we need French art to affirm strongly all its legitimate glories in order first to console and brace us, and then to encourage itself to seek other [glories] . . . However, what marks out, in our eyes, the importance of this thousandth performance of so completely a French masterwork is the fact that it sets everything back in place and that it appears to me as a milestone destined to stand out in the history of public taste, indeed of *opéra comique*.[3]

Opéra comique, Bertrand pledged, should become 'something more masculine and sinewy (because comedy does not exclusively mean feminine smiles, superficial gaiety [or], even less, trivial merriness)'.[4] Performing French music and masculinising French art would thus constitute patriotic acts, bestowing cultural identity on and power to the defeated France. The newly founded Société Nationale de Musique's motto 'Ars Gallica' became the all-embracing battle-cry for the next decades, and protectionist legislation not only ensured that institutions such as the Opéra, the Concerts Colonne and Concerts Lamoureux employed French musicians but also made certain that they performed new French music for at least a specified amount of time each season.[5] French discourse on music contributed to and reflected these nationalist undertakings to redefine French music as an inherently national art through essentialising 'Frenchness' in music and masculinising both France's musical heritage and her overcoming of Germanic influences. Independent of a given writer's aesthetic or political allegiances, such discourse proclaimed the new French music as the most vital art in Europe.

The French defeat in 1871 was a pivotal event in the forging of cultural identity in nineteenth-century France. Perceived as the victory of a Prussia that 'founds its force on the development of primary education and on the identity of army and nation',[6] the débâcle challenged France's identity as a nation-state.[7] Finding a French 'collective identity' became a central preoccupation for the Third Republic,[8] especially given that, as Ernest Renan put it in 1870, 'once one has rejected the principle of dynastic legitimisation, there is nothing but the right of nationalities, that is, natural groups determined through race, history and the will of the people, to give a basis to the territorial limits of states'.[9] Symbols referring to the 'heroic past' and 'glory' represent the 'social capital' on which such Republican national identity could be established after the humiliating defeat of the corrupt Second Empire with its cosmopolitanism, *grandes cocottes* and operettas,[10] thus creating a link with the purer and glorious days of the earlier periods of the *Ancien Régime* and the French Revolution.

This process of forging a national identity after the Franco-Prussian war was, however, characterised by an antagonistic debate between two theoretical positions: one (appropriated by the Republican left) based on Sieyès's revolutionary concept of a free association of like-minded individuals, sharing similar concepts under the same law; the other (defended by the right) referring to Joseph de Maistre's traditionalist concept of nationality as a common destiny into which one is born.[11] The two positions on defining nationality – in Finkielkraut's terms, 'nation-contrat' (contractual nationality) versus 'nation-génie' (spiritual nationality)[12] – led to sharp conflicts over the question of who and what is French, culminating in the 'war of the two Frances' during the Dreyfus affair.[13] The debate started out as a reaction to the defeat by a nation whose identity, in France, had been defined in cultural instead of political terms ever since Madame de Staël's *De l'Allemagne* (1810).[14] Therefore the issue of cultural legitimisation became an important topic in the debate. Whereas Republicans such as Renan and Fustel de Coulanges refuted the notion of race, language and birth as the decisive elements of creating nationhood, they defended a 'community of ideas, interest, affections, memories and hopes' as its foundation.[15] Thus, soon after its election in 1879, the new left-wing government of Grévy and Ferry appealed to the Republican memory in installing the 'Marseillaise' as the national anthem (1879) and 14 July as the national holiday (1880).[16] Here, cultural symbols and historical events were appropriated for political ends and inscribed with meaning, but they were not – as in the case of the right – perceived as concretising of the French national soul as such. This is where a 'patriotic' left-wing Republican approach towards building nationhood differs fundamentally from the 'nationalist' right, which continued to refer to blood, soil and Catholicism as the foundation of national identity. Catholicism – in Maurice Barrès's words – was 'the expression of our blood',[17] and nationhood represented the mystical rooting of all members in the essence of its historical and racial selfness; thus the collision course between the nationalist movement of the right and the laicist Republican government (from 1879) was inevitable.[18]

Whether to create cultural symbols or to identify a genuinely French inheritance, references to the past became an important element in the discourse of both left and right throughout the Third Republic. Whereas the interpretations of such references could take on a wide range of political, social and cultural meanings, some strategies of approaching these issues were very similar. One of those discursive strategies consisted of the attempt to 'masculinise' French culture, either implicitly or explicitly – as in Bertrand's assessment of *opéra comique* above. 'Masculine' and 'feminine' were loaded terms when used in political and aesthetic discourse of the late nineteenth century, but they were particularly meaningful in France after the 1871 defeat, for the reciprocal connection made between women's emancipation and the loss of the war called into question the virility both of France and of Frenchmen.[19] As for aesthetic discourse, 'masculine' and 'feminine' transcended the specific human body and became signifiers that used sexual difference as a powerful metaphor to categorise political and cultural manifestations in accordance with a value system embodied in late nineteenth-century French society. In order to be successful, metaphors need to refer to concepts on which a relatively clear consensus exists within a shared cultural context. Such concepts offer a system of signs that abbreviate the world with its infinite complexity and variation.[20] These abbreviations – which, according to Nietzsche, can be described as 'solidified metaphors'[21] – allow for individual interpretations without the necessity of explication.[22] This is the epistemological context in which the terms 'masculine' and 'feminine' operated at the time.[23]

The terms 'masculine' and 'feminine' constituted a referential system which could be used either in direct reference or in allusion. Thus the novelist Joséphin Péladin was able to describe Chopin and Brahms[24] as 'feminine', but Beethoven and Wagner, on the other hand, as 'masculine'.[25] The two terms could also be evoked through substitution ('virile' for 'masculine) or allusion (thus the reference to the 'lovely flowers' of French folk-song in a German publication points towards its 'feminine', even 'effeminate', character).[26] But 'masculine' and 'feminine' were not only categorising and describing terms, they also implied a value judgement. Masculine qualities such as virility, strength, structure, logic, concision and coherence were character traits celebrated in popular, philosophical and educational literature in nineteenth-century France, whereas softness, confusion, decadence, weakness and sweetness were deemed less positive attributes, not only with respect to life in general but also as manifestations of culture.[27] The undertaking of restoring pride in France and her culture, shared by both right and left with similar fervour, thus needed to emphasise their 'masculine' qualities. With respect to music, several topics became particularly important after 1870: the representation of patriotic subjects; the acknowledgement of music's role in education as a valuable tool for instilling a sense of national conscience in French citizens; the heritage of popular music and French art music (whether as common memories or expression of the national soul); and the writing of (music) history. Although all of these issues were addressed soon after the end of the war, the exploitation of patriotic subjects presented the most immediate form of response.

Defending 'la patrie': patriotism through music

The musical world in France responded to the Franco-Prussian war through militaristic rhetoric in its journals, the composition of numerous patriotic songs such as 'La Française'[28] and a patriotic choice of subjects for vocal music. Thus the return of Pauline Viardot from her adopted Baden-Baden to Paris was celebrated as a 'true conquest by France over the German musical world',[29] and Henri Heugel found it necessary to incite his compatriots to a more nationalist support of French music as a patriotic act.[30] Patriotism was clearly the motive behind the choice of text for the 1871 *Prix de Rome* competition: an adapted fragment of Jules Barbier's play *Jeanne d'Arc* containing the scene of Jeanne's call to save France. The choice takes up Jules Michelet's earlier interpretation of Jeanne d'Arc as the incarnation of 'the French collectivity and the French soul', 'transforming her into a Republican heroine and symbol of a non-monarchical nation'.[31] The Republican Jeanne is not the devout virgin of pro-royalist interpretations of the legend, but the masculinised embodiment of the French people:

> And one should not be surprised if the people appear here in the guise of a woman, if a woman passes from patience and sweet virtues to virile ones, those of war, if a saint becomes a soldier.[32]

This masculinised reading of the heroine is reflected in the edition of selected pieces from the prize-winning cantata by Gaston Serpette. The cover represents Jeanne d'Arc as an androgynous figure in full armour, wearing the beret well known from portraits of great Renaissance kings such as François I (see Figure 1).[33] Indeed, this engraving could be seen as an example of drawing together various cultural references in a way that Renan had argued would help forge a Republican national identity.

Two years later, on 8 November 1873, Barbier's complete *Jeanne d'Arc* was staged with music by Charles Gounod at the Théâtre de la Gaîté, and its patriotic appeal was evident, especially with respect to Jeanne's martyrdom, underlined by Gounod's poignant Marche Funèbre:

> Under the transfigured form of Jeanne d'Arc, it was our country itself that appeared to all; from the orchestra stalls and the boxes, there was an outburst of ardent enthusiasm; it was France, loved even more in her disasters, that was acclaimed; and in this explosion of all that which these Parisian hearts, boasters of scepticism, had confined until now, suddenly the national sentiment of our glories and our misfortunes was awakened.[34]

Figure 4.1

Gounod's music, in particular the Marche Funèbre and the chorus *Nous fuyons la patrie* – 'the *Super flumina Babylonis* of the invaded and repressed France'[35] – was perceived as strengthening the emotional impact of the play's patriotic message. Although the role of Gounod's music was rather secondary in this context, his contribution was received not just as a major new work by one of France's leading composers but as a patriotic act.

Three years later, the newly built Palais Garnier gave as its first new opera the première of Mermet's *Jeanne d'Arc*. Again this was clearly a patriotic choice, but the subject alone was no longer enough to guarantee the work's success. And by the end of the decade, Jeanne d'Arc had become too controversial a figure to be used for Republican ends without ambiguity. Maurice Agulhon identifies 'un contre-culte nationaliste autour de Jeanne d'Arc' as one of the means of the nationalist right to fight the Republic with its own symbolic impersonation in 'Marianne'.[36] Although the history of Jeanne d'Arc remained one of the most popular topics in French music,[37] patriotic criteria for the choice of subject were slowly superseded by more nationalist considerations of developing a French music of the avant-garde, especially in the context of the reception of Wagner,[38] who had soon been assigned the role of a cultural giant within the camp of the enemy against whom developments in French art were measured. As in the case of other issues such as schooling, the German comparison never disappeared, and, although the selection of operatic subjects was still linked to political factors, the arguments about such topics and their sources became more and more focused on aesthetic and cultural issues.[39]

Educating healthy 'French' citizens

However, patriotic concerns were still present in other parts of French cultural life. Renan claims that widespread popular education as a decisive element in Germany's victory became a national obsession in Third-Republic France, and French educational reforms after 1871 emphasised patriotic issues in their teaching programmes.[40] Although music had already been introduced into primary education towards the end of the Second Empire in 1865, it received a new Republican function of developing a national conscience in the school system after 1870, justified not only by educational ideals derived from Plato's *Republic* and Aristotle's *Politics* but even more through its ability to forge a sense of collectivity by way of choral singing.[41] The German educational system provided both a model and a measuring stick, and justification for French educational practice was often sought by comparison with it.[42] Thus, when Louis-Albert Bourcault-Ducoudray[43] was asked to report on choral singing in French secondary schools, he came to the conclusion that Germany had its vibrant musical and artistic culture because of the ideas of Luther and their reception:

> Luther thus created, with unprecedented success, opportunities for his fellow believers to express collective religious feeling; at the same time as he made evident the usefulness of music in applying it to an elevated and civilising aim, he taught Germany, once and for all, the function and virtue of 'great art', inculating therein a love and respect for it forever.[44]

Music, Bourcault-Ducoudray asserted, had an educating mission, creating '"unity" in the heart of a nation',[45] and, properly applied, choral singing would produce a 'sacred trembling in young hearts' with reference to the heroic past of France.[46] Bourcault-Ducoudray not only provided a theoretical justification for the educational value of music but also composed 'patriotic' songs specifically for schools. His 'chant scholaire,' 'Esprit de la France!' offers a perfect example of the nationalist if not revanchist spirit of some such pieces, emphasising heroism, patriotism and male qualities in general. The diatonic setting in march rhythm underlines the text's message:

Esprit de la France,	Nous sommes toujours
Inspire à nos cœurs	La race fidèle
Les saintes ardeurs,	A l'être si belle
La mâle espérance!	De paix et d'amour.
Afin qu'on proclame	Mais si l'on outrage
Nos rudes travaux,	Le sol des aïeux,
Allume en notre âme,	Aux champs du carnage
La généreuse flamme	Nous courons comme eux![47]
Des héros!	

This educational role of music was by no means trivial: it was the key to nationalising French art and to creating both a healthy musical taste and healthy French citizens. As early as 1872, *L'Art musical* published a defence of music as part of higher education, stressing these aspects of mental and physical health.[48] In 1910, Jules Combarieu went much further, writing that: music is a 'school of solidarity', even a 'school of attention and discipline,' for pupils who need to give the same attention to their conductor 'as soldiers to their colonels on a field of manoeuvre'.[49] In the practice of choral singing, melody and rhythm intensify all feelings expressed in the text, which is why music is an ideal tool in patriotic education:

> The verbal phrase fades; the melody engraves. For example, you may give a lesson to the children on patriotism, on military courage, on the necessity of believing in victory when one has to pay with one's own life: you will find it easy to move and to interest them. But make them then sing the *Chant du départ*: 'La victoire en chantant nous ouvre la barrière . . .' Which of these two lessons will provide the deepest and most long-lasting effects? It will certainly be the second.[50]

But choral singing achieved even more for the French Republic: 'music educating both ear and voice, so important in a democracy; music teaching to speak clearly – and to listen'.[51]

Although such discourse refers to earlier concepts, as, for example, the emphasis on developing physical and spiritual health – to which reference is often made with respect to the Orphéon movement – it takes on a different and much more Republican slant here. Plato's ideal republic, Aristotle's ideas of music's 'ethos', the glorious memory of the 'chants révolutionnaires' in the first revolution[52] and the perceived success of choral training in Germany formed the mainstays of the argument to give vocal music a new weight in French public education. Choral singing is the form of musical practice which is the chief object of such masculinising rhetoric: virtue, power and glory are recurring terms.[53] However, so invigorating a musical education is useful not only for boys, but also for girls. The ideology of 'Republican motherhood' – the exaltation of 'the crucial part [women] would play in nurturing and educating the Republic's new-born citizens'[54] – had lost nothing of its attraction since the early nineteenth century, in particular because 'the decline of the old gender order accelerated in the aftermath of the revolutionary Commune and France's humiliating defeat in the Franco-Prussian war (1870–71).'[55] One major French concern thereafter was that France's birth-rate was the lowest in Europe.[56] Campaign followed campaign to fight against this form of decay; the question of national health developed into a public neurosis. Not only was motherhood understood as the 'patriotism of women' (Dumas) through repopulating the nation, but women's health and education were perceived as essential to the breeding of a strong and healthy race:

> The mother makes the race. It is she who gives vigour, intelligence and the foundations of education; the stronger and more intelligent she is and the more noble her character, the more powerful will be the race.[57]

Thus, in the project of educating 'Republican' mothers, choral singing again held a central place. Not only would it provide 'localised gymnastics' to prevent sore throats and respiratory problems[58] – an important factor in a period of rampant tuberculosis – but it would form women spiritually and intellectually. Furthermore, such choral singing would prevent them from preferring vulgar music-hall songs and their environment over the 'pure and sublime joys of ensemble music'.[59]

Cultural migrations I: 'la bonne et saine chanson française . . .'

It was not only choral singing in schools that was used to instil patriotism and health in future French citizens and their mothers, keeping them from the temptations of the café-concert. The same function was fulfilled by the newly founded co-educational 'universités populaires' and choral societies for working-class women, such as Ernest Chebroux's L'Œuvre de la Chanson Française.[60] As Mary Ellen Poole has shown, one of the central musical focuses of these institutions was 'la bonne et saine chanson française', rallying socialist, Republican and right-wing forces in the shared undertaking of revitalising 'true' French musical culture after 1870. These practical projects relied heavily on an industry of collecting, editing and researching French folk-songs headed most prominently by Julien Tiersot, who played a central role in the theoretical and practical mediation of the *chanson populaire*.[61]

As with the introduction of music into primary education, French interest in national folk music pre-dates the beginning of the Third Republic. It was mainly a literary movement, fuelled not only by contact with German literature and philology[62] but also by the French encounter with the English folksong movement and historical novels.[63] Thus from the 1830s to the 1860s the collecting of French folksongs concentrated on the presentation of poetic anthologies either by collectors such as Charles Nisard or by poets inspired by the German and English Romantic movements. One well-known example of such poets is Gérard de Nerval with his *Chansons et légendes du Valois*, published as part of his *Les filles du feu*,[64] which he presented as a response to the cultural challenges posed by France's two powerful neighbours whose creative artists had apparently not been alienated from the inspirational source of a national folk culture.[65] During the 1850s, a government-sponsored collection primarily of folksong texts led to an increase in the number of poetic anthologies before 1870.[66] However, the two most influential studies of the musical aspects of French *chansons* appeared in the late 1880s within the space of three years, during a crucial moment for the survival of the Third Republic. Both Weckerlin's *La Chanson populaire* (1886) and Tiersot's *Histoire de la chanson populaire en France* (1889)[67] can be interpreted as attempts to grasp and define an essentially French national heritage in the face of both external and internal threats, from Bismarck's Germany on the one hand, and General Boulanger's right-wing attack on the Republican government on the other. Both books offer almost perfect examples of the process of masculinising popular music in an act of nationalist appropriation, not only through their descriptive vocabulary but also by their authors' scholarly way of taking intellectual control over this repertoire.

Weckerlin and Tiersot presented French folksong as an answer both to external challenges against France's music – particularly Wagner – and to scepticism among the French themselves regarding the possibility of a specifically French national tradition of (vocal) music. Rousseau's classic verdict that the French language was – as Daniel Heartz has put it – 'expressive only of ideas, not sentiments; [that] it had no marked accent'[68] had been perpetuated throughout French music criticism of the nineteenth century, beginning with Julien-Louis Geoffroy, the influential opera critic of the *Journal des débats* from 1800 to 1814.[69] It surfaced periodically to discursive prominence as a 'topos obligée', for example in Stendhal's widely read *Vie de Rossini* (1824). Weckerlin's argument is based on his division between on the one hand, 'le peuple', close to their roots, and on the other the aristocracy with its universalist art music, a division that he dates back to the Middle Ages with its troubadours.[70] For Weckerlin, following a line of argument reminiscent of Hippolyte Taine, it is folksong that truly expresses 'the type, specific physiognomy and characteristic rhythms' of a people.[71] Because of her specific location and history, France proves to be 'the kingdom of song, for the French are born singers'.[72] Superior in her natural musical skills to any other nation, France's popular culture proves to be vibrant, vital and masculine in its strength, a direct expression of the 'génie français'. Weckerlin carried forward these arguments from Gaston Paris's preface to his *Chansons du XVe siècle*, published in 1875 (by the same publisher as Weckerlin's), and unequivocally undertaken as a patriotic act by one of France's leading philologists.[73] Both Paris and Weckerlin attributed Rousseau's essential musical quality of 'true sentiment' to France's folksongs (whereas they decry its loss in French art music, which is alienated from its source),[74] and at the same time they inscribed the aesthetic principles of classic *tragédie* such as *clarté* and *simplicité* as national characteristics presenting direct artistic articulation of the French people through the *chanson populaire*. Both Paris and Weckerlin are careful in expressing their claim for French superiority within the European context, even with respect to Germany. Thus Gaston Paris hid his claim in a footnote spreading over four pages, and limited his comments in the text to the following:

> Another interest attached to the old *chansons* is their importance for comparative literature. Whatever will be the final word in a just born science on the date, origin and relationships of the popular poetry of Roman and Germanic nations, it is already certain that the [poetry] from France will have to hold a significant place in the depicting of these relationships and in the study of these origins.[75]

Julien Tiersot's book, written at almost exactly the same time as Weckerlin's (when Tiersot began to work as Weckerlin's assistant at the Bibliothèque du Conservatoire), took all these points one step further. His foreword spelled out what the other two texts only implied, referring not only to Rousseau but to an even older concept which by then had acquired the status of an important topos in French culture, the notion of the 'translatio studii'. This concept, which originated in the idea of philosophic progression 'through time and space until it reaches France'[76] in the sixteenth century, was based on the belief that cultures followed a necessary trajectory from primitive beginnings to a period of splendour, followed by decline. In the Paris of François I, the 'home of the greatest cultural achievements was thought to have shifted from its origins in the East to Greece, Rome, modern Italy and finally France as each old civilisation became exhausted and corrupt'.[77] By the eighteenth century, this concept of cultural progression in the direction of France had become a widely used topos underpinned by new theories of environmental influence, especially through the climate. Writers such as d'Espiard in his *Essais sur le génie et le caractère des nations* (1743) based their defence of France's cultural superiority on an amalgam of the new 'scientific' ideas on climate with the older notion of the 'translatio studii'.[78] During the nineteenth century, these notions retained an important place in aesthetic discussions and were developed still further, fuelled by the Republican metaphor of France as the 'new Rome'.[79] Tiersot clearly referred to the concept of the 'translatio studii' in his attempt both to justify the superiority of a French national culture and to attribute cultural value to the *chanson populaire*. He says at the very outset of the book:

> Greece had exerted her sovereign influence over the entire civilisation of antiquity. Creator and then disseminator of all the arts, she had brought them to the highest perfection that the ancient world had known, and had spread amongst all civilised peoples the accomplished types of serene maturity and sober elegance that she had produced. In music, her influence was considerable . . . Through Rome, who had become the pupil and imitator of Greece, the influence of Greek art was exerted on the greater part of the Roman empire . . . This rich Greco-Latin culture flourished to the highest degree in Roman Gaul.[80]

Thus, within a few sentences, Tiersot introduced the foundation of French culture through Greece and Rome and set France at the head of this 'Greco-Latin' cultural field. France, he continued, was unique because it not only assimilated the two different genres of Greco-Roman music (theatre and religious music) and the truly Latin form of North Italian popular music ('une troisième forme lyrique, cette fois purement latine'),[81] but also because the French were able to amalgamate these influences with their 'celtic' heritage and its 'particular artistic instincts'.[82] The superiority of this sophisticated French form of cultural eclecticism becomes immediately obvious when compared with the neighbouring Germanic tribes whose music Tiersot characterised through the following tale, loosely based on Tacitus' *Annals*:[83]

> Tacitus mentions the savage war-songs through which the Germans excited each other in the battles. Around King Chlodevech, the Frank warriors sang epic songs which consecrated the memory of their national hero Siegfried during meals and in war council. At the occasion of the first battle in Gallia between the [invading] Franks of [Chlodevech] and the legionnaires of Aétius, the Franks were camping on a

> hillside and celebrated the marriage of one of their leaders to the sound of songs and dances sung in chorus; these noises revealed their presence to the Romans; they were taken by surprise: their taste for resounding music was the reason for their first defeat.[84]

Indeed, Tiersot used here the authority of an author well known to every French *bourgeois*, given that Tacitus was a staple in French secondary education.[85] In the context of the late 1880s in Paris, the political undertones of Tiersot's rendering of the tale are obvious: Wagnerian noise could well be the reason for Germany's cultural – at least – defeat when faced with a nation whose cultural values were based on the assimilation of the most noble and vibrant cultures in human history.

Victor Cousin's influential theory of eclecticism had not only become the 'official philosophy of Louis-Philippe's reign' during the July monarchy[86] but also persisted during the Third Republic as the Republican model for artistic progress in France.[87] In an interesting rhetorical strategy, Tiersot turned this to his advantage. Like Paris and Weckerlin, he saw a split between an art music becoming more and more decadent and subject to foreign influence and a folk music that remained virile and truly French and which possibly represented the seed of a renewed French cultural identity. The *chanson populaire* is the only cultural remnant of the ideal world of the Middle Ages, embodying the virtues of the France of Jeanne d'Arc, to whom both Paris and Tiersot refer.[88] The notion of a medieval 'golden age' was not new in the 1880s – Romantic fascination in the earlier nineteenth century with champions such as Viollet-le-Duc had paved the way – but by then the concept had become a powerful image as the counter-world to a materialistic, decadent and corrupt present. At this central point in his argument Tiersot uses the full register of masculinising rhetoric, insisting on the non-flowery, concise, logical, profound and vital qualities of the *chanson populaire*:

> We find again this same *chanson* [of the times of Jeanne d'Arc] still alive at the end of our nineteenth century ... Rhyme is unknown in it; at most, it is replaced by assonance, the last remnant of the versification traditions of the Middle Ages.[89] ... Its phrase is short and clear; the right word leaps from it with a splendour that even the most erudite verse would envy; and always an admirable concision, no superfluous development: the narration aims straight for its goal with logical and natural deductions, without lingering on anything useless; or else, the sentiment is expressed in simple but profound and penetrating words. And on this verse are admirable melodies, short and concise like them, but of intense appeal and inexhaustible vitality.[90]

In Tiersot's concept of the *chanson populaire* and its history, French folk music stands at the beginning of all Western art music, its genres as well as its harmonic language.[91] His quest for 'historical truth' enables him to re-read music history, presenting the musical language of the French people, and thus an inherently national music, as art music's true basis:

> One has to go back to the Middle Ages, and one will see these two arts [Gregorian chant and *chanson populaire*], the first and primitive forms of French music, play in concert with respect to the creation of opera, a role exactly similar to the one which we have seen them play in studying the creation of harmony.[92]

This statement is part of a substantial chapter on the *mélodie populaire* on stage, in which Tiersot traces the role of folksong in the creation and development of music theatre. It begins with a lengthy quotation from the third book of Wagner's *Oper und Drama* that immediately marks this chapter as a response to the impact of Wagner's theories and music. Thus Tiersot traces music theatre back to one major French work, Adam de la Halle's *Le Jeu de Robin et Marion*,[93] which he would later edit and write about.[94] Throughout the rest of the book, he judges music, especially French opera, with respect to its relationship with folksong. *Opéra comique*, for example, is hailed as a truly French genre because it grew out of the French people's musical language, and a successful *opéra comique* will always show this affinity with French popular music, as for example François-Adrien Boieldieu in *La Dame blanche*.[95] When in 1894 the thousandth performance of Ambroise Thomas's *opéra comique*, *Mignon*, was celebrated as a major event in French music, Tiersot praised its popular elements in an article entitled '*Mignon* et la chanson française'. Here Tiersot claims that Thomas's music corresponded so well to the language of the *chanson populaire* that two of his *romances* had become part of that tradition. Tiersot describes them being orally transmitted and sung on the streets and in villages by 'the people' without knowledge of their origin as works of a specific composer. This process of popular appropriation had proven their quality as true folk-songs.[96]

With this book, Tiersot offered a powerful philosophy of French music and its history that would find a nationalist and right-wing reception in the circles of the Schola Cantorum. Although Tiersot was later to align himself with the Schola and its ideals, the present book stands in the context both of patriotic and Republican attempts to define French music[97] and of French Wagnerism. Tiersot never denied his fascination with Wagner and saw the composer's strength in his ability to draw on his national popular culture. But Tiersot's book proposed a French model as an answer to this challenge, suggesting a genuinely French identity for musical language. He was able not only to assimilate the 'Wagnerian' references to the Middle Ages into his theory but also the 'Latin' qualities of *clarté* and *simplicité*, redefining these as characteristics embodied in French cultural expression *sui generis* instead of the 'aristocratic' and universalist context of the *Pléiade*, the poetic circle of the Renaissance that is usually perceived as the historical foundation of France's artistic glory.

Tiersot's study marks the beginning of what might be called the French 'folksong consensus'.[98] Like the reception of Wagner, the reference to popular music as an inspirational source for a truly French music became a shared topos of French aesthetic discussions.[99] It found its way in the writings of a wide variety of authors, ranging from Wagnerian and anthroposophist Edouard Schuré to the biographer of Massenet, Louis Schneider.[100] When in 1906 the Schola Cantorum began the publication of *Les Chansons de France*, a trimestrial journal dedicated to folksong research, the first issue contained supporting letters not only from Frédéric Mistral, Vincent d'Indy and Pierre Lalo but also from the director of the Conservatoire, Gabriel Fauré.[101]

Musical heritage and the 'new' French music

The vibrant, masculine and truly French *chanson populaire* was not the only foundation on which a renewed French music would be based. Fiamma Nicolodi has recently demonstrated the powerful nationalist potential of the myth of 'early music'.[102] Whereas before 1870 any reference to earlier music had often been part of either universalist scholarly projects, such as Farrenc's *Le Trésor des pianistes*, or movements for the renewal of religious music as in the case of Choron, the overwhelmingly nationalist appropriation of past French music began to flourish mainly in the aftermath of the Franco-Prussian war. This was directed in two ways: on the one hand, the publication, study and performance of French (and other 'Latin'; i.e. Italian) early music not only in order to create a 'canon' of French musical masterpieces but also to provide models of a truly French musical language; on the other, the (re-)evaluation and aesthetic defence of traditional genres such as *opéra comique* and new genres such as French orchestral song.

This interest in early music reflects similar concerns to those of the folksong revival. In fact, the main champions of the regeneration of popular music – for example, Tiersot, Weckerlin, Bourcault-Ducoudray, Bordes and d'Indy – were also key figures in the early-music movement. The division between popular and 'high' art with respect to *chansons françaises* was perceived as only liminal, and their use for patriotic and nationalist definitions of French art through both left and right was almost identical, as were the rhetorical strategies ascribing masculinity to this repertoire. An interesting example for this *modus operandi* is Henry Expert's preface to the first volume of his series *Les Maîtres musiciens de la Renaissance française* (1894),[103] where he explicitly refers to the virile qualities of French Renaissance music:

> However, from the first hours of the sixteenth century, in the vigour of a male and fruitful youth, music rejected the rigid formalism of the primitives [i.e. the music of the Ars Nova]; linked to an erudite technique,

> conscious of her expressive energies, [music] could attempt the interpretation of feelings; she possessed from now on this *secret and almost unbelievable virtue of moving the hearts in one way or another* (Calvin). And to begin with, the secular spirit, this powerful Gallic foundation nurtured by the Renaissance, appears fully in secular music . . . And while the poetic school of Marot and the Pléiade gave music its most beautiful jewels, fervent Humanism tried, under the pen of erudite musicians, to revive the likes of Horace and Virgil, Ovid, Catullus and Martial.[104]

Again, the virility of the French musical heritage is linked to the powerful symbolic imagery of France as the 'new Rome', with the concept of the 'translatio studii' serving as justification. In an interesting twist, Expert also ascribes this masculine musical quality to both Catholic and Protestant sacred music of the French Renaissance, given that the churches had no choice but to respond to this 'triumphant spirit' of the sixteenth century.[105] Furthermore, the expressive qualities of Renaissance music make it an ideal point of historical reference if Rousseau's verdict on French music's lack of expression and Wagnerian demands on the expressive role of music are kept in mind.[106] As with the *chanson populaire*, these early works provided models of a French music which satisfied the requirements of an inherently French musical language.[107] Eventually such collections would constitute a 'canon' of French musical heritage – whether of the 'race' or of a cultural association – and create a French tradition of referential masterpieces.[108] In his *La Musique et les musiciens français*, Albert Lavignac makes it clear to young composers that traditional French qualities were always part of past artistic achievements, whereas their negation would necessarily lead to awkward and thus ridiculous works:

> It is impossible to finish this chapter [on the national French style] without urging young French composers to concern themselves before anything else with conserving the characteristic qualities of our national art, which have always been its glory, which one finds in all great eras and which are *clarity, elegance* and *sincerity of expression*. It is the only way for them to be natural and to succeed in creating a proper style, a personality; because every time that they stray from these traditions inherent to the race, to the genius of [French] language as to the French spirit, they will only be awkward imitators and plagiarists; they will remind us of people who speak a foreign language badly with a ridiculous accent.[109]

Thus it is not necessary to look across the Rhine for musical guidance because France's own glorious past provides rich inspiration and shining examples. Lavignac's nationalist approach is deeply rooted in the proclamation of a racial heritage as expressed in the idea of the 'nation-génie', but similar forms of argument – now referring to a common cultural past in the wake of Renan's ideas – can be found in writings of declared Republicans such as Camille Saint-Saëns.

This attitude becomes particularly evident with respect to *opéra comique*, a genre much discussed in the early Third Republic. More than any other form of musical drama, *opéra comique* could be re-appropriated as a national operatic genre in the ambivalent context of French Wagner reception, whereas *grand opéra* was much more problematic because of its more cosmopolitan history and appeal. However, *opéra comique* had carried the stigma of being judged a feminine genre since the eighteenth century. Both plot and music were often judged as facile, naïve, charming, *à la mode* and cloying.[110] It was not only described in these feminised terms, but was also a genre which was thought to be suited to women composers such as Sophie Gail, Lucile Grétry, Caroline Wuiet, to name just a few from the eighteenth century. Bertrand's already cited demand that *opéra comique* needed to become more masculine was echoed in writings such as Camille Bellaigue's extensive discussion of *opéra comique* in his study *Un siècle de musique française*[111] and in reviews of opéra-comique performances. An interesting case is the first performance of Camille Saint-Saëns's *Phryné* in 1893, which was clearly conceived as a work reviving traditional characteristics of earlier *opéra comique*.[112] For Saint-Saëns, one of the ways to 'masculinise' *opéra comique* was to use alexandrine verse, the 'noble' metre of classical French tragedy, for both sung and spoken text. This corresponds to his earlier theories that the renewal of French opera was to be found in, amongst other things, a return to classical rhythm in both text and music.[113] Saint-Saëns not only attempted to include elements of the *tragédie* but also the modes of ancient Greek music. These modes had not been tainted by Wagnerian chromaticism and were thus 'pure' and promising for musical progress.[114] The première of *Phryné* was celebrated as a significantly French event after the first Parisian performance of Wagner's *Die Walküre* just two weeks earlier at the Opéra, and critics did not miss the opportunity to emphasise once more the traditional French (i.e. Latin) qualities of *clarté*, *esprit* and *justesse* in comparison to Wagner's ungainly Germanic noise.[115]

But it was not only in the revival of traditional French genres such as *opéra comique* that the French attempted to represent inherently French musical characteristics. Avant-garde forms such as French orchestral song were discussed in similar terms. In the case of this genre, the notion of intrinsic French musical qualities was reflected in the lively discussions about its merits; and although the answers were slightly different in their orientation, some issues such as the specific aesthetic value of French prosody were linked to the glorious tradition of French vocal music. But orchestral song – as opposed to orchestrated song – also had an innovative aspect: France appeared as the creator of a new, advanced genre of symphonic vocal music.[116] These 'poèmes pour chant et orchestre' began their life in the context of *Weltanschauungsmusik* and musical experiments in the 1870s and 1880s in Paris, when composers such as César Franck, Henri Duparc and Camille Saint-Saëns tried to revive French music outside the opera house. Orchestral songs were symphonic music in the strong sense of the term, with its aesthetic meaning being seen in the same manner as that of symphonies and symphonic poems. The boundaries were fluid, and structures such as sonata form (e.g. in Saint-Saëns's *La fiancée du timbalier*) or cyclic musical organisation of several movements (as in Ropartz's *Quatre poèmes d'aprés l''Intermezzo' d'Henri Heine* or Ernest Chausson's *Poème de l'amour et de la mer* – reflected these aesthetic claims in musical terms. French absolute music (in particular symphonies) demanded a model of explication which would take German achievements into account. Thus French symphonic music of the *fin de siècle* was represented in the writings of musicians as different as d'Indy and Saint-Saëns as flourishing, inventive and taking on the baton in the relay race of nineteenth-century Beethoven reception.[117] Yet works of a genre such as orchestral song could be easily defended as genuinely French, given the clearly established link to the past.

Cultural migrations II: Reading national music history

This reading is congruent with contemporary notions of music history. The writing of music history reaches back to the encyclopaedic eighteenth century with works such as De la Borde's *Essai sur la musique ancienne et moderne* (1780). As for the nineteenth century, during the decades before 1870 some major historical surveys reflected the growing interest in founding, justifying and integrating French and others' music and aesthetic judgement in a historical lineage.[118] In particular François-Joseph Fétis, influenced by Victor Cousin's synthetic concept of eclecticism and Auguste Comte's evolutionary model of linear progress, proved to be one of the most powerful writers of music history before 1870.[119] After the Franco-Prussian war, a panoply of music histories swept France, and 1879 saw the introduction of a new class in music history at the Conservatoire.[120] Books on music history had many purposes, serving for example as textbooks for classes at the Conservatoire and, later, in secondary schools. In the field of music journalism, historical accounts – usually of a specific topic such as the history of harpsichord music – became an essential branch of the trade, published mainly in the specialist musical press, from *Le Ménestrel* to *Musica*. However, the notion of linear artistic 'progress', which Fétis had already perceived as full of problems[121] – even if it still represented the aesthetic mainstay of the early Third Republic[122] – gave way to a wide variety of approaches to the construction of music history that echoed the different aesthetic and political currents outlined above.

All these French music histories were faced with the difficulty of assessing and evaluating French music, both in a historical and a contemporary context, particularly with repect to the overwhelming aesthetic and musical presence of German music. Thus these historical constructions had to create readings that would represent France in a central position within European music and its history. The now familiar model of the 'translatio studii', strengthened by its 'scientific' support through recent Darwinian and Taineian philosophies, proved particularly useful in this endeavour, for it allowed French writers to achieve two goals: on the one hand, they could ascribe to France a key role as 'enabler' of the development of German music in the late eighteenth and the nineteenth centuries, thus continuing the path of cultural migration from France to Germany; on the other, the model provided a helpful tool to redirect this migration to contemporary France by representing German culture as reaching a period of decadence after the death of Beethoven or Wagner – paradigmatically formulated in Debussy's famous *bon mot* on Wagner as a glorious sunset erroneously mistaken for a sunrise.[123]

Thus, for example, Albert Soubies, a declared adherent of the philosophical concept of eclecticism, places the influence of Rousseau at the beginning of Germany's national artistic awakening. Indeed, 'the influence of Rousseau on the other side of the Rhine was considerable',[124] and it was Rousseau's ideas that allowed the Germans to find their own national voice, completely developed for the first time in the towering *œuvre* of Beethoven that epitomised the virile traits of this new, powerful German music whose influence would be predominant in nineteenth-century Europe, particularly with respect to symphonic music.[125] Soubies's masculinisation of Beethoven's music was typical for the period, not only in the composer's French reception but also in Germany and England.[126] For the eclectic Soubies, German achievements held a positive place, even with respect to contemporary French music:

> As for France, finally, whose characteristics in art have always been a clear-sighted and delicate eclecticism, intelligent and fine combination, [and] the skilful adaptation of very diverse elements, one knows with what brilliance, with what abundance of resources we have, in what M. Lavoix has called 'the century of Beethoven', received and put in its true light the German tradition.[127]

Soubies's reference to German achievements implied a demand for their acculturation, their transfer back to France. His rhetoric stands in the context of a post-war relationship between France and Germany which was determined by cultural competition. Through cultural imports, new ideas could be infused into French music, offering a catalyst to its further development.[128]

Other writers such as Vincent d'Indy who opposed such an eclectic theory gallicised the lineage from Beethoven. Instead of assimilating Germanic concepts in an eclectic manner, d'Indy's hero, César Franck, developed – in ways similar to those outlined by Tiersot for the Latinising of folksong – what he encountered in Beethoven's music into an essentially French composition technique:

> With Franck, the inspired French continuer of the immortal German symphonist, begins a new and so far *exclusively French* period. The value and power of the best works belonging to this period rely on all the innovations of Beethoven and on the *cyclic* construction finally understood and realised. Under this benign influence, the traditional sonata form has already recovered, at least in our country, a vitality and youth that are truly surprising after half a century of decadence and oblivion ... It falls to France to continue and to realise the transformation of sonata form, clearly indicated by Beethoven: not one of his German successors, in fact, knew how to or seriously wanted to attempt this truly *cyclic* renovation, the sole means of giving life to this beautiful form which was atrophying and seemed close to disappearing, at least in Germany, despite the timid endeavours of Schumann and Brahms. Thus the *cyclic* tradition can be considered as transmitted *directly* from Beethoven to César Franck.[129]

D'Indy clearly uses this masculinising rhetoric with respect both to the old and now surpassed German style (i.e. Beethoven) and to the new French sonata form in order to emphasise the vitality and youth of a triumphant new French school. Like Debussy with Wagner, d'Indy identifies the moment of decline with the death of a key Germanic figure, spelling out what Debussy implied: that the new way forward in music was to be found in France.

The concept of the decadence of German music, either after Beethoven (with respect to absolute music) or after Wagner (with respect to opera) and culture's new dynamic haven in the France of the Third Republic, pervades all levels of music history right through to educational literature such as Laure Collin's highly popular *Histoire abrégée de la musique et des musiciens* or Elise Vigoureux's *Manuel d'histoire générale de la musique à l'usage des classes de solfège*.[130] These authors implicitly (and sometimes explicitly, like d'Indy) used the gender metaphor to feminise current developments in Germany and to masculinise the French future. Authors might choose the eclectic model, like Soubies, or a more nationalist model emphasising the 'national soul' expressed through music, like Lavoix in his *La Musique française*;[131] however, they all rose to the challenge to find and apply an explicatory model for the ambivalent cultural migration between France and Germany. As Werner and Espagne have shown, the issue of cultural relationship in this case has been determined by competition particularly after 1870–71, given that the French defeat has been ascribed not only to military reasons but also as a 'result of a cultural inferiority'.[132] The arts of other countries such as Italy – a major reference point in Stendhal's time – became less important in discourse after 1870. Whereas music journalism had to react to new 'others' such as music from Russia, adapting models and metaphors to new situations,[133] music histories from 1870 to 1914 were fixated on a bilateral relationship between France and Germany.

Discourses on a national music in France after 1870 reveal similar masculinising tendencies, as can be observed in Imperial Britain, the Germany of the Weimar Republic – with its discussion of 'Neue Sachlichkeit' and 'Moderne' – or the United States immediately after the Second Word War.[134] It appears as if these cultures needed to redefine and consolidate their aesthetic values in times of political instability (either in defeat or expansion) by emphasising accepted cultural values that met a need for reassurance in threatening times. Given that the shared notion of 'masculinity' represented the highest and healthiest concept in the cultural and social hierarchy of Republican France, its constant presence in the cultural discourses of the *fin de siècle* is anything but unexpected. It played an important role in redefining and appropriating French music past and present for the endeavour of patriotic and nationalist self-definition of both the French right and left in all their different shades. In the same way that right and left colluded during the period between 1870 and 1914 to keep women in the home – to produce either healthy young republicans or good French subjects – they perpetuated masculine ideals in their aesthetic and historical discourses on music. To develop a healthy, vibrant and truly French art had become a major concern in a culture that could see the threat of decadence and effeminacy not only in the world of their enemies but also at home.[135]

Notes and References

1 I wish to thank the British Academy for a research grant enabling me to spend the necessary time in Paris in order to conduct my research for this chapter. I am grateful to Linda Phyllis Austern, Tim Carter, Katharine Ellis, Andrea Musk and Steve Stanton for their most helpful comments on earlier versions of this chapter. Such versions were also presented as papers at the University of Southampton, City University, London, and King's College, London; I am indebted for the insightful and challenging comments and questions by staff and students.
2 Stéphane Wolff, *Un demi-siècle d'opéra-comique* (Paris, 1953).
3 Gustave Bertrand, 'Opéra-Comique/Hérold/1000e représentation du *Pré aux Clercs* – Rentrée de Mme Carvalho', *Le Ménestrel*, 37, 1870–71, pp. 361–2: 'Disons enfin, et c'est là-dessus que nous aimons le plus à insister que la millième représentation du *Pré aux Clercs* est une fête pour l'école française. Nous avons besoin, en ce moment plus que jamais, que l'art français nous affirme hautement toutes ses gloires légitimes, pour nous consoler d'abord et nous réconforter, et puis pour s'encourager lui-même à en chercher d'autres. . . . Or, ce qui fait avant tout, à nos yeux, l'importance de cette millième représentation d'un chef-d'œuvre si absolument français, c'est qu'elle remet toutes choses en leur rang, et qu'elle m'apparaît comme une borne milliaire destinée à marquer dans l'histoire du goût public, en fait d'opéra-comique'.

4 Gustave Bertrand, 'Opéra-Comique/Hérold/1000e représentation du *Pré aux Clercs*', p. 362: 'quelque chose de plus mâle et de plus nerveux dans le comique (car enfin qui dit comédie, ne dit pas exclusivement jolis sourires féminins, gaieté superficielle [ou] encore moins joyeusetés triviales)'.

5 On the conditions of subsidy for the concert societies, see Annegret Fauser, *Der Orchestergesang in Frankreich zwischen 1870 und 1920*, Freiburger Beiträge zur Musikwissenschaft, Vol. 2 (Laaber, 1994), pp. 141–54. For documents relating to state subsidies for the concert societies, see Archives Nationales, Paris, F^{21}4626. For the Opéra, see Frédérique Patureau, *Le Palais Garnier dans la société parisienne, 1875–1914* (Liège, 1991), with a list of archival sources on pp. 471–6.

6 Ernest Renan, 'La Guerre entre la France et l'Allemagne' (1870), *'Qu'est-ce qu'une nation?' et autres essais politiques*, ed. by Joël Roman (Paris, 1992), p. 104: 'La Prusse fonde sa force sur le développement de l'instruction primaire et sur l'identité de l'armée et de la nation'.

7 On the question of nationalism and nation-state in more general terms, see Heinrich August Winkler (ed.), *Nationalismus*, 2nd edn. (Königstein/Taunus, 1985); Eric J. Hobsbawm, *Nations and Nationalism since 1870: Programme, Myth, Reality* (Cambridge, 1990); Gil Delannoi and Pierre-André Taguieff (eds.), *Théories du nationalisme: Nation, nationalité, ethnicité* (Paris, 1991).

8 Joëlle Caullier, *La Belle et la Bête: L'Allemagne des Kapellmeister dans l'imaginaire Français (1890–1914)* (Tusson/Charente, 1993), p. 60.

9 Ernest Renan, 'Lettre à M. Strauss' (1870), *'Qu'est-ce qu'une nation?'*, p. 120: 'Il est clair que, dès que l'on a rejeté le principe de la légitimié dynastique, il n'a y plus, pour donner une base aux délimitations territoriales des Etats, que le droit des nationalités, c'est-à-dire des groupes naturels déterminés par la race, l'histoire et la volonté des populations'.

10 Ernest Renan, 'Qu'est-ce qu'une nation?' (1882), *'Qu'est-ce qu'une nation?'*, p. 54: 'Un passé héroïque, des grands hommes, de la gloire (j'entends de la véritable), voilà le capital social sur lequel on assied une idée nationale'.

11 See Alain Renaut, 'Logiques de la nation', in Gil Delannoi and Pierre-André Taguieff (eds.), *Théories du nationalisme*, pp. 33–8; Alain Finkielkraut, *La défaite de la pensée* (Paris, 1987), pp. 22–69. Finkielkraut quotes de Maistre's famous observation: 'Il n'y a point d'homme dans le monde. J'ai vu dans ma vie des Français, des Italiens, des Russes. Je sais même grâce a Montesquieu qu'on peut être persan; mais quant à l'homme, je déclare ne l'avoir rencontré dans ma vie; s'il existe, c'est bien à mon insu' (p. 28).

12 Alain Finkielkraut, *La défaite de la pensée*, p. 44.

13 Pierre Birnbaum, 'Nationalisme à la française', in Gil Delannoi and Pierre-André Taguieff (eds.), *Théories du nationalisme*, pp. 125–38; Danny Trom, 'Frankreich: Die gespaltene Erinnerung', in Monika Flacke, *Mythen der Nationen: Ein europäisches Panorama*, exhibition catalogue (Berlin, 1998), pp. 129–51.

14 See Wolfgang Leiner, *Das Deutschlandbild in der französischen Literatur*, 2nd edn. (Darmstadt, 1991), pp. 79–95 and 154–80.

15 Fustel de Coulanges, 'L'Alsace est-elle allemande ou française?' (1870), in Ernest Renan, *'Qu'est-ce qu'une nation?'*, p. 260: 'Ce qui distingue les nations, ce n'est ni la race, ni la langue. Les hommes sentent dans leur cœur qu'ils sont un même peuple lorsqu'ils ont une communauté d'idées, d'intérêts, d'affections, de souvenirs et d'espérances. Voilà ce qui fait la patrie'.

16 Maurice Agulhon, *La République de Jules Ferry à François Mitterand, 1880 à nos jours* (Paris, 1990), p. 24.

17 Given in Pierre Birnbaum, 'Nationalisme à la française', p. 134: 'l'expression de notre sang'.

18　Geneviève Bernard-Krauß ('Nationalismus und Internationalismus in Frankreich von 1870 bis zum zweiten Weltkrieg', Proceedings of the Quinquennial Conference of the International Musicological Society, Madrid 1992, *Revista de Musicologia*, 16 (1993), at pp. 658–60) attempts to distinguish between three phases of nationalist musical awakening in France between 1870 and 1914. However, her linear and chronological model reflects neither political differentiations nor the complex intertwinings and parallel developments of the various positions in French musical life after 1870.

19　Edward Berenson, *The Trial of Madame Caillaux* (Berkeley, 1992), pp. 114 and 116–17.

20　See Werner Stegmaier, 'Weltabkürzungskunst: Orientierung durch Zeichen', in Josef Simon (ed.), *Zeichen und Interpretation* (Frankfurt am Main, 1994), pp. 119–41.

21　Josef Simon, *Philosophie des Zeichens* (Berlin and New York, 1989), p. 263.

22　Paul Ricoeur, 'Die Metapher und das Hauptproblem der Hermeneutik', in Anselm Haverkamp (ed.), *Theorie der Metapher*, 2nd edn. (Darmstadt, 1996), pp. 356–75.

23　On the use and meaning of these terms in nineteenth-century France, see Marcia J. Citron, *Gender and the Musical Canon* (Cambridge, 1993), pp. 120–44; Katharine Ellis, 'Female Pianists and Their Male Critics in Nineteenth-Century Paris', *Journal of the American Musicological Society*, 50 (1997), pp. 353–85; Annegret Fauser, 'Lili Boulanger's *La princesse Maleine*: A Composer and her Heroine as Literary Icons', *Journal of the Royal Musical Association*, 122 (1997), pp. 100–6; Annegret Fauser, '*La Guerre en dentelles*: Women and the *Prix de Rome* in French Cultural Politics', *Journal of the American Musicological Society*, 51 (1998), pp. 83–129; Jeffrey Kallberg, 'The Harmony of the Tea Table: Gender and Ideology in the Piano Nocturne', *Representations*, 39 (1992), pp. 102–33; Jann Pasler, 'The Ironies of Gender, or Virility in the Music of Augusta Holmès', *Women and Music: A Journal of Gender and Culture*, 2 (1998), pp. 1–25; Deborah L. Silverman, *Art Nouveau in Fin-de-Siècle France: Politics, Psychology and Style* (Berkeley, 1989), pp. 63–106; Tamar Garb, *Sisters of the Brush: Women's Artistic Culture in Late Nineteenth-Century France* (New Haven and London, 1994), pp. 105–52; Tamar Garb, *Bodies of Modernity: Figure and Flesh in Fin-de-Siècle France* (London, 1998), pp. 25–53.

24　The French reception of Brahms reveals some specific traits. He was not at first perceived as a symphonist in the tradition of Beethoven (the German reception model) but the composer of small-scale pieces in the wake of Schumann. See Edouard Lalo, *Correspondance*, ed. Joël-Marie Fauquet (Paris, 1989), pp. 14 and 123–4.

25　Joséphin Péladin, *Istar* (1888), quoted in Michel Cadot, 'Un ardent wagnérien: Joséphin Péladin (1858–1918)'; Annegret Fauser and Manuela Schwartz (eds.), *Von Wagner zum Wagnérisme: Musik, Literatur, Kunst, Politik* (Leipzig, 1999), p. 478.

26　Karl Bartsch, *Alte französische Volkslieder* (Heidelberg, 1882), p. iii: 'diese liebliche Blüten des französischen Volksgeistes'.

27　The connotations of such gendered value judgements are discussed in the works cited in note 22. A blatant example of the use of the gender metaphor in Vincent d'Indy's aesthetics is given in Marcia J. Citron, *Gender and the Musical Canon*, p. 136.

28　Gustave Nadaud's 'La Française' shared with Rouget de Lisle's 'Marseillaise' and Alfred de Musset's '*Le Rhin allemand*' the favour of the Parisian public in 1870–71.

29　'Nouvelles diverses', *Le Ménestrel*, 37, 1870/71, p. 374: 'Mme Pauline Viardot est de retour à Paris, avec l'intention formelle d'y résider désormais. Voilà une bonne fortune pour l'art du chant français. Mme Viardot, abandonnant sa villa de Bade pour reprendre possession de son ancienne habitation de la rue Douai, n'est-ce pas là une vraie conquête faite par la France sur l'Allemagne musicale?'

30　H. Moreno (i.e. Henri Heugel), 'Semaine théâtrale', *Le Ménestrel*, 38, 1872, p. 91.

31 Susan Dunn, 'Michelet and Lamartine: Making and Unmaking the Nationalist Myth of Jeanne d'Arc', *Romantic Review*, 80 (1989), pp. 404 and 407.
32 Jules Michelet, *Histoire du Moyen-Age*, Vol. 5 (Paris, n.d.), pp. 15–16, quoted in Susan Dunn, 'Michelet and Lamartine', p. 408.
33 For a short survey on the different appropriations of Jeanne d'Arc, see Danny Trom, 'Frankreich: Die gespaltene Erinnerung', pp. 136–40. He shows there how the 'militaristic' Jeanne was used in Republican iconography, whereas the young devout country girl figures mainly in the Catholic and nationalist representations of the myth.
34 Marc Gérard, 'Un peu de patriotisme', *Le Gaulois*, 11 November 1873, p. 1: 'Sous la forme transfigurée de Jeanne d'Arc, c'était la patrie même qui apparaissait à tous; des fauteuils d'orchestre et des loges, un ardent enthousiasme éclatait; c'était la France, plus aimée encore dans ses désastres, qu'on acclamait; et dans cette explosion de tout ce que ces cœurs parisiens, fanfarons de scepticisme, avaient contenu jusqu'alors, s'est réveillé tout à coup le sentiment national de nos gloires et de nos revers'.
35 Benedict, 'Chronique musicale', *Le Figaro*, 11 November 1873, p. 3: 'C'est le *Super flumina Babylonis* de la France envahie et refoulée'. Benedict refers here to Psalm 137, an interesting reference insofar as the psalm not only laments Jewish captivity but also incites revenge.
36 See Maurice Agulhon, *Marianne au pouvoir: L'imagerie et la symbolique républicaines de 1880 à 1914* (Paris, 1989), p. 326.
37 Composers who took up the subject between 1870 and 1894 include Alfred Bruneau, Théodore Dubois, Benjamin Godard, Charles Lenepveu and Charles Marie Widor. Emile Huet offers a bibliographical survey of more than 90 pages in his *Jeanne d'Arc et la musique: Essai de bibliographie musicale* (Orléans, 1894).
38 On Wagnerism, see Sieghart Döhring and Sabine Henze-Döhring, *Oper und Musikdrama im 19. Jahrhundert*, Handbuch der musikalischen Gattingen, 13 (Laaber, 1997), pp. 282–96; Annegret Fauser and Manuela Schwartz (eds.), *Von Wagner zum Wagnérisme*; Manuela Schwartz, *Wagner-Rezeption und französische Oper des Fin de Siècle: Untersuchungen zu Vincent d'Indy's 'Fervaal'*, Berliner Musik Studien, 18, (Sinzig, 1999).
39 The relationship between opera and political context was not only crucial with respect to France but also other countries such as *fin de siècle* Italy. See for example Jürgen Maehder, 'Die italienische Oper de Fin de siècle als Spiegel politischer Strömungen im umbertinischen Italien', in Udo Bermbach and Wulf Konold (eds.), *Der schöne Abglanz: Stationen der Operngeschichte. Oper als Spiegel gesellschaftlicher Veränderung* (Berlin and Hamburg, 1992), pp. 181–210.
40 Alexander Schmidt, 'Deutschland als Modell? Bürgerlichkeit und gesellschaftliche Modernisierung im deutschen Kaiserreich (1871–1914) aus der Sicht der französischen Zeitgenossen', *Jahrbuch für Wirtschaftsgeschichte* (Berlin, 1992), p. 234.
41 For an attempt to understand the music of his time in terms of Aristotle, see Camille Bellaigue, 'Les idées musicales d'Aristote', *Etudes musicales*, troisième série (Paris, 1907), pp. 1–28.
42 The German system of education with its inclusion of music was also cited by English reformers of the late nineteenth century. See Vic Gammon, 'Folk Song Collecting in Sussex and Surrey 1843–1914', *History Workshop: A Journal of Social Historians*, 10 (1980), p. 78.
43 Already in 1869, Louis-Albert Bourcault-Ducoudray (1840–1910) had founded a choral society with the explicit aim 'to encourage people to sing choral music', and over the years music education developed into a 'patriotic obsession' for him; see Jann Pasler, 'Paris: Conflicting Notions of Progress', in Jim Samson (ed.), *Man and Music: The Late Romantic Era from the Mid-19th Century to World War I* (London, 1991), p. 394.

44 Louis-Albert Bourcault-Ducoudray, 'L'Enseignement du chant dans les lycées', *La Revue musicale*, 3 (1903), p. 725: 'Luther a donc créé, avec un succès inouï, des occasions pour ses coreligionnaires d'exprimer le sentiment collectif religieux; en même temps qu'il rendait l'utilité de la musique évidente en l'appliquant à un but élevé et civilisateur, il renseignait l'Allemagne, une fois pour toutes, sur la fonction et la vertu du "grand art", et lui en inculquait à jamais l'amour et le respect'.
45 Ibid., p. 727: 'faire "l'unité" dans le cœur d'une nation'.
46 Ibid., p. 728.
47 Louis-Albert Bourcault-Ducoudray, *Esprit de la France!* (Paris, 1901). Another example for such a piece is Camille Saint-Saëns' 'Hymne à la France', specifically written for secondary schools.
48 Mark de Thémines, 'La Musique dans les lycées', *L'Art musical*, 11 (1872), pp. 177–8.
49 Jules Combarieu, 'L'Etude du chant à l'école primaire', *La Revue musicale*, 10 (1910), pp. 314–17 and 339–43, at p. 315: 'elle est une école de solidarité'; 'elle est une école d'attention et de discipline . . . [car l'attention] doit être entière, absolue, comme celle des soldats devant leur colonel sur un champ de manœuvre' (p. 315).
50 Ibid., p. 316: 'La phrase verbale estompe; la mélodie engrave. Par exemple, faites à des enfants une leçon sur le patriotisme, sur le courage militaire, sur la nécessité d'avoir foi dans la victoire quand il faut payer de sa personne: il vous sera facile de les toucher et de les intéresser. Mais faites-les chanter ensuite le *Chant du départ*: "La victoire en chantant nous ouvre la barrière . . ." De ces deux leçons, quelle est celle qui produira les effets les plus profondes et les plus durables? Ce sera certainement la seconde'.
51 Ibid., p. 316: 'la musique [chorale] faisant l'éducation de l'oreille et celle de la voix, si importante dans une démocratie; la musique apprenant à parler nettement – et à écouter!' Katherine Bergeron refers to a similar concept with respect to French art song in her current research on the *mélodie française*.
52 Bourcault-Ducoudray unequivocally refers to both in his report 'L'Enseignement du chant dans les lycées', p. 725: 'Il lui faut, pour vivre, des sentiments réels, vivants, palpitants, qui aient besoin de se formuler et de s'épancher en un flot musical. En France, ces occasions n'ont jamais existé, ou du moins, si elles ont existé, c'est à une seule époque, pendant la première Révolution. En 1792, l'Etat voulut employer les arts et surtout la musique à exalter des sentiments "réels", comme le fit l'antiquité grecque.'
53 This form of masculinising rhetoric could include militaristic vocabulary, in particular with respect to German choral practice. See, for example, the short notice on a choral meeting in Vienna in 1888, published under 'Nouvelles Diverses: Etranger' in *Le Mnestrel*, 54 (1888), p. 70: 'L'Alliance chorale allemande, connue sous le nom de *Sngerbund*, et qui ne compte pas moins de 63,512 chanteurs – une arme – donnera son prochain grand festival, qui sera le quatrième, Vienne, en 1889.'
54 Edward Berenson, *The Trial of Madame Caillaux*, p. 106.
55 Ibid., p. 103.
56 A short survey of the statistics appears in Jann Pasler, 'Paris: Conflicting Notions of Progress', p. 395. A more detailed analysis is quoted in Karen Offen, 'Depopulation, Nationalism, and Feminism in Fin-de-Siècle France', *American Historical Review*, 89 (1984), pp. 648–76, and Hartmut Kaelble, *Nachbarn am Rhein: Entfremdung und Annäherung der französischen und deutschen Gesellschaft seit 1880* (Munich, 1991) (esp. chapter 2).
57 Dr H. Thulié, 'Variétés. La Femme. Fonctions sociales', *L'Harmonie sociale*, 8 April 1893, quoted in Anne Cova, *Maternité et droits des femmes en France (XIXe–XXe siècles)* (Paris, 1997), p. 36: 'La mère fait la race. C'est elle qui donne la vigueur, l'intelligence et la base de l'instruction; plus elle sera forte et intelligente, plus son caractère sera noble, plus la race sera puissante'.

58 Jules Combarieu, 'L'Etude du chant à l'école primaire', p. 316: 'La musique enfin considérée comme une gymnastique locale; il est reconnu que les personnes ayant l'habitude de chanter sont beaucoup moins sujettes que les autres aux maux de gorge et aux accidents des voies respiratoires'. Katharine Ellis has discovered similar justifications in the context of an earlier experiment by Adolphe Sax promoting wind-playing for women; see Katharine Ellis, 'The Fair Sax: Women, Brass-Playing and the Instrument Trade in 1860s Paris', *Journal of the Royal Musical Association*, 124 (1999), pp. 221–54.

59 Camille Saint-Saëns, 'L'Enseignement du chant dans les lycées', *La Revue musicale* 4 (1904), p. 11.

60 On the musical education of working-class women, see Mary Ellen Poole, 'Gustave Charpentier and the Conservatoire Populaire de Mimi Pinson', *19th-Century Music*, 20 (1997), p. 234.

61 I borrow the term 'mediation' (as a form of transmitting cultural artefacts and concepts mediated through the collector's or writer's political, social and aesthetic ideas) from Dave Harker, *Fakesong: The Manufacture of British 'Folksong' 1711 to the Present Day* (Milton Keynes and Philadelphia, 1985). I am grateful to Steve Stanton for drawing my attention to this book.

62 Reinhart Meyer-Kalkus, *Die akademische Mobilität zwischen Deutschland und Frankreich (1925–1992)*, DAAD-Forum: Studien, Berichte, Materialien, 16 (Bonn, 1994), p. 22. See also Michael Werner, 'Le Prisme franco-allemand: à propos d'une histoire croisée des disciplines littéraires', in Hans Manfred Bock, Reinhart Meyer-Kalkus and Michel Trebitsch (eds.), *Entre Locarno et Vichy: Les relations culturelles franco-allemandes dans les années 1930*, 2 vols. (Paris, 1993), pp. 305–6. See also Michael Werner and Michel Espagne (eds.), *Transferts. Les Relations interculturelles dans l'espace franco-allemand (XVIIIe et XIXe siècle)* (Paris, 1988).

63 For example, James Macpherson's *Fragments of Ancient Poetry* (1760–63), which contained the Ossian poems, and the novels and poetry of Walter Scott. For a Marxist interpretation of the folksong movement in Britain since 1700, see Dave Harker, *Fakesong*.

64 Gérard de Nerval, *Les filles du feu*, ed. Béatrice Didier (Paris, 1972), pp. 166–78; on Nerval's interest in popular culture, see Paul Bénichou, *Nerval et la chanson folklorique* (Paris, 1970), esp. pp. 177–84.

65 Gérard de Nerval, *Les filles du feu*, pp. 168–9: 'Est-ce dont [sic] la vraie poésie, est-ce la soif mélancolique de l'idéal qui manque à ce peuple pour comprendre et produire des chants dignes d'être comparés à ceux de l'Allemagne et de l'Angleterre? Non, certes; mais il est arrivé qu'en France la littérature n'est jamais descendue au niveau de la grande foule; les poètes académiques du dix-septième et du dix-huitième siècle n'auraient pas plus compris de telles inspirations, que les paysans n'eussent admiré leurs odes, leurs épîtres et leurs poésies fugitives, si incolores, si gourmées'.

66 On these earlier collections and their political meaning, see Jane F. Fulcher, 'The Popular Chanson of the Second Empire: "Music of the Peasants" in France', *Acta musicologica*, 52 (1981), pp. 27–37.

67 Jean-Baptiste Weckerlin, *La Chanson populaire* (Paris, 1886); Julien Tiersot, *Histoire de la chanson populaire en France* (Paris, 1889). During the time in which both books were written, Weckerlin and Tiersot were employed as librarians in the Bibliothèque du Conservatoire: in fact, Tiersot was Weckerlin's assistant from 1883 to 1909, when he succeeded him as head librarian.

68 Daniel Heartz, 'Jean-Jacques Rousseau', in Stanley Sadie (ed.), *The New Grove Dictionary of Music and Musicians*, 20 vols. (London, 1980), 16, p. 272. The most influential passage stems from Rousseau's *Lettre sur la musique française* (1753), in

which he describes a hypothetical language, easily recognisable as French, and its effects on music: 'une [langue] qui ne serait composée que de sons mixtes, des syllabes muettes, sourdes ou nasales, peu de voyelles sonores, beaucoup de consonnes et d'articulations, et qui manquerait encore d'autres conditions essentielles dont je parlerai dans l'article de la mesure. Cherchons, par curiosité, ce qui résulterait de la musique appliquée à une telle langue. Premièrement, le défaut d'éclat dans les sons des voyelles obligerait d'en donner beaucoup à celui des notes; et, parce que la langue serait sourde, la musique serait criarde. En second lieu, la dureté et la fréquence des consonnes forceraient à exclure beaucoup de mots, à ne procéder sur les autres que par des intonations élémentaires; et la musique serait insipide et monotone: sa marche serait encore lente et ennuyeuse par la même raison; et quand on voudrait presser un peu le mouvement, sa vitesse ressemblerait à celle d'un corps dur et anguleux qui roule sur le pavé'. Quoted in Catherine Kintzler, *Poétique de l'opéra français de Corneille à Rousseau* (Paris, 1991), pp. 459–60. Catherine Kintzler gives an excellent overview of Rousseau's aesthetic concepts and their immediate influence on pp. 333–514. On Rousseau's ideas on music in general, see also Peter Gülke, *Rousseau und die Musik* (Wilhelmshaven, 1984). With respect to his reception in France in the eighteenth and early nineteenth centuries, see Jane F. Fulcher, 'Melody and Morality: Rousseau's Influence on French Music Criticism', *International Review of the Aesthetics and Sociology of Music*, 2 (1980), pp. 45–56.

69 See Katharine Ellis, 'A Dilettante at the Opera: Issues in the Criticism of Julien-Louis Geoffroy, 1800–1814', in Roger Parker and Mary Ann Smart (eds.), *Opera and Ballet: Criticism from the Revolution to 1848* (Oxford, 2000).

70 Jean-Baptiste Weckerlin, *La Chanson populaire*, pp. iii–iv: 'Les troubadours se trouvant sous notre plume, nous en profitons pour dire que leur répertoire aristocratique n'ayant rien de commun avec la chanson du peuple, nous n'avons pas à en parler. On n'a qu'à examiner les œuvres de Thibaut de Champagne ou de Charles d'Orléans . . ., et l'on verra bien qu'aucune de leurs chansons n'a passé dans le répertoire populaire, que ces deux littératures étaient scindées, aussi différentes l'une de l'autre que l'étaient les grandes classes de la population française, l'aristocratie et le peuple'.

71 Ibid., p. 3: 'Les chansons populaires d'un pays expriment mieux son type, sa physionomie spéciale, ses rythmes particuliers, caractéristiques, que la musique des compositeurs de ce même pays, parce que l'art étant universel, ne peut avoir comme type tel ou tel pays, tandis que la chanson du peuple reste circonscrite dans un rayon, déterminé généralement par la même langue ou le même dialecte'.

72 Ibid., p. 3: 'La France est le royaume de la chanson, car le Français naît chansonnier'.

73 Gaston Paris, *Chansons du XVe siècle, publiées d'après le manuscrit de la Bibliothèque nationale de Paris par Gaston Paris et accompagnées de la musique transcrite en notation moderne par Auguste Gevaert* (Paris, 1875).

74 Ibid., p. ix: 'Par une réaction remarquable, elle [la poésie populaire] s'est dégagée à l'époque où la littérature proprement dite est le plus éloigné de la nature, de la simplicité et du sentiment vrai'.

75 Ibid., p. vi: 'Un autre intérêt s'attache aux vieilles chansons, c'est leur importance pour la littérature comparée. Quel que soit un jour le dernier mot d'une science qui naît à peine sur la date, l'origine et les rapports de la poésie populaire des nations romanes et germaniques, il est sûr dès aujourd'hui que celle de la France doit occuper dans le tableau de ces rapports et dans l'étude de ces origines une place prépondérante'.

76 Margaret W. Ferguson, 'The Exile's Defense: Du Bellay's *La deffence et illustration de la langue françoyse*', *Publications of the Modern Language Association of America*, 93

(1978), pp. 280–1, quoted in Jeanice Brooks, 'Italy, the Ancient World and the French Musical Inheritance in the Sixteenth Century: Arcadelt and Clereau in the Service of the Guises', *Journal of the Royal Musical Association*, 121 (1996), p. 148. The notion of the 'translatio studii' – which refers to cultural transfer – needs to be understood in the context of the political concept of 'translatio imperii': 'Dieser Theorie liegen antike Konzepte einer Nationalcharakterlehre zugrunde, die im Mittelalter unter eschatologischen Vorzeichen zu Transfertheorien der Weltherrschaft ausgebaut wurden (translatio-imperii-Theorien), die in der Neuzeit aus ihrem heilsgeschichtlichen Kontext herausgelöst wurden und nunmehr in Gestalt transnationaler Geschichtsphilosophien entfaltet werden . . . Es gibt Leitnationen der Menschheitsgeschichte, deren Bewegungsverlauf zeitweilig identisch ist mit der weltgeschichtlichen Entwicklungsstruktur. Dies bedeutet, daß sich die Menschheitsgeschichte realisiert über die Teilgeschichte von Kulturräumen, von Nationen und Epochenumschwüngen'. Thus, for example, the French Revolution could be understood as the revolution of humanity. See Jörn Garber, 'Peripherie oder Zentrum? Die "europäische Triarchie" (Deutschland, Frankreich, England) als transnationales Deutungsmodell der Nationalgeschichte', in Michel Espagne and Michael Werner, *Transferts*, pp. 98–9.

77 Jeanice Brooks, 'Italy, the Ancient World and the French Musical Inheritance', p. 148.
78 See Werner Oechslin, 'Le goût et les nations: débats, polémiques et jalousies au moment de la création des musées au XVIIIe siècle', Edouard Pommier (ed.), *Les Musées en Europe à la veille de l'ouverture du Louvre* (Paris, 1995), pp. 367–414, esp. pp. 381–385. I wish to thank Matthias Waschek for bringing this article to my attention.
79 See Edward Berenson, *The Trial of Madame Caillaux*, pp. 103–17.
80 Julien Tiersot, *Histoire de la chanson populaire en France*, p. i: 'La Grèce avait exercé son influence souveraine sur la civilisation de l'antiquité tout entière. Créatrice, puis vulgarisatrice de tous les arts, elle les avait portés au plus haut point de perfection que le monde ancien ait connu, et avait répandu parmi tous les peuples civilisés les types accomplis de maturité sereine et de sobre élégance qu'elle avait produits. En musique, son influence fut considérable . . . Par Rome, devenue l'élève et l'imitatrice de la Grèce, l'influence de l'art grec s'exerça sur la plus grande partie de l'Empire romain . . . Cette riche culture gréco-latine était au plus haut point florissante dans la Gaule romaine'.
81 Ibid., p. ii.
82 Ibid., p. iii.
83 Cf. Tacitus, *The Annals of Imperial Rome*, trans. by Michael Grant (1956) (Harmondsworth, rev. edn. 1971), pp. 61–2. The episode related by Tacitus in *Annals* 50–51 has little bearing on Tiersot's tale which freely adds names to the Roman description, especially the one of Siegfried, for Tiersot most probably Wagner's hero, given the musical reference. I wish to thank Tim Carter for providing the Tacitus reference.
84 Julien Tiersot, *Histoire de la chanson populaire en France*, pp. iii–iv: 'Tacite fait mention des sauvages chants de guerre dont les Germains s'excitaient les uns les autres dans les combats. Autour du roi Chlodevech, les guerriers franks chantaient, aux repas et dans les assemblées guerrières, les chants épiques qui consacraient la mémoire de leur héros national Siegfried. Lors de la première bataille qui fut livrée en Gaule entre les Franks de Chlodion et les légionnaires d'Aétius, les Franks, campés sur une colline, célébraient les noces d'un de leurs chefs au son des chansons et danses chantées en chœur: ces bruits relevèrent leur présence aux Romains; ils furent surpris: leur goût pour une musique éclatante fut cause de leur première défaire'.

85 Wolfgang Leiner, *Das Deutschlandbild in der französischen Literatur*, p. 17.
86 Katharine Ellis, *Music Criticism in Nineteenth-Century France: 'La Revue et Gazette musicale de Paris', 1834–1880* (Cambridge, 1995), p. 35.
87 Jann Pasler,'Paris: Conflicting Notions of Progress', p. 398. See also Annegret Fauser, 'L'art de l'allusion musicale', *L'Avant-Scène Opéra*, 161 (September-October 1994), pp. 126–9.
88 On the ideal world of the Middle Ages in French *fin-de-siècle* imagery, see Annegret Fauser, 'Die Sehnsucht nach dem Mittelalter: Ernest Chausson und Richard Wagner', in Wolfgang Storch and Josef Mackert (eds.), *Les Symbolistes et Richard Wagner: Die Symbolisten und Richard Wagner* (Berlin, 1991), pp. 115–20.
89 With this sentence, Tiersot reinstalls France's own medieval poetic traditions, offering an essentially French alternative to the Wagnerian theories of versification which were much discussed during the 1880s and 1890s in Paris. On the reception of Wagner's poetic ideas through translations, see Jean Louis Jam and Gérard Loubinoux, 'D'une *Walkyrie* à l'autre: Les adaptations françaises de Wagner', in Annegret Fauser and Manuela Schwartz (eds.), *Von Wagner zum Wagnérisme*, pp. 401–30. On Wagner's concept of versification, see Reinhart Meyer-Kalkus,'Richard Wagners Theorie der Wort-Tonsprache in "Oper und Drama" und "Der Ring des Nibelungen"', *Athenäum: Jahrbuch für Romantik*, 6, 1996, pp. 153–195.
90 Julien Tiersot, *Histoire de la chanson populaire en France*, pp. vi–vii:'Nous retrouvons cette même chanson encore vivante à la fin de notre dix-neuvième siècle ... La rime y est inconnue: tout au plus est-elle remplacée par l'assonance, dernier reste des traditions de la versification du moyen âge ... Sa phrase est courte et nette; le mot juste y ressort avec un éclat qu'envierait le vers le plus savant; et toujours une concision admirable, point de développement superflu: le récit va droit au but, par déductions logiques et naturelles, sans s'attarder à rien d'inutile; ou bien le sentiment s'exprime en des mots simples, mais profonds et pénétrants. Et sur ces vers sont d'admirable mélodies, comme eux simples et concises, mais d'une saveur intense et d'une inépuisable vitalité.'
91 Such appropriations can be found in other countries as well, as for example in England. See Robert Stradling and Meirion Hughes, *The English Musical Renaissance, 1860–1940: Construction and Deconstruction* (London, 1993), p. 23.
92 Julien Tiersot, *Histoire de la chanson populaire en France*, p. 489:'[I]l faut aller jusqu'au moyen âge, et l'on verra ces deux arts, formes premières et primitives de la musique française, jouer de concert, dans la création du théâtre lyrique, un rôle exactement semblable à celui que nous leur avons vu en étudiant le création de l'harmonie'.
93 Ibid., p. 495.
94 See Julien Tiersot, *Sur le Jeu de Robin et Marion d'Adam de la Halle* (Paris, 1897). This perception of Adam de la Halle's *Jeu de Robin et Marion* goes back to Fétis in his article 'Adam de la Halle,' in Franois-Joseph Fétis, *Biographie universelle des musiciens et Bibliographie générale de la musique* (Paris, 2nd edn., 1860), 1, pp. 12–13. I wish to thank Katharine Ellis for this reference.
95 Julien Tiersot, *Histoire de la chanson populaire en France*, p. 529.
96 Julien Tiersot,'*Mignon* et la chanson française', *Le Ménestrel*, 60 (1894), pp. 155–6.
97 The book celebrates, for example, the Republic and the French Revolution in an entire chapter on the patriotic strength of folk music as expressed in the 'Marseillaise'. See Julien Tiersot, *Histoire de la chanson populaire en France*, pp. 275–86. Tiersot concludes this passage with the following judgement: '[œuvre] où n'en revit pas moins avec une rare intensité l'esprit de la race française, et même, fait curieux à signaler au sujet d'un chant révolutionnaire, sa tendance à rester constamment fidèle à ses plus anciennes traditions' (p. 286).

98 I borrow the term from Dave Harker, *Fakesong*. The rhetorical strategies employed in the research and mediation of English folksong rely on similar concepts to the French, drawing on nationalist and essentialist interpretations. The central text in this respect is Cecil Sharp, *English Folk-Song: Some Conclusions* (London, 1907).
99 See Jane F. Fulcher, 'Wagner in the Cultural Politics of the French Right and Left before World War I', in Annegret Fauser and Manuela Schwartz (eds.), *Von Wagner zum Wagnérisme*, pp. 137–54.
100 See Edouard Schuré's foreword to the 1902 edition of his *Histoire du Lied ou la chansons populaire en Allemagne* (Paris, 1902), and Louis Schneider, *Das französische Volkslied* (*Die Music*, ed. by Richard Strauss, 28/29) (Berlin, 1908).
101 *Les Chansons de France: Revue trimestrielle de musique populaire*, 1, 1906, pp. 4–6.
102 Fiamma Nicolodi, 'Nationalistische Aspekte im Mythos von der "alten Musik" in Italien und Frankreich', in Helga de la Motte-Haber, *Nationaler Stil und europäische Dimension in der Musik der Jahrhundertwende* (Darmstadt, 1991), pp. 102–21. Katharine Ellis is currently researching a book on the reception of early music in nineteenth-century France which will give more detailed insights into this very complex reception history. The political implications of the early-music revival form an important part of Jane F. Fulcher's study, *French Cultural Politics and Musical Aesthetics from the Dreyfus Affair to the First World War* (Oxford, 1998).
103 Henry Expert, *Les Maîtres musiciens de la Renaissance française*, 1: Orlande de Lassus, *Premier Fascicule des Mélanges* (Paris, 1894), pp. i–vi.
104 Ibid., pp. i–ii: 'Toutefois, dès les premières heures du XVIe siècle, dans la vigueur d'une mâle et féconde jeunesse, la musique a rejeté le formalisme rigide des primitifs; rompue à une technique savante, consciente de ses énergies expressive, elle peut tenter l'interprétation des sentiments: elle possède désormais cette *virtu secrette et quasi incredible à esmouvoir les cueurs en une sorte ou en l'autre* (Calvin). Et d'abord, l'esprit laïque, ce puissant fonds gaulois fécondé par la Renaissance, apparaît pleinement dans les musiques profanes ... Et tandis que l'école poétique de Marot et la Pleiade donnent à la musique leurs plus beaux joyaux, l'Humanisme fervent s'essaie, sous la plume de savants musiciens, à faire revivre les nombres d'Horace et de Virigile, d'Ovide, de Catulle et de Martial'.
105 Henry Expert, *Les Maîtres musiciens de la Renaissance française*, p. ii: 'A ces chants où éclate et triomphe l'esprit de la Renaissance, l'Eglise répond par les chef-d'œuvres de son art sacré'.
106 On the 'metaphysical' qualities of music in the context of Wagner reception, see Katharine Ellis, 'Wagnerism and Anti-Wagnerism in the Paris Periodical Press, 1852–70', in Annegret Fauser and Manuela Schwartz, *Von Wagner zum Wagnérisme*, pp. 51–83; Annegret Fauser, 'Die Sehnsucht nach dem Mittelalter'; Manuela Schwartz, *Wagner-Rezeption und französische Oper*.
107 Similar phenomena can be observed in other art forms. Debora Silverman shows, for example, how the rococo revival of the 1890s in the *art-nouveau* movement became politicised within a 'profoundly nationalist discourse'. See Debora L. Silverman, *Art Nouveau in Fin-de-Siècle France*, pp. 8–9 and 142–58.
108 A similar form of canon creation through the publication of editions took place in Germany during the nineteenth century. See Philip Brett, 'Text, Context, and the Early Music Editor', in Nicholas Kenyon (ed.), *Authenticity and Early Music: A Symposium* (Oxford and New York, 1988), pp. 85–6.
109 Albert Lavignac, *La Musique et les musiciens français* (Paris, 1895), p. 431–2: 'Il est impossible de terminer ce chapitre sans exhorter les jeunes compositeurs français à s'attacher avant tout à conserver à notre art national les qualités caractéristiques qui en ont toujours fait la gloire, qu'on y retrouve à toutes les grandes époques, et qui sont: *la clarté, l'élégance* et *la sincérité d'expression*. C'est pour eux la seule manière

d'être naturels et d'arriver à se créer un style propre, une personnalité; car toutes les fois qu'ils voudront s'écarter de ces traditions inhérentes à la race, au génie de la langue comme à l'esprit français, ils ne seront jamais que des imitateurs maladroits et des plagiaires; ils feront penser à des gens qui parlent péniblement une langue étrangère avec un accent ridicule'.

110 These terms recur in countless criticisms and other writings on *opéra comique*. Marie-Claire Mussat quotes some of these remarks in her 'Diffusion et réception de *l'opéra comique*', in Herbert Schneider and Nicole Wild (eds.), *Die Opéra Comique und ihr Einfluß auf das europäische Musiktheater im 19. Jahrhundert* (Hildesheim, 1997), pp. 283–96.

111 Camille Bellaigue, *Un siècle de musique française* (Paris, 1887), pp. 1–141.

112 For a brief discussion of this subject, see Annegret Fauser, 'Saint-Saëns: *Phryné*', in Sieghart Döhring (ed.), *Piper Enzyklopädie des Musik-theaters*, Vol. 5 (Munich, 1994), pp. 521–2.

113 Camille Saint Saëns, 'La poésie et la musique' (1881), *Harmonie et mélodie* (Paris, 1885), pp. 257–66.

114 In a late letter to his friend Camille Bellaigue, he claims that his chorus 'C'est Phryné, quand elle passe' is 'en pure mode grec, le 2e ton du plain chant.' Letter from 27 February 1919, F-Pn, l.a. Saint-Saëns 116.

115 This essentialist opposition of Latin qualities and Germanic metaphysical bombast has its roots in the eighteenth century, with texts by writers such as the Marquis d'Argens (see Werner Oechslin, 'Le goût et les nations') and aesthetic debates as expressed by the 'querelles des Gluckistes et Piccinistes'. Through Fétis it became part of the French Wagner reception as early as 1852. See Katharine Ellis, *Music Criticism in Nineteenth-Century France*, pp. 206–18, and Katharine Ellis, 'Wagnerism and Anti-Wagnerism in the Paris Periodical Press, 1852–70'. A comprehensive collection of press reviews of the first performance of *Phryné* is kept in the 'Dossier d'œuvre: *Phryné*', Bibliothèque de l'Opéra, Paris.

116 On French orchestral song, see Annegret Fauser, *Der Orchestergesang in Frankreich zwischen 1870 und 1920* (Laaber, 1994), esp. pp. 59–139.

117 See the brief discussion in Annegret Fauser, *Der Orchestergesang in Frankreich*, pp. 11–15. Brian Hart has examined the aesthetics of the symphony in his 'The Symphony in Theory and Practice in France, 1900–1914' (PhD diss., Indiana University, 1994), esp. chapter one. See also Brian Hart, 'Wagner and the *Franckiste* "Message-Symphony" in Early Twentieth-Century France', in Annegret Fauser and Manuela Schwartz (eds.), *Von Wagner zum Wagnérisme*, pp. 315–37.

118 For a still fascinating discussion on the foundation, historic dimensions and implications of music history, see Carl Dahlhaus, *Grundlagen der Musikgeschichte* (Köln, 1977), esp. his chapters 'Historismus und Tradition' (pp. 91–117) and 'Historische Hermeneutik' (pp. 120–38). In the latter, Dahlhaus discusses the implications of 'the theory of historic understanding', developed in the nineteenth century (p. 121). On the philosophical context of German nineteenth-century music criticism and history, see Carl Dahlhaus, *Klassische und romantische Musikästhetik* (Laaber, 1988), pp. 219–90.

119 On Fétis's role in the development of music history, see Katharine Ellis, *Music Criticism in Nineteenth-Century France*, pp. 33–45.

120 See Rémy Campos, '"Mens sana in corpore sano": l'introduction de l'histoire de la musique au Conservatoire', in Emmanuel Hondré, *Le Conservatoire de Musique de Paris: Regards sur une institution et son histoire* (Paris, 1995), pp. 145–71. The first holder of the chair of the *Classe d'histoire générale de la musique* was Louis-Albert Bourcault-Ducoudray (p. 146).

121 Katharine Ellis, *Music Criticism in Nineteenth-Century France*, pp. 44–5.

122 See Jann Pasler, 'Paris: Conflicting Notions of Progress'.
123 Claude Debussy, 'L'Influence allemande sur la musique française' (1903), in François Lesure (ed.), *Claude Debussy: Monsieur Croche et autres écrits* (Paris, 2nd edn. 1987), p. 67: 'Wagner, si l'on peut s'exprimer avec un peu de la grandiloquence qui lui convient, fut un beau coucher de soleil que l'on a pris pour une aurore . . .' Decadence and decline were detected not only in Germany's music but also in her musical life. See, for example, the gleeful note in 'Nouvelles Diverses: Etranger', *Le Ménestrel*, 54 (1888), p. 70: 'Un signe de la décadence du thâtre lyrique en Allemagne. L'Opra grand-ducal de Darmstadt, qui, il ya quelques années, était au premier rang des scénes allemandes, a été obligé pour relever l'état de ses finances, de faire appel au genre de l'opérette. *Le Baron des Tziganes*, de Johann Strauss, y a été représenté, pour la premiére fois, le 5 février dernier'.
124 Albert Soubies, *Histoire de la musique allemande* (Paris, 1897), p. 194: 'L'influence de Rousseau fut considérable au delà du Rhin'.
125 Ibid., p. 290.
126 On the gendered British Beethoven-reception, see Maria McHale, 'The Discourse on Gender in British Writings on Music 1880–1914' (MA diss., City University, London, 1997).
127 Albert Soubies, *Histoire de la musique allemande*, p. 291: 'Pour la France, enfin, dont la caractéristique, en art, a toujours été l'éclectisme clairvoyant et délicat, la combinaison intelligente et fine, l'habile adaptation d'éléments très divers, on sait avec quel éclat, quelle abondance de ressources a été, chez nous, dans ce que M. Lavoix a nommé "le siècle de Beethoven", recueillie et mise en valeur la tradition allemande'.
128 For an excellent discussion of the implications of cultural transfer, see Michel Espagne and Michael Werner, 'Deutsch-französischer Kulturtransfer als Forschungsgegenstand: Eine Problemskizze', *Transferts*, pp. 11–34.
129 Vincent d'Indy, *Cours de Composition musicale* (deuxième livre, première partie), rédigé avec la collaboration de Auguste Sérieyx d'après les notes prises aux Classes de Composition de la Schola Cantorum (Paris, 1919), pp. 391 and 421–2: 'Avec Franck, génial continuateur français de l'immortel symphoniste allemand, commence une période nouvelle et *exclusivement française* jusqu'à présent. La valeur et la force des meilleurs œuvres appartenant à cette période reposent sur toutes les innovations beethovéniennes et sur la construction *cyclique* enfin comprise et réalisée. Sous cette influence bienfaisante, la traditionnelle forme Sonate a déjà reconquis, dans notre pays tout au moins, une vitalité et une jeunesse vraiment surprenantes après un demi-siècle de décadence et d'oubli. [. . .] C'est à la France qu'il devait appartenir de poursuivre et de réaliser la transformation de la Sonate, clairement indiquée par Beethoven: nul de ses successeurs allemands, en effet, n'avait su ou voulu tenter sérieusement cette véritable rénovation *cyclique*, seule capable de rendre la vie à cette belle forme qui s'étiolait et semblait près de disparaître, en Allemagne tout au moins, malgré les timides essais de Schumann et de Brahms. La tradition *cyclique* peut donc être considérée comme transmise *directement* de Beethoven à César Franck.'
130 Laure Collin, *Histoire abrégée de la musique et des musiciens*, 7th edn. (Paris, 1891); Elise Vigoureux, *Manuel d'histoire générale de la musique à l'usage des classes de solfège* (Marseilles, 1904).
131 H. Lavoix fils, *La Musique française* (Paris, 1891), p. 6.
132 Michel Espagne and Michael Werner, 'Deutsch-französischer Kulturtransfer als Forschungsgegenstand', p. 15.
133 Jann Pasler showed this in her paper 'Making Alliances through Music: Russia as Embraced by the French', read at the International Conference on Nineteenth-Century Music, Surrey, 14–17 July 1994 (to be published).

134 For a feminist re-reading of American canon formation after the Second World War see Nina Baym,'Melodramas of Beset Manhood: How Theories of American Fiction Excluded Women Authors' (1981), in Elaine Showalter (ed.), *The New Feminist Criticism: Essays on Women, Literature and Theory* (London, 1986), pp. 63–81. On the implications of masculinised music theory and history for historical and current judgement and canon formation, see Marcia J. Citron, *Gender and the Musical Canon*, pp. 15–43 and 120–45.
135 See Eugen Weber, *France: Fin de Siècle* (Cambridge, MA, 1986), pp. 9–26.

5.
Against Germanic Reasoning: The Search for a Russian Style of Musical Argumentation

MARINA FROLOVA-WALKER

> *Symphonic development in the technical sense* is just like German philosophy – all worked out and systematized . . . When a German thinks, he *reasons* his way to a conclusion. Our Russian brother, on the other hand, starts with the conclusion and only then might amuse himself with reasoning. That's all I have to say to you about symphonic development.
>
> Mussorgsky[1]

Russia provides us with one of the earliest examples of a nationalist music school, and, as many would agree, this school became the most ambitious, productive and influential of all, for the Russian intelligentsia came to see music as a vital tool of nation-building, second only to literature in this respect. It is hardly surprising, then, that in Russia the historiography of this music is primarily a mythology of musical nationalism. Russian critics and musicologists have sustained and encouraged these myths almost throughout the past century-and-a-half, due to the intellectual, and later political, dominance of nationalism in its bourgeois and Stalinist forms; the only brief hiatus occurred in the second and third decades of this century, when a cosmopolitan modernism was in the ascendant, eventually to be stifled by Stalin. But much more puzzling is the fact that Western critics who were not bound by such ideological constraints and obligations served, more often than not, as mouthpieces for this same nationalist mythology. While the Russians were preoccupied in constructing an identity for themselves that was self-consciously in opposition to the characteristics of Western music, Westerners indulged themselves in constructing an exotic quasi-oriental identity for Russian music, happily reproducing Russian nationalist mythologies for their own purposes.

Had Glinka produced at least one complete symphony, the history of nineteenth-century Russian music could have been very different. Instead of discussing the problems which dogged Russian efforts to work within this genre, we might instead be musing upon the special predilection of the Russian mind for symphonic argument. While Glinka's operas and programmatic orchestral works were enthusiastically mined by succeeding generations of nationalists, he failed to leave even a single example of the symphony to posterity, so that his would-be disciples found themselves stranded, bereft of any authoritative Russian symphonic model. Worse still, the absence of any Glinka symphony was no mere oversight on the part of the older master, but the result of intractable problems which he had already encountered. As Glinka confessed:

> I had written the first part of the Allegro and the beginning of the second part of [my] Cossack symphony in C minor (Taras Bul'ba). I was unable to continue with the second part, which I found unsatisfactory. When I gave the matter some thought, I found that the development of the Allegro (Durchführung, développement) I had begun in the German manner, while the general character of the piece was Little Russian. I discarded the score, and Pedro [his secretary] destroyed it.[2]

What are we to make of this? Firstly, we must understand that Glinka was well able to write a development based on established methods (as his early sonata-based works testify) – the difficulties did not lie here. Secondly, he perceived these methods to be an inalienable characteristic of German music, incompatible with the Russian or other local colours he was attempting to evoke. Thirdly, the project he mentions would not in any case have inaugurated a grand tradition of Russian national symphonies, for the intended character of the work was 'Little Russian'; that is, Ukrainian. His problems with indelibly German development techniques would equally have arisen had he wished to compose a symphony in his Spanish style. But successive generations of Russian composers unanimously ignored this last qualification, and transformed Glinka's rather casual remark into a polemical cornerstone of musical nationalism. As Glinka, now posthumously a national hero, was elevated to ever more rarified heights, his every word was presented in the form of an ordinance for future generations.

Let us now examine the origins of the problem symphonic development posed for Russian composers. We must return to that watershed in Russian music history, the 1836 premiere of Glinka's *A Life for the Tsar*, for it was from this moment on that music could be regarded as a possible vehicle for Russian nationalist discourse. As a newcomer, music had to learn from the experience of the main player in the nationalist game, literature.

From the earliest stirrings of nationalism in the eighteenth century, the Russian language received the greatest attention, and the state of literature was in time understood to reflect the state of the nation. In the course of the next hundred years, owing to the conscious efforts of men of letters, a new, more monolithic Russian national language grew out of many diverse dialects; a multi-volume dictionary and a systematic grammar of the language were published, and the lexical set was expanded, so that it traversed the centuries from ancient epic to modern science. The borders between rural and urban, oral and written, and low and high began to dissolve, and after a century of development in this manner Pushkin's great example finally ensured that it was seen to be fit even for the most exalted works of literature. By the 1830s, cultural nationalism was taking stock of its achievements, constructing a pantheon for its heroes; Pushkin was accordingly mythologised, even within his own lifetime, as the first national poet and the founding father of Russian literary language. It was not long until Glinka was hailed as music's Pushkin, the first national composer and the founding father of Russian musical language; this endowed the next generation of composers with a consciousness of their weighty responsibilities to the nation.

The possession of an uncontaminated, originary language was the most important nation-defining criterion in early nationalist writings. It was claimed that such a language was a natural phenomenon guaranteeing the organic unity of a nation, and that this irreplaceable heritage had to be protected from the dilution of foreign borrowings and developed only from its source. Music appeared no less plausible a subject for such rhetoric. The natural phenomenon in this case was the whole body of folk music found among the Russian-speaking peoples, viewed as a monolith, without regard for the many significant regional differences that would exercise the ethnomusicologist today.

This is the 'mother tongue' of Russian composers, who, protecting it from harmful foreign influence, were to develop it carefully into a national language of art music. If an original language possesses not only its original vocabulary but original syntax and grammar as well, then national music should not only draw its melodic material from folksong but also should use national metres and rhythms, national harmony, and supposedly original methods of development of its material.[3] And it is at this point that Glinka's rejection of Germanic development, if presented as a nationalist statement, can be brought into play. A composer who wants to speak Russian in his music, not only ought to use the vocabulary of his nation (folksong or folk-inspired material) but also make sure that his musical grammar is not contaminated by foreign constructions (such as Germanic symphonic development). This is how a myth was born, a myth about the possibility and even the imperative of specifically Russian thematic procedures.

A second justification of this myth soon followed, now at the deeper level of national character; this was pithily stated by Mussorgsky in the epigraph at the head of the present essay. Now, it seemed, a Russian composer embarking on a development section had to be true not only to his material but also to his national self. Mussorgsky's idiosyncratic language makes it difficult to convey the range of possible meanings he might have intended. Here is the epigraph once more, as rendered by Richard Taruskin:

> When a German thinks, he reasons his way to a conclusion. Our Russian brother, on the other hand, starts with the conclusion and then might amuse himself with reasoning.

Taruskin's version is elegant, but rather interpretative – perhaps of necessity, given the obscurity of Mussorgsky's language. The reader might, however, find the following translation useful for comparison; I have sacrificed elegance here for the sake of a more literal rendering:

> When a German thinks, he first expatiates [or rambles, waffles], then delivers the proof. Our Russian brother first supplies the proof [or *perhaps better:* gets to the point straight away], and then amuses himself with waffling.

Taruskin's verb 'reason' is rather more flattering to the German than Mussorgsky's *'razvodit'*; Russian in fact lacks any lexical item equivalent to the concept of *ratio* or reason, and the verb Mussorgsky has chosen evokes the aimless spreading of water. The point of the comparison was primarily to dissuade Rimsky-Korsakov from developing his material in ways that seemed distinctly Germanic to Mussorgsky. And he was, of course, always happy to mock German ways (this had become a minor Russian tradition – a well-known example is to be found in the farcical portrayal of German generals in *War and Peace*). But we can also see this quotation to be a symptom of the anti-rationalistic sentiments commonly found in nineteenth-century Russian writings. One can perceive here one hundred and fifty years of Russia's jealous observation of her civilised and prosperous Western neighbours.[4] Russia's failure to compete with the West on Western terms was only too obvious, and reflection upon the fact generally left Russians embittered. But Russia's emerging national consciousness soon devised a way of escaping this humiliation: what Russians took to be the values of the West, they portrayed as vices; and conversely, they made the opposite of each Western virtue into a Russian value. Western rationality, creative initiative, worship of success and so on were exaggerated so much as to appear pathological, while Russian intuition, contemplation and underachievement were offered as their healthy counterparts. Perverse as this may seem, it allowed the Russian nation to develop a pride in itself, and indeed formed a basis for Slavophile thought. The Slavophiles went on to construct an ideal image of original innocence (rather than mere ignorance) in pre-Petrine Russia, under the wise ministrations of the Eastern Church. Ivan Kireyevsky, the most eminent of the Slavophiles, called upon Russia to return to its true path:

> In the West, theology became rational and abstract, while in the Orthodox world it retained the inner integrity of the Spirit; in the West the

forces of intellect are split, while here there is a striving for a live totality; *there you have mind moving towards truth through a logical chain of ideas, here, a striving for truth through the inner elevation of consciousness towards cordial integrity and intellectual concentration;* . . . there you have scholastical and juridical universities, while in ancient Russia there were monasteries of prayer that enjoyed a concentration of the supreme knowledge within their walls.[5]

The classical, pagan world which Russia did not inherit is essentially *the triumph of formal reason over everything else* inside and outside the human being – of pure, naked reason, based on nothing but itself . . . the Roman church is distinguished by the same triumph of rationalism over . . . supreme spiritual insights . . . The Inquisition, Jesuitism – all traits of Catholicism are the fruit of the same formal intellectual process . . . That same Protestantism that Catholics reproach for its rationality can be traced back to the rationalism of Catholicism. In this last triumph of formal intellect over faith and tradition a sharp mind could already see the entire destiny of Europe [as unfolded up to the] present: . . . the new philosophy . . . industrialism as a foundation for society, philanthropy based on calculated self-interest, a system of education based on stimulating envy, Goethe, the crown of new poetry . . . who kept changing the notion of beauty like Talleyrand his governments [etc., etc.][6]

Of course many of Kireyevsky's Russian contemporaries thought the very things he condemned should characterise any civilised modern society. It seems that symphonic development fell into the same category. Our aim here is to find out if Russian composers ever managed to devise any alternative.

The example of a clearly non-Germanic structure usually cited is Glinka's symphonic fantasy *Kamarinskaya*, the work based on two folksongs whose far-from-obvious melodic resemblance is developed through a chain of ostinato variations. The idea, fresh enough in itself, of reconciling two contrasting entities acquires additional interest from its choice of thematic material, which was given rather than composed. Although the next two generations of Russian composers claimed to be playing by the *Kamarinskaya* rules when they produced numerous overtures and fantasies on Russian or foreign themes, they never recaptured the tautness of Glinka's structure, nor its independence from Germanic methods of development. Not only was the brilliance of Glinka's musical pun never reproduced, but while the double-variation form he created was self-sufficient, they had to reach out for the crutches of sonata allegro, as in Balakirev's Overture on Three Russian Themes and *Russia*, or in similar works by Rimsky-Korsakov and Glazunov.[7] In Rimsky-Korsakov's Piano Concerto, a Russian folk theme is indeed used as the basis for a chain of variations, but these are unabashedly Lisztian in character and technique – an indication of the fact that by this stage (1884) any type of variation form, and not merely the characteristic changing-background type created by Glinka, was accepted as a token of Russian-style thematic treatment.

But the real testing-ground for Russians was, of course, the symphony itself: was their cast of mind original enough to change the course of the genre, which had acquired a certain rigidity by the time they approached it? Indeed, there exists a distinct, immediately recognisable Petersburg style in the symphonies of Borodin, Balakirev, Rimsky-Korsakov and the younger Glazunov. What, then, was the original, or paradigmatic, Petersburg symphony? Cui spoke thus of Rimsky-Korsakov's First Symphony:

> It is Russian because only a Russian could have written it, because there is no trace of musty Germanic stuff, but both the ideas and their development could have emerged only here [in Russia].[8]

Just to what extent this was wishful thinking is demonstrated by Rimsky-Korsakov's later remark, made after he had edited and re-orchestrated the symphony in the 1880s:

> What a shameful work it was, not in the youthfulness of its ideas, but rather in its total incompetence! O Russian school! O Stasov! O Balakirev![9]

And 'O Cui!' we could well add, since Rimsky-Korsakov's frank assessment of his first magnum opus is perhaps not overly harsh. Much more seminal for the New Russian School were the first symphonies of Balakirev and Borodin. Although nearly thirty years separate the dates of their completion (Borodin's in 1867, Balakirev's in 1893), both symphonies passed through Balakirev's workshop at the same time – indeed, Balakirev was responsible for a large proportion of the finished products his pupils turned out at this time. Balakirev's St Petersburg archives demonstrate that all the material for the first movement of his own symphony was ready in the 1860s:[10] the first 246 bars underwent little revision, and it is most likely that the remainder of the highly original structure was planned out at this stage, since the other fragments to be found in the 1860s sketches appear in the same keys that we find in the finished work. And Balakirev was, of course, playing his work to his younger friends and discussing it at the very time when Borodin was working on his own first symphony.

A comparison of Balakirev's and Borodin's first movements brings out obvious similarities:

- Both movements are replete with motivic-thematic work, so that there is hardly any contrast between expository and developmental writing.
- Both the first and second subjects within each movement are closely related.
- Both are remarkable for the number of pedal-note passages (usually on V) which appear in both expected and unexpected places.

- Both seem to deviate from conventional sonata form more than any other sonata movement in Russian music of the time (including earlier and later works of their own).

The approach to symphonic development in Balakirev's workshop was lively and ingenious; clever motivic and contrapuntal tricks guaranteeing symphonic sophistication were encouraged, but the form itself was not subject to any inherited doctrines (and, indeed, Balakirev did not know the A. B. Marx schemes at that stage). As Rimsky-Korsakov observed:

> A certain kind of musical fragment or period was held in greatest esteem, such as preparations, extensions, short but characteristic phrases, dissonant progressions (but not of the enharmonic kind), sequential growths, abrupt closures, etc.[11]

In effect, Balakirev was teaching his friends how to build symphonies from the material of the striking and inventive themes they had brought to the workshop, to be honed and admired there; their work was to be filtered through Beethoven, Schumann and Liszt, whose music was the staple diet prescribed by Balakirev. But we must pause to ask: can this be reconciled with the aesthetic and moral scorn Mussorgsky displayed for Germanic approaches to symphonic development?

In order to answer this question, we look now at the form of both these first movements, for this was the aspect which has always been considered least Germanic; if we then discover that even in this respect Germanic models were being followed, we will be able to judge how distant were Mussorgsky's sentiments from the compositional procedures of his colleagues. Borodin's First is marginally the simpler of the two, so we shall discuss it first. Its recapitulation is followed by a second development, which reworks the sections of the development proper, presenting them in a different order; this gives the old material a new dramatic profile. Framed by a slower introduction and coda, the allegro falls into two halves (see Figure 5.1).

Another curious feature is the absence of any closing section in such an expansive and thematically rich exposition. Later, we encounter a majestic build-up leading to a grand cadence; this passage might easily have served to end the exposition, but instead it appears in the middle of the development, and the cadence itself is in the distant A major (bars 166–204). This build-up is reproduced at the end of the entire movement in the tonic E flat (bars 455–483), embedding the tritone E♭ – A in the structure of the movement. This relationship is unorthodox but clear, and is thrown into relief by the vagueness and ambiguity of the movement's tonality elsewhere. For example, the structure of the secondary area of the exposition is elusive; it is probably best to interpret the exposition on a three-, rather than two-key model, the initial E♭ being succeeded first by B♭ and then g.[12] Another unusual feature is that, in the recapitulation, the secondary area is not straightforwardly transposed, but introduces some unexpected keys once again, while the interval of transposition varies. All these strategies are indeed surprising and indicate a serious re-thinking of sonata procedures. But are they unprecedented?

Figure 5.1. Borodin, First Symphony, first movement.

Introduction		Exposition					Development		
slow	fast								
bar 1		54	91	115	131	152	166	204	233
eb	V of Eb	Eb	Bb	D	Bb-g	g	V of A	A-Ab	Ab-Db-V of Eb
[a]	[ab]	a	b	c	d	[ad]	a	d[e]	ad, c, b

Recapitulation				Development 2			Coda	
							fast	slow
301	338	362	378	407	427	448	483	513
Eb	Eb	Gb	D-b-c	Ab	ped. on c	V of Es	V of Eb	Eb
a	b	c	d	ad	e	a		[ad]

a = main theme; b = transitional theme; c = "introduction" to "secondary" theme
d = "secondary" theme; e = "episode"

Note. Square brackets indicate that material from the designated theme is used, although that theme is not presented in its original form.

If we were to single out the one composer whose influence in Borodin's First is paramount, this would undoubtedly be Schumann. Some of the symphony's Schumannisms are readily discernible on the surface, e.g. the main theme of the finale, see Example 5.1a and 5.1b for comparison; but the debt to Schumann is also evident at a deeper level.

Example 5.1a. Borodin, Symphony No. 1 (Finale)

Example 5.1b. Schumann, Symphony in D minor (Finale)

Borodin was introduced to Schumann's music by his wife-to-be (a fine pianist) at the most romantic time of his life; a few years later, Borodin would have been reacquainted with the piano sonatas in particular when they were studied within Balakirev's circle. And it is in these three works that Schumann's most daring experiments with sonata form may be found. Only recently have these unorthodox forms received the analysis they deserve, first and foremost in the work of Linda Roesner, who termed them 'parallel forms'.[13] Their most important feature is their restatement of all the development material after the recapitulation, a procedure endowing the whole with a bipartite structure (the second part is a mere transposition of the first). Roesner gives several examples of this: the rejected version of the finale of the Second Sonata (presto passionato in g), and the outer movements of the Third Sonata; she also shows that a similar principle was involved in the construction of the piano Fantasia's outer movements. To this list the finale of the First Sonata can be added; indeed, it would seem to be an extension of the parallel principle on two levels: each half of the finale itself contains two sections (see Figure 5.2). But in tonal terms the parallelism is not fully consistent due to the change of the transposition interval (a minor third between E♭ and C, a tritone between A and E♭, and, finally, a perfect fourth between f# and b).[14]

Figure 5.2. Schumann, First Sonata, finale.

1	2	3	3a	2a	1	2	3	2b	Cad	dev	epi-sode	retr	
A	a	E♭	E♭	V of E♭	e♭	A	f#	A	--f#	f#			
1	2	3	3a	2a	1		3	2b	Cad	dev	epi-sode	etr	1+ coda
A	a	E♭	E♭	V of C	c		E♭	c	E♭	--c	b		Fis

Note. Most of the themes are represented here by numbers, since treating them according to sonata or any other form would be artificial; however, some gestures are so obviously sonata-generated that naming them by function - cadential closure, start of 'development', episode, retransition - is most appropriate.

It seems most likely that Schumann's piano sonatas (above all, the F sharp minor) were the inspiration behind Borodin's experimentation in his First Symphony. Two stages of Borodin's structure hint at the 'parallel' principle: the tritone relationship at the core of it is a literal reproduction of Schumann's central pair of keys in the finale of Op.11, and the idea of a shifting interval of transposition can be traced back to the same source. Moreover, while Schumann's 'parallel' forms can be reduced to neat symmetrical tonal diagrams (see Roesner),[15] there are also certain signs of tonal symmetry in Borodin, even apart from the tritone A-E♭: the secondary area in the exposition outlines D-B♭-G (a g-minor triad, a major third up from the tonic E♭), and in the recapitulation it is G♭[F#]-D-B (a b-minor triad, a major third down from the tonic).

Let us now examine the other work in question: the first movement of Balakirev's First Symphony. This has puzzled commentators for nearly a century now and, although it was judged to be inspired and convincing,[16] and although its unorthodox form has received a lucid account,[17] no attempt has been made to trace the source of its structural oddities beyond the whim of the composer. Yet I think the key to the form of the first movement lies in its intended programmatic content, which can be deduced from Balakirev's remark in the margins of the incomplete piano score from the 1860s: 'the descent of the Holy Spirit'. This remark is attached to the passage which can now be found at bar 247 of the published score (the fortissimo arrival at an E♭ major triad; see Example 5.2).

Example 5.2. Balakirev, Symphony No. 1, first movement, The descent of the Holy Spirit

It is precisely at this point that the 1860s score breaks off. We may suggest that, although Balakirev's programme for the symphony was never completely revealed, it does not mean that he discarded it. The E flat major climactic chord, then, stands as a turning-point: what was a more than conventional sonata allegro up to this moment completely changes its course, and we can explain this change with reference to the event mentioned by Balakirev in the score. Without exercising too much interpretative licence, it would seem obvious enough that 'the descent of the Holy Spirit' must bring about some radical *transformation* of everything that precedes. And this is exactly what happens in the completed score (Balakirev returned to the composition in the 1890s). The climax of bars 247–255 does not remain triumphant, but immediately slips from the E flat major triad to a half-diminished seventh stating the 'secondary' theme, which up to this moment was characterised by its interrogative and plaintive intonation and thus could be seen as representing a subjective, lyrical human element. The descent of the Holy Spirit, the meeting of man with God, brings confusion, fear, trembling, awe – and, in conveying this, Balakirev's climax can be compared with similar moments in Beethoven's Ninth or Schumann's Third.

But before long, in bar 271, the confusion is strikingly resolved in the new key of B major, where we encounter the first of the transformed characters, the movement's main theme (cf. Example 5.3).

Example 5.3. Balakirev, Symphony No. 1, first movement

It has acquired an up-beat and an appoggiatura, and has become softer and gained an ascending profile. It is important to note that we never hear the main theme again in its original form: its transformation is irreversible. In bar 291 there is another entry, and now the character seems to be genuinely new: it is a theme introducing a new rhythmic figure and a bold octave leap, while before the music moved in crotchets and quavers and favoured conjunct motion (I still recall my first impression that this was out of style). But since we have now left the world of the exposition, we are in B major (a heavenly key in relation to the earthly C?) and we should not be surprised at this new theme of unreserved joy. Bars 318–330 introduce the transformed (with a different stress pattern and re-harmonised) closing theme, which confirms the key of B major and convinces us that what we have just heard was a kind of second exposition. Will there be a development to follow? Indeed, we hear the secondary theme in its original form (still complaining and asking questions) combined with the main theme in its new guise and moving in a regular developmental sequence. But in bar 350 it arrives at a dominant pedal of E major and we are about to witness its *gradual* transformation into an affirmative character – this time it happens before our eyes – and the transformation is complete by bar 368; once again, the transformation is irreversible. A fugato on the dotted-rhythm theme brings us to a dominant pedal of C major in bar 400 (retransition?), then the motto comes in, participating in the build-up, and in bar 433 we finally return to C major for a recapitulation, so to speak, which reproduces the closing theme, the main theme and then the secondary theme in that order, all in their new, transformed guise. The movement ends with a fast triumphant coda, arriving at the climax in a chorale version of the motto (see Figure 5.3).

Figure 5.3. Balakirev, First Symphony, first movement.

Bar	Section	Key	Material
bar 1	Introduction	C	Two motives: A (also functioning as motto) and B
26	1st subject	C	Main theme a (based on A)
62	2nd subject	e -eb-...G	'Secondary' theme b (based on B)
130	closure	D of G - G	closing theme c (based on A)
153–	'false start' of development	Eb...D of C	c, then A
190	proper start of development	C-a -D of C-C	a developed
247	climax	Eb	
248		~ D of h	climactic b
271	'2nd exposition' theme 1	D of H	a* (a transformed)
291	theme 2	H	d
318	closure	H	c* (c transformed)
330–		gis-cis-D of H /ii of E	b+a*, gradually transforming into b*
368	theme 3	E	b*
384	retransition	E~ D of C	fugato on d and motto (A)
430	'recapitulation'	C	c*, then a*, then b*
499	Coda	...C	material of c, b, then A as chorale

The thick line indicates the end of the 1860s score.

As with Borodin's First, it is possible to trace this form to Western sources. Apart from the obvious influence of Lisztian principles, the form more specifically brings to mind Schumann's D Minor Symphony. Being a cross between a symphonic cycle and a one-movement work, it has a most unusual first allegro, which can be properly understood only in relation to the whole of which it forms a part. It starts with a deceptively conventional sonata exposition, even with repeats, but then goes astray in the development, introducing two new themes, one march-like, one lyrical, as if it is the exposition of a new sonata movement. There is no recapitulation of the original exposition material, although it is permanently present in accompanimental textures: instead, the return to the tonic features the new lyrical theme transformed into a march as a grand closing gesture (which is similar to Balakirev's procedure).

We have so far found that large-scale symphonic forms, starting from the respective first symphonies of Balakirev and Borodin (two of the best candidates), fail to sustain nationalist claims that they represented uniquely Russian forms; let us now see whether any unique Russian approach might nevertheless emerge from an examination of smaller scale techniques, of shaping phrases into larger periods. One of the most obvious traits of the Petersburg composers in this respect is the use of repetition on different levels, from single motives or 2-bar phrases to whole paragraphs: a characteristic example would be the first movement of Rimsky-Korsakov's Sinfonietta. This feature won a mixed response from critics – here, for example, is Taneyev's sour response to Glazunov's First Symphony (1881):

> Its shortcomings are those of Glazunov's teachers: *a lack of experience in form*, much as Cui displayed in his *Tarantella* (for example, the first section of the development consists of numerous repetitions of an 8- or 12-bar phrase with a modulation at the end, which is every time the same – a close on the dominant chord, then a crescendo and resolution of the dominant onto a triad – this, being repeated several times in a row, is rather tedious); *an inability to constuct long periods*, which are replaced by the most intolerable mannerism of the Petersburg composers, that endless and meaningless repetition of a one- or two-bar motive, resulting in something importunate, tiresome and evincing in the listener not merely boredom, but boredom coupled with animosity, an impression of something laborious and impotent.[18]

While Taneyev assigns such repetition to a simple lack of ability or training, others see in it an original method of developing ideas. A rather curious defence of the Five's symphonic argumentation is found in the writings of Mikhail Gnesin from the 1940s and 1950s. He attempted to portray the trait not so much as truly national, but as socially progressive and therefore of special value for Soviet audiences. What Taneyev criticised as an 'intolerable mannerism of endless repetition' (with Tchaikovsky's approval), Gnesin hailed as the 'analytical method' akin to that of the sciences. Here is Gnesin's description of the Five's method:

> Creative work begins . . . with the scrupulous selection of a meaningful and expressive thematic germ (idea) . . . Thematic repetitions (constantly re-evoking the idea) guard against the intrusion of elements that are not directly relevant to the design, or those that would neutralise it. Melodic and rhythmical variants of the theme in different sections of the work, enriching it with important and sometimes unexpected details, allow us the better to perceive the main contours and foundations of the theme. Ever-changing harmonic progressions surrounding the theme present it every time in a different light. Textural variety contributes to the commentary on the theme. Transferring the theme into different keys sharpens our perception of it, causes us to hear it in a new environment, and also strengthens our impression of it by increasing the number of its appearances. All of these are different ways of *analysing the theme* . . . Making sure that every new statement of the theme (or every new section of the work) is not lacking in richness when compared to the previous one is as natural as searching for more and more convincing arguments while proving some point.[19]

By shrewd wording Gnesin introduces the *theme* as a natural object. This metaphor would work to some extent only for literally quoted folk tunes as something one may indeed select and then analyse. But the rest of the thematic material used by the composers in question was of their own invention – their pride in their artistry never allowed them to efface their own authorship. There seems to be much less sense in analysing their own creations than given objects, and thus Gnesin's justification for substituting the new and striking word 'analysis' for the traditional 'development' or 'variation' falls apart. And he himself sometimes turns from the analysis metaphor to the traditional 'argument' one. But beware: the Five's argument, according to Gnesin, is totally different from the style of argument found in Beethoven and Tchaikovsky, for these latter felt free to abandon the main theme and create 'associative' or 'nearly accidental' thematic connections, justifying them at a later stage: 'they were not at all afraid of their conceptions being metaphysical', Gnesin says. For those who are not sufficiently familiar with Soviet rhetoric, 'metaphysical' was a swear-word, opposed to 'dialectical' and meaning, according to Gnesin, 'a lack of grounding in the objective study of life processes'. Gnesin's idea is clear: Beethoven and Tchaikovsky lose this round, while the Five win because they employed a more 'realist' method. (I present this to the reader as a sample of the contorted arguments used in defence of the Five's nationalism during the Soviet period, and not as a coherent or interesting argument in its own right.)

If we move from Soviet Russia to the West, we find that Gerald Abraham, like Gnesin, regards the Petersburg tendency towards repetition as a special viable 'method' (rather than a lazy and tedious mannerism); but, unlike Gnesin, he is not so much interested in locating these musical methods within the categories of Soviet dogma; rather, he finds them truly Russian, or, even better, 'semi-oriental', arising from that non-Germanic mentality promoted by Mussorgsky. 'A love of monotony, of endless repetitions' can be explained by the Russians' inspiration from oriental art, or indeed by the Russian mind's 'natural affinity with Eastern mentality'.[20] Borodin's mind in the first movement of his Second Symphony 'seems to return again and again to the same point, viewing it from different angles, instead of moving definitely forward from one position to another in the Western way'; his 'semi-oriental mentality is never more fully revealed than in this movement'.[21] And in general:

> For real intellectual understanding of Russian music one almost needs an entirely new set of postulates. The Russian mind is essentially so naïve, naïve even in ingenuity ...[22]

Now the first Russian symphony which adopted the repetitive manner in a thorough-going fashion was Borodin's First (Balakirev's First began in this manner, but did not sustain it after the first-movement exposition). The first allegro seems to be propelled by the omnipresent syncopated motive, just as we find so often in Schumann. Most of Schumann's allegros are monorhythmic, as determined by their first bar, and in their turn they can be traced to Schumann's youthful fascination with Beethoven's Seventh. When we read some of the critical accounts of Schumann's symphonies, it is hard to miss their kinship with Taneyev's complaints about the Petersburg composers:

> If you examine [Schumann's] orchestral pieces closely, you will find that he was often forced to repeat single bars or groups of bars in order to spin out the thread further, because the theme itself is too small for such continuation. Sometimes even the theme itself is formed through the repetition of this or that phrase. On account of these ... rhythmical repetitions, his larger pieces for the orchestra naturally become monotonous.[23]

It seems natural to suggest, then, that the Petersburg school was influenced by Schumann's symphonic allegros at least as much as by the ostinato variations of Glinka's *Kamarinskaya* (the only source normally given for 'Russian repetition'), if not to a greater extent. The principles of *Kamarinskaya* may have been emulated elsewhere, perhaps in slow movements or finales, but not in first movements. And so another 'deeply national' trait can be traced back to Germany.

As we have just seen, nationalist claims that symphonies could be written in Russian amounted to little or nothing. Of course, we have a lot of Russian symphonic music which is original, striking and fresh, but we owe it to the talented and inventive minds of individuals such as Borodin and Balakirev, rather than to some mysterious 'Russian Spirit' speaking through them. Yet it seems that some Western critics are prepared to support the nationalist myths of a Russian musical language, and a Russian Spirit, and would probably be totally lost without it. This trend started with Gerald Abraham, who accepted such claims at face value:

> Russian musical language had to grow from itself, or rather (if I may mix metaphors) to form its own channel. Traditional methods would have corrupted the purity of the young growth and perhaps even stifled it altogether.[24]

Abraham, as we have seen, also had a clear picture of the naïve Russian mind, defying the forward thrust of Germanic argument. But strangely, his critique of Glazunov, seemingly strengthening the 'Russian Spirit' theory ('nothing ever happens to those ideas ... the flow of music never gets anywhere ... there is no growth, not even a sense of direction'), is supposed to prove that 'Glazunov learnt to speak music with a Russian accent, but not to think musically in Russian'.[25] Abraham's notion of authentic Russianness seems so diffuse that we can only suppose that he awards or withholds it according to his personal tastes rather than according to any concrete musical properties he observes.

It would be pointless to revive these views, had they not remained in currency up to the present today. David Brown, at the end of his *Tchaikovsky*, attempted to 'put the finger on the very essence of Russian creativity'.²⁶ The key to it he found in the concept of 'inertia', which he drew from Goncharov's celebrated novel, *Oblomov*; now, for Russians, the eponymous hero is characterised by 'laziness' or 'idleness', but this would preclude many of the applications which Brown wants to make, as we shall see (indeed, some of the composers concerned were, if anything, industrious to a fault).²⁷ From 'inertia', which Brown takes as a key concept for the understanding of Russian history in general, he proceeds to folksong as 'the clearest clue to the characteristics of a nation's musicality', and finds it 'a concentric, not an onward moving creation', evolving 'as a series of variations against a simple protoshape'.²⁸ Even if we could grant that Brown managed to find a single song expressing this supposed national character among the repertoires of thousands of diverse local traditions, is variation against a 'protoshape' a characteristic only of Russian folksong? Many geographically remote traditions across the globe contain songs in a narrow vocal range, rotating around a set of three or four pitches – clearly they cannot all partake of Russian inertia.

Next, inevitably, *Kamarinskaya* comes into play – 'a decorative, not an organic creation . . . static rather than dynamic'.²⁹ A number of other observations on Russian national characteristics are made, including, for some reason, Russian proficiency in chess; 'why not figure-skating?' which Russians dominate as well, we might ask. But of course, this would be difficult to trace back to the supposed Russian inertia which the examples were designed to confirm. We might have imagined that this inertia gave birth to the 'static' music of Borodin or Glazunov, but then, to our surprise, we find that Tchaikovsky's *Pathétique* is offered as the end product.³⁰ It would be hard to believe that any listener could have failed to perceive the tension and suspense of this symphony's first movement. The tension is strong enough to override both the break between the first and second subjects and the rounded form of the second subject itself: the suspense of the narrative is too powerful to be dissipated by any deviation. Only strong prejudices can force one to make a connection between this music and Russian 'inertia'; in this case, two prejudices are at work: the presumed intrinsic difference of Russian music in general from the Germanic mainstream, and the traditional bias in Western musicology against Tchaikovsky the symphonist. This bias is encapsulated in the words of Martin Cooper: '[they [Tchaikovsky's symphonies] may be fine music but thay are poor symphonies'.³¹ This view seems a little too old-fashioned to be reiterated in the twenty-first century: it stems from the tradition, in the nineteenth century, of evaluating all symphonies according to a single paradigm; namely, the Beethoven symphony.³² This paradigm may do justice to Brahms, but, even within the Austro-German symphony, it serves Bruckner and Mahler badly; since no one at present would think of judging Bruckner or Mahler by 'strict academic tests . . . [that is] the manipulation of sonata form in the appropriate movements'[33], why should Tchaikovsky still be made a victim of this outmoded approach?

Western perceptions of the Petersburg symphonies (by Borodin, Balakirev, Rimsky-Korsakov, Glazunov) were equally shaped by the application of the Beethovenian symphonic paradigm, be it wittingly or unwittingly. Yet the Five and their successors were no devout followers of Beethoven, although they wanted to buy into the prestigious tradition he represented, to emulate it and, if possible, to outshine it. Indeed, they took the most prestigious genre within German art music – the symphony – but sought, as their model, the most recent examples of that genre from the hand of a leading German composer. It was their misfortune (as far as their long-term reputation was concerned) to choose Schumann as their model symphonist, for, eminent though he indeed was, his symphonies came to be regarded as relatively marginal to his *oeuvre* and to the history of the genre at large. In this way, the marginalisation of their symphonies by Western critics was to some extent conditioned by their choice of Schumann as a model.

The clouding of Russian music history by nationalistic mythologies was not, therefore, merely a later accretion from music historiography, but began with the composers themselves. The stories they created to account for the authentic derivation of their music from the depths of the 'Russian Spirit' worked so powerfully upon their imagination that they soon appeared unable to distinguish between the facts of their compositional processes and the fictions they had so colourfully woven for a public willing to believe. It is therefore necessary to acknowledge the existence of a large gap between the history of their nationalist rhetoric and the history of their compositional practices. On the one hand, we have the myth of Russian music following the route mapped out in *Kamarinskaya*, we have Mussorgsky's stance against Germanic reasoning and Cui's over-zealous praise of Rimsky-Korsakov's 'Russian' developmental procedures. On the other hand, the two examples discussed earlier, from Balakirev and Borodin, both pivotal for the development of Russian nationalist music, certainly did not constitute a revolt against the German symphony; quite the contrary, for they reveal a profound understanding and ingenious assimilation of the Schumann model.

The striking similarities between the supposedly Russian traits of the Petersburg symphonies and the devices found in Schumann's symphonies prompt us to question the validity of this perceived Russianness. Is the repetitive character of a Rimsky-Korsakov symphony evidence of his non-Western mentality or did it stem from his strong concern about motivic-thematic coherence, a concern that he and his compatriots shared with Schumann? All too often, Western musicologists have not looked beyond the myths represented by the first option, simply because these suit their preconceptions about the exoticism of Russian music. And so the myths invented by Russian composers in the nineteenth century are perpetuated and rechanelled according to the purposes of a very different audience.

Notes and References

1. Mussorgsky's letter of 15 August 1868, as translated in Richard Taruskin, *Stravinsky and the Russian Tradition: A Biography of Works Through 'Mavra'* (Berkeley and Los Angeles, 1996), Vol. 1, p. 137.
2. From the letter to Kukol'nik of 12 November 1854, quoted in A. Orlova, *Glinka's Life in Music: A Chronicle*, trans. R. Hoops (Ann Arbor, 1988), p. 597. There was as yet no established Russian term for what we call a 'development' section, hence Glinka's parenthetical inclusion of the German and French terms, which his Russian contemporaries would have been sure to recognise.
3. In this essay I shall only discuss the issue of development, since the problems of folksong as 'mother tongue' and 'national' harmony were touched upon in my article "On *Ruslan* and Russianness", *Cambridge Opera Journal*, 9, 5 (1997), pp. 21–45.
4. See Liah Greenfeld, *Nationalism: Five Roads to Modernity* (Cambridge MA., 1992), pp. 190–274.
5. I. V. Kireyevsky, 'O kharaktere prosveshcheniya Yevropï i yego otnoshenii k prosveshcheniyu Rossii', *Moskovsky sbornik* (1852), quoted in N. Troitskaya, 'Ot yevropeiskogo romantizma k pravoslavnomu votserkovleniyu', in *Russkaya tsivilizatsiya i sobornost*, ed. Ye. Troitskiy (Moscow, 1994), p. 106.
6. I. V. Kireyevsky, *Kritika i estetika* (Moscow, 1979), pp. 147–53.
7. Richard Taruskin, 'How the Acorn Took Root', *Nineteenth-Century Music*, 6, 3 (1983).
8. Cui's letter to Rimsky-Korsakov of 27 December 1863, see N. A. Rimsky-Korsakov, *Polnoye sobranie sochineniy: Literaturnïe proizvedeniya i perepiska* (Moscow, 1955–82), Vol. 5, p. 254.
9. Rimsky-Korsakov's letter to Kruglikov of 23 February 1884, see N. A. Rimsky-Korsakov, *Polnoye sobranie sochineniy*, Vol. 8a, p. 136.
10. Most of the relevant material can be found in the Manuscript Department of the Russian National Library, Fund 410, the Archive of the St Petersburg Conservatoire and the Manuscript Department of the Russian Institute for Arts History.
11. N. A. Rimsky-Korsakov, *Letopis' moey muzikal'noy zhizni* (Moscow, 1982), p. 30.
12. The idea of a three-key exposition was brought into the workshop by Balakirev (see his letter to Rimsky-Korsakov, 24 April 1862, published in N. A. Rimsky-Korsakov, *Polnoye sobranie sochineniy*, Vol. 5, p. 18). Balakirev's model was Schumann's Third Symphony (first allegro); Schumann, in turn, borrowed the idea from Schubert.
13. Linda Correll Roesner, 'Schumann's "Parallel" Forms', *Nineteenth-Century Music*, 14, 3 (1991), pp. 265–78.
14. Charles Rosen came to similar conclusions in his *Sonata Forms* (New York and London, 1980), pp. 296–310.
15. Roesner, 'Schumann's "Parallel" Forms', pp. 272, 274, 277.
16. Gerald Abraham, *On Russian Music* (London, 1939), pp. 185–6.
17. Edward Garden, *Balakirev: A Critical Study of His Life and Music* (London, 1967), pp. 324–6.
18. Taneyev's letter to Tchaikovsky of 9 September 1882, see P. I. Tchaikovsky, and S. I. Taneyev, *Pis'ma* (Moscow, 1951), p. 85.

19 M. F. Gnesin, *Mïsli i vospominaniya o N. A. Rimskom-Korsakove* (Moscow, 1956), pp. 77–8.
20 Gerald Abraham, *Borodin: The Composer and His Music* (London, n.d.), pp. 20–1.
21 Ibid., p. 38.
22 Gerald Abraham, *Studies in Russian Music* (London, n.d.), p. 9.
23 Felix Weingartner, *The Symphony since Beethoven*, trans. M. B. Dutton (Boston, 1904), extracts reprinted in *Schumann and his World*, ed. Larry Todd (Princeton, 1994), pp. 375–84 (p. 377).
24 Abraham, *Studies in Russian Music*, p. 30.
25 Abraham, *On Russian Music*, pp. 236–40.
26 David Brown, *Tchaikovsky: A Biographical and Critical Study*, Vol. 4 (London, 1991), p. 424.
27 On the role of this concept in the construction of Russian national identity, see Marina Frolova-Walker, 'All Russian Music is So Sad: Two Constructions of the Russian Soul, Through Literature and Music', paper given at the IMS Congress (London, 1997), proceedings to be published by Oxford University Press.
28 Brown, *Tchaikovsky*, p. 422.
29 Ibid., p. 423.
30 Ibid., p. 425–7.
31 Martin Cooper, 'The Symphonies', in Gerald Abraham (ed.), *The Music of Tchaikovsky* (Port Washington, 1969), p. 24.
32 See more on this in Sanna Pederson,'On the Task of the Music Historian: The Myth of Symphony after Beethoven', *Repercussions* 2 (1993), pp. 5–30.
33 Cooper,'The Symphonies', p. 24.

6.
Horn Calls and Flattened Sevenths: Nielsen and Danish Musical Style

DANIEL GRIMLEY

The recent revival of interest in Scandinavian music from the turn of the century, following the Grieg anniversary in 1993, raises issues which are central to discussions about the nature of musicological writing. Both analytical and historical modes of music criticism have been dismantled as, amongst other things, white, male-oriented and ethnocentrically biased towards the Austro-German tradition. Within the supposedly pluralist context of such criticism, the importance and quality of much Scandinavian music should have been more broadly acknowledged, but this has not been the case. Scandinavian music has been peripheralised within the academic community on account of its 'geographical otherness', but the sense of Northern identity which is apparently so alienating within these works is poorly understood by critics working within the perceived 'mainstream' continental European repertoire.

Considering the popularity of Nielsen's music in the concert hall (there are currently over half a dozen different cycles of his symphonies available on compact disc), and his widely acknowledged importance in the history of twentieth-century music, it is remarkable that his work has received such little critical attention.[1] What is worse, the existing critical literature has so far addressed an unusually narrow range of issues. This problem has been raised by the American scholar Mina F. Miller.[2] According to Miller, the relatively undeveloped nature of Nielsen research may be accounted for by both difficulties in obtaining primary and secondary reference material, and by the formidable language barriers encountered by non-Danish speakers. She writes:

> if more recent scholars have failed, on the whole, to formulate and address new stylistic questions in their research on Nielsen, this fact is associated with major limitations in the resources available: the lack of translation of significant sources, the dearth of studies in English, the limited accessibility of relevant books and journals, and the restricted admittance to primary source materials in the Carl Nielsen Archive (Copenhagen).[3]

I do not wish to detract from the very real difficulties surrounding access to source materials mentioned by Miller. Nevertheless, I would argue that her reading circumnavigates the most important issues in Nielsen scholarship. I should suggest rather that Nielsen's music has been neglected for two more ideologically motivated reasons: first, an unwillingness to stray from canons of musicological discourse which may be chronologically, generically, geographically or even racially exclusive; second, a more specific but no less intense methodological problem arising in the analysis of turn-of-the-century works that do not conform to familiar formal patterns.

The issue of nationalism and music is a deeper problem in historical musicology as a whole. For Carl Dahlhaus, for instance, 'nationalism' can only be understood as a collection of historical ideas or 'facts':

> Nationalism, the belief in the spirit of a people as an active creative force, is an idea with a character and function which it is simplistic to identify with the phenomenon of a national style ... if applied rigorously, however, a distinction between national style as a musical fact and nationalism as a creed imposed from without is far too crude to be an accurate reflection of the historical and aesthetic reality.[4]

Dahlhaus argues that the issue of national style in music belongs largely in the domain of reception history, but that it is no less 'an aesthetic fact' for being formed at a 'secondary stage'. By historicising the concept of national style so completely, however, Dahlhaus risks losing sight of the way in which nationalism became a discourse within which composers consciously worked. Likewise, the way in which musical nationalism becomes subsumed entirely within a process of political modernism is epistemologically problematic. In *Nineteenth-Century Music*, for example, he writes:

> the urge toward abstraction was a quality which Sibelius, ostensibly a rhapsodist, took up in a deliberately modernist spirit. It is also one of the key features of the structuralist thought that took possession of music under the aegis of that process of rationalisation diagnosed by Max Weber. Thus, however slight Sibelius's connection with modern twentieth century music [!], it would be wrong to call a work like his Fourth Symphony a late-romantic relic in need of special geographical pleading to justify it aesthetically in the midst of musical modernism.[5]

Dahlhaus's argument is contentious because of his elevation of modernism as some absolute historical category. Furthermore, it is unclear why the 'special geographical pleading' for Sibelius's work should be a bad thing, unless the historical significance of a work of music (or art, for that matter) is in inverse proportion to its sense of locality. This is a problematic worldview to advance, since some music, notably nineteenth-century Austro-German symphonies, have very rarely been considered nationalist whereas other music, Scandinavian works particularly, have invariably been considered so. Dahlhaus himself noted:

> it is precisely Russian, Czech, Hungarian and Norwegian historians of music who should be particularly sensitive about the concept of a 'national school', for the very expression implies, tacitly but unmistakably, that 'national' is an alternative to 'universal' and that 'universality' was the prerogative of the 'central' musical nations. *The term 'national school' is a covert admission that the phenomenon it describes is peripheral.*[6]

That is not to deny that all 'musical nationalisms' are fictitious constructs which have little directly to do with ethnic difference in terms of wealth distribution or political ideology. As the title of Benedict Anderson's influential book *Imagined Communities* suggests, nation-states are ultimately little more than a function of political and economic entities, so that the sense of place conveyed by some musical works is inevitably the product of some kind of collective cultural imagination[7]. That should not detract us, however, from the extent to which such musical nationalisms have become an integral part of our musical culture. It is easy to turn Dahlhaus's historicism back on itself and argue that the very modernism which he elevates above national difference is itself a nationalist project.

More promising work towards what Peter Alter has called a 'functional-based typology of nationalism'[8] has been carried out by John Hutchinson.[9] Hutchinson has distinguished between *political* nationalists, who are essentially modernist in outlook and therefore seek to reject traditional 'ethnicities' in favour of a 'cosmopolitan rationalist conception of the nation that looks forward ultimately to a common humanity transcending cultural differences', and *cultural* nationalists, for whom the nation is perceived as 'a complex of individualities, each one of which has equal rights and value to the community'.[10] The most radical aspect of Hutchinson's work, and what makes it particularly relevant to the present study, is the way in which he has re-evaluated political orientation between the two 'nationalisms'. The view of cultural nationalism as an essentially conservative, retrogressive movement, as proposed by Ernest Gellner and Hans Kohn, is mistaken, according to Hutchinson, since 'this evocation of the folk on the part of intellectuals and the intelligentsia is, first, a dynamic vision of the nation as a high civilisation with a unique place in the development of humanity and, secondly, a corresponding drive to recreate this nation which, integrating the traditional and the modern in a higher level, will again rise to the forefront of world progress'.[11] Not only does Hutchinson's model describe the pan-Scandinavian movement of the mid-nineteenth century exactly, but more importantly it challenges the notion that the Scandinavian nations were somehow 'backward', or 'behind' their European counterparts. 'Cultural nationalism', with which I align the Danish nationalist movement of which Nielsen's music was a part, 'disavows the passive isolationism of the traditionalists and presents the nation as a progressive culture in active contact with other societies'.[12] Hutchinson goes some way towards providing a theoretical context for a new reading of Nielsen's music where, contrary to critics such as Adorno,[13] the expression of a sense of place is no longer indicative of aesthetic inadequacy.

Considering the lack of critical interest in Scandinavian music, it is not surprising that the nineteenth-century Danish poet Jens Peter Jacobsen (1847–85) is best known to musicologists as the author of the cycle of poems that served as the text for Arnold Schoenberg's massive tone-poem *Gurrelieder* (1901).[14] Relatively neglected during his lifetime, Jacobsen's work largely came to prominence through the advocacy of Georg Brandes, the most influential literary critic in Denmark in the 1870s and 1880s. Jacobsen's poetry was closely associated with the young authors of what Brandes called 'the modern breakthrough', notably Sophus Claussen (1865–1931, Nielsen's exact contemporary) and Johannes V. Jensen (1873–1950). These poets were associated with Nielsen during his lifetime, and together they signal a shift away from the national romanticism of mid nineteenth-century Danish literature to a more localised social realism.[15] Jacobsen was also a significant poet for Nielsen. Two early song cycles, FS 12 and 14 (1890–92),[16] are settings of Jacobsen's poetry, though on a much more modest scale than Schoenberg's monumental conception.

The first four lines of *Har Dagen sanket al sin Sorg* articulate a regular iambic heptameter that gradually breaks down as the poem progresses. The prevailing 6/8 duple metre of Nielsen's setting, the last of his FS 12 collection, is a response to this initial regularity: the opening half-bar anacrusis suggests the weak–strong stress of the iambic metre of the poem. Nielsen parallels the tension between stable and unstable verse-forms that underpins Jacobsen's poem using means other than metre. Nielsen's setting is essentially through-composed, but the return of the opening material from bar 10 onwards in bars 31–36 and the strong harmonic contrast of the middle section (largely in A flat major, as against the C minor of the opening and close) suggest a tripartite form. In her persuasive discussion of the early song collections, Anne-Marie Reynolds finds an even more direct link between poem and music.[17] For her, the terseness of the formal return in bar 33 creates a sense of ambiguity, which conveys 'both a sense of continual movement (through contrast) and stasis (through recurrence) appropriate to the image of spirits gliding across the heavens, as well as to the aimless tirelessness of their activity'.[18] The generic history of ternary forms in the nineteenth century, however, suggests that the recapitulation of the opening material is often reconfigured so as to disguise the moment of return: the use of extensive *fiorature* in the A' sections of many of Chopin's nocturnes is a classic example of this procedure, but the same is also true of the terseness of the second movement of Sibelius's Fourth Symphony. Instead, the day-night antithesis of Jacobsen's poem suggests other dualities, such as the changing of the seasons. Indeed, the astral guardians of his poem might not only be the stars of the winter night sky but also the *aurora borealis*, a phenomenon particularly associated with Northern latitudes.

The final bars (cf. Example 6.1) are the most striking part of the whole song, since Nielsen reduces the music to its fundamental harmonic components.

The voice finishes in bar 43 without cadencing on a tonic chord, and the piano postlude dies away in a series of echoes similar in effect to the *diminuendo* of the opening two bars of the song. Though the piano reiterates the early c^1-eb^1-g^1 arpeggio three times, the music only settles on C minor in the very final bar. In the meantime, the piano oscillates between Eb and Ab^7, pivoting on an eb^1-g^1 dyad in a compression of the song's principal

Example 6.1. *Har Dagen sanket al sin Sorg* FS 12/6 (closing bars)

harmonic regions. In effect, Nielsen reassembles cadential syntax in a diatonic haze, the final tonic conclusion reached without local preparation and with the plagal motion Eb^{4-3} repeated until it ceases to sound like a dissonance.

Such conclusions are a characteristic feature of Nielsen's music. Many of his slow movements, from *Har Dagen sanket al sin Sorg* onwards, conclude with a similar kind of horn fifth rich sonority in spite of the absence of structural perfect cadences. In one sense, these chords can be heard as vastly expanded plagal cadences, the heavy subdominant orientation of such codas often the result of an insistent flatwards drift throughout the movement as a whole. In another sense, these chords represent a kind of *elementalisation*, achieving closure by compressing the harmonic argument of the movement into a single diatonically complex chord or progression. By the term 'elementalisation', I understand a process akin to what Schoenberg called 'liquidation'.[19] Like liquidation, elementalisation is explicitly goal-directed, but, whereas liquidation is aimed at the elimination of musical detail 'until only uncharacteristic [features] remain', the purpose of elementalisation is the reduction of music to its simplest constituent parts, whether harmonic, motivic, melodic, textural or rhythmic. Elementalisation can operate at any structural level, but it is at its most powerful when used in conjunction with large-scale parameters such as voice leading or motivic *Fortspinnung*. As a technique, elementalisation is a common procedure in late nineteenth-century music, where it usually becomes associated, in the Romantic imagination, with the uncovering of some deep or spiritual truth.[20] Often, the process becomes foregrounded in a single epiphanal moment that becomes the focus of the whole work. Elementalisation is a particularly recurrent feature of many of Nielsen's works which are often concerned with music in its purest and most uncorrupted state.

Genrebillede, the first song of the FS 14 set, begins with a similar horn-rich sonority as the coda of *Har Dagen sanket al sin Sorg*. In the later song, this is an archetypal gesture: the slowly oscillating horn calls of the opening bring to mind numerous similar gestures in Romantic Lieder, from *An die ferne Geliebte* and 'Der Lindenbaum' (*Winterreise*) onwards.[21] This is a satisfying response to Jacobsen's text, the pale and stylised imagery of which is conveyed by the laconic title 'Genrebillede' (Genre Picture). Jacobsen's poem is commonly read as an ironic commentary on the creative process. As the page struggles with his love poem, the syntax of Jacobsen's verse begins to fragment and break apart, to an even more marked degree than in *Har Dagen sanket al sin Sorg*. The central four lines of *Genrebillede* can hardly be read as a regular quatrain, but the final four lines seem to regain some sense of metrical order just as the page discards poetry for the more immediate medium of his horn.

The importance of the horn call goes far beyond that of being an early-Romantic symbol of absence or loss, since the whole song is saturated in horn sounds. Horn fifths are commonly understood as both an opening and a closing gesture. In fact, this semantic ambiguity is part of their appeal in Classical and early-Romantic works which play on notions of closure and formal circularity.[22] Nielsen's song begins in a state of almost total inactivity: the slow oscillation from I to V defines the harmonic rhythm for much of the rest of the song. But the opening is also a cadential gesture that is frustrated in the second bar: the rhythmic diminution of the neighbour-note motion f^1-eb^1 (3 – 2) (cf. Example 6.2), which implies a I – V progression, is underpinned by a static tonic pedal. The triadic entry of the voice is similar to *Har Dagen sanket al sin Sorg* again, and the emphasis on 6 (bb^1) in bar 4 creates a complex compound-fifth texture based on db-ab, ab-eb and eb-bb.

Despite the near-motionlessness of the opening bar, the neighbour-note oscillation is a pregnant motivic cell. Combined with the swinging fourths and fifths of the opening horn call it produces the 1 – 3 – 5 – 6 contour of the voice's initial entry. Furthermore, the minim neighbour-note motion creates the bass descent from Db to Cb (8 – b7) in bar 5. Flattened sevenths in Nielsen's music are usually treated in two ways: firstly as an ethnic model flavouring from Danish folk music, and secondly as a result of modal mixture. The first interpretation stresses Nielsen's supposed relationship with a collective Danish musical consciousness, planting Nielsen's music firmly in the Danish soil. The second takes the opposite view, since modal

Example 6.2. *Genrebillede* FS 14/1 (opening)

mixture is customarily discussed as one of the ways in which composers sought to move away from conventional diatonic harmony in the second half of the nineteenth century. Nielsen's music therefore becomes merely a case study in a much larger historical narrative. It is towards this 'emancipation of the dissonance' view that Reynolds is inclined:

> Surely Nielsen, along with his contemporaries, drew on mixture in his symphonic compositions simply as a means of broadening the notion of 'key' to include chords derived from both major and minor forms of the scale.[23]

In fact, flattened sevenths function in two entirely different ways to those outlined above. First, they can be heard as a kind of baroque 'hyperconsonance',[24] an accented appoggiatura or consonant skip to the fifth degree of a structural tonic chord. Second, they operate in a purely voice-leading context, as in the example from *Har Dagen sanket al sin Sorg* examined above. The latter is the case here in *Genrebillede*. The C♭ in bars 5 and 6 functions as an appoggiatura to B♭, strongly reinforcing the modulation from I to V/E flat minor. Indeed, the harmonic progress of the song is strikingly similar to *Har Dagen sanket al sin Sorg*: by treating a barely-established tonic as an applied dominant, Nielsen quickly pivots the music towards the subdominant, initiating a large-scale tonal ascent towards the structural dominant that is only attained at the climax of the song. The subsequent emphasis on the flattened seventh (D♭) of E flat minor in bar 10 of *Genrebillede* is a pun on the stability of 1, since, in spite of the cadential horn fifths, the tonic note in bars 1–2 is supported by a harmony that does not receive tonicisation.

Like the harmonic compression in the closing bars of *Har Dagen sanket al sin Sorg*, the way in which the whole design of *Genrebillede* rests on the image of a horn call is a kind of elementalisation. In both songs, the horn functions as a symbol of an archetypalised Danish musical style. The appropriation of this most Germanic of musical images is both an assimilationist and isolationist gesture. In *Genrebillede* in particular, the horn call is associated with the notions of thematic and harmonic unity, balance and structural closure that are the tenets of the German musical canon. Similarly, the subject matter and versification of Jacobsen's poems recalls Heine and Eichendorff. Nielsen's songs might therefore be placed beside mid nineteenth-century song collections such as Schumann's *Liederkreis*. A more salient comparison, however, is with Mahler, whose *Wunderhorn Lieder* were written at approximately the same time as Nielsen's Jacobsen songs. Horn calls in Mahler's music invariably either stand for some kind of retreat from the contemporary world into a fairy-tale Romantic Arcadia (in the cow bells episode in the first movement of the Sixth Symphony, for example) or announce the appearance of a stylised heroic figure (the opening of *Das Lied von der Erde,* or the first movement of the Third

Symphony). In Nielsen's music, horn calls are associated rather with the uncovering of a more 'real', arcane Truth. They are not so much Arcadian as *archaic*. The climaxes of *Har Dagen sanket al sin Sorg* and *Genrebillede* are intended to represent the uncovering of a pure musical state that is distinctly Nordic in tone and character.

Nielsen's preoccupation with the elemental constituents of his musical language invites a comparison with the work of a contemporary Danish painter, Vilhelm Hammershøi (1864–1916).[25] Much of Hammershøi's work, which consists largely of studies of quiet or unpeopled interiors, bleak open landscapes and views of various historical sites in Copenhagen and other locations on Zealand, is characterised by an extreme tendency towards a geometrical division of space that verges on the minimalist. Though his painting remains unquestionably representational, Hammershøi's overriding concern for formal arrangement in pictures such as *Open Doors (White Doors)* ['Aabne døre (Hvide døre)'] of 1905, for example, seems almost abstract.[26]

Landscapes are an underrated part of Hammershøi's output. Though his pictures invite comparison with the work of Danish 'Golden Age' painters such as Christen Købke (1810–1848) Hammershøi's landscapes are remarkable for their emptiness. Objects which normally provide some sense of orientation, such as roads, trees, buildings or coastlines, are either omitted or reduced to mere geometric inflections of the whole. The low horizons, rolling hills and the interplay of land and water which characterise Danish scenery are depicted with a vastly reduced range of colours – various shades of greys, greens and luminous marine-blues. Similarly, Hammershøi's choice of viewpoint can seem incidental. There are no precipitous cliffs or rocky outcrops, which were the characteristic features of nineteenth-century Romantic landscapes. Equally, Hammershøi resists the domestication of the landscape that often marks the work of Golden Age Danish painters. In mood, Hammershøi is closest to Peder Severin Krøyer's[27] picture, *Summer evening on the South Beach at Skagen* ('Sommeraften på Skagens sønderstrand', 1893), a painting which has since become the archetypal *fin-de-siècle* Scandinavian image. Both Krøyer's and Hammershøi's landscapes are suffused with a glowing blueness, suggesting the long 'blue' twilight of the Scandinavian summer. This blue light is the subject of Krøyer's painting, but the two figures in the foreground provide a sense of focus, leading the eye onwards along the curving line of the shore into the blue distance beyond. Though his evocation of an end-of-the-century twilight is undeniably powerful, Krøyer's figures humanise the landscape so that the final impression is of containment rather than expansiveness. In contrast, because Hammershøi's landscapes are unpeopled, his paintings evoke an altogether more elemental sense of nature.

In *Landscape, Lejre* (1905), (cf. Figure 6.1) Hammershøi creates a sense of temporal and visual distance that is entirely different in mood to Krøyer's

Horn Calls and Flattened Sevenths 133

Figure 6.1. *Landscape, Lejre*

more populous and immediate landscape vision. In both of Hammershøi's paintings, the sense of perspective is entirely flat, almost decorative save for the lack of detail in the foreground. Attention is focused on the middleground of the painting, but the low horizon prevents the eye from forming any sense of scale. Consequently, the feeling of space and unenclosure is potentially enormous. *Landscape, Lejre* is organised by the asymmetrically placed clumps of trees on the hilltops in the middle distance, and the dreamlike, apparently unordered, progression of the clouds which occupies over half the painting. Though the painting lacks visible human presence, the gentle curve of the hills resembles burial mounds, suggesting a more distant Golden Age in Danish history. Likewise, the virtual absence of any man-made feature in either work presents an image of an untouched, idealised past.

Hammershøi reduces landscape to its barest and most essential constituents. The depiction of burial mounds is significant, however, since ancient archaeological sites have a privileged place in the Danish historical imagination. Excavations in the early nineteenth century, at a time when Danish scholars were also involved in the editing of the medieval Icelandic sagas of Snorri Sturlason, appeared to provide evidence of a rich cultural heritage. The extensive collection of lurs (large Bronze Age Horns) in the Royal Museum, Copenhagen, were likewise believed to point to a pre-Christian musical practice. Hammershøi's painting therefore has two points of chronological reference: one evoking an idealised idyllic past, and the other the Biedermeier 'Golden Age' of Danish Art at the beginning of the nineteenth century, when popular pan-Scandinavian feelings were at their most intense and richly expressed. It is tempting to draw a direct analogy between Hammershøi's imagined Danish identity and the semiotic significance of the horn call (at its most literal, as *lur*) in Nielsen's music as a symbol of Danish musical style. Nielsen's music is saturated in horn calls to an exceptional degree. Works such as *Genrebillede* evoke the sound of the *lur* explicitly and Nielsen's incidental music for the play *Hagbarth og Signe* by the Danish Romantic poet Adam Oehlenschläger[28] includes a quartet of Lurs. The real significance of the comparison, however, is that both Hammershøi's and Nielsen's work can be seen to enact a process of elementalisation, in which Danish identity is explicitly associated with a state of extreme simplicity and sparseness.[29] Far from consisting simply of a few neutral landscape metaphors, Hammershøi's paintings and the pastoral topics in Nielsen's music are important points of focus.

Nielsen's attachment to the Danish soil is well documented, not least by Nielsen himself in his biography *Min fynske barndom* and the panegyric entitled 'The Song of Fünen' at the end of his collection of essays, *Living Music*. With only the slightest hint of irony, Nielsen could write that 'even the trees dream and talk in their sleep with a Fynsk lilt'.[30] As Jørgen I. Jensen has observed, however, the apparently eternal image of Nielsen as farm lad or country boy is merely the product of a long-running Danish myth that stretches from the linguist Rasmus Rask and Hans Christian Andersen to Nielsen and beyond.[31] For Nielsen, Funen constitutes some kind of concentrated, purified Danishness, precisely because of its distance from the cosmopolitan (for which, read 'continental') milieu of the capital city on Zealand. Furthermore, his permanent residence in Copenhagen and travels throughout Europe later in life appear to have inspired Nielsen with a heightened awareness of his own local identity. When writing his biography at the end of his life, he embodied his imagined Funen-Danish identity in a description of his brother:

> Whenever I think of Sophus . . . it is with some landscape as a background, something very Danish or, rather, intensely Funen: his placid blue eyes, neither sad nor merry, and his every movement, rather slow, unassuming and tentative, had a kind of awkward grace. I think I can say that there had never lived a better, purer, and more self-contained person than him.[32]

Nielsen's pronounced regionalism is, of course, a familiar nationalist strategy, and one which is far from being exclusively Danish. In effect, the emphasis on a highly localised, even parochial, childhood background has become a response to a sense of marginalisation from a perceived cultural mainstream, which may be located in Copenhagen or, equally, abroad. In other words, the evocation of childhood innocence inevitably invokes notions of an aesthetic purity which is subsequently corrupted by engagement with the wider (adult) world. At the same time, Nielsen is actively engaged with the construction of a collective Danish identity in his music, just as Hammershøi's choice of artistic subject matter amounts to a commentary on Danish notions of style, form and landscape.

It is commonly agreed that the second movement of the Third Symphony (1911) is the most literal evocation of the Danish landscape outside Nielsen's programmatic works, and it forms an interesting comparison with the two songs discussed above, where questions of Danish style are less evident. In a letter Nielsen himself talked of 'a broad, landscape Andante which is quite different from any of my other works'.[33] A possible explanation for the exceptional nature of the movement has been provided by David Fanning, who notes that Nielsen originally sketched a text for the vocal parts in the second half of the movement: 'All thoughts disappear. Ah! All thoughts disappear[,] I lie beneath the sky'.[34] It might be suggested that, in its lack of dark (minor-key) colouring, the symphony is a decidedly un-Scandinavian work, especially when compared with the bleak tone of Sibelius's Fourth Symphony, composed at exactly the same time as the *Espansiva*. Arguably, however, the glowing, almost over-bright, major-key quality of Nielsen's Third is the product of a particularly extreme Scandinavian diatonicism that stretches back to Franz Berwald's *Sinfonie Singulière*

(1845) and pieces such as Grieg's *Klokkeklang* Op.54/6. The closing bars of Sibelius's Second Symphony (1901–2), for example, seem especially close to much of the *Espansiva*, and it was the apparent 'healthiness' of the finale that attracted Max Brod to Nielsen's work. In a letter to the composer from Prague, Brod wrote:

> I can only say that this work, especially the last movement (which I have already played four times with my brother), almost elevates and fortifies me *morally*. It seems to me that you are beginning to sing about a happy, work-rich [arbeitsreichen] and yet arcadian-naïve future for Mankind. That certainly awakens hope! One believes in that humanity! – That is how it has moved me, and I am now looking for a way of expressing it openly.[35]

If the explosive opening of the *Espansiva* sounds like the musical embodiment of the 'modern breakthrough' for which Georg Brandes had made an impassioned call in Danish art and literature thirty years before, however, the following Andante pastorale evokes a intense stillness that more closely resembles Nielsen's Jacobsen songs.

Heard in the context of the symphony as a whole, the second movement functions as the arcane or 'timeless' antithesis to the aggressive modernism of the first. Whereas the dynamic tonal movement of the Allegro is chaotic and virtually unstoppable, the Andante unwinds a series of gentle melismata underpinned by apparently immovable pedal points. Despite their seemingly irreconcilable differences, however, the first and second movements are inextricably linked in terms of thematic substance. So much so, in fact, that there is some justification for regarding the second movement as a mirror image of the first, rather than as its opposite. The triadic opening figure of the Allegro (cf. Example 6.3a), for instance, becomes massively slowed-down to form the string melody of the prelude of the Andante; the chromatic b# which inflects the theme in the Allegro is omitted in the Andante, in favour of a pure, white-note C major (cf. example 6.3b).

Examples 6.3a and 6.3b. *Sinfonia Espansiva* (first and second movement correspondences).

Similarly, the various oscillating layers of the second subject group of the first movement (cf. Example 6.4a) produce the complex multi-layered ostinato texture of the second half of the slow movement (cf. Example 6.4b). The opening horn call of the Andante (cf. Example 6.4c) is the product of just such oscillating patterns in the Allegro.

Example 6.4a, 6.4b and 6.4c. *Sinfonia Espansiva* (first and second movement correspondences).

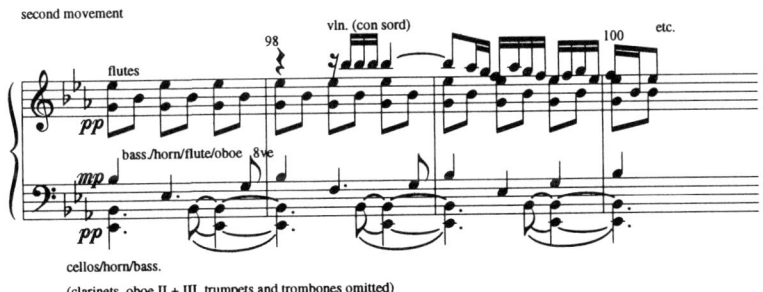

Equally notable is the way in which the canon of the introductory link in bars 84–97 of the Andante (cf. Example 6.5a) is an augmentation of the dramatic syncopated passages at bars 86–99 in the Allegro (cf. Example 6.5b).

Example 6.5a and 6.5b. *Sinfonia Espansiva* (second and first movement correspondences).

The obsessive acciaccaturas in bars 694–698 of the Allegro, which first emerge 'organically' in bar 191 and become increasingly prominent as the Allegro progresses, do not feature in the second movement, however. Instead, they become the predominant feature of the finale, notably at the apotheosis of the chorale theme in bars 174–190. It is possible to trace other important parallels between movements in the *Espansiva*. As has often been noted, for example,[36] the third movement works towards a D major passage (bar 173ff) that anticipates the opening tonality and thematic profile of the finale. Less commonly observed, however, is the way in which the third movement transforms the oscillating ostinatos of the first movement into what Fanning has termed a 'warning signal'.[37] Similarly, the long B flat major passage after the central climax of the fourth movement (bars 226–280) is a return to the subdued dynamic level, the dense multi-layered textures and flat-side tonality of the Andante.

One of the most striking features of the first movement is the way in which the music can appear to become tied in minimalist knots: the insistent, albeit accelerating, repetition of the opening As is the catalyst for a series of places where the music momentarily appears unable to break out of its circular pattern. This tendency reaches its climax in the *tranquillo* section in bars 656–683, where Nielsen accumulates three different oscillating layers out of the accompanimental figuration of the second subject group: Nielsen reduces the music to a series of elemental rhythmic patterns. The second movement could be heard as an extended development of this proto-minimalistic technique. The whole of the second half of the movement gets stuck, as it were, on an E flat major chord, so that the focus of musical attention is upon the interaction between the various different oscillating strands in the orchestra, the return of the opening string theme within the texture, and the distant entry of the voices, which weave an improvisatory melodic line in counterpoint with the first and second violins. What makes such passages Danish in both movements is that they represent another kind of elementalisation. The sudden emphasis on rhythm and the brief cessation of harmonic motion produce a stylised, archaic effect so that, as in *Har Dagen sanket al sin Sorg* and *Genrebillede*, Nielsen returns to the most basic components of his musical language.

Ultimately, Danish musical style in Nielsen's work, like all national styles, is a dialectical concept based as much on notions of difference as of collectivity. The meanings of symbols such as horn calls and flattened sevenths are associative rather than intrinsic. From an analytical and critical point of view, however, if we are to move beyond understanding nationalism in purely historical terms, we must be prepared to treat it as an aspect of musical signification. Only then might we begin to appreciate the 'northerness' in Nielsen's music which has so far proved so telling but elusive.

Notes and References

1   One might hope that the publication of Jack Lawson's Nielsen biography (London, 1997) and David Fanning's analysis of the Fifth Symphony (Cambridge, 1997) might encourage more academic interest in Nielsen's music.
2   Miller produced the first modern critical edition of Nielson's music, a volume of the complete piano works (Copenhagen, 1982). An official Nielson editon based in the Royal Library, Copenhagen, is now well advanced.
3   Mina Miller, *Carl Nielsen: A Guide to Research* (New York, 1987), p. xiv.

4   Carl Dahlhaus, 'Nationalism and Music', in *Between Romanticism and Modernism: Four Studies in the Music of the late Nineteenth Century*, trans. Mary Whittall (Berkeley, 1980), p. 85.
5   Dahlhaus, *Nineteenth Century Music*, trans. J. Bradford Robinson (Berkeley, 1989), p. 368.
6   Dahlhaus, 'Nationalism and Music', p. 89 (my italics).
7   Benedict Anderson, *Imagined Communities: Reflections on the Origin and Spread of Nationalism*, rev. edn. (London, 1991).
8   Peter Alter, *Nationalism* (London, 1989), p. 28; originally published in German as *Nationalismus* (Frankfurt, 1985).
9   J. Hutchinson, *Modern Nationalism* (London, 1994).
10 Ibid., p. 128.
11 Ibid., p. 128.
12 Ibid., p. 131.
13 Adorno's 'Glosse über Sibelius' (from the *Impromptus*, published in the *Gesammelte Schriften*, 17, pp. 247–52) offers a famously vituperative response to what might be called the national-landscape tradition in early twentieth-century music.
14 Jacobsen's work enjoyed particular vogue in Germany in the early years of the twentieth century. Zemlinsky also set some poems by Jacobsen, and Rainer Maria Rilke intended to write a monograph on Jacobsen.
15 See Jørgen I. Jensen, *Carl Nielsen: Danskeren* (Copenhagen, 1991) (in Danish), and 'Carl Nielsen: Artistic Milieu and Tradition', in *The Nielsen Companion*, ed. Mina Miller (London, 1994), pp. 58–77, for a detailed discussion of the relationship between Nielsen and Danish symbolism. Jensen shows, for instance, how Nielsen became associated with the circle involved in the publication of the symbolist periodical *Taarnet* in 1893–4 and suggests that powerful comparisons can be drawn between Claussen's poetry and many of Nielsen's large-scale works, such as the *Hymnus Amoris* and the Fourth Symphony.
16 FS numbers refer to the catalogue of Nielsen's works originally compiled by Dan Fog and Torben Schousboe. For an up-to-date and comprehensive listing, see the excellent CD-ROM, Carl Nielsen: Mennesket og Musikken ed. Knud Ketting (Copenhagen: AM Multimedia, 1998).
17 Anne-Marie Reynolds, 'The Early Song Collections: Carl Nielsen Finds his Voice', in *The Nielsen Companion*, pp. 399–453.
18 Ibid., p. 408.
19 '*Liquidation* consists in gradually eliminating characteristic features, until only uncharacteristic ones remain, which no longer demand a continuation. Often only residues remain, which have little in common with the basic motive.' (Arnold Schoenberg, *Fundamentals of Musical Composition* ed. Gerald Strang and Leonard Stein [London, 1967], p. 59 and *passim*.).
20 Examples include most of Sibelius's symphonies (including *Kullervo*), Mahler's First and Second Symphonies (though the Fifth and Seventh, which work towards similarly elemental conclusions, are more problematic), Elgar's Second Symphony and even Stravinsky's *Symphony of Psalms*.
21 See Charles Rosen's *The Romantic Generation* (London, 1996), pp. 116–24, for a discussion of the semiotics of the horn call in early Romantic songs.
22 This is the premise of the first movements of Haydn's Symphony No. 67 in F and Beethoven's Sonata Op.81a *Les Adieux*, for example.
23 Reynolds, 'The Early Song Collections: Carl Nielsen Finds his Voice', p. 425.
24 I use the term 'hyper-consonance' to refer to notes which lie strictly outside the diatonic collection but which serve to highlight the diatonic effect and, in so doing, cease to be heard as dissonant.
25 Nielsen may have known Hammershøi through their mutual acquaintance, the

painter Jens Ferdinand Willumsen (1863–1958). Nielsen stayed with Willumsen in Paris from February to April, 1891; Hammershøi was in Paris until March, but there is no evidence that the two Danes met on that occasion. Hammershøi is mentioned only once in Nielsen's published correspondence; in a letter dated 18 February 1916, Anne Marie Carl Nielsen wrote to her husband that 'Hammershøi was buried today – it was melancholy and his sweet little wife was inconsolable. Fini (Henriques) played in church and it was very moving.' ('Idag blev Hammershøj [sic] begravet – det var melankolsk og hans lille søde gode Kone var utrøstelig. Fini spillede i Kirken og det var stemningsfuldt.') Quoted in Nielsen, *Dagboger og Brevveksling med Anne-Marie Carl-Nielsen*, ed. Irmelin Eggert-Møller and Torben Schousboe, (Copenhagen, 1983) (2 Vols.), p. 405. Unless stated otherwise, all translations are mine.

26 See *L'universe poétique de Vilhelm Hammershøi, 1864–1916* (Paris) the catalogue of the first major Hammershøi retrospective outside Denmark held at the musée d'Orsay, 17 November 1997–1 March 1998, for a comprehensive survey of his work.

27 The Norwegian painter Peder Severin Krøyer (1851–1909) was Hammershøi's teacher and the founder of the Frie Studieskoler in Copenhagen in 1882.

28 Oehlenschläger is a pivotal figure in early Scandinavian Romanticism. His grand tour of Europe brought him into contact with many of the leading intellectuals of the early-nineteenth century; he met Henrik Steffens in Halle, Goethe in Weimar and Tieck in Dresden. The neo-classical tragedies of Schiller were the model for his own heroic dramas, *Axel og Valborg* and *Baldur hin Gode*, based on figures from Norse mythology, but much of his work also betrays the influence of Walter Scott.

29 Nielsen's music for *Hagbarth og Signe* has been recorded by the Odense Symphony Orhcestra under Tamás Vetö (Kontrapunkt CD-32188, 1994), which gives an excellent idea of the sound of the lurs.

30 Nielsen, *Levende Musik* (Copenhagen, 1925), published in English as *Living Music*, trans. Reginald Spink (London, 1953), p. 72.

31 See Jensen, *Carl Nielsen: Danskeren*.

32 Nielsen, *Min fynske Barndom* (Copenhagen, 1927), published in English as *My Childhood on Funen*, trans. Reginald Spink (London, 1953), p. 47.

33 'en bred landskabelig Andante, som er noget forskjellig fra min tidligere Arbejde'; letter dated 7 October 1910, quoted in Nielsen, *Breve*, ed. Torben Meyer and Irmelin Eggert-Møller (Copenhagen, 1954), p. 111 (in Danish).

34 ('Alle Tanker svundne. Ah – ! Jeg ligger under Himlen.') 'Nielsen' in *A Guide to the Symphony* ed. Robert Layton (London, 1995), p. 358. There is a photograph of the relevant pages of the manuscript reproduced in Birgit Bjørnum and Klaus Møllerhøi (eds.), *Carl Nielsens Samling: Katalog over komponistens musikhåndskrifter i Det kongelige Bibliotek* (Copenhagen, 1992), p. 286 (plate vii). See also the editorial commentary by Niels Bo Faltmann in the new critical edition of the Third Symphony (Copenhagen, 1999), xiii.

35 'Ich kann Ihnen nur sagen, dass mich dieses Werk, namentlich der letzte Satz (den ich mit meinem Bruder schon 4 mal gespielt habe), förmlich moralisch erhoben und befestigt hat. Sie scheinen mir da ein Lied anzustimmen von einer glücklichen, arbeitsreichen und doch arkadisch-unschuldigen Zukunft der Menschheit. Da erwacht wieder die Hoffnung! Man glaubt an das Menschengeschlecht! – So ist es mir ergangen und ich suche jetzt eine würdige Form, um dieses öffentlich zu sagen.' Letter dated 17 May 1913, quoted in Karl Claussen, 'Max Brods breve til Carl Nielsen', *Oplevelser og Studier omkring Carl Nielsen* (Tønder, 1966), p. 26.

36 See Simpson, *Carl Nielsen: Symphonist*, p. 70, and, more explicitly, Fanning, *Nielsen: Fifth Symphony*, p. 358.

37 Fanning, *Nielsen: Fifth Symphony*, p. 21.

7.
Following Grieg: David Monrad Johansen's Musical Style in the Early Twenties, and His Concept of a National Music

STÅLE KLEIBERG

It is often said that some of Grieg's works tend towards the kind of extended tonality which was developed in the first decades of our century. *Slåtter* Op.72 is of course the most notable example of this. What we see here is not only the emergence of a new style, but a new harmonic and tonal idiom. It is quite easy to look upon this work as a precursor of Bartók's harsh and dissonant style from around 1910. However, it is difficult to imagine that Bartók's so-called *barbarism* would have emerged without the new harmonic and tonal processes which form the basis of Debussy's musical style. It was Debussy, after all, who really opened the door to a new tonal landscape. He concentrated on a few corners of this landscape while Stravinsky and Bartók explored others. Yet, although the soundworld and aesthetic orientation of their music are very different, the structural foundations have much in common, founded in a similar approach to extended tonality.

Grieg's *Slåtter* Op.72 is, then, an important antecedent of this kind of extended tonality, functioning at the level of the structural foundation of the music. But this piece is something of a special case within Grieg's output. In discussing other Grieg works we tend to focus on *impressionistic* features, such as the technique of creating static harmonic fields and reducing the directional forces of harmony in other ways, and in so doing, we are really discussing the nascent stages of a new style and not a new structural foundation. These elements of style are thus viewed as an extension of a more traditionally functioning tonal structure. The so-called 'impressionistic' elements of style in Grieg's music are best regarded, then, as characteristic features of Grieg's personal style – a matter of surface detail rather than structure.

If, in many 'transitional works', we look at the development from a tonality based on functional harmony towards an extended and freer tonality, it may be difficult to decide if we are dealing with surface structures or with components of a new structural basis. That it gives meaning to distinguish between the surface and structural basis should at least be uncontroversial. An obvious example of this is found in the violin cadenza at the end of the third movement in Mozart's *Ein musikalischer Spaß*. When, right in the middle of the clearest C major, Mozart interweaves a whole-tone scale, we are not witnessing a new structural principle but a break with a clearly defined structural basis. Here, the intended comical effect is achieved (cf. Example 7.1).

Example 7.1. Mozart's *Ein musikalischer Spaß*, end of the third movement.

This comical effect is certainly not found in the 'transitional works' from the beginning of our century, as here the surface structures are integrated in the style. They threaten the structural basis, but have not undermined it, nor replaced it.

Slåtter aside, it is principally in the generation of composers after Grieg that Norwegian music comes to terms with an extended tonality which functions at deeper structural levels. I will concentrate on one of these composers, namely David Monrad Johansen. The connections to Grieg are clear. Indeed his admiration of Grieg was the principal impetus for Monrad Johansen as a composer. This admiration also resulted in a major Grieg biography which he published in 1934. However, it was his encounter with French music which gave real vitality to his creative powers. In 1919 he received a grant which enabled him to go to Paris and what he encountered there was of crucial significance to him as a composer.

French contemporary music was first introduced to Monrad Johansen by Alf Hurum, a legendary figure in Norwegian music history who left Norway for Hawaii, where, among other things, he established the Honolulu Symphony Orchestra! It was Hurum who put Monrad Johansen to work studying Debussy's music, and the piano suite *Nordlandsbilleder* (Pictures of Nordland), Op.5, composed at the end of 1918 and the beginning of 1919, is the first work where we can clearly see the fruits of these studies. But which Debussy works did Monrad Johansen study? It is obviously the late Debussy, the Debussy we meet in the piano preludes, and even in the *Etudes*. Thus it was not only the general atmosphere of Debussy's music which fascinated Monrad Johansen. On the contrary, we see in *Nordlandsbilleder* and the other works from around 1920 that he concerned himself with the structural principles underlying Debussy's qualitatively new kind of tonal language. In this way he was very much a figure of his own time, and was not simply trying to add spice to outmoded procedures.

The lesson to be learned from studying the *Etudes* is that only the imagination sets limits for the development of the constructive principles in music. If we want to let the interval of the fourth comprise the central structural element of an entire movement, we can devise constructive principles which make this possible; likewise if we want to foreground sonorities in a complementary relationship. It was a material revolution – a focusing on new horizons just waiting to be explored – that Debussy launched in his later works. His last piano work, *Etudes,* presents us with much more than pianistic studies. The basis of each of the twelve pieces is a simple musical structure. This structural element is thematised, so to speak. It becomes the central element giving form to an entire piece. We might say that each piece thus explores one musical element, and in this way the *Etudes* are studies in compositional technique and musical structure as much as in pianistic technique. These are the concerns – essentially structural – that Monrad Johansen found so stimulating, as an analysis of his *Nordlandsbilleder* will reveal.

Nordlandsbilleder

The piano suite *Nordlandsbilleder* was published in 1919, four years after Debussy's *Etudes*. His immensely interesting sketchbook from these years tells us that Monrad Johansen started this piece in 1918. We will return to this sketchbook later, but let us first analyse the work in its final version.

The whole-tone scale is a basic structure in this work, and it is not used as a surface Debussyan phenomenon but as a part of the raw material itself. Of course, music is not created out of pure raw material. The structures in their raw forms must be organised according to structural *principles*. The principle adopted by Monrad Johansen was to organise his whole-tone material predominantly on what we can call the *juxtaposition of complementary sonorities deduced from the same mode.*

I will illustrate this with a closer analysis of the second piece in the suite, *Den lille Stengud* (The Little Stone God). In the introductory bars of this piece it is obvious that Monrad Johansen has consciously moved away from the interval of the third as the basis for harmonic structures. Rather he uses the interval of the second, and both the construction of the chords and the nature of their progression are drawn from one of the two possible whole-tone scales. I will call this transposition whole-tone scale no. 1, and the other possible transposition (i.e. the transposition from C sharp) whole-tone scale no. 2.

So far we have been talking about a rather primitive principle. It becomes more interesting when Johansen juxtaposes sonorities which are derived from one whole-tone scale with sonorities which are derived from the other (cf. Example 7.2).

Example 7.2. *Den lille Stengud*, bars 1–4

We find a number of examples of such complementary sonorities in this work. Let us illustrate this by looking more closely at bars 15 to 20. Juxtaposition of complementary sonorities from the two whole-tone spheres is the underlying principle for this whole section. The chord which follows the arpeggio figure in bar 15 has whole-tone scale no. 1 as its basis. This is followed by a complementary chord where the scale foundation is whole-tone scale no. 2. Then a third chord follows (bar 16) where it is once again whole-tone scale no. 1.

Example 7.3. *Den lille Stengud*, bars 15 and 16

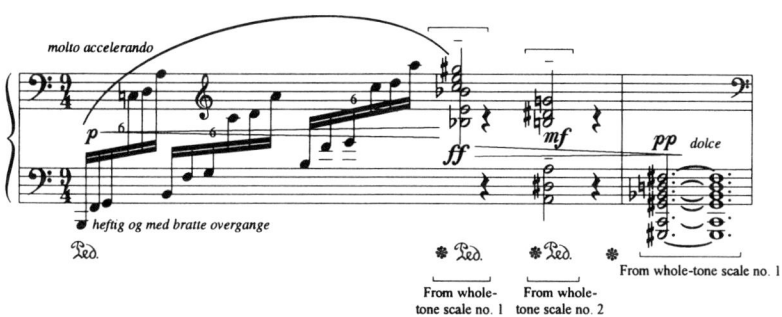

The underlying whole-tone structure emerges even more clearly in the next two bars, 17 and 18 (cf. Example 7.4). The chord which is arpeggiated over several octaves at the beginning of bar 17 contains all the notes in whole-tone scale no. 2. The rising arpeggio figure is accompanied by a crescendo and all this leads to a central chord which clearly functions as a complementary sonority in relation to the preceding one. The scale foundation for the central chord is thus not whole-tone scale no. 2, but rather whole-tone scale no. 1. As a complementary sonority for this, a chord based upon whole-tone scale no. 2 is introduced, and finally a six-note chord in bar 18 follows which has whole-tone scale no. 1 as its scale foundation.

Example 7.4. *Den lille Stengud*, bars 17 and 18.

One formal characteristic of these pieces is their episodic nature. This is well illustrated in *Den lille Stengud* with the transition from bar 18 to 19. In bar 19 we are given a new, highly contrasted section. The transition is abrupt, but it is not without connective strands. The choice of notes in the four first beats of bar 19 is related to whole-tone scale no. 2. Near the end of the bar (with elements of A#, F#, C, and D) he refers fleetingly to the other whole-tone sphere, i.e. the one based upon whole-tone scale no. 1. In bar 20 (cf. Example 7.5), with two exceptions, the pitches are once again related to whole-tone scale no. 2. The one exception is the D. The other is the element of the E which comes exactly in the middle of the bar, and which is the goal towards which the first half of the bar leads (cf. the high point of the crescendo). The bar is symmetrically constructed and the E, which thus breaks out of the whole-tone sphere, functions as an axis. Before this axis we have an ascending movement accompanied by a crescendo. After the axis we have a symmetrical response – a descending movement accompanied by a decrescendo.

Example 7.5. *Den lille Stengud*, bar 20.

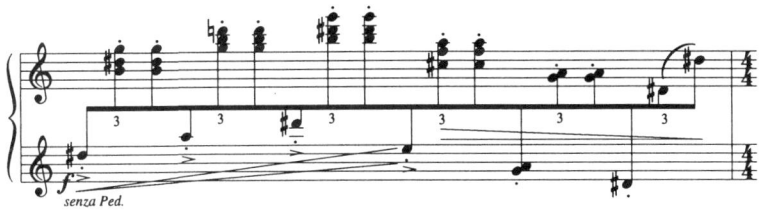

Near the end of the piece we also find a clear example of the significance the whole-tone structure has in this piece. The chord progression in bar 46 and the first half of bar 47 uses whole-tone scale no. 2 as its scale foundation. This is followed by a modal cadence in A aeolian (cf. Example 7.6).

Example 7.6. *Den lille Stengud*, bars 47 and 48.

We find a similar combination of whole-tone and modal harmony at the beginning of the piece. We have seen how Monrad Johansen in the five first bars alternates between the two whole-tone spheres. In bar 6 (cf. Example 7.7) he draws away from the whole-tone sphere. The chords built of seconds are replaced by triads, mainly in parallel motion and related to an F aeolian mode. This opening passage cadences in bar 8, and it is followed by a new phrase in A flat major where modal harmonic progressions are replaced by more traditional functional harmony.

Example 7.7. *Den lille Stengud,* bars 5 to 13.

Such functional harmony thus finds a place within the music, but no longer as the dominant structural principle.

Before we move on from the significance of the whole-tone scale in this work we can look at examples from two of the other pieces in the suite. The first piece, *Kvinneprofil* (Woman's Profile), further illustrates the juxtaposition of complementary sonorities from the two whole-tone spheres, notably at bar 26 (cf. Example 7.8). The first eight notes here form a group from whole-tone scale no. 2. A new group of eight tones is placed as a complementary sonority to this group. The scale foundation for this is whole-tone scale no. 1. After this, a new eight-tone group follows based upon whole-tone scale no. 2.

Example 7.8. *Kvinneprofil,* bar 26.

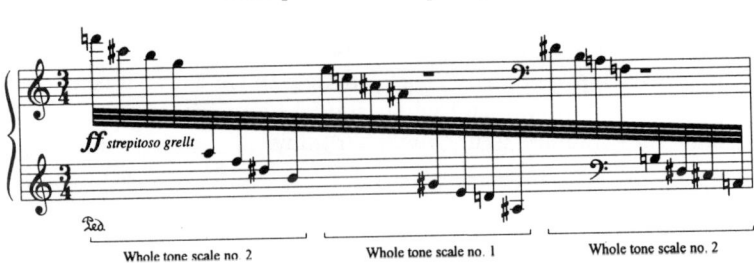

The third piece, *Rensdyr* (Reindeer), illustrates another way in which Monrad Johansen uses the whole-tone structures. In *Rensdyr* the dominant force is not juxtaposition of complementary sonorities from the two whole-tone spheres, but the simultaneous presentation of whole-tone elements and elements related to other tonal spheres.

We see this most clearly in bars 45 to 49, where the scale foundation for the melodic material in the right hand is whole-tone scale no. 1, while the accompaniment figure in the left hand is related to E♭. The whole-tone structure is thus incorporated in a polymodal context (cf. Example 7.9).

Example 7.9. *Rensdyr*, bars 45 to 49.

Scale foundation in the upper system: whole-tone scale No. 1

The main part of this piece commences in bar 19 and here Monrad Johansen indicates a key signature. The beginning and end of the main part are clearly related to E flat as the tonal centre. However, Monrad Johansen does not indicate either E flat major or E flat minor. On the contrary, the key indicated is D flat major or B flat minor. But the tonal centre in bars 19 to 28 is unquestionably E flat because of the ostinato constructed from an arpeggiated E flat chord in the left hand. What Monrad Johansen has thus done is to indicate not E flat minor but E flat dorian, and this scale foundation is maintained consistently in bars 19 to 27. In bar 28 the dorian-scale foundation is clearly replaced by a polymodal structure. As we can see in Example 10, the whole-tone scale is also present here, but only as one of three simultaneous components. The scale foundation for the lowest system is whole-tone scale no. 1. In the upper system we find two elements. The descending line of sixteenths is chromatic, while the underlying line of eighths is diatonic. Which diatonic scale we have here is impossible to determine with any degree of certainty, but for the sake of simplicity we can call it a C major element. Bar 32 is entirely identical to bar 28, with the exception that everything is transposed one octave up. Bar 30 is also parallel to these two bars, but here everything is transposed up a perfect fourth, which means that the lower system is now related to whole-tone scale no. 2.

Example 7.10. *Rensdyr*, bar 28 and 30.

Scale foundation in lower system: whole-tone scale no. 1

Scale foundation in lower system: whole-tone scale no. 2

The polymodal principle is also the basis for the succeeding bars. Two different modal spheres are juxtaposed from the end of bar 33 up to and including bar 39. The lowest system contains tones in a pentatonic scale built on E♭. While it is possible to interpret the upper system in many ways, I choose to see it as D dorian. This is substantiated, for example, at the beginning of bar 33, where the E♭7 chord in the lower system is part of a polychordal structure. The material in the upper system appears to have D as its pitch centre. Two tonal spheres related to each other by a minor second are thus placed together in a polymodal structure. The minor second is the central interval in this piece, while the central interval in the previous piece, *Den lille Stengud*, was a *major* second. In bars 33 to 40 the relation between the two tonal spheres is thus identical to the minor second central interval (cf. Example 7.11).

Example 7.11. *Rensdyr*, bars 33 to 39.

The polymodal principle also proves to be the basic structure in the piece's introductory section. The scale foundation in the upper system is a pentatonic scale built on G. This pentatonic melody is coupled with a line in the left hand which gives a consistent minor second below. The scale foundation for the left hand is thus a pentatonic scale built on F#. Of course, it is open to discussion if this should be classified as a pure voice coupling or as a real polymodality. However, whichever way you classify the opening bars, they are clearly based on a polymodal principle.

Example 7.12. *Rensdyr*, bars 1 to 4.

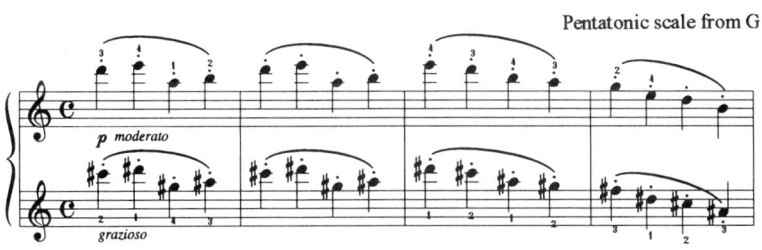

It may appear as if it is a kind of polymodality which is also the basis for the following bars (cf. Example 7.13). While the left hand has a pedal point consisting of the pitches A and D# (i.e. a triton), the right hand has motives which appear to belong to another modal or tonal sphere. This is also the case in bar 11. What is happening in the upper system here at the beginning of the bar is related to whole-tone scale no. 1. As a contrasted sonority we find a motif which is related to one or other D minor sphere. The A-D# tritone interval which comprises the pedal point in the left hand is not in whole-tone scale no. 1, nor can it be united tonally with the D minor sphere. Thus different tonal or modal spheres are united here. This is present again in the last half of bar 10. The descending line of sixteenths in the right hand are purely chromatic, while the descending line of eighths are related to whole-tone scale no. 1. As a third element we have the A-D# tritone pedal point (cf. Example 7.13).

But we cannot interpret bar 9 and the first part of bar 10 in a similar way. The motivic material in the upper system moves both above and below the tritone in the left hand. The two elements are thus not in clearly separate registers and the pianist has no possibility of separating them by means of contrasted timbres. Moreover, there is nothing in the choice of pitches indicating that we have two different tonal or modal planes. Everything must be related to the same starting-point, and when this is done it becomes clear that the basic structure is the octatonic scale (Messiaen's mode 2), which is especially familiar from works by Janáček and Stravinsky but which has a history stretching back to the early nineteenth century.

Example 7.13. *Rensdyr*, bars 9 to 12.

Octatonic scale. Transposition from C

Monrad Johansen may not have employed the octatonic scale consciously, but it is not the only place where it forms a basic structure in this piece. In bars 40 to 45 (cf. Example 7.14) we again witness a polymodal section. In the lower system a chord consisting of the pitches E♭, B♭ and D♭ is arpeggiated in an ostinato movement. E♭ of course comprises the root of the chord. Above this we have arpeggiated chords in a melodic movement which clearly belongs to another tonal or modal sphere. The pitches are grouped in three diminished seventh chords. Together, the pitches in these three chords form the same transposition of the octatonic scale which we have already seen in bars 9 and 10. That it is this scale which actually is the basis for this section becomes even more obvious if we isolate the melody pitches alone. These then comprise the six first tones of the scale.

Example 7.14. *Rensdyr*, bars 39 to 44.

We also find Messiaen's mode no. 3 as a scale foundation in this suite. The opening motive in *Kvinneprofil*, the first piece in the suite, is presented in the first two bars and the scale foundation here is Messiaen's mode no. 3 (cf. Example 7.15a). It is true that this scale foundation is quickly left, in bar 3, in favour of a chromatic elaboration of the motif. However, the motif returns in bar 13 and it is the same transposition of mode no. 3 which is the foundation for the motif here as in the opening bars. Furthermore, this time it is harmonised and, with the exception of the II-V cadence in bars 16–17, the harmonic material is also derived from Messiaen's mode no. 3 (cf. Example 7.15b).

Example 7.15a. *Kvinneprofil*, bars 1 to 3.

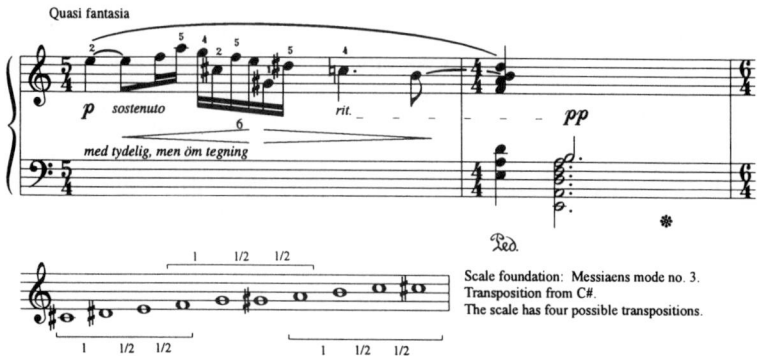

Example 7.15b. *Kvinneprofil*, bars 13 to 18.

The last time this motif appears is near the end of the piece, at bar 30 (cf. Example 7.16). The motif here is identical to the opening bars, but it is followed by a new motif which functions as a kind of commentary. The immediate experience is as if this motif is composed of tones from two complementary spheres. Some bars earlier, in bar 26, we find one of the many examples of the principle of juxtaposing complementary sonorities from the two possible whole-tone spheres. In bars 31 and 32, however, the complementary sonorities cannot be derived from the two whole-tone scales. In the extension of bar 30 we are still in Messiaen's mode no. 3. Thus this is not a shift of mode, only a change to other transpositions of the same mode. The first part of the commentary motif in bar 31 relates to mode no. 3 in its transposition from C. Of course, this could also have been derived from whole-tone scale no. 1. However, seen in the light of both the preceding and the following bars this is an unlikely reading. It is far more probable that we experience the first four notes of the commentary motif in bar 31 as a new transposition of mode no. 3. This transposition is thus established as a complementary sonority for the mode no. 3 sphere we find in bar 30. Moreover, half of the commentary motif relates to yet another transposition of mode no. 3, a transposition from D#.

Example 7.16. *Kvinneprofil*, bars 30 to 33.

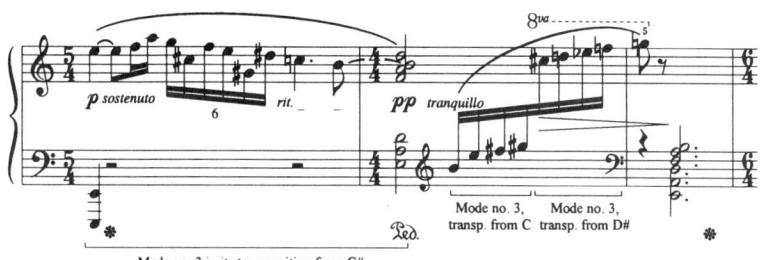

After this there follows a chromatic elaboration of the opening motif and this is also followed by the commentary motif, which is composed of complementary sonorities from different transpositions of Messiaen's mode no. 3. The scale foundation in the first half of the motif is mode no. 3 transposed from C#. The scale foundation in the second half is mode no. 3 in its transposition from C (cf. Example 7.17).

Example 7.17. *Kvinneprofil*, bars 34 and 35.

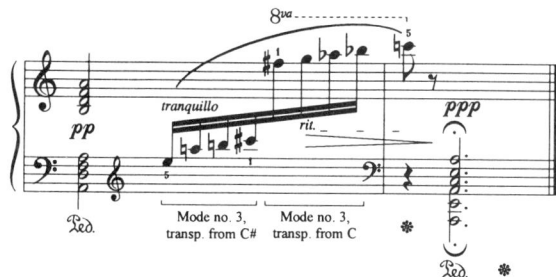

Conclusion

It is clear from this analysis of the piano suite that tonality based upon functional harmony has been replaced by other basic principles. In the suite's second and third pieces, *Den lille Stengud* and *Rensdyr*, it appears that Monrad Johansen's point of departure is a central interval – a major second in *Den lille Stengud* and a minor second in *Rensdyr*. The central interval is not only used as a sonority but to generate more basic controlling and structural principles. In the case of *Den lille Stengud,* and to an extent *Kvinneprofil*, the basic principle is the juxtaposition of complementary sonorities from the two possible whole-tone spheres. In the case of *Rensdyr*, however, the whole-tone structures, together with pentatonic and octatonic material, are incorporated as a component in an overarching polymodal structure, and the polymodal principle thus becomes a basic structural principle in this piece.

In addition to the use of whole-tone and octatonic material (Messiaen's modes nos. 1 and 2) there are also elements of mode no. 3, as we noted in our analysis of *Kvinneprofil*. The opening motif of this piece is again structured in accordance with the now familiar principle where sonorities from different transpositions of the same mode are juxtaposed in a complementary way.

The last piece in the suite, *Mot fedrenes fjell* (Towards the Mountain of Our Forefathers), does not comprise more than a page. It is based upon a far more conventional modality which requires no elaboration here. But it may be worth noting that these elements strengthen the links with Debussy. What is significant here is not just the use of chromatic symmetries (especially those based on the whole-tone scale), but the co-existence of these with traditional modal and pentatonic scales and even with more traditionally functioning diatonic harmonies. What is involved here is a tonal synthesis very much in the manner of Debussy.

The influence of late Debussy is indeed undeniable, but there are also other basic structures which point beyond Debussy, and especially a polymodal organisation of basic structures which points at times to Bartók. With this in mind it is hardly correct to characterise *Nordlandsbilleder* and the other Monrad Johansen works from the years around 1920 as delayed impressionism. For Monrad Johansen, studying Debussy did not encourage him merely to imitate. He was not interested in extracting phenomena from the musical surface, but rather in gaining a greater insight into the musical material and a dawning awareness of new and alternative ways of working with the musical material. Precisely because he was able to grasp this basic structural level he was able to use the experiences gained in a way which resulted in a uniquely personal form of artistic expression.

Synthesis: Norwegian and French impulses

We have focused on the French impulses in Monrad Johansen's music, but no examination of this composer is complete without also looking at the *Norwegian* impulses which contributed to shaping him as a composer. In the compositions which follow immediately after *Nordlandsbilleder* we witness an increasing interest in Norwegian folk art in general and Norwegian folk music in particular. In the sketchbook mentioned earlier it is evident that this interest in Norwegian folk art was also present in the years 1918–19. In the sketches from these years we find examples of harmonised Norwegian folk-songs together with titles which allude to old Norwegian folk poetry. Moreover, the title of opus 5 – *Nordlandsbilleder* – as well as some of the titles of the pieces in the suite tell us that Norwegian nature was a powerful source of inspiration for the composer. This especially applies to the landscape that Monrad Johansen knew from his childhood, the scenic beauty of Nordland, which was also where Knut Hamsun spent his childhood.

Thus on the one hand the sketchbook refers to Norwegian nature and culture, and on the other to his studies of Debussy. The extensive section on Debussy comprises relatively systematic studies of the use of melody, scales and harmony in some of Debussy's piano works. He scrutinises the musical texts for certain elements and then comments upon them. Most of Monrad Johansen's comments focus, of course, on the areas which interest him and which he feels correspond to his own ideas. Among all the positive evaluations, however, there is one negative comment. This applies to Debussy's melodic idiom. After having carefully studied seven of Debussy's piano works, where he paid special attention to the melodic aspect, he states:

> His [Debussy's] melodic idiom has a light and smooth feel to it, it is very flexible, with much movement in whole steps (without necessarily using the whole-tone scale). There is a degree of calm in the expression, but at the same time there is a certain objectivity, I do not find a heart in the melody, but that is perhaps not intended either.[1]

Thus Debussy's melodic idiom is too 'cool' for Monrad Johansen. He was aware that its expressive character was quite different from anything he himself would have wanted. The melodic expression in Norwegian folk-songs was certainly closer to Monrad Johansen's heart. He said that it was particularly the Ole Sandvik collections of folk music from the *Gudbrandsdal* area which had significance for his development as a composer. It was thus the interplay between French and Norwegian impulses which fed his creative power, enabling him to develop further as a composer. This is especially evident in the works which follow immediately after *Nordlandsbilleder*. In *Syv sanger* (Seven Songs), written to the verses of old Norwegian folk poetry, the melodic style is more expressive, more clearly shaped and has more of a sense of the folksong than Debussy's melody. In the preface to this composition he states that after returning from Paris in 1920 he did not know which direction he wanted to take. The impressions he had been exposed to were so overwhelming that he was disheartened. However, as soon as he related them to something domestic, more precisely the old Norwegian folk-songs and folk melodies, he managed to assimilate the impressions from his stay in Paris into his own style. Through a pure coincidence he happened upon Landstad's *Norske Folkeviser* (Norwegian Folk Songs):

> Springing from the pages of this book I was engulfed by a swarm of colours and sights, pictures of Norwegian nature and Norwegian folkways, but not as I knew them from our national–romantic art. No, this poetry took me even further back, to more distant times, to the Norwegian middle ages, perhaps even further back. There was something

fantastic about them, not the least because the poems intimated more than they expressed.²

This idea that the poem should intimate more than it expresses is a central ideal in symbolist poetry, especially in Mallarmé. The poet should, according to Mallarmé, not mention or portray things, but rather allow them to evolve in the reader's consciousness. In the study *Sur l'Évolution Litteraire* he says:

> *Mentioning* an object is to remove three quarters of the poetic pleasure, which consists of feeling one's way towards the answer: *suggesting*, that is the goal. It is a true application of this mystery which comprises the symbol: to conjure an object in order to show a condition of the soul, or vice-versa, to choose an object and from this object to release a condition of the soul, through a number of intimations.³

What Monrad Johansen points out as particularly inspiring about the old Norwegian folk poetry thus corresponds to a central principle of symbolist poetry. Monrad Johansen certainly was not deeply versed in Mallarmé's poetry, and far less his poetics, but the parallel is no less interesting because of this. Quite the contrary, it is a key to a deeper understanding of both the differences and similarities between Debussy and Monrad Johansen. If we allow Mallarmé's poetics to comprise the framework for interpreting Debussy's music we will find striking parallels which go far beyond the ideal of intimation as an artistic tool. Let us continue to examine the use of melody, the element where Monrad Johansen fails to find agreement between his own expressive world and that of Debussy.

When Monrad Johansen finds Debussy's melody to be 'objective', it is because of the extensive use of circle and pendulum movements. The melodic lines often go from one point to another and then back again. It is not uncommon that the distance between the two points is a tritone, so that in tonal terms a floating and directionless feeling is created. This way of using melody is made objective in the sense that it is not experienced as a musical parallel to a linguistic expression or to an emphatic gesture. Thus it is not primarily perceived as being an expressive correlate to some speaking subject. On the contrary, what is important is the melodic *object*.

This agrees to a striking degree with the poetics of Mallarmé. According to him it is *the poem's* and not *the poet's* voice which should be heard. Emotions should be released on the basis of the objects one chooses or conjures up, as Mallarmé himself puts it in the above quotation. In other words, emotions should not be expressed with rhetorical emphasis and power. This is the same idea which we find in T. S. Eliot's 'objective correlative of a feeling'. A rhetorical proclamation of the poet's own feelings is quite simply a bad method of expressing feelings in artistic form. Emotions must, according to Eliot, be expressed through an *objective correlative*. External objects and sensations must be presented in such a way that the emotions one wants to thus impart are evoked in the recipient.

Perhaps Monrad Johansen favoured the aesthetics of expression a little too much for him to agree without reservation with such an uncompromising a-rhetoric ideal. It is true that he was fascinated by the ability of folk poetry to intimate more than to express and this represents a tendency to objectivise in relation to the Romantic's emphasis on subjective expression. The question is, however, how far he was willing to lead this tendency to objectivisation. His comments on Debussy's melody clearly indicates that there were limits for him. In his evaluation of harmonic and tonal structures in Debussy's music, Monrad Johansen is totally positive towards the ambiguous feelings they create. However, he feels that the directionless quality so often found in Debussy's melodies is too objective. He feels more attracted to the modal melodies found in Norwegian folksongs.

Thus it is in the interplay between Norwegian and French impulses that Monrad Johansen found his own voice. As I mentioned earlier the initial creative impetus for Monrad Johansen as a composer was his deep admiration for Grieg and his works. To take the tradition Grieg had created further was therefore one of his central goals. What enabled him to develop and extend Norwegian traditions in a productive way was, however, his encounter with contemporary French music. Monrad Johansen was deeply fascinated by Debussy's music, but he was aware that he was in search of another mode of expression. The great value of the meeting with Debussy's music was that he acquired new insights into musical structures and techniques of composition. It was precisely these ideas and tools which enabled him to develop further a musical tradition in which Norwegian nature, literature and history are central elements.

David Monrad Johansen's view of music in the interwar period

Let us now look more closely at how Monrad Johansen viewed music in the interwar period. In examining his interest in Norwegian folk art we touch upon a more controversial aspect of the composer. In 1924 he gave a lecture at the Kristiania music teachers' association entitled: *Nationale værdier i vor musik* (National Values in Our Music). The lecture was printed in the major daily *Aftenposten* the same year and it has since been treated as the most important source of the ideology underlying nationalist endeavours in Norwegian music in the interwar period. Monrad Johansen emerged as the standard-bearer for this nationalist movement in music and it is very much for this that he is remembered today. But in his music he had already moved in other directions by the end of the 1920s. Then there was another trip to Paris, where he spent much time with Fartein Valen. Valen's influence is noticeable in the university cantata *Ignis Ardens*, and after a study tour in Berlin he wrote a number of orchestral works of a high quality. Stylistically these are in a neo-classical style, far removed from the homophonic national style he strived for in the monumentally constructed *Voluspaa*, which is based upon a poem from the *Elder Edda*. However, Monrad Johansen's name is far more associated with *Voluspaa*, incorporating as it does his national ideals, than with the rest of his major works.

There has been a tendency to see a connection between his national view of music in the interwar period and his unfortunate political decision of 1940.[4] Some of the things he said could perhaps be interpreted in this way, but if we compare the lecture of 1924 with all his writings in the interwar period we find that there are far more statements which bear witness to an entirely different politicisation of the concept of nationality.

What Monrad Johansen speaks about might be described as a musical–linguistic struggle. He appears to draw direct parallels between verbal language and musical language and argues in a way which has strong associations with parts of the New Norwegian linguistic movement, especially the politically most radical wing. From the reformation in 1536 until 1814 Norway was ruled from Copenhagen. The written language for Norway during these years was Danish, and one of the most important tasks for Norwegian artists and intellectuals in the nineteenth century was to create a written language. Two different camps emerged from this task: one wanted to Norwegianise the Danish, while the other favoured a more radical solution. For them, the formulation of a written Norwegian language had to be based on the Norwegian way of speaking; in other words the language of the people as it mainly existed in the rural communities. These were the proponents of a 'New Norwegian'. It was claimed that to create what could truly be called a written Norwegian language could only be achieved by comparing Norwegian dialects and finding as many common points as possible, and from this basis a grammar could be established.

A central figure in this camp was the Norwegian author Arne Garborg, who lived from 1851 until 1924. David Monrad Johansen and his family lived for a period with Hulda Garborg, Arne Garborg's widow. It is not possible to say if it was here that he became familiar with Arne Garborg's ideas of nationality. We cannot speak of any complete merging of ideas, but there are obvious similarities regarding Garborg's ideas as they are expressed, for example, in his little-known book: *Den ny-norske Sprog- og Nationalitetsbevægelse* (The New-Norwegian Language and Nationality Movement).

For Garborg a nation is a cultural area where the people share common ideas: there is a direct relationship between culture-specific concepts and ways of thinking and cultural expression. This emerges most obviously in language and therefore it is of major and dramatic significance if a person is deprived of the possibility of expressing himself in the language he feels is his own. Garborg shows, using examples both from the Norwegian language and from other cultural areas, how linguistic and political oppression are one and the same thing. This oppression may be represented by an external occupying power, or by a cultural group in the same political and geographic area. The result in both cases is the same: the oppressed linguistic and cultural group is deprived of the possibility of expressing itself in a way which is in accordance with its thoughts and concepts. One is forced to undertake what Garborg calls 'self-translation' and in the wake of this comes self-censorship. If there is a Norwegian nationality it will 'reveal itself by materialising in an independent form', says Garborg.[5] The language of the people represents such a form and it was therefore this which would form the basis for the formulation of a written Norwegian language.

We find much the same ideas in Monrad Johansen in his argument for the formation of a national music language. One might have many misgivings about drawing direct parallels between verbal and musical language, but unfortunately we cannot begin to debate this issue here. We must rather be content with examining the fact that Monrad Johansen himself draws such a direct parallel. His idea appeared to be that not only had the political and verbal language of Norway been oppressed, but also the music language. To give an example of this he referred to the manner in which Edvard Grieg's music was often received in Germany. Sarcastic comments such as *Norwegerei* and *er norwegert* were not uncommon and, in the lecture of 1924, he quotes from a letter Grieg wrote in 1906 complaining about the chauvinistic cultural attitudes he had often encountered from the German critics. But Monrad Johansen did not only refer to Grieg. He believed there were also other cultural areas which had been oppressed by German music culture. French music 'lacked the language itself to make it valid. Under such circumstances it was clear that it could easily be prey to foreign conquerors', he wrote in a letter to *Aftenposten* in 1928.

He returns to the French example often. 'The French spirit and the French musicality can only be expressed through the laws the material itself dictates, and not through style and form forced upon them from external sources', he said in an article in 1936.[6] This reveals clear associations with Garborg. Both felt that cultural expression had to be national to be authentic. For Garborg this meant simply that it had to be culturally determined. Thus his concept of nationality is not the antithesis of internationality. Quite the contrary, the international aspect is dependent upon the national aspect, as coexistence with equal parts cannot be realised through an international culture, but only through reciprocal acceptance and understanding of each other's culture.

It is doubtful if Monrad Johansen shared the same perspectives regarding the relationship between the national and international culture, but the constant references to other nations' music-language 'liberation' makes it difficult for us to attribute chauvinistic attitudes to him. The idea that nations must be able to maintain their cultural and political identity is very much in contrast to a significant part of the basic ideas behind Monrad

Johansen's national music endeavours in the interwar period. Seen from this point of view, his political choice in 1940 is an action which stands in stark contrast to his view of music in the interwar years, and is not a natural consequence of it.

The parallel to Garborg also has its limitations. A main point in Garborg's argument is that the cultural-specific aspect is not found in the language's material aspect, i.e. in the vocabulary itself. What binds the language to the cultural-specific concepts and ways of thinking is its structure. Therefore, what Garborg calls the Norwegianising strategy, where it is felt that it is sufficient to add Norwegian words and expressions to a foreign language, will never succeed. This strategy is actually based upon a national-romantic illusion, he says.

However, Monrad Johansen's actualisation of Norwegian music elements never leaves the material plane, so we are left with the disparity between what he proclaimed were the ideas for his music and what in fact his ideas were. In Norwegian folk music he found a limited number of specific characteristics, and he 'Norwegianised' his impressionist or rather symbolist basis by approaching these elements. But this is not bad music because of this. We must not allow our evaluation of Monrad Johansen as a theorist to influence our evaluation of Monrad Johansen as a composer. Monrad Johansen's music holds an unchallenged place among the most outstanding works in Norwegian art music. What we see more clearly today than in the time when the national issue raged is that his music is not only Norwegian, but also clearly reflects the contemporary trends in European music.

The best of his music measures up well to this double perspective: it is authentically Norwegian, yet it takes its place among the most significant products of European culture.

Notes and References

1. Sketchbook 9575:757, p. 111, Norwegian Music Collection, University of Oslo Library.
2. Preface to *Syv sanger*, Op.6, Noreg Edition, No. 72, Oslo.
3. Stéphane Mallarmé, *Sur l'Évolution Littéraire,Œuvres complètes* (Paris, 1945), p. 869. Quoted here according to Haugen, Arne Kjell, *Mallarmés Poetikk* (Oslo, 1966), p. 74.
4. Monrad Johansen became a member of Quisling's National Assembly.
5. Arne Garborg, *Den ny-norske Sprog- og Nationalitetsbevægelse. Et forsøg paa en omfattende Redegjørelse formet som polemiske Sendebreve til Modstræverne.* (The New-Norwegian Language and Nationality Movement. An attempt at a comprehensive report formed as polemic letters to opponents) (Oslo, 1982), p. 15. First published in Kristiania in 1887.
6. The article was published in the *Allers* family magazine, No. 47, 21/11/1936.

8.
Moniuszko and Musical Nationalism in Poland[1]

MICHAEL MURPHY

In the aftermath of Poland's tri-partition at the hands of the Russians, Prussians, and Austrians in the final decade of the eighteenth century, Polish nationalists focused on regaining independence. Polish nationalism flourished despite the fact that there was no national state and very limited industrial and economic modernisation. In this context, intellectual and cultural activities assumed a political tenor in which politics and art were inseparable. As the influential revolutionary and historian Maurycy Mochnacki stated:

> Hence literature is . . . a nation's conscience. This leads us to conclude that a nation without its own original literature . . . is only a collection of people in a space defined by arbitrary borders, and not yet of a moral collective. It is not enough for us to exist; we have to *know* we exist.[2]

Cultural nationalism in Poland was concerned with forging and expressing a national consciousness.

In Polish romantic nationalism the idealisation of peasant culture was inextricably linked with the political claim for social revolution, a revolution that was essential to the process of constructing the Polish nation. The failure of that social revolution is central to the genesis of the most important romantic nationalist opera, *Halka*, by Stanisław Moniuszko (1819–1872). In this chapter I will examine how social politics in nineteenth-century Poland vitally conditioned this work. The context for the discussion of Moniuszko's construction of nationalism is provided in the initial survey of social structures in late eighteenth-century Poland, the subsequent analysis of different strains of Polish nationalism and a brief survey of the theoretical works of literary and musical theorists. After examining Moniuszko's nationalism, I will question the historiographical notion of a Polish national school by considering the discontinuities that existed between Moniuszko and his contemporaries. In conclusion, I will briefly examine the break with the nationalist tradition that came with the short-lived Young Poland era.

Social and political background

The Polish nation at the end of the eighteenth century was comprised solely of the noble estate.[3] The peasantry (*lud*), although the largest social class, had no access to political institutions but existed in a semi-feudal relationship with their Polish masters for the majority of the nineteenth century. They did not exhibit a national consciousness until after their emancipation and subsequent exposure to education in the latter part of the nineteenth century. In this regard, it is worth recalling the memoirs of one Galician peasant who witnessed the change of government from Austrian imperialism to Polish independence:

> As for national consciousness ... the older peasants called themselves Masurians, and their speech Masurian. They lived their own life, forming a wholly separate group, and caring nothing for the nation. I myself did not know that I was a Pole till I began to read books and papers, and I fancy that other villagers came to be aware of the national attachment in much the same way.[4]

The persistence of local and imperial identities created a crisis for the nationalists in the mid-nineteenth century. I will return to this crisis when I consider the events of 1846 in Galicia.

The Polish Commonwealth in the late eighteenth century was a multi-ethnic and multi-linguistic republic comprised of Poles, Lithuanians, Ukrainians, Ruthenians, Belorussians and, in the western regions, Germans. As Andrzej Walicki notes, 'One could speak the Ruthenian language but nevertheless consider oneself, and be considered by others, as a Pole ('gente Ruthenus, natione Polonus').[5] In the latter years of the nineteenth century, political nationalism was to take hold of the various ethnic groups who sought their own political independence based on cultural identity, thus bringing them into conflict with a specifically Polish nationalism. These developments do not concern us here, however.

A typology of Polish nationalism

Theorists of Polish nationalism have identified different strains of nationalism in mid nineteenth-century Poland. My preference is for Wanda Taylor's typology of nationalism wherein she identifies six categories of nationalists: the conservative romantics, the romantic messianists, the romantic socialists, the romantic democrats, the liberals and the positivists.[6] The romantic socialists were the most radical group of the revolutionaries based in Poland, and they sought full emancipation for the peasants by violent revolution, not only as a socio-economic process but as a vital part of nation-building.[7] Taylor summarises their project thus:

if we understand nationalism in the strictly political terms of social equalisation, then the romantic socialists not only qualified as nationalists but provided the most obvious form of national expression ... The fight for independence was seen as a popular movement originating and run entirely from below and directed as much against the feudal landlords as against the governments of the foreign occupants ... The nationalism of the romantic socialists originated from the premise of 'cultural' expression, due largely to political circumstances, developed into a strongly political conception of class conflict.[8]

It is this strain of nationalism that has the greatest explanatory power for my discussion of musical nationalism with respect to Moniuszko's *Halka*.

The champion of the romantic socialists was Edward Dembowski, a committed disciple of Mochnacki's vision of 'ennobling' the population, where every Pole, regardless of class, would be a member of the political nation.[9] Dembowski's philosophy of history contrasted the 'latinised' culture of the gentry with the 'original' Slavic nation. In particular, he believed that the religious beliefs of the peasantry were tainted by the Roman faith of their Polish masters.[10] He frequently criticised those intellectuals who equated the *szlachta* customs with Polish national character, and to promote his own views he frequently attired himself in peasant clothes and went into the countryside to 'preach the revolutionary gospel' to the peasants.[11]

The most notable contribution to the radical, nationalist historiography came from Joachim Lelewel, whose treatise 'The Lost Citizenship of the Peasant Estate in Poland' (Poznań, 1851) claimed that the land had been taken from the *lud* by the *szlachta*.[12] Under the impress of German romantic thought, the role of the peasants in Polish history and the development of the nation became theorised in a wholly romantic way. Consequently, the search ensued for the historical and cultural origins of the nation in the peasantry.[13] The romantic disenchantment with the Enlightenment and the influence of Western ideas on Polish thought fundamentally challenged the feudalism of the old order, and politicised the cultural concerns of Polish intellectuals. This change of world view provided a seminal impetus to musical nationalism.

Polish national style

The influence of German thought on Polish musical culture came to prominence in the career of one of the most important figures of Polish musical life in the early nineteenth century, Józef Elsner. In his theoretical writings, Elsner examined the metronomy and rhythmic nature of the Polish language.[14] His intellectual project represented a modern, Romantic reaction to earlier Enlightenment attempts at codifying Polish prosody; e.g. his 'Treatise on the Metric and Rhythmic Features of the Polish Language' was in direct opposition to the classical theories of his predecessor, Tadeusz Nowaczyński.[15] Significantly, Elsner's work was banned by the Russian censor due to the centrality of 'nationality' in his thesis.[16] In making the connection between language and music, Elsner compared poetic metres with the rhythms of Polish folk dances (e.g. the trocaic in the mazurka and the spondaic in the krakowiak). His ideas were widely debated, and they formed a central part of the musical creativity of contemporary composers, writers and critics. However, these theoretical dispensations ultimately led to a formulaic approach to musical composition, and those composers who did not adhere to this aesthetic were severely criticised. Moniuszko's works represented the embodiment of this nationalist aesthetic.

Moniuszko

Moniuszko's career must be read against the demographic shift of the post-1830 era. He was born into a cultured and landed *szlachta* family in Ubiel in Belorussia. After his early education in Warsaw and Vilnius he completed his musical studies in the Singakademie in Berlin (1837–1840). A number of his songs were published by Bote and Bock in Berlin in 1840, and were received favourably by Leipzig's *Allgemeine Musikalische Zeitung*: one review noted that his ballad, *Trzech Budrysw*, breathed the national spirit in words and music. Shortly after this success Moniuszko wrote:

> I feel the growing strength of my talent which makes me so different from the multitude ... You must know your own value, so others will take notice of you and respect you! From now on this will be my maxim.[17]

However, this sense of individualism was not to remain with Moniuszko for long. His failure to retain his inherited estates obliged him to support his large family on his income from teaching piano and playing the organ. His straitened circumstances dictated that he join the ranks of the many *déclassé* nobles who were forced to abandon their family estates and move to the urban centres in search of posts. Taylor describes the emergence of these intellectuals as a professional class that stemmed from the 'landed' tradition but 'developed an understanding of society and social relations that distanced it from the conservative aristocratic world-view'.[18] It was in this social ferment that Moniuszko became a professional composer of 'national' status. This process got under way in Vilnius in the early 1840s.

Śpiewnik domowy (Domestic Songs)[19]

In an article announcing his first volume of *Śpiewnik domowy* (Vilnius, 1842) he drew a clear distinction between the new Romantic aesthetic of music, which was characterised by 'an expression of place, national character of peoples, their games, festivals, traditions, etc.', and the earlier 'European' mimetic notion of music 'as a language expressing thought, feeling, passion, expressing different phenomena in a physical world'.[20] Moniuszko thus aligned himself with the modernist trends in Polish national romanticism. In acknowledging the recent researches of Polish theorists that informed the development of 'national singing', he noted a lack of songs for domestic singing. His own songs, therefore, were his 'modest contribution' to this expansion of the national repertoire. Central to the aesthetic of the beauty of national song was the 'local echo of our childhood memories' which will relate directly to 'people born and reared on Polish soil'.[21] He noted that, although his songs contained 'various types of music, their drift and character are national'. The unique 'Polish-ness' of these songs lies in the presence of national dance genres and rhythms (krakowiak, mazurka, kujawiak and polonaise), and the proliferation of text settings by the national poets Mickiewicz, Malczewski, Syrokomla, Odyniec, Witwicki and Pol.

These songs were immediately recognised as an important innovation in Polish musical culture. Ironically, the first important review came as a mixed blessing to Moniuszko. The prolific historical novelist and music critic, Józef Ignacy Kraszewski, addressed himself thus to the composer:

> We would like the inspired compositions of Mr Moniuszko to take the place of the limpid and pale songs popular in Warsaw of which so many can be seen on each piano and heard everywhere, which are always the same, always slide off one's soul and can never get into it. Therefore we kindly ask Mr Moniuszko to descend to the level of the general public and make his songs easier. Later, when his readers become acquainted with his music, he will be gradually able to make his compositions more difficult.[22]

This was a seminal articulation of Polish musical nationalism. While it accords with Moniuszko's desire to supplant the hegemony of European music, it also showed that Moniuszko's role as a 'national' composer was subject to the favour not only of the Russian state censor but also to certain elements of the Polish élite. In the end, the tension between Moniuszko and the conservative élite led to his unease with the hegemony of nationalism in Polish musical culture.

Halka: Genesis

The success of the first volume of Moniuszko's songs was consolidated in 1846 with the successful Warsaw première of his opera buffa, *Loteria* (The Lottery).[23] As a result, Moniuszko was fêted in the literary salons of the capital, where he came into contact with writers, journalists and other artists.

It was at a *soirée musicale* in the literary salon of the Łuszczewski family that Moniuszko met the future librettist of *Halka*, Włodzimierz Wolski.

Wolski was a member of the *cyganeria warszawska* (Warsaw bohemians), a group of revolutionaries and poets who followed Dembowski, and whose writings were published in Dembowski's *Przegląd Naukowy* (*Scientific Review*).[24] This weekly journal was dedicated to 'literature, knowledge, and art', and was heavily influenced by Dembowski's Hegelian philosophy of history. Its contributors advocated a national philosophy of Poland's history in which the peasantry were identified as the source of the nation. (It is worth noting that *Przegląd Naukowy* differed significantly from its apolitical rival, *Biblioteka Warszawska*, which sought to provide a neutral forum for intellectual debate unconnected with the nationalist struggle.)

Dembowski was vigilant regarding the young generation of writers, only classifying them in the 'New School' if they professed progressive tendencies. Despite his own political activities, Dembowski wrote solely on the importance of intellectual activities for the national cause. In particular, he attached great significance to the philosophy of 'creativity' – in contradistinction to the idea of 'imitation' – in the pursuit of national renewal. In the spirit of Mochnacki and other influential Polish Hegelian philosophers, Dembowski promoted the idea that art was imbued with a mission to serve the cause of national realisation and independence.

Wolski enjoyed Dembowski's favour as a 'progressive' writer, and thus had his poetic drama *Ojciec Hilary* (Father Hilary) published in *Przegląd Naukowy* in 1843, the heyday of the journal.[25] However, because of the decline of the journal in 1845–1846 due to the arrest of many of its contributors, another of Wolski's poems, *Halszka*, on the peasant question was censored by the Russian Warsaw office. However, *Halszka* remained in circulation in the literary salons, where Moniuszko came in contact with its author.[26]

After their initial meeting, Wolski and Moniuszko immediately set about transforming the poem into an opera. *Halka* was ready for performance by the following year. However, such were the conditions of the time that during the disturbances precipitating the 'Spring of the Peoples' there was little chance of having it performed in Warsaw.[27] Instead, Moniuszko directed the first performance in the foyer of his in-laws' hotel in Vilnius on 1 January 1848.[28] It was not until 1 January 1858 that it received a performance in Warsaw.

The decision by the board of directors of the Wielki Theatre to revive *Halka* came in the period after the death of Nicholas I, when a more liberal administration emerged with Aleksander II (reigned 1855–1881).[29] Indeed, it was with considerable surprise that Moniuszko read in the Warsaw press of the forthcoming performance.[30] With the permission of the board of directors, Moniuszko and Wolski frantically expanded the libretto to its present four-act version.

Halka: Plot

The plot of the opera is the familiar tale of the peasant girl who falls in love with a nobleman who eventually abandons her to marry one of his own class. When Halka is told by her peasant suitor of her master's deception she goes insane and throws herself from a precipice as the wedding ceremony is taking place. As most commentators demonstrate, the 'national spirit' is powerfully expressed in the Polish dances which celebrate the various traditions of Poland's past: the polonaises celebrate the noble tradition while the mazurkas and highland dances celebrate the spirit of the peasants, much in the manner of Mickiewicz's *Pan Tadeusz*. As is obvious from the original publicity posters, these dances were one of the major attractions of the opera.

Halka: Social politics – Galicia (1846)

It is possible, however, to recover a political element in the inspiration of the work. As Witold Rudziński reminds us, the opera was 'a passionate response to the events of 1846'.[31] The events of that year can only be explained by reference to the aftermath of the 1830–1831 uprising. In the wake of the confiscation of lands that resulted from the brutal repression of the uprising, the issue of land ownership and conversion of labour to rents was highly controversial. The peasants were primarily concerned with security of tenure and the prospect of freehold, 'which would sever once and for all the connection of village and manor.'[32] Although the Polish landlords sympathised with the nationalist movement, they were alarmed at the claims that national freedom would necessitate a social revolution, and they were particularly frightened at the linking of the agrarian issue with the national cause. But they were also frightened by the prospect of the Austrians initiating peasant reform over their heads. The upshot of these fraught years occurred in 1846 in western Galicia when the Polish gentry, with the backing of the Polish Democratic Party, staged an uprising as part of wider 'Napoleonic' plans to restore 'historic Poland' (i.e. the restoration of the pre-partition boundaries). Central to this conspiracy was the emancipation of the peasants. The peasants, however, violently suppressed the insurrection in the name of the Austrian Emperor. While the role of Metternich's government in instigating the peasant revolt is a moot point, it is fair to say that the peasants had been treated harshly by their Polish landlords. Furthermore, the fixity of tenure which they had enjoyed since the eighteenth century explains their loyalty to the Austrian government.[33]

When Dembowski heard of the peasant revolt he went to Kraków, where he attempted to convince the peasants that the gentry's uprising was in their best interests. In his pamphlet 'To All Poles Who Can Read' he attempted to enlist the peasants for the national cause, declaring: 'We, the people; we, the peasants; we, the Poles.'³⁴ However, two days later he was killed by Austrian troops and the uprising was suppressed. In light of the successful pro-Habsburg *jacquerie*, the Austrians were concerned that the peasants would demand their independence as a reward for their patriotism. The outcome, in Austrian Poland, was the abolition of serfdom in 1848.

This affair highlighted a number of difficult realities for the romantic nationalists: firstly, peasant serfdom was abolished as a result of the failure – rather than the hoped-for success – of their grand nationalist project; and secondly, it highlighted the precarious position of the nationalists as the new intellectual class *vis-à-vis* the interdependence of the ancient classes. Deep divisions ensued amongst Polish intellectuals over the peasant question. While conservatives wanted stringent measures to contain the peasants, the revolutionary romantics sought full emancipation.

To briefly illustrate this division, we may contrast the politics of Zygmunt Krasiński and Julisuz Słowacki.³⁵ Krasiński expressed his grave reservations about social change in many anti-revolutionary works which he published under various pseudonyms.³⁶ The peasant rebellion against the gentry convinced Krasiński of the correctness of his conservative position. By contrast, Słowacki addressed himself thus to the defeated *szlachta* in his *Voice From Exile to the Brethren in Poland*:

> Ye are standing now on the edge of the abyss, people of noble stock, death and hell are under your feet, and up there, overhead, God and Poland. Recognize God's hand in your punishment and thank the Father in Heaven who sent it for your improvement . . . Have regard for the crude russet coat because this is the dress of the future soldiers who will win Poland's freedom.³⁷

For the revolutionary romantics, the alternative to idealising the peasants in the aftermath of 1846 was to admit that local identity and imperial loyalty were in danger of exploding their national philosophy and the Romantic concept of the Polish nation.

In this context, Wolski's *Halszka* sustained the Romantic view of the peasants as victims of their Polish masters. Consequently, Moniuszko's *Halka* is firmly in this radical, revolutionary, Romantic tradition. Clearly, the opera was more than just an expression of the 'national spirit': it was vitally informed by the social question at the core of Polish nationalism.

Halka: Nationalism and music

As one would expect, the opera is replete with the peasants' complaint of their fate at the hands of their Polish masters. But Halka herself represents the Polish nation in a particular way. Dahlhaus noted that she appropriated the 'elevated style' reserved in Aristotle's rules of social standing for 'kings and potentates'.³⁸ In fact, this is the 'ennobling' of the *lud* as advocated by

Mochnacki and Dembowski. Halka's language is decidedly overcharged throughout the opera: she typically refers to herself in the third person (e.g. 'But her wings are no longer white, they are red, redded by her own blood, She is flapping her wings, and, like a stone, she is falling to the ground').[39] And her music frequently registers an elevated style (e.g. her Italianate G minor aria in the second act). Moreover, the first notes of the overture in D minor strike a tragic tone, thereby situating the work at the apex of musical genres in Poland. The generic import of French Grand Opera was unmistakable in these and other gestures, and Hans von Bülow compared the opera with Halévy and Auber.[40] Clearly, Moniuszko's contravention of social conventions directly challenged the socio-political aspirations of the Polish élite. Indeed, the use of the grand style for Halka's music is arguably the most potent of nationalist gestures in the opera with respect to Poland's national philosophy.

The great tragic moment in the opera occurs in the penultimate scene with Halka's suicide. Her initial impulse to avenge herself by setting fire to the church in which her master is getting married is supplanted by the impulse for self-sacrifice.[41] Most crucially, her suicide is vitally conditioned by a religious consciousness. At the beginning of the second act she had identified herself with the Holy Virgin of Częstochowa grieving at the foot of the cross. In the final act, at the moment when she decides to kill herself, the peasant choir chant the words 'For the sake of martyrdom of your son, have pity on your people'.[42] This is sung to the tune of a Polish folksong which Halka also sings, thus representing a powerful moment of shared consciousness between Halka and the villagers. Moreover, it specifically foregrounds the theme of universal salvation. The stage direction at this point indicates that 'realising that setting fire to the building will mean vengeance at the cost of innocent lives, she throws away the burning faggot'.[43] It is then that she apostrophises her master: 'I am going to die and I forgive you'.[44] This redemptive moment invokes the ideology of Polish Messianism. I use the term 'Messianism' in the sense in which Walicki defines it: 'It is a belief in a redeemer, individual or collective, mediating between the human and the divine in the soteriological process of history.'[45] This understanding of millenarism is formed by a specifically religious consciousness allied to social revolutionism and the notion of the 'religions of the oppressed'. Polish Romantic Messianism, therefore, is not solely a form of political thinking: Walicki identifies one of its strands as 'an ardent search for religious consolation combined with a bitter sense of having been let down by the traditional religious authority (the condemnation of the Polish insurrection [1831] by Pope Gregory XVI'.[46] If we add to this Dembowski's belief that the faith of the peasants had been corrupted by their latinised masters, then Halka's self-sacrifice challenges the villagers' devotional Catholicism and their passive witness to the sexual politics of their masters. Halka's suicide, therefore, embodies the ideology of Messianism to the degree that it challenges the existing social order.

However, despite the powerful drama in this scene the opera ends abruptly with a celebration for the newly-weds: the peasants are forced to sing a happy song for their master and his bride. Jim Samson notes the 'ambivalent' ending in an 'affirmative D major' (the parallel major of the opening D minor), and wonders 'if this is an ironic play on different levels of meaning or simply a response to the censor'.[47] While there is no definitive solution to this quandary, a consideration of the compositional history of this finale suggests that this conclusion would not have been Moniuszko's preferred choice. Firstly, Moniuszko and Wolski considered a number of different conclusions to the opera, one of which was a peasant uprising. Unsurprisingly, they rejected this idea as it would not pass the censor.[48] Another ending called for Halka's rescue by her faithless *szlachta* lover: while this was the ending of the first Vilnius version, the subsequent 1858 version concluded with Halka's suicide and is now the accepted *dénouement*. Indeed, Moniuszko's intention of composing a tragic opera in the grand style would have been incompatible with the heroine's ultimate rescue. Thus, despite the abrupt and ambivalent ending, the tragic integrity of the opera is sustained. Moreover, Moniuszko emphasises the religious consciousness surrounding Halka's suicide. As already mentioned, this is a striking parallel with the central tenets of Messianism. Furthermore, if we consider that Moniuszko did contemplate a peasant revolution, then we can see that the Messianist philosophy of a new moral and social polity would have been realised. However, the final scene maintains the social status quo. In the end, it seems that censorship truncated the revolutionary thrust of the opera.

Halka: Reception

The first important review of *Halka*, and the one which set the terms for the subsequent reception of the work, was written by Hans von Bülow in a long article in the *Neue Zeitschrift für Musik*.[49] As one would expect, the majority of his essay was taken up with discussion of musical details, comparisons with other operas and friendly advice to the composer. With regard to the nationalistic aspects of the opera, however, he placed the greatest emphasis on cultural nationalism. In particular, he wasted no time in defusing the opera of political motivation. He began his review thus:

> It is always a welcome occurrence when nations generally regarded as living in a state of oppression and therefore suffering in a kind of peculiar existence of their own find a satisfying outlet for their deep-seated and legitimate national aspirations by abandoning the futile and inflammable game of playing politics in favour of aesthetic activity. For it is only in the realm of the spirit that impassioned dreams can be converted

into noble reality, a reality that becomes the more undeniable the more ideal are the forms through which the national spirit seeks expression.[50]

In suggesting that musical culture could drain off political anxieties, he welcomed the recent awakening of the 'national spirit' in Poland which had 'spoken through the medium' of the composer 'in its most spiritual and therefore its richest form of expression, that of poetry and music'.[51] Along with this thoroughly German reading of the work, Bülow observed that the cream of the Polish aristocracy 'were united (as several papers reported) in giving an especially positive expression to the consciousness of the nation by the considerable personal interest they showed for the author'.[52] What Bülow meant by the 'consciousness of the nation' is demonstrated admirably when he quoted a 'cultured Polish lady' who characterised Moniuszko and his opera thus:

> c'est un poète slave: il rend avec un sentiment profond et vrai la mélancolie, l'exaltation, le passion sauvage, le résignation pieuse de la race lithuanienne. Son opéra *Halka* renferme des beautés très saisissantes pour nous autres.[53]

These *bon mots* prompted Bülow to conclude that Moniuszko had presented 'a lively and picturesque musical rendering of the contrast between peasant and noble, between village and manor'.[54] However, his general cultural discourse was tempered by the more pragmatic statement that 'more than one of the members of the audience might well be justified in complaining of verbal assault and it might be impossible to explain away the *animus injurandi*'.[55] Indeed, Bülow acknowledged that Halka 'is intended to represent the oppressed peasantry, and her tragic end preaches a philippic against this feudal nonsense' (i.e. 'the immoral tyrannical treatment of its subjects by the Slav aristocracy').[56] These remarks, however, do not measure fully the political weight of the opera. Bülow's praise of the 'picturesque' rendering of the relationship between the ancient classes is undercut by the fact that Moniuszko and Wolski had contemplated a peasant uprising in the opera. However, the most significant political import of the opera was the original impulse behind Wolski's *Halszka* (i.e. to produce a work that idealised the peasants in the aftermath of their pro-Habsburg *jacquerie*. Thus, Halka was more than a representation of the 'oppressed peasantry' or an expression of the 'national spirit': her 'elevated style' was the very essence of Dembowski's national philosophy, and her redemptive self-sacrifice resonated with Messianism.

A national school?

Moniuszko's main influence on Polish musical culture after 1865 was primarily symbolic. From 1866 until his death in 1872 he was Professor of

Harmony and Counterpoint in the Institute. Alongside Moniuszko were Zygmunt Noskowski and Władysław Żeleński, and the legacy of their pedagogy was the consolidation of a conservative national style. If any group of Polish composers deserve to be called a national school it is those who worked in the Institute in the final decades of the nineteenth century. However, Polish musicology has typically regarded Chopin, Moniuszko and Kolberg as the 'essence of the Polish national school'.[57] This notion presents a homogenous view of Polish musical culture that contrasts with the discontinuities that existed amongst these same contemporaries. As is often noted, Chopin never considered himself to be part of a national school of composers. He expressed his dismay at the provincialism of those who imitated him[58] and in relation to Kolberg's folklorist activities he remarked 'it would be better to have nothing'.[59] Furthermore, he remained famously silent on the Polish question despite the presence of Mickiewicz and other significant Messianists and nationalists in Paris. Rather, his individualism is neatly (if inscrutably) captured in a letter to his family in 1845 regarding three newly composed mazurkas:

> at this moment I am not with myself, but only as usual in some strange outer space. Granted, it is only those *espaces imaginaires* . . . I am a real blind Mazur. So, not seeing far, I have written three new mazurkas.[60]

If, as Jeffrey Kallberg has suggested, Chopin did respond to the Messianism that pervaded Paris in the 1830s, there is little evidence that Mickiewicz's mature discourses on Messianism made any impact on Chopin in the mid 1840s.[61] The above letter and the mazurkas to which he referred date from the year after Mickiewicz had completed his famous lectures at the Collège de France (1840–1844) in which he advocated passionate bloodletting on the scales of Providence for the sake of Poland.[62] Chopin's statement and his late mazurkas seem far removed for all that.

Although Moniuszko, in his introduction to *Śpiewnik domowy* (see note 20), expressed the hope that a national school would emerge from the researches of Polish scholars and musicians, it is fair to say that he was dubious about the limitations placed on him by conservative nationalists. As early in his career as 1850, in response to an article in which he was compared with Meyerbeer and was named as Chopin's successor, Moniuszko privately observed: 'I can only compose for home [*dom*], internal use, a field in which one cannot unfortunately spread one's wings.'[63] It would be incorrect to blame nationalist orthodoxy alone for his discontent: due regard must be given to the crippling restrictions placed on performing opportunities and civic freedom in Poland under Russian rule. Moniuszko was at the mercy of the Russian bureaucrats in Warsaw and in his beloved Vilnius, and he also expressed frustration with the standard of orchestral playing in Warsaw. However, he was also impatient with the insular attitudes of the Polish élite: we may recall that Kraszewski had exhorted him 'to descend to the level of the general public' in his songs (1842).⁶⁴ Moniuszko's frustration with Kraszewski was exacerbated fifteen years later when the latter claimed that Chopin's late mazurkas had lost touch with the national soul, and that Apolinary Kątksi's mazurkas were of higher artistic value.⁶⁵ Moniuszko's response identifies a fundamental problem at the heart of nationalist musical culture in Poland:

> Apolinary Kątski attempts to reflect as clearly as possible the character of his nation, which Mr. Kraszewski justifiably heard clearly in the vigour and bluster of these mazurs as the traits of his noble brotherhood [*szlachta*]. Chopin spoke only for himself...With what interest would we hear those mazurkas which Chopin could play for us back in the homeland and how differently would look those that Kątski could write in Paris. Chopin's mazurkas are jewels of universal music; Kątski's mazurkas are dear only to us . . . the two are artistically far apart though both are near to our hearts.⁶⁶

It is true that there was no small degree of personal animosity towards both Kraszewski and Kątksi in this reply. Indeed, Moniuszko was disingenuous in his remarks on Kątksi: he began the above article by proclaiming his admiration for Kątksi's talent, and he even went so far as to write: 'I love his mazurkas like my own.' However, this contrasts with his admission to Aleksander Walicki in 1852 that Kątksi was 'very incompetent in his art, very clever in small tricks, unbearable in mazurkas and even in performing them'.⁶⁷ His opinion of Kątksi had deteriorated even further when he wrote to Sikorski on the subject of Kątksi's music two years later.⁶⁸ Thus, when Kraszewski praised Kątksi at Chopin's expense, Moniuszko concluded his reply by advising Kraszewski to stay out of musical affairs and to concern himself with literature.

However, Moniuszko's comments extend deeper than personal rivalry. While Kraszewski's elevation of Kątksi over Chopin was an acute instance of insularity, Moniuszko's reply challenged the more traditional reception of Chopin as 'the worthiest representative our nation'.⁶⁹ For Moniuszko, Chopin was primarily a 'universal' composer, who 'spoke only for himself'. By clearly distinguishing between the national and the universal, Moniuszko placed Chopin outside of the specifically domestic world to which himself and Kątksi belonged.

Młoda Polska w muzyce (Young Poland in music)

Notwithstanding the informal musical education rendered in the pages of such journals as *Echo Muzyczne, Teatralne i Artystyczne* in the final two decades of the nineteenth century, and the broadening of musical taste with the founding of the Warsaw Philharmonic Hall in 1901,⁷⁰ Polish musical culture retained its ultra-conservative dynamic into the early twentieth century. The emergence of a cohort of young, modernist composers known as *Młoda Polska* led to a sharp conflict with the old guard.[71] In response to a concert in 1907 which included Szymanowski's Concert Overture, the arch-conservative critic, Aleksander Poliński, chastised the group thus:

> What kind of Poland is this that does not serve the nation as Chopin and Moniuszko did? . . . These composers [Young Poland] seem to be under the influence of an evil spirit which corrupts their work and tries to deprive their music of its individual and national original tone, turning them into parrots that imitate Wagner and Strauss.[72]

Such cultural protectionism prompted Adolf Chybiński, a champion of the Young Poland group, to remark that 'There is an ignorance which does not exist in Western countries, in fact in Western countries they could not imagine such ignorance as it is here.'[73] It is not surprising, therefore, that the young generation of the 1900s reacted against the insularity of their forebears by imitating their modern European counterparts. Where other nations sought an alternative to Germanism in the post-1870 era, Young Poland actively sought it out in an attempt to modernise Polish music.

Just how conservative this culture was is illustrated by the fate of Karłowicz's *Lithuanian Rhapsody* (1906). While the most advanced of Karłowicz's symphonic poems embraced the musical language of Wagner and Richard Strauss, the *Lithuanian Rhapsody* was different in style (i.e. its form was traditionally episodic in the manner of Smetana's *Vltava* (1874), it quoted folk tunes that the composer had collected in his native Lithuania, and these folk tunes were treated in a manner that recalls the so-called 'changing-background' technique of Glinka and the Russian nationalists). Moreover, while Karłowicz tirelessly promoted his other works in Poland and abroad, he consistently withheld the *Lithuanian Rhapsody* from performance. As I have argued elsewhere, this was most probably because it would answer to the prescriptions of the conservative nationalists with whom Karłowicz was constantly in conflict.[74] That it was posthumously received as a 'national' work supports such a notion. Poliński greeted the première of the *Rhapsody* (given eighteen days after the composer's death in February 1909) in triumphant nationalist rhetoric. He noted that the composer 'shows pure Polish soul . . . [and] one should consider the Rhapsody as the pearl of Karłowicz's work and as a model for all the Young Poland Composers'.[75] While Karłowicz never clearly stated his reasons for withholding the work, other than to say it required a high degree of subtlety in performance, it is reasonable to assume that Poliński's attitude realised the composer's fear that the work would be lionised by the traditional nationalists.

Coda

The exchange between Kraszewski and Moniuszko calls into question Dahlhaus's claim that nationalism 'seemed to suspend or resolve the conflict between the avant-garde and popular taste.'[76] That Kraszewski made his remarks nearly a decade after Chopin's death shows that these works were not assimilated into Polish musical culture. Paradoxically, it was only with the advent of Young Poland, and the break with nationalist musical culture, that the more advanced of Chopin's musical techniques were made available for Polish music.

Notes and References

1. I am grateful to the Arts Faculty Fund of University College, Cork, for its research grant. I also want to thank Beata Oziębłowska for her translations of some of the Polish texts quoted in this chapter.
2. Maurycy Mochnacki, *On Polish Literature in the Nineteenth Century* (Warsaw, 1830), quoted in Donald Pirie,'The Agony in the Garden: Polish Romanticism', in Roy Porter and Mikuláš Teich (eds.), *Romanticism in National Context* (Cambridge, 1988), p. 328.
3. The nobility can be subdivided into three groups: the aristocrats (*magnateria*), the gentry (*szlachta*) and the petty nobility (*drobnaszlachta*). The latter were the largest group, and were so poor that they were almost indistinguishable from the peasants except for their pretensions and their literacy.
4. J. Slomka, *From Serfdom to Self-Government* (1941), quoted in Elie Kedourie, *Nationalism* (London, 1960), p. 120. See also Kazimierz Dobrowolski, 'Peasant Traditional Culture', in Teodor Shanin (ed.), *Peasants and Peasant Societies* (Harmondsworth, 1971).
5. Andrzej Walicki, *Philosophy and Romantic Nationalism: The Case of Poland* (Indiana, 1994), p. 68.
6. Wanda Taylor,'Aspects of Cultural Nationalism in the Congress Kingdom of Poland in the 1840s' (MLitt diss., Oxford University, 1987). Taylor constructs her classification as a complementary system to that of Stefan Kieniewicz's in *The Emancipation of the Polish Peasantry* (Chicago, 1969), and Walicki's in *Philosophy and Romantic Nationalism*. These groups may briefly be described as follows: the conservatives were Catholic aristocrats who believed strongly in their traditional feudalism; the Messianists were concentrated in Paris after 1831; the romantic democrats sought to dismantle feudalism and create a new social order without resorting to violent revolution; the liberals wanted to replace feudalism with capitalism as a matter of modernisation but without reference to social and national ideologies – they were drawn predominantly from the wealthy *szlachta* and saw themselves as political centrists opposed to socialism, violent revolution and religious conservatism; the positivists were opposed to romanticism, and turned to French positivism for matters of economic methodology – their contribution to Polish life came after the 1863 uprising when they absorbed the liberals and democrats. We may further note that there was a formidable group of conservative *émigrés* who gathered themselves around Prince Adam Czartoryski, the former foreign minister to Alexander I, and president of the national government until he left Poland in August 1831. Czartoryski's supporters regarded him as the future king of a restored Poland. There was

strong opposition, however, from the revolutionary left, who published a declaration in July 1834 signed by 2,840 Polish exiles stating that he was an enemy of the emigration. See Leslie, *Reform and Insurrection*, pp. 3–4.

7   Taylor notes that her category of romantic socialists corresponds to Kieniewicz's revolutionary democrats. I have chosen to use Taylor's nomenclature so as to remain consistent with her overall analysis.
8   Taylor, 'Aspects of Cultural Nationalism', p. 145 and 151.
9   See Walicki, *Philosophy and Romantic Nationalism*, p. 30.
10   Ibid., p. 212.
11   Ibid., p. 208.
12   His work had a profound effect on Mickiewicz, and he was a frequent guest in the Moniuszko home in Warsaw in the late 1820s.
13   Famous examples are the activities of the ethnographer, Zorian D. Chodakowski, and the composer, ethnographer and folklorist, Oskar Kolberg.
14   See Rosemary Hunt, 'Moniuszko's Musical Treatment of Texts by Mickiewicz' (PhD diss., University of London, 1980), Chapter 4.
15   Elsner, *Rozprawa o metryczności i rytmiczności języka polskiego* (Warsaw, 1818). For an analysis of Elsner's thesis, see Hunt, 'Moniuszko's Musical Treatment of Texts by Mickiewicz', p. 55. See also Pirie, 'The Agony in the Garden', for the debate which raged within Polish letters between the supporters of the Enlightenment and the new Romanticism.
16   By focusing on the essential 'softness' of the Polish language that results from the accent on the penultimate syllable, he argued that 'masculine endings' should not be incorporated from French and German.
17   Letter to his wife dated 6 July 1840, Berlin, quoted in B. M. Maciejewski, *Moniuszko, Father of Polish Opera* (London, 1979), p. 33.
18   See Taylor, 'Aspects of Cultural Nationalism', Chapter 2.
19   *Śpiewnik domowy* is variously translated as 'Home Song Book,' 'Domestic Songs' or 'Songs for Domestic Use'.
20   Moniuszko, 'Śpiewnik domowy', in *Tygodnik Petersburski*, No. 72 (22 September 1842), published in Witold Rudziński (ed.), *Stanisław Moniuszko: Listy Zebrane* (Collected Letters) (Kraków, 1969), pp. 601–3.
21   Like Mickiewicz and most other Poles, Moniuszko was taught Niemcewicz's *Śpiewy historyczne* (Historical Songs, 1816) in childhood, the subject matter of which embraced Polish history from the tenth to the early nineteenth centuries.
22   J. I. Kraszewski, article on *Śpiewnik domowy* in *Athenaeum* (1842), quoted in Aleksander Walicki, *Stanisław Moniuszko* (Warsaw, 1873), p. 89.
23   Józef Sikorski, the future editor of *Ruch Muzyczny* (Musical Movement) and founder of the Warsaw Music Society, was seminal in getting it performed.
24   *Przegląd Naukowy* was founded in 1842 at a time when Dembowski was on the run from the Russians for conspiratorial activities. The title of the journal embraces the idea of 'learning', including philosophy and history.
25   *Ojciec Hilary* dealt with the peasant question.
26   Wolski's poem was based on the romantic tale, *The Mountain Girl*, by Kazimierz Wójcicki who was one of the active figures in Polish ethnography.
27   *Przegląd Naukowy*, for example, was disbanded and its editors were arrested.
28   This was the original two-act version, and was given a concert performance because there were no available resources for a staged version. It was not given a full performance in Vilnius until 1854.
29   The period of Alexander II's reign brought about a number of significant improvements in Polish musical life: the establishment of the journal *Ruch Muzyczny* (Musical Movement) in 1857, the opening of the Warsaw Music Institute in 1861

and the Warsaw Music Society in 1870, and the establishment of the journal *Echo Muzyczne, Teatralne i Artystyczne* (Musical and Artistical Echo) in 1877. Moniuszko was made Artistic Director of the Warsaw Opera in 1858, and later he became Professor of Harmony and Counterpoint in the Institute from 1866 until his death.

30 For his reaction to the announcement of *Halka's* revival, see his letter to August Iwański dated October 1857, quoted in Maciejewski, *Moniuszko*, pp. 57–8.
31 W. Rudziński, *Stanisław Moniuszko, Studio i materiały* (Kraków, 1955), Vol. 1, p. 127.
32 Leslie, *Reform and Insurrection*, p. 58.
33 See Leslie, *Reform and Insurrection*, pp.14 and 57. Walicki claims that Metternich's administration skilfully encouraged the slaughter of the Galician gentry; see his *Philosophy and Romantic Nationalism*, p. 284. See also T. W. Simons Jr., 'The Peasant Revolt of 1846 in Galicia: Recent Historiography', *Slavic Review*, 30, 4 (1971), pp. 795–817.
34 Quoted in Walicki, *Philosophy and Romantic Nationalism*, p. 220.
35 Krasiński and Słowacki were Mickiewicz's greatest rivals.
36 His conservative stance reflected his family background: he was the son of General Count Krasiński and Maria Radziwiłł' who maintained good relations with the partitioning powers. See Julian Krzyżanowski, *A History of Polish Literature* (Warsaw, 1978), pp. 287 ff., and Pirie 'The Agony in the Garden', p. 332.
37 Quoted in Walicki, *Philosophy and Romantic Nationalism*, p. 284.
38 Carl Dahlhaus, *Nineteenth-Century Music*, trans. J. Bradford Robinson (Berkeley, 1989), p. 223.
39 Moniuszko, *Halka: Score* (Kraków, 1951), p. 351.
40 See Hans von Bülow, *Neue Zeitschrift fur Musik*, 20 (12 November 1858), and 21 (19 November 1858), quoted in Maciejewski, *Moniuszko*, p. 78.
41 Moniuszko, *Halka: Score*, p. 448.
42 Ibid., p. 449.
43 Ibid., p. 455.
44 Ibid., p. 458.
45 Walicki, *Philosophy and Romantic Nationalism*, p. 240.
46 Ibid., p. 242. The conflict between traditional Catholicism and Messianism is illustrated by the fact that Mickiewicz's Paris lectures were banned by the Catholic Church.
47 Jim Samson, 'Halka', in Stanley Sadie (ed.), *The New Grove Dictionary of Opera* (London, 1992), Vol. 2, p. 603.
48 See Gerald Abraham, *Essays on Russian and East European Music* (Oxford, 1985), p. 159. Abraham refers to Leon Schiller's discussion of the various finales in his introduction to the 1953 Polskie Wydawnictwo Muzyczne edition.
49 See note 40 above.
50 Bülow, quoted in Maciejewski, *Moniuszko*, p. 67.
51 Ibid.
52 Ibid., p. 69.
53 'He is a slavic poet; he portrays with a true and profound feeling the melancholy, the exaltation, the wild passion, the pious resignation of the Lithuanian race. His opera, *Halka*, embodies wonderful beauties.' Ibid., p. 78.
54 Ibid., p. 72.
55 Ibid., p. 70.
56 Ibid.
57 E. Dziębowska, 'On the Polish National School', in Z. Chechlińska and J. Stęszewski (eds.), *Polish Musicological Studies* (Kraków, 1985), Vol. 2, p. 140.
58 See Zofia Chechlińska, 'Chopin Reception in Nineteenth-Century Poland', in Jim Samson (ed.), *The Cambridge Companion to Chopin* (Cambridge 1992), p. 218.

59 In a letter to his family dated 19 April 1847, published in Opieński and Voynich (eds.), *Chopin's Letters*, p. 325.
60 In a letter to his family dated 20 July 1845, published in Henryk Opieński and Ethel L. Voynich (eds.), *Frédéric Chopin: Chopin's Letters* (New York, 1988), p. 285. The mazurkas in question were Op.59 A minor, A flat major, F sharp minor, composed and published in 1845.
61 For a discussion of the relationship between Messianism and nationalism in Chopin's music in the 1830s, see Jeffrey Kallberg, 'The Rhetoric of Genre: Chopin's Nocturne in G Minor', *19th-Century Music*, XI, 3, 1988, pp. 238–61.
62 See Walicki, *Philosophy and Romantic Nationalism*, pp. 247 ff. and *passim* for a discussion of Mickiewicz's mature philosophy of Messianism.
63 In a letter to Sikorski dated 23 December 1850, quoted in Rudziński (ed.), *Stanisław Moniuszko: Listy Zebrane*, pp. 160ff.
64 See note 22 above.
65 Kraszewski, 'Listy do redaktora' [Letters to the Editor], *Gazeta Warszawska*, 1857, No. 80, published in Stefan Świerzewski, *J. I. Kraszewski i polskie życie muzyczne XIX wieku* (J. I. Kraszewski and Polish musical life in the nineteenth century) (Kraków, 1963), pp. 169 ff.
66 Moniuszko, 'Parę uwag z powodu listów J. I. Kraszewskiego do *Gazety Warszawskiej*' (A few remarks on J. I. Kraszewski's letters to the *Warsaw Gazette*), *Ruch Muzyczny*, 1857, No. 11, p. 84, quoted in Dziębowska, 'On the Polish National School', p. 144.
67 Letter to Aleksander Walicki dated 11 June 1852, quoted in Rudziński (ed.), *Stanisław Moniuszko: Listy Zebrane*, p. 182. Kątski often gave his mazurkas programmatic titles (e.g. Sobieski, Batory).
68 Letter to Józef Sikorski dated 3 June 1855, quoted in Rudziński (ed.), *Stanisław Moniuszko. Listy Zebrane*, pp. 203 ff.
69 M. A. Szulc, article about Chopin in *Orędownik naukowy*, 26 (17 June 1841), quoted in Chechlińska, 'Chopin Reception in Nineteenth-Century Poland', p. 217.
70 Arthur Nikisch, Richard Strauss and Siegfried Wagner conducted in the Warsaw Philharmonic Hall in the early 1900s.
71 *Młoda Polska w muzyce* refers to the music publishing company set up by Karol Szymanowski, Grezgorz Fitelberg, Ludomir Różycki, Apolinary Szeluto and Prince Władysław Lubomirski in Berlin in 1905. Mieczysław Karłowicz was not a formal member of this short-lived group but he was a key figure in the Young Poland era. See my 'An Aesthetical and Analytical Evaluation of the Music of Mieczysław Karłowicz (1876–1909)' (PhD diss., University College, Cork, 1994).
72 Poliński, concert review in *Kurier Warszawski*, 110 (22 April 1907), quoted in Teresa Chylińska, *Karol Szymanowski*, trans. A. T. Jordan (New York, 1973), p. 33.
73 Quoted in Kornel Michałowski, 'Adolf Chybiński a Młoda Polska w muzyce', in *Muzyka Polska a modernizm* (Kraków, 1981), p. 109.
74 See my 'Karłowicz's *Lithuanian Rhapsody*: An Expression of Polish Romantic Nationalism or a Skeleton in the Closet?', *Irish Musical Studies*, 5 (Dublin, 1996), pp. 205–13.
75 Alexander Poliński, concert review in *Kurier Warszawski*, 58 (27 February 1909), quoted in Murphy, 'Karłowicz's *Lithuanian Rhapsody*', p. 211.
76 Dahlhaus, 'Nationalism and Music', in *Between Romanticism and Modernism*, trans. Mary Whitall (Berkeley, 1980), p. 99.

9.
Music and Nationalism in Italy

JOHN ROSSELLI

In its engagement with music, Italian nationalism is anomalous twice over. First, up until Italian unification in 1859–1860 nationalists had no need to identify a geographical area called 'Italy' for which political nationhood must be won, hence they had no need to enlist music among other cultural expressions as a means of identifying it. Secondly, nationalism began to take shape at a time when the educated élite throughout Europe (except France) believed that Italian music was supreme. Nationalists need not exalt their people's music when others had already done the job for them; still less need they discover it.

If we accept definitions of nationalism such as Renan's, according to which the will for unity matters far more than pre-existing objective factors;[1] if, further, we agree with Gellner that nationalism is, in one respect, 'the imposition of a high culture on society',[2] and in another the deliberate forging of group identity through political action aimed at achieving 'multi-symbol congruence among a group of people defined initially by a single central symbol',[3] we have to conclude that, for Italian nationalists in the run-up to political independence and unity, music called for no exercise of will, did not have to be imposed and, as a symbol, was already fully defining.

At most, the words and the musical idiom of the chief Italian form, opera, might serve to communicate nationalist feeling which had already been roused by other means. The part music played in nationalist agitation has, however, been a good deal blown up by legends put about after the achievement of political nationhood and repeated ever since. It was indeed after political unification, amid widespread discontent with its results, that nationalist discourse came to engage seriously with music.

Neither in the eighteenth nor the early nineteenth century did anyone doubt where Italy was, although it was politically divided among a number of states (at most times between nine and eleven, but reduced to five for the last few years of the Napoleonic wars) and some of these states depended on empires based outside the area – first Spain and Austria, then

France, then, from 1814, Austria alone. As a physical unit, Italy was clearly bounded by the Alps and the sea; Italian high culture, like that of ancient Greece or India, was well understood to be shared, and was embodied in the Italian language, even though this was a mostly official and literary medium and most people spoke local dialects. A few border or outlying areas whose élites shared Italian culture, musical culture included, might raise questions about their identity (examples are Trieste, the Ionian Islands, Malta), but such questions were seldom articulated during the nation-building years 1790–1860.

Italian music was therefore that which was created in the Italian cultural area and enjoyed by the élite – chiefly, in those years, opera. Folk music aroused little interest: it was not called upon (as in the Celtic areas of the British Isles, or in Eastern Europe) to witness to the essential identity of the nation. The examples of folk music that began to appear in print between about 1840 and 1850 were often influenced by comic opera, with which folk music had a symbiotic relationship, particularly in Naples and Venice; most Venetian patriotic songs in the revolutionary years 1848–1849, were the work of professional composers, as were many so-called Venetian folk-songs.[4] Serious studies of folk music only began to appear at the end of the nineteenth century.[5]

Music – which was virtually co-terminous with opera – had in Italy its 'fatherland', or so the radical nationalist leader Giuseppe Mazzini wrote in an 1836 essay on the 'philosophy of music'. He was, however, uttering a truism rather than a polemical assertion. Mazzini was dissatisfied with the state of Italian music, but he had no doubt that in this art 'the land of Porpora and Pergolesi' – eighteenth-century composers who, in his day were honoured rather than performed – was supreme.[6] In the previous generation the musicologist Charles Burney had declared that music was 'a manufacture in Italy': a trading country like Britain as a matter of course imported it as it did wine or tea.[7] The modern section of his *General History of Music* (1789) concentrated on Italian opera as self-evidently the most important genre.

The pre-eminence of (Italian) opera had always been contested in France. By Mazzini's day it was contested in the German-speaking countries as well (and among music lovers elsewhere who prized the German symphonic tradition). This, however, did not stop Italian composers, singers and musicians from triumphing throughout Europe and the Americas, and even, by the 1820s, in Paris; the operas they brought with them drew élite audiences and earned vast sums; their virtual monopoly was such that one of the earliest American opera singers, appearing in New York with an Italian company, was made to feel 'a foreigner in her own country'.[8] In Italy itself, the German symphonic tradition attracted only a small minority; theoreticians habitually dismissed it as too 'learned' and too centred on harmony and orchestration.[9] Italians therefore had no cause to feel that their music was an index of deprivation or inferiority. Nor did they need to characterise it as national: music was simply what Italians produced.

The first serious internal criticism of Italian opera came from the 'Jacobin' minority who welcomed the French revolutionary armies in 1796–1799. Literary men had often complained of the excessive importance given to singers and to decorative music at the expense of the words, but the same literary men went on writing for the lyric theatre; their reforms did not go beyond a striving after austere declamation and coherent drama, as in the libretti Ranieri de' Calzabigi wrote for Gluck (*Orfeo ed Euridice*, 1762; *Alceste*, 1767), which had no patriotic or national content and could be first performed in Vienna, then adapted for Paris.

With the short-lived conquest by French revolutionary ideals, however, democratic authors in positions of influence accused serious opera of being the plaything of aristocrats, effete, luxurious, even 'lascivious' – a term so used by the poet Ugo Foscolo in his famous ode 'Dei sepolcri' of 1806. They set out to purge the genre by banning castrati, the chief exponents of virtuoso singing, and by promoting high-minded republican tragedies such as they themselves wrote.[10] This attempt came to little, however. Under the Napoleonic regime from 1801, castrati were reinstated and florid music still ruled; so did censorship. At most, some libretti embodied the austere virtues attributed to ancient Greece and republican Rome, with a transparent allusion to the modern 'patriots', some of whom had perished, for instance in the crushing of the 1799 republic at Naples.[11]

The 'patriotic' critique of opera was to continue – albeit underground. An anonymous verse of 1833 contrasted the heroic Venetians of the Fourth Crusade with their descendants, content to applaud the latest opera.[12] In 1847 a Tuscan historian urged the closure of all music schools in favour of schools teaching useful crafts, on the grounds that music merely pleased the senses – cultivating 'arias, trills, and vocal ornaments' kept the young from thinking and turned them into 'sheep'[13] – while in Milan, after the outbreak of revolution in 1848, some democrats denounced 'lascivious' operatic music as an argument for closing down La Scala: let it give way to the sound of guns.[14]

Patriotism of this kind expressed a universal ideal of republican virtue and, in its early form up to the 1820s, largely accepted the influence of France as the guiding '*grande nation*'. It had in common with nationalism only a revulsion for what was felt to be a lack of manly, warlike ardour and the urge to make good the deficiency. Its moralistic attack on opera paralleled that of the ultra-conservative Cardinal Vicar of Rome, who in 1838 investigated the influence 'lascivious' theatre melodies were having on church music.[15] Though denounced by both extremes as hedonistic, opera in these years remained the premier entertainment for the upper classes and the focus of their social life.[16]

In the Restoration period, between 1814 and 1846–47, attempts at revolution in parts of Italy (which were briefly successful in 1820–21 and 1831) were the work of small minorities, again moved by universal ideals – either of parliamentary liberalism under aristocratic guidance or of full-blown democracy. The poets Giacomo Leopardi and Alessandro Manzoni spoke for many of the élite in lamenting the indolence of Italians and their dependence on a foreign power, Austria, but only a small group, led by Mazzini in the early 1830s, looked for political unity for the whole of the Italian peninsula, to be achieved through popular revolt and self-determination. (The alternative, a take-over by Piedmont, the only Italian state independent of Austria, was envisaged only for the northern plain; to Piedmontese monarchs and statesmen this was a traditional goal, to be taken no further.)

The great majority were still intensely local-minded. When, in 1843, the publication of Vincenzo Gioberti's *Of the Moral and Civil Primacy of the Italians* set off a prolonged debate, this centred not on the making of a unified nation but on the possibility of creating in Italy a federation or confederation of existing states, freed from Austrian hegemony and perhaps headed by the Pope – a notion further encouraged by the election in 1846 of the so-called 'Liberal' Pope Pius IX. The tumultuous course of the 1848 revolutions was to show that conflicting aims among the various social classes and local élites stood in the way of such an outcome. Rather than a concerted move towards nation-building, historians now tend to see these years as striving after modernisation, common to parts of both the ruling and the dissenting élites; they have also stressed the difficulties governments had, both before and after unification, in modernising Italy when they had to deal with fragmented and often resistant élite groups.[17]

In the three decades before 1848, Italian opera was a repository of, at most, cultural nationalism – a hankering after the lost glories of the past, and a pursuit of noble, even heroic, behaviour in the present, which might imply a call to political action but not to the making of a unitary Italian state.

We need to clear the ground of legends which, when looked into, turn out to have originated in late nineteenth-century anecdotal writings; their authors' reading of nationalist sentiment into the early works of Verdi and even Bellini goes on being reproduced in modern accounts, though the cavalier misuse of evidence by two of these authors – Gino Monaldi and 'Folchetto' (Jacopo Caponi), both highly influential – has been exposed.[18] Besides accepting such 'evidence' uncritically, modern writers have often failed to look at historical context: supposed attitudes of 1842 have been 'verified' by an appeal to what were undoubtedly attitudes of 1846 or 1848. Because the Italian context changed so swiftly, particularly during the 1840s, no such 'verification' can hold water.

A clear example is the prevalent contention that Bellini's *Norma* (1831) was a nationalist opera because it showed a subject people rebelling against a foreign empire. It was so interpreted by Italian audiences in the immediate run-up to the 1848 revolutions, when the prophecy that the hand of God would 'free Gaul from the enemy's eagles' triggered demonstrations, as did other opportune tags in libretti. In 1838, however, *Norma* had played in Cremona before the visiting Austrian Emperor; not only was there no hitch, but the performers lined up to sing a hymn in the Emperor's praise, to general cheers and applause.[19] The opera's 'nationalist' meaning was read into it after it had been performed up and down Italy for a decade and a half.

A crucial example is that of the young Giuseppe Verdi. Few now seriously maintain that earlier composers were nationalists. Rossini was an ironic conservative; the big aria in his *L'Italiana in Algeri* (Venice, 1813), 'Pensa alla patria' ('Think of the fatherland'), sometimes cited as evidence of nationalism, was a propaganda piece aimed at exhorting young subjects of Napoleon's Kingdom of Italy (a territory comprising about a third of the peninsula) to fight in the desperate German campaign that followed the retreat from Moscow – this at a time when the Napoleonic regime was deeply unpopular in Venice and another third of Italy had been annexed to France.[20] Later, in his Paris years, Rossini composed operas on themes of liberation, notably *Guillaume Tell* (1829), because such themes were welcome to the French middle-class audience. The 1848 revolution in Bologna gave him a serious fright and he became implacably opposed to 'progress' of any kind, though after Italian unification had come about he persuaded himself that he had always favoured it – behaviour which is common (and as a rule sincere) after a nationalist movement has triumphed.[21]

Like many other composers, Bellini was wholly non-political; when he in turn wrote for Paris an opera based on the English revolution (*I puritani*, 1835), he assured his friend and agent that, for Italian consumption, the word 'liberty' and 'every liberal expression' could go, and so could the very title of the work.[22] Giovanni Pacini, successful from the 1820s to the 1850s, was frankly reactionary even after unification.[23] Donizetti may have shown concern for the glory of Italy in a letter of 1840[24] (the letter's authenticity is questionable), but that did not prevent him from accepting, in 1842, a post in Vienna as court composer to the Austrian Emperor, the alleged oppressor of his country.

The test case is Verdi, who made his operatic debut in 1839 at the age of 26. His early period of prolific production, in the 1840s, was a time of increasingly heated debate over the chances of achieving Italian independence, as well as full-blown Romanticism in the arts. The accepted view – which is only now beginning to be questioned – is that he was from the start a nationalist, that his early operas gave voice to straightforward 'Risorgimento' nationalist feeling, and that contemporary audiences understood them to do so. Statements to this effect are usually capped with the report that audiences shouted 'Viva Verdi' as a means of cheering King

Victor Emmanuel II of Piedmont, who fought Austria in 1849 and again in 1859, as the future king of a united Italy (VERDI was an acronym of Vittorio Emanuele Re d'Italia). This slogan was indeed used, but only after Victor Emmanuel had made the provocative speech on 9 January 1859 that set off a crisis and led to the outbreak of war on 29 April. The slogan was first uttered at La Scala about the end of January,[25] but after June 1859 (after March 1861 officially) Victor Emmanuel was indeed king of Italy, so it was no longer needed.

One author – an anthropologist working from a structuralist perspective – has felt able to dismiss the whole of Verdi's supposed share in the Risorgimento, together with the Risorgimento itself and the idea of Italy as a nation, as a 'myth'.[26] Though Verdi's nationalism has been much exaggerated, this approach ignores the mood at once reflected and generated by his music and his actual political stance. In the earlier part of his career that stance was not fully clear. In the 1830s he was strongly anti-clerical and seems to have been a covert republican, hence a liberal, and perhaps even a democrat. After the outbreak of revolution in 1848 Mazzini won him over to enthusiastic support for Italian unity – an outlook he was to maintain, though in socially and politically more cautious terms, for the rest of his life. He composed an overtly patriotic opera, *La battaglia di Legnano*, for Mazzini's short-lived Roman Republic of 1849. The opera was based on the twelfth-century struggle of north Italian cities against the German-based Emperor Frederick Barbarossa which was seen as a parallel to the 1848 revolt of Milan and Venice against Austria.

This, however, does not necessarily mean that Verdi was a nationalist during the years when he was writing the earlier 'Risorgimento' operas. Some evidence suggests that, if he was one, he was hardly intransigent: he wrote a cantata for the Austrian Emperor's birthday, and took trouble to dedicate *I lombardi alla prima crociata* (1843), very much a 'Risorgimento' opera, to his own sovereign, the Austrian Archduchess Marie-Louise, Duchess of Parma.[27] Even after the fall of Mazzini's Rome he was pragmatic enough to recycle *La battaglia di Legnano* in the despotic states restored under Austrian hegemony with a bowdlerised libretto and the title shifted to the Dutch revolt against Spain; he did remark that 'to keep [in the work] all the ardour for fatherland and liberty without ever mentioning fatherland or liberty is a mighty hard task', but added 'all the same, one can try'.[28]

Verdi's own intentions and outlook are one question, but what his early operas meant to audiences when they were first performed is quite another. Stories (uncorroborated) to the effect that audiences quickly detected allusions to Italian slavery and independence and even broke into cries of 'War! War!' have always run up against the fact that the operas had to be approved before the first performance by a censorship which was strictly enforced in all the Italian states, while the police dealt summarily with disturbances – political or otherwise.

All we know about the workings of such censorship up to 1848 shows that it was concerned in the first place with morality and religion: it specially guarded against the representation of clergy and religious ritual or language and, in the face of the Romantic cult of violent emotion, took a stand against multiple killings, suicide and adultery, especially if they were made blatantly obvious. As a rule it banned words thought dangerous by autocratic governments, such as 'liberty' and 'chains': *Guillaume Tell*, a story of revolt against medieval Austria, in its Italian version, in some states, had to have its location changed to an area not under Austrian rule.[29]

Italian librettists, however, exercised self-censorship and did not, by and large, put forward texts which were unlikely to pass. In Verdi's *Attila* (1846), Pope Leo the Great (who miraculously prevents Attila from taking and sacking Rome) appeared as 'an ancient Roman', though this supposed historical event was well known to many in the audience; his *Ernani* (1844) ends with one suicide rather than, as in Victor Hugo's play, three. Censorship was for the most part a matter of revision here and there by officials who were themselves Italian literary men.[30] If the censor did not forbid the performance of an opera, we may wonder just how nationalistic it was understood to be at the time of its first performance.

The early Verdi operas which are most often identified as nationalist – *Nabucco* (1842), *I lombardi*, *Ernani* and *Attila* – all passed the censor: the last with no difficulty whatever, the first three with only minor ones. These difficulties, significantly, had to do with religion, not with politics: the Archbishop of Milan objected to the heroine's prayer 'Ave Maria' in *I Lombardi* (it was merely reworded as 'Salve Maria'; the opera got away with showing the sacrament of baptism), while in *Nabucco* the censor was concerned to make sure that the acting of the parts of Zaccaria (a crypto high priest) and Nabucco (a king who demands to be worshipped as a god) should be discreet. However, it is true that he secured the removal from an early version of the *Ernani* libretto of the word 'liberty' and of a mention of Brutus and the Gracchi, Roman republican leaders of popular revolt; he probably also induced the librettist of *Nabucco* to remove the word 'fetters' from the final chorus of rejoicing, though 'chains' still figured elsewhere in the work. Neither of these passages was, in context, clearly applicable to Italy.[31]

The censor took no notice of Ezio's celebrated address to Attila 'You shall have the whole world, leave Italy to me', which was said much later to have triggered demonstrations in Venice in March 1846, but for which there is no contemporary evidence. In 1846 this line – derived from Werner's German tragedy of 1808 – did not necessarily refer to a united Italy or even to the complete expulsion of Austria. Some people thought the whole idea illogical: the librettist Temistocle Solera explained that Ezio (Aetius, a historical figure) was inviting Attila to conquer both the eastern and the western Roman Empire but to let him rule Italy.[32] Since the western Roman Empire was centred on Italy, that could mean only that Attila would be

Ezio's suzerain – in principle not unlike the federation some Italian nationalists still had in mind in 1846, with some states, as before, under Austrian Habsburg princes but no longer directly ruled from Vienna. The libretto also went out of its way to compliment the audience on the foundation of their city – a ploy going back to Metastasio's *Ezio* (Venice, 1728), which was presumably welcome at a time when many Venetians still hankered after the old republic (which they were to restore briefly in 1848).

True, as conflict heightened in the months leading up to February 1848, lines which had not troubled the censor might have changed their meaning for the audience, like those already quoted from *Norma*. Since the election of Pius IX, audiences had cheered the word 'pio' ('pious', but also Pius in Italian) whenever it came up, while in *Ernani* some managements had got the chorus to alter their praise of Charles V from 'O sommo Carlo' to 'O sommo Pio', setting off huge applause which the police tolerated: no one could be against the Pope, and the expectations he had aroused were still vague though great. When demonstrations could be that opportunistic, Ezio's address too may – though we have no clear record of it – have been reinterpreted as a wholehearted call for independence.

What counted at this late stage was not the original intentions of the composer and librettist but the audience's use of the theatre – the regular meeting place of the élite – to demonstrate their feelings. The theatre had long seen faction fights, on occasion virtual local civil wars, centred on the merits of rival singers or dancers, but perhaps this served as a means of expressing wider conflicts – although these were more likely to be local than national.[33] In the crucial winter of 1847–48 members of the audience generally demonstrated against (and some would have supported) the authorities.[34]

The best-known example of a nationalist element in Verdi's early operas – whether intended or as perceived by audiences – is provided by a string of choruses, in particular the chorus of ancient Hebrews in their Babylonian exile, 'Va, pensiero, sull'ali dorate', from *Nabucco*. This has since become an unofficial Italian national anthem, though it remains unspecific enough to have been adopted in 1996–97 by the Northern League, the political party that wants Northern Italy to secede from the rest of the country and form a new state called 'Padania'. 'Va, pensiero' expresses nostalgia for a lost fatherland; only with the entrance of the Hebrew leader Zaccaria does the subsequent fast section (not usually mentioned as part of the legendary 'nationalist chorus') include a call to action and a prophecy that Babylon will be destroyed.

This chorus was successful enough for Verdi to repeat the effect in *I lombardi* ('O signore, dal tetto natio', another expression of nostalgia for the homeland); *Ernani* included a rebels' chorus as a call to action against Charles V ('Si ridesti il Leon di Castiglia'), though the Emperor presently won them over by his magnanimity. It has, however, become clear that –

contrary to reports sometimes falsified by Verdi's early biographers – 'Va, pensiero' aroused no particular enthusiasm among the original Milan audience, who were far more struck with other passages; in Venice, where (unlike Milan) the opera was not a great success, the figure of Zaccaria was thought boringly 'sacerdotal' and after the first performance one of his arias was cut out. In the 1848–49 revolutionary period, when audiences were free to express nationalist sentiments, 'Va, pensiero' and 'O signore, dal tetto natio' were little cultivated and were even described as not positive or martial enough, while *Attila* could be said to show a humiliating period of Italian history.[35] Acceptance of the great choruses as nationalist anthems did not in fact precede but followed the achievement of national unity – a clear instance of reading back.

Although the ground has to be cleared of myths, Verdi's early works do earn their description as 'Risorgimento' operas – but by musical means rather than by specific allusions in the text. Their headlong energy and, in many places, soaring grandeur are fitting for a collective struggle: in them 'a people found its voice'.[36] The question, as usual, with music is: just what do these qualities express? Which people are they addressed to, and what sort of collective act might they inspire it to perform? A further complication is the increasing role, since the late eighteenth century, of the chorus within serious opera, and of the military band in all kinds of music-making.

One example of the many choruses is the one in *La clemenza di Tito* (1791). Mozart and his librettist purposely made this more dramatic; in the original Metastasio text of 1734 which they adapted it had been celebratory. The opera, in any case, remained impeccably monarchist. Later Italian operas generally used the chorus to build up a big scene of crisis and resolution in the Act 1 finale, and often elsewhere, as in Rossini's serious operas, especially *Mosè in Egitto* (1819), *Maometto II* (1820) and *Semiramide* (1823).[37]

Military bands got a tremendous fillip from the wars of the French Revolution and Napoleon; throughout the period 1796–1814 armies crossed Italy or garrisoned its cities. Even in Restoration Italy, bands were much in evidence. Under Austrian rule in Venice, excellent military and naval bands (one at least with a Venetian conductor) played in St Mark's Square and did much to popularise operatic and other music; only after 1858, late in the Austrian period, did nationalist Italians boycott them.[38] In Rome on Easter Sunday 1829, military bands outside St Peter's were so loud that the choir could not sing the anthem.[39]

This military influence was such that, in Italian opera from the 1810s on, band instruments and quick march tunes are often featured at what strike later generations as inappropriate moments, even in the serious Rossini operas already mentioned. Bellini, often thought of as an 'elegiac' composer, wrote an incongruous march for a crucial scene in *Norma*, and a martial duet in *Puritani* ('Suoni la tromba') that was equally effective whether, as in Paris, the two captains sang of 'fatherland' and 'liberty' or, as in Italian productions, 'glory' and 'loyalty'. Besides using the band, Verdi's early operas at times blatantly double the vocal parts with trumpets to work up excitement.

In the year after *Puritani*, Mazzini's essay called for Italian music –which was then stuck in 'forms without soul, sounds without thought', the mere 'plaything of an imperceptible minority' – to renew itself by embodying a 'concept' at once 'regenerative' and in tune with the 'progressive movement of the universe'. It should bring about a synthesis of the Romantic self – 'the "I" restored to its mission' – and of the collective in its local, national and historical character. Rossini, in Mazzini's opinion, had not done any of this, though there were glimmerings in Act 3 of *Otello*, and in *Mosè, Semiramide* and *Tell*; in fact the composer, though a titan, was the embodiment of music for music's sake: his style was 'positive, cutting, materialistic ... without shadow, without mystery, without twilight', representative of a people without God, without a supreme law or an eternal faith. According to Mazzini, the 'languid' Bellini had likewise been unprogressive, whereas Donizetti showed a touch of the epic spirit, had developed throughout his career and might disclose powers as yet hidden.[40]

The real hope was that a 'Genius' would one day unite the powers of music and poetry and of the Italian melodic and the German harmonic tradition; he would thereby 'rise to spheres as yet unattempted, draw from Art secrets so far unsuspected, diffuse in Raphael-like melodies, through an uninterrupted harmony, a shadow of that Infinite our souls aspire to.' Mazzini's only practical advice – confined, like his essay as a whole, to opera – was that in place of decorative arias composers should make more use of dramatic accompanied recitative or arioso, should consider adopting a kind of leitmotiv, and should above all bring forward the chorus as the 'solemn and complete representation of the popular element'.[41]

Mazzini's 'Genius' may appear in some ways to be a description of the mature Wagner; but his call was in fact answered within three years by the emergence of the young Verdi. Though a modern scholar might think Rossini's mature serious operas did embody in their choruses the suffering of nations,[42] Italian contemporaries seem to have made little of this; they may have agreed with Mazzini, or a likelier explanation is that, by the 1840s, those operas, by now twenty or so years old, may no longer have had much to say to a public keen on novelty. Verdi's early operas, on the other hand, clearly did use the chorus, as in the opening scene of *Nabucco*, to show a whole people arrayed, with its men and women and its priestly caste. They showed epic conflicts, profound emotions, and groups of men and women imbued with spirituality.

What spirit, though? The Tuscan poet Giuseppe Giusti, an undoubted nationalist, after *Macbeth* (1847) urged Verdi to write something more national: a foreign, fantastic subject could not express 'the kind of sorrow that now fills the minds of us Italians . . . the sorrow of a people that feels the need of a better destiny . . . of one who has fallen and desires to rise . . . of one who repents and longs for regeneration'. Verdi agreed but pointed to a lack of adequate librettists – not a very convincing or, perhaps, convinced reply.[43] A year earlier Giusti, in his poem 'Sant'Ambrogio', had written of hearing the chorus 'O signore, dal tetto natio' from *I Lombardi* in a Milan church full of Austrian soldiers; this had prompted him to overcome his hatred of the foreign occupier and to feel instead a sense of brotherhood with the ill-treated conscripts from Bohemia or Croatia, lands of the empire themselves oppressed, perhaps as much as Italy.

Giusti's nationalism may have hardened, as with many others, between 1846 and 1847; it may also be that in the 1846 poem he got it right – that Verdi's choruses embodied a sense of human community, wider than any political nationalism. In Italy they no doubt contributed to the sense of 'belonging together' that may be defined as cultural nationalism. So too Verdi's operas' formidable musical energy – culminating in *Il trovatore* (1853), on the subject of medieval chivalry and Spanish at that – helped to suggest a new Italian capacity for valour, without having anything specific to say or even hint at about the political destiny of the nation.

La battaglia di Legnano apart, Verdi ignored Giusti's advice to concentrate on Italian subjects that would reflect Italian suffering and arouse Italian ardour. When, in *Les Vêpres siciliennes* (1855), he took up another classic story of Italian revolt, open to nationalist interpretation, this was for Paris, where the requirement was a typical '*grand-opéra*', heavy with spectacle, rather than a searing patriotic drama. True, a patriotic drama would have been out of the question in Italy: the 1850s were years of reaction (though also of administrative modernisation); the censorship was much harsher than it had been before 1848. Like *La battaglia*, *Les Vêpres* toured Italy in a bowdlerised form, this time with the action shifted to Portugal.

Even after Italian unification, however, Verdi wrote no music that could be construed as nationalist. He handled themes of brotherhood, self-sacrifice, freedom and patriotism (*La forza del destino*, 1862; *Don Carlos*, 1867; *Aida*, 1871), but without reference to Italy. It was left to a lesser musician, Ruggero Leoncavallo, to create in 1893 what he saw as a 'national poem' – an opera about the Medici: he wanted, he wrote, 'a great feeling of *Italianness* to hover constantly in its musical aura'.[44]

Some years earlier, in the 1870s, debate had shifted from ostensible subjects to musical style. From the 1850s, symphonic music had gained in popularity in Italy, at first through the Paris grand operas of Meyerbeer with their ingenious orchestration and ambitious historical themes but, increasingly in the last third of the century, through performances of Beethoven's symphonies and other works in the Franco-German orchestral tradition. 'Quartet societies' proliferated (not necessarily limited to chamber music). Wagner's operas made a belated entry from 1871.[45]

These changes were hotly contested on grounds that must be called nationalistic. Verdi himself wrote that German symphonism was fine in its way, but Italian composers should stick to their own tradition: 'the Germans should stay German and the Italians Italian'. A curriculum for music students, he advised, should set them to work on the best of old Italian music: 'let us go back to the old – it will be a step forward'.[46] As happened so often, Verdi's practice was to contradict his theory: he distilled his innovative, highly personal late style from his familiarity with a wide range of new German and French music as well as from his own earlier experience.

In his advice, however, Verdi represented a considerable body of Italian opinion. With the coming of nationhood, many had lost confidence in the primacy of Italian music. This was partly because of the greater ease of travel and communication that marked the late nineteenth century – opening minds to what was going on beyond the Alps – but also because of a wider disappointment in the nation which was brought about by the Risorgimento. The new Italy soon came to seem inadequate: beaten in war (by Austria in 1866, even by Abyssinia in 1896), its bourgeois Liberal politics hemmed in by an unreconciled Catholic Church and a nascent working class, economically weak – sustained by emigration – and unable to play a leading part in European alliances or in the scramble for colonial power.

In this climate, many criticised the operatic tradition represented by Verdi, like the young Arrigo Boito, a member of a self-conscious avantgarde group who in 1863 published a poem calling for the restoration of Italian musical art, 'now befouled like the walls of a brothel'. Others stood out against the encroachment of foreign music. Nationalists either contested its value (for Italian ears at least) or sought to take the credit for Italy for such distinguishing marks of the now dominant symphonic tradition as sonata form.[47]

The influential critic Francesco D'Arcais complained in 1886 that younger composers all neglected the essence of Italian music, melodic invention, in favour of eclecticism and especially Germanism. He claimed that, on the international artistic scene, 'Italy gives little and imports a great deal. . . .though politically risen again to the dignity of a nation, and on the way to commercial and industrial prosperity [a somewhat premature statement], in the arts and letters she has instead become more than ever the handmaiden and the slave of other nations'.[48]

On a more workaday level, it took time for a pioneer concert series in Turin to overcome prejudice against symphonic music: at an early performance of Wagner's *Tannhäuser* overture a well-known concert-goer shouted 'Out with the barbarians!'[49] Music publishers who promoted Wagner and the new French opera composers (Lalo, Thomas, Massenet) were accused of being anti-Italian or of having 'sold out to the foreigner'. However, when Wagner's Italian publisher was bought out by Ricordi, the

Ricordi house magazine, which had led the anti-Wagner camp, fell silent.[50] None of this prevented French composers and, eventually, Wagner from winning over both the intellectuals and audiences, although but as late as 1911 the first performance of *Der Rosenkavalier* at La Scala was greeted by a shower of leaflets from the upper gallery, protesting against the dominance of foreign composers at the expense of Italians.[51]

A subtler nationalist strategy was to appropriate the foreign aesthetic and discover that Italy had thought of it first. The decadent, ultra-nationalist poet Gabriele D'Annunzio identified himself with Wagner's music dramas, but the hero of his novel *Il fuoco* (1900), an obvious self-projection, announced the coming of a new art that would 'continue and crown the immense edifice [built up by] our elect race'. At its source would be the Florentine composers of early opera, who had worked out the principles of music drama two and a half centuries before Bayreuth, and above all Monteverdi, 'the divine Claudio . . . a heroic soul, purely, essentially Italian!' The mythologising of Monteverdi as the founder of opera and a guiding light for the future of Italian music was to be taken up in the Fascist period by the composers Gianfrancesco Malipiero and Luigi Dallapiccola among others, and was widely influential.[52]

In 1911, the critic Fausto Torrefranca launched a campaign not only against German influence but against the Italian operatic tradition, especially as represented by Puccini. He promoted the collection of folk music, to be carried out in scholarly fashion, and worked for the rediscovery of the Italian harpsichordist composers of the eighteenth century (G. M. Rutini, Platti, etc.); their works, he maintained, had led to the creation of sonata form and ought to replace those of C. P. E. Bach, Haydn, Mozart and minor German composers in the syllabus for piano students in the conservatories.[53] He thus managed to subsume the German tradition while repudiating it, an ambiguity characteristic of much nationalist discourse.

The disgrace brought by the Fascist regime so discredited Italian nationalism that post-war Italy has been one of the least nationalist societies in Europe; a few small groups apart, what nationalist aspirations there have been have aimed at autonomy or even independence for regions within the country. This means that the rediscovery and re-evaluation of early nineteenth-century Italian opera over the past forty-odd years has gone on with virtually no emphasis on its possible role as a carrier of nationalism. That role was always exaggerated; so was the alleged unity of the Italian nation. Italy's substantial cultural unity within diversity is something the age of European integration can take in its stride.

Notes and References

1 See E. Renan, 'What Is a Nation?' (1882), in A. Zimmern (ed.), *Modern Political Doctrines* (London, 1939), p. 190.

2   See E. Gellner, *Nations and Nationalism* (Oxford, 1983), p. 57.
3   See P. Brass, *Language, Religion and Politics in North India* (Cambridge, 1974), pp. 9–10.
4   See R. Carnesecchi, *'Venezia surgesti dal duro servaggio'*: *La musica patriottica negli anni della Repubblica di Manin* (Venice, 1994), and L. Sirch, 'Le canzoni in dialetto veneziano di Antonio Buzzolla', in F. Passadore and L. Sirch (eds.), *Antonio Buzzolla: Una vita musicale nella Venezia romantica* (Rovigo, 1994), pp. 327–69, and P. Zappalà, 'La musica patriottica di Antonio Buzzolla', in Passadore and Sirch (eds.), *Antonio Buzzolla*, pp. 403–23.
5   See R. Leydi, 'Italy: Folk Music', in Stanley Sadie (ed.), *The New Grove Dictionary of Music and Musicians* (London, 1980), and F. B. Pratella, *Saggio di gridi, canzoni, cori e danze del popolo italiano* (Bologna, 1919).
6   See G. Mazzini, 'Filosofia della musica', *Scritti letterari editi ed inediti*, 4 Vols., Edizione Nazionale degli Scritti di G. Mazzini, Imola, Galeati, Vol. 2 (1910), pp. 119 and 146.
7   See Charles Burney, *A General History of Music*, 2 Vols., ed. F. Mercer (London, 1935), Vol. 2, pp. 671–2.
8   C. L. Kellogg, *Memoirs of an American Prima Donna* (New York, 1913), pp. 40–1.
9   See S. Maguire, *Vincenzo Bellini and the Aesthetics of Early Nineteenth-Century Italian Opera* (New York, 1989).
10 See John Rosselli, 'Governi, appaltatori e giuochi d'azzardo nell'Italia napoleonica', *Rivista Storica Italiana*, 93 (1981), pp. 357–8, and Rosselli, *The Opera Industry in Italy from Cimarosa to Verdi: The Role of the Impresario* (Cambridge, 1984), p. 77.
11 See F. Lippmann, 'Un'opera per onorare le vittime della repressione borbonica del 1799 e per glorificare Napoleone: *I Pittagorici* di Vincenzo Monti e Giovanni Paisiello', *Musica e cultura a Napoli dal XV al XIX secolo* (Florence, 1983), pp. 281–306, and G. Morelli and E. Surian, 'Come nacque e come morì il patriottismo nell'opera', Fondazione Giorgio Cini, *Opera e libretto* (Florence, 1990), pp. 101–36, and M. Nocciolini, 'Il melodramma nella Milano napoleonica: teatro musicale e ideologia politica', *Nuova Rivista Musicale Italiana*, 29 (1995), pp. 5–30.
12 See G. Morelli and E. Surian, 'La musica strumentale e sacra e le sue istituzioni a Venezia', G. Arnaldi and M. Pastore Strocchi (eds.), *Storia della cultura veneziana*, 6 Vols., (Vicenza, Neri Pozza, V/1, 1985), (pp. 401–27) p. 427.
13 A. Zobi, *Manuale storico di economia toscana* (Florence, 1847), pp. 323–4.
14 See Rosselli, *The Opera Industry in Italy from Cimarosa to Verdi*, pp. 76–7.
15 L. M. Kantner, *'Aurea Luce': Musik an Skt. Peter in Rom 1790–1850* (Vienna, 1979), Vol. 339, p. 174.
16 A. Ghislanzoni, *Storia di Milano dal 1836 al 1848*, appended to his *In chiave di baritono* (Milan, 1882), p. 135; and Rosselli, *The Opera Industry in Italy from Cimarosa to Verdi*, pp. 3–4, 39–46.
17 See M. Meriggi, *Il regno Lombardo-Veneto* (Turin, 1987), and L. Riall, 'Elite Resistance to State Formation: The Case of Italy', in M. Fulbrook (ed.), *National History and European History* (London, 1993), pp. 46–68, and Riall, *The Italian Risorgimento: State, Society, and National Unification* (London, 1994), and D. Laven, 'Law and Order in Habsburg Venetia 1814–1835', *Historical Journal*, 39 (1996), pp. 383–403, and Laven, 'Austria's Italian Policy Reconsidered: Revolution and Reform in Restoration Italy', *Modern Italy* (1997), 2, 1997, pp. 3–33.
18 See F. Walker, *The Man Verdi* (London, 1962), pp. 47, 92, 150–1, 284–6, 355–6, and Roger Parker, *'Arpa d'or dei fatidici vati': The Verdian Patriotic Chorus in the 1840s* (Parma, 1997), pp. 20–7, 33–4.
19 See E. Santoro, *Il teatro di Cremona*, 4 Vols. (Cremona, 1969–72), Vol. 2, pp. 231–2, 262.
20 See R. J. Rath, 'Economic Conditions in Lombardy and Venetia, 1813–1815, and their

Effect on Public Opinion', *Journal of Central European Affairs*, 23 (1963), pp. 267–81, and A. Zorzi, *Venezia austriaca* (Rome-Bari, 1985).
21 See R. Osborne, *Rossini* (London, 1986).
22 See V. Bellini, *Epistolario*, ed. L. Cambi (Milan, 1943), pp. 401, 452, 479.
23 See G. Pacini, MS correspondence with ex-Grand-Duke Leopold of Tuscany, Fondo Pacini, Biblioteca Comunale, Pescia.
24 See G. Zavadini, *Donizetti: Vita, musiche, epistolario* (Bergamo, 1948), p. 522.
25 See C. Gatti, *Il Teatro alla Scala nella storia e nell'arte (1778–1963)*, 2 Vols. (Milan, 1964), Vol. 1, pp. 130–1.
26 See B. Pauls, *Giuseppe Verdi und das Risorgimento. Ein politischer Mythos im Prozess der Nationenbildung* (Berlin, 1996).
27 See M. J. Phillips-Matz, *Verdi* (Oxford, 1993), pp. 51, 145–6.
28 F. Abbiati, *Giuseppe Verdi*, 4 Vols. (Milan, 1959), Vol. 2, p. 274.
29 See G. Radiciotti, *Gioacchino Rossini: vita documentata*, 3 Vols. (Tivoli, 1927–1929), Vol. 2, pp. 126–7, and M. Viale Ferrero, 'Guglielmo Tell a Torino (1839–40) ovvero una "procella" scenografica', *Rivista Italiana di Musicologia*, 14 (1979), pp. 378–94.
30 See Rosselli, 'Censorship', in Stanley Sadie (ed.), *The New Grove Dictionary of Opera* (London, 1992), and J. Budden, *The Operas of Verdi*, 3 Vols. (London, 1973–1981), Vol. 1, pp. 143–4, 167.
31 See Budden, *The Operas of Verdi*, Vol. 1, p. 11, and Parker, 'Arpa d'or dei fatidici vati'. The Verdian Patriotic Chorus in the 1840s, pp. 85–6, and M. Conati, *La bottega della musica. Verdi e la Fenice* (Milan, 1983), pp. 159–60.
32 Ibid., pp. 169–70.
33 See Rosselli, *The Opera Industry in Italy from Cimarosa to Verdi*, pp. 157, 160–2, 167–8.
34 See P. Ginsborg, *Daniele Manin and the Venetian Revolution of 1848–49* (Cambridge, 1979), pp. 72, 76, 78–9, 81.
35 See Parker, 'Arpa d'or dei fatidici vati'. The Verdian Patriotic Chorus in the 1840s, pp. 86–97, and A. L. Bellina and B. Brizi, 'Il melodramma e la musica strumentale', in G. Arnaldi and M. Pastore Strocchi (eds.), *Storia della cultura veneta*, 6 Vols. (Vicenza, Neri Pozza, VI, 1986), p. 450.
36 P. Gossett, 'Becoming a Citizen: the Chorus in "Risorgimento" Opera', *Cambridge Opera Journal*, Vol. 2 (1992), pp. 41–64.
37 See P. Isotta, 'I diamanti della corona. Grammatica del Rossini napoletano', in G. Rossini, *Mosè in Egitto, Moïse et Pharaon, Mosè* (Turin, 1974), pp. 195–260.
38 See Zorzi, *Venezia austriaca*, p. 347, and Rosselli, 'La vita musicale a Venezia dal 1815 al 1866', in Fondazione Giorgio Cini, *Venezia e l'Austria. Atti del convegno, Venezia ottobre 1997* (Florence, forthcoming).
39 See Kantner, 'Aurea Luce'. *Musik an Skt. Peter in Rom 1790–1850*, p. 132.
40 See Mazzini, 'Filosofia della musica', pp. 123–9, 138–4, 146–52, 158–64.
41 Ibid., pp. 151–7.
42 Gossett, 'Becoming a Citizen: The Chorus in "Risorgimento" Opera'.
43 See Walker, *The Man Verdi*, p. 157.
44 L. Zoppelli, 'The Twilight of the True Gods: *Cristoforo Colombo, I Medici* and the Construction of Italian History', *Cambridge Opera Journal*, 8 (1996), p. 258.
45 See S. Martinotti, *Ottocento strumentale italiano* (Bologna, 1972), and M. De Angelis, *La musica del Granduca* (Florence, 1978), and M. S. Miller, 'Wagner, Wagnerism and Italian Identity', in D. C. Large and W. Weber (eds.), *Wagnerism in European Culture and Politics* (Ithaca, 1984).
46 See Budden, *Verdi* (London, 1985), pp. 107–8, 121–3, 128, 151–2, and G. Verdi and A. Boito, *The Verdi-Boito Correspondence*, ed. M. Conati and M. Medici (Chicago, 1994), p. 125.

47 See Rosselli, *Music and Musicians in Nineteenth-Century Italy* (London, 1991), pp. 99–105, 122–35.
48 F. D'Arcais, 'Un maestro di musica italiano: Amilcare Ponchielli', *Nuova Antologia* (third series) Vol. 55 (1886), pp. 459–74
49 G. Depanis, *I concerti popolari e il Teatro Regio di Torino*, 2 Vols. (Turin, 1914–1915), Vol. 1, pp. 22–5, 49–51, 65–70.
50 See Rosselli, *Music and Musicians in Nineteenth-Century Italy*, p. 104, and Miller, 'Wagner, Wagnerism and Italian Identity'.
51 See Gatti, *Il Teatro alla Scala nella storia e nell'arte, (1778–1963)* Vol. 1, p. 246.
52 See A. Dell'Antonio, 'Il divino Claudio: Monteverdi and Lyric Nostalgia in Fascist Italy', *Cambridge Opera Journal*, 8 (1996), pp. 271–84.
53 See F. Torrefranca, 'Problemi del dopoguerra musicale', *La critica musicale*, 1 (1918), pp. 33–9, 57–66, 88–92.

10.
The Tone of Defiance[1]

JOE RYAN

The virgin art

Like the nature of nationalism itself, the introduction of the vulgate into the serene region of musicological dissertation serves on a number of levels, not least here, in that it questions any remaining assumption that music retains a hallowed otherness. It can be argued that for too long music has occupied the high ground, regarded as a virgin art untainted by practicalities. Unsullied and mysterious, it was an expression for those within the circle possessed of a sufficiently refined sensibility. Such a critique might well emanate from a socialist or populist commentator; it is not employed in such a manner here but reflects rather first, that music was not always so precious and second, that a legacy of romanticism has been the rarefaction of the art to a level that is unhealthy. Music has for too long been content in its proud insularity, and, as a result, it has proved resistant to the comprehensive critical approach mentioned above. This has been to the detriment of the art. The current Irish experience is that many people of good disposition and training will lead busy contented lives with only a cursory brush with the great Western canon of music. This must of necessity occasion concern and indeed a concern that requires to move beyond the defensive and look to the measures required to enhance the understanding between the exponents, particularly the creators, and their community. A purpose of this chapter is to pose this problem and to look both to the history of music in Ireland and to wider studies to see if together they can cast light on the matter.

The early preparation for this undertaking was constructively informed by *Music and Society: The Politics of Composition, Performance, and Reception.*[2] The editors note in their introduction a transformation in the approaches to the study of arts and humanities:

> These changes ... have led to a systematic investigation of the implicit assumptions underlying critical methods of the past two hundred years,

including prominently the assumption that art constitutes an autonomous sphere, separate and insulated from the outside social world.[3]

However, they proceed to note that:

> The only one of the arts that has remained largely untouched by such redefinitions of method and subject matter in its academic discipline is music.[4]

This prompts the conclusion that music consciously supports the ideology of autonomy.[5] The purpose of their volume is thus to propose a reinterpretation of music study, and crucially one qualified by context. This approach is applauded by one contributor, Janet Wolff, then Reader in the Sociology of Culture at the University of Leeds who asserts that:

> Culture, however, is a social product, and the study of culture and the arts must accordingly be sociologically informed.[6]

A fellow contributor to *Music and Society*, Rose Rosengard Subotnik, a disciple of Adorno, takes a similar contextualist view and argues that:

> the notion of an intimate relationship between music and society functions not as a distant goal but as a starting point of great immediacy, and not as an hypothesis but as an assumption.[7]

One of musicology's most pertinent legacies is the awareness of the changing view of music and of music's interaction with the broader environment. The five years that separate the publication of Denis Stevens's *Musicology: A Practical Guide* (1980)[8] and Joseph Kerman's seminal *Musicology* (1985)[9] describe a giant leap in the perceptive approach to the art. This chapter within this present volume of studies is one positive response to this call for music to be cognisant of the broader environment. Just as the introduction of the vulgate ruffles the normal staid currency of academic discourse, so is contextualism challenging the erstwhile rarefied consideration of matters of high music by positivist musicologists. This tendency is not universally welcomed; some committed and reasonable musicians hold that the mystery is the essence of an abstract art and moreover that too pragmatic a scrutiny cannot but fail to preserve the spiritual core of the art. The central defence of those desirous to resist a more interdisciplinary approach lies in the very nature of the art as the expression par excellence free from representational qualities. But even here music is, according to Theodor Adorno, not absolved from wider nuances:

> If music is privileged above all other forms by the absence of illusive imagery – the fact that it does not paint a picture – then it nonetheless has participated energetically in the illusory character of the bourgeois

work of art; this it does by means of its specific interests with the domination of conventions.¹⁰

The non-referential character of pure music remains its intrinsic quality: it acts as a brake on those who are too eager to decode. However, the case for a broader sweep in musical studies is not a charter for limitation; there is no attempt at a reductionist approach. Music does not require to be revisited in order to fit its environment. It is rather that music emerges within a context; and that context shapes the music that emerges. To be sensitive to the ambience is better for understanding the music and perhaps, more importantly, such an informed approach may supply a greater appreciation of how this and future generations might fashion a more vibrant musical life.

This essay was written at an especially apposite time (1998). In a year of notable Irish musical anniversaries it was pre-eminently the approaching millennium and the bicentenary of the 1798 rebellion that made it a pertinent time to reflect on the interaction between nationalism and musical expression. A true millenary study will inevitably reflect on the course of music over the course of centuries and seek to give some account or at least an opinion on that passage. Such an appraisal is subjective; it depends on the benchmark. What can be recorded with confidence is that there is a body of opinion whose assessment is that the largely jejune musical record of the last century was not in keeping with what one might reasonably expect of a people with a musical reputation, particularly one that has achieved and carefully consolidated political sovereignty, and furthermore a nation with all that accrues to a young educated population enjoying unprecedented economic prosperity. Our reflective millenarian will understandably be puzzled. It is consistent with the thrust of the argument presented here that the roots of this situation are to be found within a wider frame and one in which nationalism features prominently.

The curse of nationalism¹¹

As ever, George Bernard Shaw is transparently clear in his approach to the matter.

> Nationalism stands between Ireland and the light of the world. Nobody in Ireland of any intelligence likes Nationalism any more than a man with a broken arm likes having it set.¹²

In truth the issue here is not whether nationalism is a good or bad thing but rather that it is indisputably a potent and pervasive influence. As a Janus-headed doctrine, nationalism has intrigued the wider historiographical community for some decades now and indeed within the Irish context schools of nationalist hermeneutics have emerged to the point where

Declan Kiberd's recent *Inventing Ireland*[13] could have employed the subtitle 'revising the revisionists'. Nationalism is no slouch itself in the matter of revisionism. Revisiting the past engendered a cultural populism that included the celebration of an emblematic music. Moreover, perception often usurps the place of reality, certainly in the shorter term. What something is can often become subordinate to what it is perceived to be. Interpretations of history will necessarily be flavoured by subjectivity. This in turn tends to provoke a reaction that can equally move too far in the attempt to address perceived misreadings. Over a period historiography can resemble the action of a metronome: a succession of extremes but with an inevitable tendency ultimately to rest in the middle.

One leading commentator and indeed player who would not, I believe, object to being observed sitting on one verge of our pendulum's swing is Conor Cruise O'Brien who in *Ancestral Voices* talks of the unacknowledged failure of cultural nationalism.[14] The contention is intriguing and prompts a series of supplementary questions. Is it reasonable to describe a nation's desire to fashion a distinctive mode as a failure? If so, at what point can one draw a line and state conclusively that it has finally foundered? Furthermore, why not acknowledge the fact? Does it cause embarrassment? Is there a political price to pay? It should be said that O'Brien's context is rooted in the conscious attempt to revive the language in the early decades of the twentieth century. Our reaction is equally conditioned by context. It depends on one's view of culture, and whether culture should carry such a focused purpose. O'Brien's phrase suggests that the proponents of a cultural nationalism act consciously and that it is calculating. It raises the question as to whether one can direct the flow of culture to substantiate some desirably predetermined view of a nation. To examine O'Brien's phrase is not to dismiss it; it has deep significance for the student of music in Ireland.

Who fears to speak[15]

> In Bodenstown churchyard there is a green grave,
> And freely around it let winter winds rave –
> Far better they suit him – the ruin and the gloom –
> Till Ireland, a nation, can build him a tomb.[16]

The events surrounding the bicentenary of the 1798 rebellion will pose questions for every thinking Irish person. One's view of Irish nationalism, of native culture, even more particularly of Irish music is framed by the individual interpretation of the events surrounding that rebellion. The complexities of that seminal passage have frequently been recast to proffer a simplified reading. That patchy and chaotic period has particular purchase on the native psyche, and looked on from a distance has been retrospectively imbued with the distinction of being the wellspring of Irish nationalism. Padraic Pearse focused this on to the person of Wolfe Tone at whose graveside in Bodenstown, County Kildare he gave a notable oration in summer 1913:

> We have come to the holiest place in Ireland; holier even than the place where Patrick sleeps in Down . . . We have come to renew our adhesion to the faith of Tone: to express once more our full acceptance of the gospel of Irish Nationalism which he was the first to formulate in worldly terms.[17]

Again perspective is all here. As in O'Brien's dialectic, whether one considers that Pearse canonised[18] or sacralised[19] [sic] Tone, there is no doubt that the former's retrospective analysis has bequeathed to us a version of Tone as the apostle of Irish nationalism. But clearly this was not synonymous with national sentiment. Musicians will readily recall Tone's response to news of the Belfast Harpers' Festival held in 1792; 'Strum, strum and be hanged'.[20] The very fact that such a festival was sponsored is evidence that antiquarian studies and an appreciation of cultural heritage were features of late eighteenth century life; the reaction suggests that Tone and his companions were more pragmatic and rationalist in their approach and that indigenous expression was not fundamental to their design. It was left to a later generation and another leading player, Thomas Davis, to point to the centrality of culture in the nationalist canon. This was not a disinterested viewpoint. As I attempted to show elsewhere,[21] Davis and like-minded colleagues were acutely conscious of, and influenced by, events within the wider European sphere. The culture of a people came to be regarded as the defining bond of the nation: it became the first prerequisite of any claim for political sovereignty. The doctrine's pivotal architect of the era was the Italian nationalist, Giuseppe Mazzini. Under his writings and actions which informed nationalist movements throughout Europe and beyond, a people could be identified through their distinctive culture, of which language was the principal badge. Ireland's claim to be adjudged one of Europe's proud and distinct nations had been measured against this criterion and had failed. Mazzini's scathing rejection was a sore blow particularly to a group such as Young Ireland whose very name tied them to the ideals of a broader European movement. It served further to concentrate energy on establishing the validity of the claim to a distinct culture, endowing a legacy of narrow enterprise that survived past the turn of the century. This raises the issue as to whether a mode of living can be consciously fashioned and indeed the further issue of the homogeneity of the community purporting to share this culture. Shaw's calculated portrayal of the Irish as a parcel of mongrels[22] concisely encompasses this latter point and acts as a foil to the more simplified readings of Tone. Davis had a decidedly focused vision of culture: a culture was a tool and a necessary one when dealing with a complex society. The ballad was employed as a form of political parable, an abridged educational medium. The utilitarian approach is evident in a ballad such as 'Orange and Green Will Carry the Day', which was set, interestingly, to the air 'The Protestant Boys':

> Orange! Orange!
> Green and Orange!
> Wave them together o'er the mountain and bay.
> Orange and green!
> Our King and Queen!
> 'Orange and Green will carry the day!'[23]

Well might Seamus Deane comment that Davis had a good heart but a cloth ear.[24] Davis's schematic thinking had a profoundly conservative hue. He was, as D. George Boyce perceptively notes, in a sense, asking Irish society to stand still.[25] Culture here was not a way of life but the idealisation of a purer past; a past that required to be restored and preserved unchanged.

As a feature of this ideal world, Davis consciously presented a sanitised version of the 1798 rebellion as a time of solidarity, a togetherness that echoed his desired unity of culture. The irony here is that other, less contriving commentators point to this episode as the source of increasing division. One such, Maire Mhac an tSaoi, in contemplating Sir Samuel Ferguson's response to the publication of James Hardiman's *Irish Minstrelsy* (1831), written explicitly with a view to preserve and illustrate a portion of ancient Irish literature,[26] adjudged the reviewer's generous perspective as a unique

> breach in the barriers of resentment, mistrust and apprehension ... [which], more particularly since 1798, had grown increasingly denser and more impenetrable between the two nations in this island.[27]

Consideration of Tone's debt to France and Davis's consciousness of wider European perceptions points critically, however, to the fact that early nationalist expression in Ireland was not defined solely in terms of the relationship with the neighbouring island. The twentieth century's war of independence, the consequent internecine strife and legacy of violent unease in the northern counties have served to produce an Anglocentric historiography; indeed, nationalism itself has served to reposition towards a more narrow focus. This prevalent wash has permeated revisionism and is now subconsciously being employed retrospectively. Those concerned to address the situation of music in Ireland would be well advised to guard against such drift.

The cases given above point to the shift in understanding of the interaction between nationalism, national sentiment and culture. In the estimation of one of the doctrine's leading observers, Ernest Gellner:

> Nationalism is a political principle which maintains that similarity of culture is the basic social bond. Whatever principles of authority may

exist between people depend for their legitimacy on the fact that the members of the group concerned are of the same culture (or, in nationalist idiom, of the same 'nation').[28]

This is a considered view given in his last book, published posthumously, and the clarity of the assertion might easily conceal the crucial reversal in the popular readings of culture's role in this intricate drama. From a small unheralded support role culture has moved forward to centre stage and is now a defining character. The notion that a people could legitimately claim political sovereignty if they could demonstrate an integrity of culture has now reversed to the point where it is culture, in the widest sense, that does the fashioning; that at very least it determines the unity of sentiment. This is culture as the soul of a nation. Seamus Deane wisely noted of Irish nationalism that 'It is a moral passion more than it is a political ideology.'[29]

In his stimulating study *The Wretched of the Earth*, Frantz Fanon, writing with all of the anger and clarity of visionary youth, calls the affirmation of culture within a colonised race a special battle-field.[30] He valued the work of such cultural antiquarians as something that 'rehabilitates us both in regard to ourselves and in regard to others'.[31] That a process of revelation and celebration took place in Ireland in the nineteenth century is accepted and it took the form that one might expect of a colonised people desirous of establishing a claim to distinctive nationhood. But it would be stretching the advantages of hindsight to claim that all such endeavour was co-ordinated and singularly focused. Some who laboured to discover the pattern of a distinguished civilisation did so without overt political motivation. Others worked with conflicting intent; but the genius of nationalism is its ability to have all of these serve its central purpose. Consider for instance, the contribution of the poet Sir Samuel Ferguson who maintained his unionist politics. Ferguson, on whom Yeats lavished the highest praise, was foremost amongst many who laboured on matters cultural not for any reason of propaganda but rather through the belief that a distinguished and diverse artistic life would enhance the lot and the image of all Irishmen. In a remark characteristic of his liberal approach, Ferguson points to music's role in the generality of antiquarian research:

> What have the Irish to boast of? The answer is short but comprehensive: their music and their architecture of the era of independence. Their music is wholly and exclusively their own, and is wholly beautiful.[32]

Others shared in this view and this work but with different motivation. A Protestant colleague and leading member of the Royal Irish Academy, George Petrie, was from the third decade of the nineteenth century concerned through a remarkable range of endeavour to substantiate Ireland's historical claim to be considered a separate and unique civilisation. Like so many of the intelligentsia that were to drive the cultural life of Ireland following the Act of Union in 1800, Petrie was of the ascendancy tradition which, in the words of Liam de Paor, 'had come to the view that there was an Irish nation, and that they constituted the Irish nation'.[33] Both Ferguson and Petrie supplied introductory essays for the publication of Bunting's *Antient Irish Music* in 1840. Petrie also, in his role as a collector of traditional airs, had earlier sent some to Thomas Moore. Despite his role as the leading member of the Society for the Preservation and Publication of the Melodies of Ireland (established in 1851), Petrie, like Moore, was in time criticised for his amateur dabbling in such matters. Sir Robert Stewart dismissed his contribution with the comment that of the laws of musical construction he knew nothing.[34] This was mild compared to the treatment meted out to Moore over succeeding generations. He has been widely castigated for what many regard as his reductionist and even bastardised version of a noble heritage. Furthermore he has faced particular political criticism for focusing too clearly on a English middle-class audience, while musicians deprecated his readiness to iron out the complexities of traditional airs in order better to dress the more even metre of his verse. He was, records one of his supporters:

> In the drawing rooms of the great . . . the cynosure of every eye when he played and sang those airs, those songs of sorrow so suggestive of his country's sufferings and his country's woes.[35]

Such abutment becomes harder to discover. Of all the many criticisms of Moore the one that lingers is the dismissive assessment of the writer Anthony Cronin, who regarded him as a bit of an embarrassment.[36]

There is indisputably some substance to the critical assessment of Moore's contribution. His is a synthetic, nostalgic and idealised vision, and one far removed from the reality of the day. This occasions difficulties for all who come to evaluate the poet's work. This moved George Saintsbury to note in an exegesis penned in 1914:

> For something like half a century it has been rare to find an estimate of Moore which, if not positively contemptuous has not been at least apologetic.[37]

And yet there is a danger of hindsight lending too much certainty in the matter. It is, after all, Moore who acts as the catalyst for this discourse and his writings disclose that he at the very least argued that his labours had a purpose beyond the commercial. In justifying his blatant proselytisation, Moore stated in the phrase that lends the title for this essay that

> It has often been remarked, and oftener felt, that our music is the truest of all comments upon our history. The tone of defiance, succeeded by the languor of despondency – a burst of turbulence dying away into softness, the sorrows of one moment lost in the levity of the next – and all that romantic mixture of mirth and sadness, which is naturally produced by the efforts of a lively temperament to shake off or forget the wrongs

> that lie upon it. Such are the features of our history and character, which
> we find strongly and faithfully reflected in our music . . .³⁸

Whether one accepts Moore's justification is essentially immaterial. All of the understandable criticism can overlook the fact that he brought to a vastly wider audience an awareness of a distinctive and valuable expression – even if what was provided was a varietal. Moreover the accepted wisdom that regards the Irish as a musical people – whether sustainable or not – owes much to the legacy of Moore.

One of his most potent critics was the composer Charles Villiers Stanford who, in the preface to his edition of Moore's *Irish Melodies*, posits that:

> there is scarcely a melody which Moore left unaltered, and as a necessary consequence, unspoilt. Whether he or his arranger was responsible for these corruptions is a matter which is lost to history; but as the name of the poet has the greater prominence in the original publication, I have laid to his door any blame which I am compelled to allot.³⁹

Stanford too in turn mediated Irish culture, or a sanitised version, for an English audience, albeit in a more musically literate way and on a far grander canvas. There are few, however, who will argue that Stanford, notwithstanding all his technical proficiency, has had the same impact as his earlier compatriot. His *Irish* symphony and especially his rhapsodies are finely crafted and are still occasionally heard in the concert hall. Where he quotes directly from folksong it is presented in a distinguished, noble garb, a dress almost embarrassingly fine. This is not to join in what Ralph Vaughan Williams terms the 'belittling' of Stanford's works.⁴⁰ However, the all too evident influence of Brahms that permeates the *oeuvre* of a creative talent that could never quite break free from the constraints of academia also renders inconsistent Stanford's critical comment on Stevenson's indebtedness to Haydn apparent in the earlier composer's arrangements.⁴¹ Moore had employed strange if understandable reasoning to defend his collaborator's musical approach:

> Sir John Stevenson has brought a national feeling to this task, which it would be in vain to expect from a foreigner, however tasteful or judicious.⁴²

Such a colloquy concerns the internal fashioning of a distinctive note, even if it is with a view to foreign consumption. Inevitably the emergence of such exotic spices also attracted the palates of intrepid musical itinerants, yet another species that thrived on the fruits of nationalism. The traditional music of such countries as Hungary and Spain has captivated composers from abroad. This is very much the Ausländer approach. It is interesting to reflect in this context on the parallels with a recent debate in Germany as to whether blood or birth is the appropriate qualification for citizenship. The

Bundestag elected for the latter, a decision which in Irish terms would figuratively have allowed Ernest Moeran to claim Irish musical nationality, as his father, the Reverend J. J. Moeran, hailed from Dublin.[43] As it was, Moeran assiduously cultivated an Irish character in some of his music and spent much time in Ireland especially on the west coast. His picturesque Irish note was a miniature echo of the more passionate and expansive application of his friend and compatriot Arnold Bax, who threw himself into matters Irish with characteristic intensity. But Bax's concern to write 'Irishly'[44] was merely an infatuation, and for both men the genuine regard for the country and its musical heritage was but an occasional influence. This picturesque appeal is just one of nationalism's intriguing bounties.

Further gifts were not so welcome. Two such were an increasing insularity and a waning national confidence. Artists laboured with the legacy for over a century. James Joyce, in Act 1 of his sole play, *Exiles*, has Robert light a cigar and with the assurance of relaxation announce to the hero, Richard, that 'If Ireland is to become a new Ireland she must first become European.'[45] Albeit from a different perspective, Ralph Vaughan Williams was of the same inclination:

> Is it possible to be a nationalist, and at the same time an internationalist? I believe that political internationalism and personal individualism are necessary complements: one cannot exist without the other.[46]

Such a theme is but one of many that currently occupy the attention of musicologists within the area of Irish musical studies. Indeed the principal lines of Irish musical history are becoming better understood, especially with the work of the current generation of musicologists. The burden of this chapter is the essential requirement that such a review be informed by context, but with the proviso that such a contextual approach be not too narrowly focused. The account of music in Ireland in the last two centuries can too readily settle on the matter of choice: composers, promoters and auditors each electing between insularity and cosmopolitanism. Such an option itself best describes how music became indentured to political events. Choices were made and the argument has been presented that the fissure that resulted between the traditionalists and those espousing a more inclusive approach worked to the detriment of musical life.[47] This was not a peculiarly Irish dilemma. The polarities of rural/urban, conservative/progressive, insular/cosmopolitan were all to the fore when, in the late eighteenth century, Jean Bapiste Leclerc cogently examined the notion of utility in music and particularly the prospect for a national music:

> The time is almost ripe, perhaps, for the establishment of a national music ... The problem that must be solved then is this: the restoration of an equilibrium between the townsfolk and the countryfolk, or rather the discovery of a half-way point at which music will serve to restrain the former and advance the latter ... In doing so we must look for a moment

at the state of contemporary music. In the final analysis we will find that
it is of two distinct kinds. One corrupts and is already too decadent to be
regenerated. The other is still pure enough to deserve protection.[48]

Like our pendulum, such a dialectic tends inevitably to focus on the
extremes; one view elevates a former more sacred, more conservative,
untainted tradition while the other argues for a tradition so inclusive as to
move away from the intimate concerns of the society from which it is born.
A culture is a shifting thing, an entity intimately linked to the reality of the
lives of those from which it grows. Fanon, although ultimately a man of
action and one dismissive of the intellectual concerned solely with matters
cultural, points to this with clarity:

> A national culture is not a folklore, nor an abstract populism that
> believes it can discover the people's true nature. It is not made up of the
> inert dregs of gratuitous actions, that is to say actions which are less and
> less attached to the ever present reality of the people.[49]

Time is a leveller in these matters. Ireland has managed its affairs since the
Anglo-Irish settlement of December 1921 with some distinction. Given the
internecine division occasioned by attitudes to partition, the subsequent
political history is notably mature and while commentators such as Joe Lee
point to the many failures and lost opportunities in the succeeding decades
there is yet much to praise. The management of the independent polity has
engendered increasing native confidence, a confidence added to by a strong
economic performance and through cultural achievements, notably in the
literary field. The need to assert distinction is not so great in such circumstances. De Paor notes this at the close of his article on 'Cultural Pluralism':

> What I am suggesting here is that time has solved or is solving many of
> the problems of the past which were rooted in the disparate cultural
> origins of different groups within Ireland. As the country has moved, first
> in one part, and then in another, from 'traditional' society to the more
> open and more mobile society of developed western capitalism, the old
> cultural distinctions have faded in significance and been merged in new
> and universal cultural forms.[50]

This is fair comment but one that does not reflect the musical situation.
Music has faired poorly in this age of consolidation. Irish musicians have
for over a century fallen foul of the divided tradition; extreme positions
have been adopted and few have even attempted the necessary reconcilia-
tion. In the central matter of the approach to folksong, a medium elevated
by nationalist sentiment, composers have elected either consciously to
abjure the offering or conversely to swallow it whole. Bartók was well
aware of the value and the danger of folksong:

> knowledge of folk songs is even more important in music [than in liter-
> ature], because folk songs can be better integrated with music. I mean

> that peasant music continually inspires the composer. Do not imagine that we are thinking of the transplantation, the assimilation, the annexation of peasant music into the classical musical inheritance. No, no. We think that peasant music gives our music its character.[51]

It is only in the second half of the twentieth century that a generation of composers has with some profit taken such an approach within the Irish context.

Perhaps Moore was unconsciously more salient and prophetic than subsequent commentators have allowed. His phrase 'The tone of defiance, succeeded by the languor of despondency – a burst of turbulence dying away into softness' could well encompass the account of music in Ireland in the face of rampant nationalism. Music was shepherded into defiance and it has taken over a century to shake clear of the resulting torpor. Art that is indentured to polity will always suffer. It was Adorno who noted that 'In Germany the National Socialist Chamber of Music (Reichsmusikkammer) has left behind a total rubbish heap.'[52] In Ireland a past expression that was idealised and even sanctified proved ultimately to be stultifying. The calculated glorification of the past bequeathed by Davis and his followers brought forth in 1947 a jaundiced response from the poet Patrick Kavanagh who had little regard for such delusions:

> Culture is always something that was,
> Something pedants can measure,
> Skull of a bard, thigh of a chief,
> Depth of dried-up river.
> Shall we be thus for ever?
> Shall we be thus for ever?[53]

If one accepts the implicit argument that culture is a living organism, one that must perforce change to reflect the ever-changing reality, then it follows that the challenge for a musically literate people is to fashion an expression that can draw on the totality of past tradition and crucially one that reflects the current living environment. This corollary places the creative artist at the centre of our cultural life as an agent of that change. In musical terms it additionally suggests that the quality and currency of new music can stand as a barometer of the musical health of a nation. This is not an argument for dismissing the past; on the contrary, current reality is informed by all that has gone before. In musical terms both the indigenous tradition and the great Western canon contribute to what we are and to be constrained to elect for one over the other is spurious. A more central difficulty lies in the growing distance between the creative artist and his audience, which in the Irish situation is a problem that can only indirectly be laid at nationalism's door. There is a clear requirement to move beyond the language of a doctrine that deals in terms of the connection between the artist and his/her ethnic society. Equally there is here an explicit rejection of Milton Babbit's contention, as cited in Kerman, that avant-garde music should retreat to the bastion of the university.[54] The concept of culture presented here has nothing to do with selective communication. Ireland's sorry record is a factor of the singular educational concentration on buttressing a distinctive civilisation evident especially in the decades surrounding the achievement of political independence in 1921 which diverted energy, attention and resources from the area of musical studies. Inevitably the achievement of political autonomy did not confer a cultural *tabula rasa*. To this day we labour with this inheritance: the vast proportion of the nation is musically illiterate and the few who seek to create through sound end up soliloquising or addressing a foreign audience. Improvements have been made, and while there are more ensembles and venues, and there is greater support for composers, the inevitable conclusion is that musical life in Ireland will not prosper until such time as the matter of general musical literacy is addressed in a co-ordinated way. The true tone of defiance should be that of a glorious expression seeking to reassert its birthright.

Notes and References

1 The title for this essay is borrowed from Thomas Moore. The poet employs the phrase in the dedication to the Marchioness Dowager of Donegal in a letter prefixed to the Third Number of the *Irish Melodies* published in 1810. A subsequent private letter of July 1810 to Lady Donegal deals with the matter of the dedication. See Lord John Russell, *Memoirs, Journal, and Correspondence of Thomas Moore*, Vol. VIII (London, 1856), pp. 83–7.
2 R. Leppert and S. McClary (eds.), *Music and Society: The Politics of Composition, Performance, and Reception* (Cambridge, 1987).
3 Ibid., p. xi.
4 Ibid., p. xii.
5 Ibid., p. xiii.
6 J. Wolff, 'Foreword: The Ideology of Autonomous Art', in *Music and Society*, p. 5.
7 R. R. Subotnik, 'On Grounding Chopin', in *Music and Society*, p. 105.
8 D. Stevens, *Musicology: A Practical Guide* (London, 1980).
9 J. Kerman, *Musicology* (London, 1985).
10 T. W. Adorno, *Philosophy of Modern Music* (Frankfurt, 1948), trans. A. Mitchell and W. Bloomster (London, 1973), p. 40.
11 The quotation is taken from G. B. Shaw's Preface to *John Bull's Other Island* (London, 1928), p. xxxiv.
12 Ibid.
13 Declan Kiberd, *Inventing Ireland: The Literature of the Modern Nation* (London, 1995).
14 C. C. O'Brien, *Ancestral Voices: Religion and Nationalism in Ireland* (Dublin, 1994), p. 89.
15 The heading is taken from the first line of the popular rebel ballad 'The Memory of the Dead' by John Kells Ingram. This ballad and its author encompass in miniature something of the complexity of the second half of the nineteenth century. Ingram was a noted Trinity classicist and brother to the lawyer, Thomas Dunbar Ingram, who became one of the leading Unionist apologists and whose hostility towards

Catholicism and the Gaelic tradition inform his lucid contributions to the debate concerning Home Rule.
16   T. Davis, 'Tone's Grave', in *Walton's Treasury of Irish Songs and Ballads* (Dublin, 1947), p. 209.
17   *Collected Works of Padraic H. Pearse: Political Writings and Speeches* (Dublin, n.d.), pp. 58–62
18   The term is suggested by D. George Boyce; see 'Past and Present Revisionism and the Northern Ireland Troubles' in D. George Boyce and A. O'Day (eds.), *The Making of Modern Irish History: Revisionism and the Revisionist Controversy* (London and New York, 1996), p. 228.
19   See C. C. O'Brien, *Ancestral Voices*, p. 99.
20   *The Autobiography of Theobald Wolfe Tone*, ed. R. B. O'Brien, 2 Vols. (London, 1893), Vol. I, p. 97.
21   See J. Ryan, 'Nationalism and Irish Music' (PhD diss., National University of Ireland, Dublin, 1991), pp. 110–18.
22   Shaw, cited in D. H. Greene and D. H. Lawrence, *The Matter with Ireland* (Dublin, 1962), p. 294.
23   In T. W. Rolleston (ed.), *Thomas Davis: Selections from His Prose and Poetry* (London, n.d. [c.1890]), p. 357.
24   S. Deane, *A Short History of Irish Literature* (London, 1986), p. 78.
25   D. George Boyce, *Nationalism in Ireland*, 2nd edn., (London, 1991), p. 164.
26   J. Hardiman, *Irish Minstrelsy*, Vol. I (London, 1831), Dedication.
27   M. Mhac an tSaoi (ed.), J. Hardiman, *Irish Minstrelsy*, Vol. I (Shannon, 1971), Introduction.
28   E. Gellner, *Nationalism* (London, 1997), p. 3.
29   S. Deane, *Celtic Revivals* (London, 1985), pp. 14–15.
30   F. Fanon, *The Wretched of the Earth* (London, 1990), p. 168.
31   Ibid., p. 169.
32   Lady Ferguson, *Sir Samuel Ferguson and the Ireland of his Day*, Vol. I (Edinburgh and London, 1894), p. 291.
33   L. de Paor, 'Cultural Pluralism', *Studies*, 67 (Dublin, Spring/Summer 1978), pp. 79–80.
34   Correspondence R. P. Stewart with Dr Purdon of Belfast (5 January 1886). Cited in O. J. Vignoles, *Memoir of Sir Robert P. Stewart* (Dublin and London, n.d. [1898]), p. 173.
35   J P. Gunning, *Moore: Poet and Patriot* (Dublin, 1900), p. 47.
36   A. Cronin, *Heritage Now* (Dingle, 1982), p. 31. It should be recorded that, taken in its context, Cronin's assessment is a tempered one.
37   G. Saintsbury, 'Lesser Poets 1790–1837', in Sir A. W. Wood and A. R. Waller (eds.), *The Cambridge History of English Literature*, Vol. XII (Cambridge, 1932), p. 102.
38   From the letter of dedication in the Third Number of the *Irish Melodies* in 1810; see n.1 above. Reprinted in E. Fleischer, *The Works of Thomas Moore esq.* (Leipsic, 1833), p. 208.
39   C. V. Stanford, Preface to *Irish Melodies of Thomas Moore* (London, 1895).
40   R. V. Williams, 'Charles Villiers Stanford', *National Music and Other Essays*, 2nd edn., (Oxford, 1987), p. 196.
41   See Preface to *Irish Melodies of Thomas Moore*.
42   See *The Works of Thomas Moore esq.*, p. 264.
43   In a close decision, the Bundestag voted on 27 March 1998 to retain a long-established law that defines German citizenship according to blood rather than birthplace.
44   This attractive adverb is taken from Bax's *Farewell, My Youth* (London, 1943), p. 47.
45   James Joyce, *Exiles* (London, 1918).

46 'Nationalism and Internationalism', *National Music and Other Essays*, p. 154.
47 See Ryan, 'Nationalism and Irish Music'.
48 J. B. Leclerc, 'Essai sur la propagation de la musique' (Paris, 1796), in P. le Huray and J. Day (eds. and trans.), *Music and Aesthetics in the Eighteenth and Early-Nineteenth Centuries* (Cambridge, 1981), pp. 240–1.
49 Fanon, *The Wretched of the Earth*, p. 188.
50 L. de Paor, 'Cultural Pluralism', p. 86.
51 P. Laki (ed.), *Bartók and His World* (Princeton, 1995), p. 230. The extract is taken from an interview with Bartók conducted by Dezõ Kosztolányi and translated by D. E. Schneider.
52 Adorno, *Philosophy of Modern Music*, p. 7.
53 P. Kavanagh, 'Memory of Brother Michael', *Collected Poems* (London, 1972), p. 84.
54 See Kerman, *Musicology*, p. 101.

11.
The Political Parlour: Identity and Ideology in Scottish National Song

STEVE SWEENEY-TURNER

> Storys to rede ar delitabill,
> Suppos that thai be nocht but fabill
> John Barbour, 1375[1]

Nomological resonances

> if a man were permitted to make all the ballads,
> he need not care who should make the laws of a nation.
> Anon. (quoted by Fletcher of Saltoun), 1704[2]

> When Political combustion ceases to be the object of Princes & Patriots,
> it then, you know, becomes the lawful prey of Historians and Poets.
> Robert Burns, 1791[3]

For both Andrew Fletcher and Robert Burns, the figures of law, nationhood and history circulate in a cultural space circumscribed by the concepts of song and poetry.

For Fletcher, nationalist member of the final Scottish parliaments of the eighteenth century, arguing incisively against the idea of an incorporating union with the British parliament, the songs and laws of a nation hold a certain equivalence, recalling, perhaps, the Greek concept *nomos* – simultaneously signifying law, custom and song. In this, the power of song to define the limits of the nation, almost a bardic power, is at the very least equal to the power of the political sphere itself, and quite possibly more so. A resonant thought, no doubt, but Fletcher was hardly alone in making this association between the political and the musical in his time and place. On Beltaine, 1 May 1707, as the last Scottish parliament closed its doors on the political independence of its nation, Chancellor the Earl of Seafield lamented,'thus endeth ane auld sang', while, in the Edinburgh streets, the sounds of church bells were heard playing'Why Should I Be Sad on My Wedding Day?'[4]

For Burns, writing 84 years after the Treaty of Union which Fletcher vainly attempted to defeat, the perceived betrayal of the nation by its political representatives gives a 'lawful' sanction to the image of the songwriter as political orator, carrier of the national *nomos* in a climate of institutional impotence. If the closure of the parliament in 1707 did indeed represent the ending of an 'auld sang' within Scottish political life, then with cultural activists such as Burns, the old song of the nation was nevertheless to be recapitulated, transposed from the law-making benches of the parliament house to those more unruly benches of the local tavern, the gentleman's club and the Masonic hall; but also, as we shall see, to the more sober, proprietous chaise-longue of the bourgeois Victorian parlour.

The national song

In all of this, no single song occupies a more crucial position than 'Bruce's Address to his Army' (1793), more commonly known as 'Scots, Wha Hae wi' Wallace Bled', which is, perhaps (along with 'Auld Lang Syne') the most famous of Burns's contributions to the popular song genre. Indeed, throughout the nineteenth century, 'Bruce's Address' came virtually to define the nomological content of Scottish cultural resistance to the UK state in becoming the unofficial national anthem in the absence of a legitimising state structure. As Marjory Kennedy-Fraser commented, her father, David Kennedy 'sang it as the prayer and vow of a whole nation' in the Burns recitals he gave throughout the British Empire in the 1870s and 1880s.[5]

Example 11.1. 'Scots Wha Hae' from Hamish MacCunn, *Songs and Ballads of Scotland* (Edinburgh, Patersons, 1892), p. 168.

214 *Steve Sweeney-Turner*

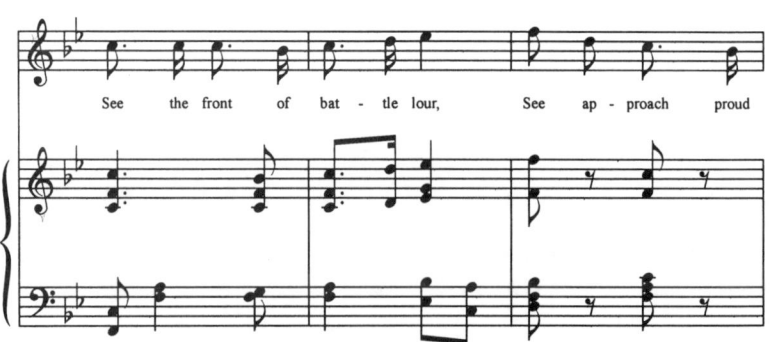

2.
Wha will be a traiter knave?
Wha can fill a coward's grave?
Let him turn and flee!
Wha, for Scotland's king an' law,
Freedom's sword will strongly draw,
Freeman stand, or freeman fa',
Let him follow me!

3.
By oppression's woes an' pains,
By your sons in servile chains,
We will drain our dearest veins,
But they shall be free.
Lay the proud usurpers low!
Tyrants fall in every foe!
Liberty's in every blow!
Let us do or die!

Despite its status as the Scottish national anthem, the language of 'Bruce's Address' is, as various commentators have noted, problematically un-Scots on two counts: (a) stanzas one to four are in Burns's characteristically Anglicised form, with non-idiomatic constructs imported from English, such as the notorious *wham* as a supposed Scotticisation of English 'whom', or, more conventionally, 'to' for *tae*, 'and' for *an*, etc.; (b) stanzas five and six are, according to David Daiches, purely in English, such that the Scots of the first four stanzas 'has been given up and the poem is revealed as an English sentimental poem on liberty'.[6] Of course, this English aspect of the final two stanzas leads to a mixture of vowel forms across the lyric as a whole, since, although in stanzas one and three we have the Scots forms *hae* and *sae* ('have' and 'so'), in the final two stanzas we find English 'woes' and 'do' (instead of Scots *waes* and *dae*). Equally, the *fa'* of stanza four transforms into the 'fall' of the final stanza, and so forth. Nonetheless, this example of what post-colonial theory calls interlinguistic practice[7] is a common marker of the majority of eighteenth- and nineteenth-century poetry and song in Scots, and merely points to the political and linguistic problematics which Scottish culture faced due to the processes of Anglicisation which had been current at least since the translation of the Bible into English, rather than Scots, under the guidance of James VI on his accession to the British throne. From that point on, if God spoke English, then political and cultural authority were soon to feel the pressure to move in a similar direction such that, by the end of the eighteenth century, even political nationalists such as Burns were producing hybrid statements in a kind of Anglo-Scots.[8]

However, within this interlinguistic orthography, it should always be borne in mind that the actual interpretative practice of readers and singers of these lyrics is often to re-Scotticise the English spellings. Furthermore, this process of linguistic re-nationalisation is encouraged by the paradoxical use of both English and Scots spellings of vowels which only make rhyming sense when transposed back into standard Scots. In 'Bruce's Address', this can be seen to operate in the two final, apparently most English of stanzas, despite Daiches' claims of an integral English text here. The overall rhyming scheme of the lyric is aaab cccb, repeated twice. In this, the final word of stanza one, 'victorie', obviously rhymes with the final word of stanza two, 'Slaverie', and in three and four we have 'flie' (flee, not fly) and 'me'. However, in the 'English' stanzas five and six, we have the half-rhyme in English of 'free' and 'die', which, of course, makes a perfect rhyme if sung in Scots as 'free' and *dee*. Within this, we have a slight disturbance on the surface of even the ostensibly English orthography of eighteenth-century Scots lyrics, a disturbance which is notationally silent but becomes activated in musical performance – a subtle rupturing of literature by music. Moreover, this musical-performative appropriation of English orthography by Scots can be characterised in the context of post-colonial linguistics as an *abrogation* of English by Scots – a disruptive practice by which the conventions of the hegemonic status of English as a 'major' language are challenged by the 'minor' language of Scots, and further, within a text which is itself intensely politicised.

The connection of Burns's political sentiments as expressed in 'Bruce's Address' with the occurrence of the French Revolution of 1790 is clear and regularly noted – his rhetorical lexis positions us between two alternatives: oppression or liberty. Nonetheless, Burns also contextualises his contemporary, politically subjugated Scotland within a specifically historical, if not fully mythic frame, recalling the so-called Wars of Independence which secured the continuation of political autonomy from the English Norman state following the Battle of Bannockburn (1314) and finally the Declaration of Arbroath (1320). Equally, there is the tradition, noted by Burns himself in a letter to George Thomson, publisher of numerous Burns songs in *A Select Collection of Scottish Airs* (1793–1841), that the tune he set the lyric to, 'Hey Tuttie Taitie', was itself played at the decisive battle of Bannockburn:

> 'Hey tutti taitie'. . . has often filled my eyes with tears. – There is a tradition, which I have met with in many places of Scotland, that it was Robert Bruce's March at the battle of Bannock-burn. – This thought, in my yesternight's evening walk, warmed me to a pitch of enthusiasm on the theme of Liberty and Independence, which I threw into a kind of Scots Ode, fitted to the Air . . . that one might suppose to be the gallant

ROYAL SCOT'S address to his heroic followers on that eventful morning . . . I had no idea of giving myself any trouble on the Subject, till the accidental recollection of that glorious struggle for Freedom, associated with the glowing ideas of some other struggles of the same nature, *not quite so ancient,* roused my rhyming Mania.[9]

But at the margins of this historical frame lies a further connection between the Scottish and French politics of liberty. 'Hey Tutti Taitie' is also associated with the Scottish archers who fought with Jeanne d'Arc against the English claims to French territories. Indeed, part of this branch of the tradition tells of Jeanne victoriously entering Orléans to the tune, with her Scottish archers, in 1429.[10] In this complex intertextual field, then, the connections between tune, lyric and the history of the Auld Alliance of Scotland and France against English imperial aspirations, whether in the heroic past or the revolutionary present, becomes self-evident.

However, the genealogy of this song becomes further problematised when we take account of the circumstances surrounding its initial publication. Burns first fully alludes to the song in a letter to Thomson dated at around 30th August 1793, and refers Thomson to the version of 'Hey Tutti Taitie' already published in Vol. 2 of Johnson's *Scots Musical Museum* (1788), the rival publication to Thomson's which Burns was also heavily involved with. Here, the two sets of lyrics are a moderately bawdy drinking song, and a Jacobite song respectively.

Example 11.2. 'Hey Tutti Taitie' from James Johnson, *The Scots Musical Museum*, Vol. 2 (Edinburgh, Johnson, 1788), p.,178.

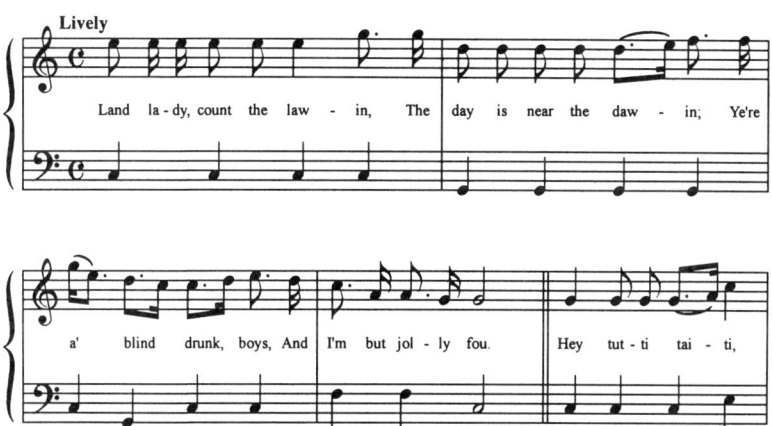

Cog an ye were ay fou,	Out upon them, fy! fy!

Cog an ye were ay fou,
Cog an ye were ay fou,
I was fit and fing to you,
If ye were ay fou.
Hey tutti &c

Weel may we a' be!
Ill may we never fee!
God blefs the king
And the companie!
Hey tutti &c

    Same Tune
Here is to the king, Sir,
Ye ken wha I mean, Sir,
And to every honeft man
That will do't again.
    Chorus
Fill up your bumpers high,
We'll drink a' your barrels dry;

Out upon them, fy! fy!
That winns do't again.

Here's to the Chieftans
Of the Scots Highland clans;
They hae done it mair than ance,
And willdo't again.
Fill up &c.

Here is to the king o' Swedes,
Frefh laurels crown his head!
Pox on every fneaking blade
That winna do't again!
Fill up &c.

But to mak a' things right, now
He that drinks maun fight too.
To fhew his heart's upright too.
And that he'll do't again.
Fill up &c.

However, Thomson, possibly due to his proprietorial feelings of rivalry towards Johnson's collection, expressed his doubts about the aesthetic merit of 'Hey Tutti Taitie' and recommended an alternative tune, 'Lewie Gordon', also suggesting various changes to the lyrics. Burns was unhappy with this state of affairs, and wrote to Thomson that one of his suggestions was 'a hacknied idea'[11] and that, in general, 'Your proposed alterations would, in my opinion, make it tame.'[12] Certainly, Thomson's suggestion that the phrase 'gory bed' in stanza one be altered to 'honour's bed'[13] would seem to pacify the lexis somewhat.

Thomson first published his version of 'Bruce's Address' to the tune of 'Lewie Gordon' in an arrangement by Kozeluch in his *Select Collection*, but this soon led to protests which finally, in 1801, forced Thomson to republish the song for the first time as Burns had initially wished, this time arranged by Haydn and displaying a strange obsession with trills in the cello and piano parts.[14] As a result of this, perhaps, but also because of the fact that 'Hey Tuttie Taitie' had already been published in Vol. 2 of the *Scots Musical Museum* when Johnson finally published the song in his Vol. 6 (1803), he was not willing to publish a simple repetition of the tune and so the following version was settled upon:

Example 11.3. 'Bruce's Address' from James Johnson, *The Scots Musical Museum*, Vol. 6 (Edinburgh: Johnson, 1803), p. 178.

'Wha will be a traitor knave?
'Wha can fill a coward's grave?
'Wha fae bafe as me a flave?
'Traitors coward! turn and flee.

'Wha for Scotland's King and law
'Freedom's fword will ftrongly draw,
'Freedom ftand and free-man fa',
'Caledonian, on wi' me.

'By oprefsion's woes and pains!
'By your fons in fervile chains!
'We will drain our deareft veins,
'But they fhall be - fhall be free.

'Lay the proud ufurpers low!
'Tyrants fall in every foe;
'Liberty's in every blow!
'Forward! let us do, or die.'

As can be seen from the two examples above, Johnson's *Museum* was intended as a collection of Scots songs arranged as simple art songs, with figured bass part for piano, or cello and harpsichord continuo. Despite this Italianate Baroque setting, the whole aim from Johnson's point of view was to ensure that:

> the original simplicity of our Ancient National Airs is retained unencumbered with useless Accompaniments & graces depriving the hearers of the sweet simplicity of their native melodies.[15]

No doubt, this expresses a typically eighteenth-century concern with the conception of traditional music as essentially pastoral ('Ancient', 'simplicity', 'native'), not to be tainted by the complex artifice of musical modernity. Nonetheless, in Johnson's *Museum*, we see this song genre being presented for a specifically bourgeois audience trained in the notational and performance techniques of the Italian Baroque style which had occupied such a high currency in Edinburgh throughout the eighteenth century.[16] Here, we are in the realm of the bourgeois parlour, the musical soirée, and the concert hall. This market was, of course, the same one which Thomson was attempting to monopolise with his *Select Collection*. However, Thomson was expressly attempting to 'modernise' the 'native' tradition, and his aesthetic models owe more to Viennese classicism than the Italian Baroque.[17] Indeed, Thomson commissioned sometimes ornate arrangements of traditional Scots material from composers such as Kozeluch, Haydn, Beethoven and Weber – collaborative choices which have become notorious for their often insensitive results. As Cedric Thorpe Davie has acerbically commented:

> As for George Thomson's elephantine *magnum opus*, it must be said at once that but for the fact that it was the means of bringing into the world several of Burns's finest creations, it can only be regarded as a joke . . . with results so ludicrous that one can listen to them only with a mixture of laughter, tears and rage. This does not prevent Teutonic lieder-singers from including them occasionally in programmes intended to be serious.[18]

The setting of Scots traditional tunes in the Viennese style is problematic not least due to their often modal character and the fact that they often operate around subtonic cadential structures (the 'double tonic') instead of the classical tonic-dominant figure. These facts led the Germanic composers who worked on Thomson's collection towards certain basic harmonic misconceptions with regard to the Scots style, as they often vainly attempted to fit the square peg of Scots modality into the round hole of Viennese tonality. Famously, Kozeluch, the arranger of Vol. 1, Set ii, of the *Select Collection*, initially complained to Thomson that the first manuscript of the Scots tunes which had been sent to him were full of basic copyist's errors. Thomson was at this point sending the tunes to Kozeluch via a colleague called Straton, who commented that, on receiving a second manuscript practically identical to the first:

> Kozeluch called on me yesterday to mention that on perusing the airs lately put into his hands, he had found most of them *une musique barbare*, which set at defiance all the rules of art that he professed . . . In reply to this . . . instead of standing up for our national music thus wantonly attacked, I left it unburthened with the epithet of 'barbarous', and, courtier-like, told M. Kozeluch that you [Thomson] relied on his knowledge and genius for the civilisation of the part of it which you had transmitted hither.[19]

Of course, despite Straton and Thomson's mild fit of nationalistic pique at Kozeluch's ethnomusical prejudice, the fact remains that Thomson's project in editing Burns's lyric was characterised by the songwriter as an exercise in 'taming' the directness of its lexis, not least in altering 'gory' to 'honour's'. Furthermore, Thomson's attempt to pacify the rhythmic angularity of 'Hey Tutti Taitie' by replacing it with 'Lewie Gordon' can surely be seen in the light of Kozeluch's accusation of musical barbarism, particularly in the context of the fact that Kozeluch composed that arrangement. More than this, however, in commissioning his final setting of the song to the original tune from none other than maestro Haydn himself, Thomson was clearly attempting to pitch for a much more classical, refined aesthetic and market than Johnson. One might comment, in Johnson's defence, that at least he had the courage to publish the mildly bawdy version of 'Hey Tutti Taitie' in his second volume, collected and edited by Burns, and with the tune's angular 'barbarity' quite untamed.

In all of this, Burns's authorship of the first published settings of 'Bruce's Address' remain securely at the level of a spectral presence. By the time that Thomson finally released a version of 'the' version which Burns had 'originally intended', Burns himself was dead some seven years, his role in sanctioning an 'authentic' setting a very corporeal impossibility. Through the internecine aspects of the Johnson–Thomson rivalries, Burns's authorial presence is only ever a fleeting, chimerical form, blown this way and that by forces outside of his presumed intentionality. The complex intertextualities which operate within the debatable borders around the traditions of folk, broadside and parlour genres is seen to operate at a high level of intensity here. Throughout, the identity of Burns's song, in both the senses of lyrical and melodic content (and their relationship to each other), is in question, with many factors of economics, aesthetics and politics combining to create a highly problematic genesis for this most famous of songs. However, in considering the various readings and uses of the song which emerged from the rapidly shifting culture of the nineteenth century, it becomes clear that the problematics of identity for this song in no way dissipated, but became even more complex.

Radical alignments

Perhaps, even today, the popular image of Burns's nationalism is that of sentimental Jacobitism, a royalism loyal to the ancient Scottish crown of the Stuart line against the succession of variously imported British monarchs, from William of Orange to the Hanoverian line of Burns's own time. Certainly, we have Johnson's Jacobite version of 'Hey Tuttie Taitie' haunting the origins of 'Bruce's Address'. Nonetheless, as many academics have been keen to emphasise in recent years (not least in the space of constitutional crisis between the devolution referenda of 1979 and 1997), and as we can clearly identify in 'Bruce's Address', the Jacobite, royalist tendency within Burns's politics also, on many occasions, elides into a Jacobin republicanism. Indeed, Burns's time was in the aftermath of the final Jacobite uprising and the brutal suppression of Highland culture following the defeat at Culloden in 1746. At this time, the political reality of nationalism in Scotland was moving swiftly away from its traditional basis in Jacobite Toryism, which was increasingly seen as a spent and defunct force with little to offer a rapidly industrialising and urbanising society. 'Bruce's Address', in its self-evident revolutionary lexis, stands very much at the edge of a shift in alternative Scottish politics from royalism to republicanism inspired by the ideals of the new France. Increasingly, these factors came together to assemble a very idiosyncratic form of Chartism in Scotland which was often overtly nationalist in its objectives.

In 1792, revolutionary nationalists such as the Glaswegian lawyer Thomas Muir established the Scottish Friends of the People as a Radical organisation with directs links to the regime in Paris, which in that year passed resolutions to aid the cause of anti-British revolution in both Scotland and Ireland (attempts to aid Welsh and Cornish Radicals also followed). Further, Christina Bewley and Marilyn Butler both claim that Burns wrote the song as a protest following the infamous trial of Muir, which resulted in the latter's transportation to Australia, a possibility alluded to in Burns's citation of 'other struggles . . . *not quite so ancient*'.[20] The urgency of Scottish activism at this time was demonstrated not least by the effects of the notorious Clearances in the Highlands – indeed, 1792 became known as *am Bliadhna nan Caorach* (the Year of the Sheep), one of the most vicious years in this early experiment in ethnic cleansing. In the Gàidhealtachd, memories of Culloden served as much to inspire a move towards republicanism as to invoke the sentimental Jacobite nostalgia which Lowland culture held so dear as an image of the Highlands throughout the nineteenth century (and beyond). It is no surprise to discover that, in the wake of such developments, 'Bruce's Address', written the following year and (possibly) in direct response to the republican cause, was translated into Gàidhlig as 'Albannaich, thug Brus mu'n Cuairt'. According to Peter Berresford Ellis and Seumas Mac a' Ghobhainn, both the original

Scots version and the Gàidhlig translation figured as the unofficial national anthem at numerous Chartist and Radical meetings and insurrections throughout the period following the French Revolution, not least in those (Scots-language) meetings which were staged in and around Paisley by that town's increasingly militant hand-loom weavers. At a meeting in Airdrie in 1819, however, the self-evident political iconography of Radicals singing 'Bruce's Address' at a public meeting prompted the authorities to arrest the entire band in retaliation, along with key members of the Airdrie Radical Committee.[21] Certainly, the song fed into the general mythos which the Scottish Radicals were assembling around the heritage of Wallace, with numerous banners at these meetings carrying logos such as: 'Sir William Wallace, like our ancestors, we'll defend our liberty and laws', 'We are the descendants of Wallace and Bruce', and so forth. On one occasion in the same year, Wallace's conjectured home-town of Elderslie also became the focus of a large Radical rally, the centrepiece of which was an assembly around Wallace's Tree, with the protesters singing 'Bruce's Address' and firing pistols into the air. As this meeting proceeded on to Paisley, they were pursued by (but successfully evaded) significant numbers of cavalry with sabres drawn.[22]

Again, for Radicals who had been incarcerated, 'Bruce's Address' became a resonant political icon around which their identity could be assembled and asserted – in the case of one group of west-coast Radicals awaiting trial in Edinburgh, the merest reference to 'God Save the King' being played as the trial judge proceeded towards the courthouse invoked a robust response in the form of the Scottish national anthem. As one of those Radicals, John Fraser, recalled:

> This we did, shouting at the utmost stretch of our voices. The whole crowd, judges and all, turned their eyes to our open cell windows, our foreheads projecting outwards as far as the iron stanchions would permit. In a little we heard John Hart rattling his keys furiously at the cell door. Opening it, he exclaimed: 'Ye're a wheen deevils; I'll put ye in chains, and shut ye up in darkness!' The latter threat he instantly executed. That was the reward we got for our Scottish patriotism.[23]

Clearly, in the Scotland of this time, the iconographic and nomological resonances of this song by Burns had very clear implications to all concerned, and its mere performance could easily have legal consequences as the political allegiance of the singer became all too self-evident. Burns himself was aware of the dangers of being associated too closely with the sentiments expressed in his own lyrics, as he intimates in a letter about publication of the lyrics in Perry's *Morning Chronicle*:

> You well know my political sentiments ... In the mean time, they are most welcome to my Ode; only, let them insert it as a thing they have met with by accident, & unknown to me. – Nay, if M[r] Perry, whose

> honour, after your character of him I cannot doubt, if he will give me an Address & channel by which anything will come safe from these spies with which he may be certain that his correspondence is beset, I will now and then send him any bagatelle that I may write. In the present hurry of Europe, nothing but news and politics will be regarded; but in the days of Peace, which Heaven send soon, my little assistance may perhaps fill up an idle column of a newspaper.[24]

In this, the risks of holding a revolutionary ideology in the Scotland of the late eighteenth century become more than clear. The political resonances of 'Bruce's Address' were self-evident to the contemporary audience, such that not only did performers of the song risk incarceration or further punishment for its mere performance but its very author, one year after its composition, recognised the dangers inherent in its message to the extent that he requested anonymity on publication of the lyrics.

The main mode of the song's initial musical publication had been through the medium of Thomson's *Select Collection* and Johnson's *Museum*, replete as those publications are with art-song pretensions of one kind or another designed for the polite middle-class metropolitan audience whose musical praxis is increasingly centred on the domestic scene of the bourgeois parlour and the public scene of the concert hall. Nonetheless, 'Bruce's Address' very rapidly became one of the central totems of Scottish Radicalism in its specifically nationalist mode. Yet the mythos which developed around this particular usage of the song did not exhaust its iconographic possibilities.

A jacobite interpolation

> in 1847 many staunch Jacobites could still express themselves strongly . . . Poets and composers (such as Lady Nairne) had kept a fascinating tradition alive and the glamour of Scott was over it all. Incidentally be it said that the purely Jacobite melodies of that period have an unmistakable essence of their own and differ considerably from the rest of our national tunes. How this came to pass has always been an interesting puzzle to me.[25]

For the *fin-de-siècle* composer Alexander Campbell Mackenzie (1847–1935), his era was not only witness to the continuation of the new Radicalisms in Scottish politics (not least the Red Clydeside movement), but also certain survivals of the eighteenth-century ideology of Jacobitism. Central to this survival, in his view, are the songwriters who were influenced by the mythologisation of Highland culture effected in the work of Walter Scott. Indubitably, Scott is the single most significant figure (besides Burns) in the gradual process by which the Gàidhlig culture of the North became popularised in the Lowlands through a series of exoticising strategies. Not least in this is the gradual reinscription of the Highlander from politically and socially volatile barbarian to pastoralised Noble Savage. Ironically, of course, the rise in popular images of the Highlands as an idyllic Garden of Eden coincided with the mass ethnic cleansing of the Clearances, in which the landscape was increasingly depopulated and made barren in order to make way for the new obsession with sheep farming. In modes of representation fully within Edward Said's concept of Orientalism,[26] the representations of the Highlands bore little resemblance to their ostensible referents. Rather, they developed as codes of signification quite external to their subject, evolving from representational traditions generated outside of the Highland scene itself.

This is in fact the reality of the mysterious glamour referred to by Mackenzie which Scott cast over the misty North, but in this it is also a question of 'an unmistakable essence' to be found within nineteenth-century Jacobite art – no doubt a question of a certain authenticity, as opposed to an obfuscating series of representational fictions. Moreover, Mackenzie refers very specifically to the songwriting work of Caroline Nairne (1766–1845) within the context of this Jacobite essentiality. Nairne was from one of the landed Jacobite families who had lost their titles in the aftermath of Culloden, yet by 1824 the threat of Jacobite militancy had well and truly dispersed, not least as a result of the Clearances, and the peerages were restored in law – an event which followed only two years after Scott had invited George IV to be the first post-Treaty of Union British monarch to visit Scotland and, notoriously, indulge in various forms of sham tartan ritual. Furthermore, as the imperial Queen Victoria began to develop an interest in the increasingly exoticised image of the Highlands, Jacobitism was back as a cultural, if not an actively political, force. Romance had finally taken centre stage in the Highland theatre.

Nairne's work represents the hard core of nineteenth-century bourgeois Jacobite song and, along with the gradual reinscription of the 1745 uprising as a heroic quest, so too came an the increasing emphasis on Burns's image not as a Radical republican figure but as a Romantic Jacobite. In this context, it is hardly surprising that Nairne relied heavily on certain of the representational codes which Burns developed from the folk traditions of the Lowlands. The pastoral scene is developed in her work to encompass an equally intense investment in the figure of the domestic, all located under the over-arching structure of sentimental Jacobitism. Nowhere is this more the case than in her own derivative of 'Bruce's Address': 'The Land o' the Leal'.

Example 11.4. 'The Land o' the Leal' from Alfred Moffat, *The Minstrelsy of Scotland* (London, Augener, 1894), p. 85.

2.
Ye aye were leal and true, John,
Ye're task is ended noo, John,
And I'll wecome you to the Land o' the Leal.
There's nae sorrow there, John,
She was baith good and fair, John,
And we grudge'd her sair to the Lnd o' the Leal.

3.
Them dry that tearfu' eye, John,
My soul longs to be free, John,
And angels wait on me to the Land o' the Leal.
Now fare ye weel, my ain John,
This warld's care is vain, John,
We'll meet and aye be fein in the Land o' the Leal.

Once more, 'Hey Tutti Taitie' resurfaces within the context of a nationalist agenda, deriving as much from Burns's version as from Johnson's earlier publication of the Jacobite version, 'Here Is to the King'. Written around 1800, 'The Land o' the Leal' combines both religious, nationalist, royalist and domestic imagery, shot through at all levels with a pervasive sentimentality. Traditionally, the song is said to have been composed by Nairne in response to the death of a friend's child and, in this, we have the stereotypical image of Nairne as female songwriter concerned primarily with the domestic. Nonetheless, the song extends from this domesticity into the religious and political fields as such, where the loyalty expressed by the Scots term *leal* is a loyalty to both faith and nation. In this, the land of the loyal is simultaneously a Catholic Heaven and a Jacobite Scotland, a land without sorrow, coldness or worry, where the family members who have gone before will once more be met.

However, the politics of this song are deeply encoded, as they so often are in the Jacobite tradition, where the figure of the secret allegiance is paramount to the survival of the loyal in the days after Culloden. Unlike the overt republicanism expressed in many Radical songs of the time, Jacobite songs tend to rely on deep levels of nuance and even innuendo for their ideology to be effectively decoded. Of course, this applies more to Jacobite songs written in Scots than to those in Gàidhlig, whose status at this time as an oral, minority language often protects the composer or singer from the metropolitan, Anglo-Scots authoritarian gaze. Yet, throughout the Scots-language genre, stock phrases operate to signify the concept of loyalty to the Stuart royal line which often require specific subcultural knowledge to be understood. In this instance, the very title of the song, which also forms the lyrics of the cadential phrases, is the key to its Jacobite content, since at this time the whole concept of loyalty within Jacobite culture was absolutely resonant with the question of monarchy.

Nonetheless, most characteristically for Nairne, we have this encoded Jacobitism overlaid with a general sentimentalism of kith, kin and Christianity (nowhere overtly revealed here as specifically Catholic) which points very clearly towards the later nineteenth-century literary genre of 'kailyaird'. Burns himself was usurped as a primary model for this genre, which tends to depict rural Scottish life within the structures of British imperial culture – Scotland as a rustic, backward, God-fearing society whose rigid moral integrity outweighs its intellectual, aesthetic or technological refinement, and where Scots is portrayed as a debased dialect of English spoken in the domestic scene between mothers and children, the old and infirm, and the village idiot (and is it not noteworthy that the only contemporary representation of anything remotely approaching the Scots language even on Scottish television channels is *Rab C. Nesbitt*?).

In the culture of nineteenth-century Scotland, then, the figure of sentiment is never far behind bourgeois representations of the nation. While Radical agitations were sweeping the towns and cities, challenging the power of industrial capitalism in new and disconcerting ways, the figure of the pastoral scene and, once more, the nation's heroic past seemed increasingly to offer a means by which the national identity could somehow be manipulated into a state of obedient passivity. Ironically, one of the most successful strategies by which this disempowering of Scottish national politics was achieved was with recourse to the history of the Jacobite cause of the eighteenth century. If the urban Radicals were dangerous in their republicanism, tainted with the fumes of modern industrial conditions, an unruly, scruffy mob hell-bent on destroying the enlightened status quo, then the heroic figure of the Young Pretender and his romanticised tribe of Celtic Noble Savages from the exotic North offered an image of a more polite, chivalrous and pastoral era. As Amy Hale has commented on a similar mythologising process within Cornish culture:

> 'industrial' and 'Celtic' do not generally share the same semantic space, and many of those working to forge 'new' Celtic nations relied on a more pastoral vision, which was actually incongruent with the reality of Cornish history. Good Celts were not supposed to be modern industrialists; they were to be rural, simple, spiritual peasants working in harmony with the land.[27]

In the Jacobite context, all one need add to this are the figures of heroic militarism and historical Romance. Nonetheless, the Young Chevalier's heroic, tragic failure on the fields of Culloden also guaranteed an inbuilt sense of redundancy within the nationalist agenda. For Nietzsche, the very structure of tragedy rests on the sacrifice of the rebellious hero to the structure of societal hegemony. Moreover, by identifying with the tragic hero, who performs actions proscribed by that society, the audience is purged of its need to personally enact its own actual rebellions, the hero's dramatic sacrifice acting as a catharsis for the antisocial desire inherent within the audience, thus restoring order within the real political field.[28] In very direct terms, the cultural Jacobitism promoted in the Lowlands, not least through the work of Scott and Nairne, offered an outlet for pride in a still extant national identity and its lengthy history, while simultaneously circumscribing that pride with the reassuring security of heroic failure. The message of tartanry in the nineteenth century is that Scottish politics are a thing of the past, even if they are also a valid reason for cultural pride. In this, a debilitating sentimentality overrides the desire for direct action. As a result, it lies in direct opposition to the Burnsian investment in Jacobitism as one of several tributaries into the wider stream of Scottish nationalism. For Burns, in invoking not only the heroic ages of Wallace and of Charles Edward Stuart, and also his invocation of specifically republican ideals derived from the French Revolution, the strategy is one of cultural and historical inclusiveness as a means of inciting the nation into direct, effective political action. Nairne's agenda, however, as a landed Jacobite whose title had been reinstated by the British state only on the implicit promise that her nationalism was cultural rather than political, involves no call to arms and, indeed, rests specifically on a certain complicity with the *status quo*. Nonetheless, the reversal of Burnsian Jacobitism which kailyairdists such as Nairne effect is by no means the most surreal reversal which these Burnsian themes have been subjected to.

Hegemonic appropriations

> My next [memory] is that of a very old and picturesque family mansion, at the foot of Stockbridge, where, in one of the immensely large rooms then let to some ancient female pensioners, dwelt my old nurse. On my visits Nannie would sit by the fireside reciting long passages from Burns by heart – and with a keen appreciation of their humour – to me.[29]

> We two had come up from dinner and were sitting in this room . . . 'Lie on the sofa there,' said she . . . In old years I used to lie that way, and she would play the piano to me: a long series of Scotch tunes which set my mind finely wandering through the realms of memory and romance . . . That evening I had lain but a few minutes when she turned round to her piano, got out the Thomson Burns book, and to my surprise and joy, broke out again into her bright little stream of harmony . . . silent for at least ten years before, and gave me . . . all my old favourites.[30]

These are two domestic images of Burns in the bourgeois parlour: the first from Mackenzie, the second from Carlyle. Archetypally perhaps, for Mackenzie, Burns is strongly associated with humour and childhood, simultaneously being the means by which his ageing nursemaid transmits to him the traditions of Scottish culture – a strongly kailyairdesque series of associations. For Carlyle, once more, the images here are of old age and the feminine. Here, he relates the final time that the ailing Jane played him Burns songs before she died – again, a strongly sentimental investment. Yet Carlyle, reclining in the parlour as Jane's 'bright little stream of harmony' flowed over him transporting him back into the Scottish landscapes of his youth, was also capable of a highly politicised reading of Burns, and one which reads from the very centre of British imperial bourgeois culture. In fact, the interval between Burns and Carlyle is at its most political over the historiographical positioning of 'Bruce's Address' itself. However, the self-evidently nationalist agenda of the song becomes deeply problematised with Carlyle, and, if Burns stands here as a prophet of the nation's historical destiny, then the question to be put to Carlyle's reading is: *which nation?* Here is the full passage on 'Bruce's Address' in his essay on Burns, replete with Carlyle's characteristically logocentric lexis:

> Why should we speak of *Scots, wha hae wi' Wallace bled,* since all know of it, from the king to the meanest of his subjects? This dithyrambic was composed on horseback, in riding in the middle of tempests, over the wildest Galloway moor, in company with a Mr. Syme, who, observing the poet's looks, forbore to speak, – judiciously enough, for a man composing *Bruce's Address* might be unsafe to trifle with. Doubtless this stern hymn was singing itself, as he formed it, through the soul of Burns; but to the external ear it should be sung with the throat of the whirlwind. So long as there is warm blood in the heart of Scotchman or man, it will move in fierce thrills under this war ode; the best, we believe, that was ever written by any pen.[31]

Here, Carlyle speaks of a reverential abstinence of speech – Syme forbears his own vocality in deference to the more seminally virile whirlwinds of Burns which have not their *acoustic* sign, but a *visual* sign of a stern, warlike countenance. In the middle of the external tempests, and in the absence of signs presented to the external ear, Burns forges the musical organism within his soul, his *prima materia*, being that which 'sings itself' to him, is communicated from beyond: a divine image, no doubt, and one which results in the warming of Scottish blood in a nationalistic fervour. Let us turn, then, specifically to the political question of the nation, which is never far from Carlyle's aesthetics. Of the post-Burnsian scene, he writes that:

> Among the great changes which British, particularly Scottish literature, has undergone since that period, one of the greatest will be found to consist in its remarkable increase of nationality. Even the English writers, most popular in Burns's time, were little distinguished for their literary patriotism, in this its best sense.[32]

> We might write a long essay on the Songs of Burns; which we reckon by far the best that Britain has yet produced: for indeed, since the era of Queen Elizabeth, we know not that, by any other hand, aught truly worth attention has been accomplished in this department.[33]

In the context of these and many other passages, we are clearly to construe that Carlyle, in direct opposition to the early nineteenth-century Radical reading, considers Burns song in general to be recoverable within the context of a *British* rather than Scottish nationalism. Certainly, he writes here against the contextualisation of Burns within the Jacobite or Jacobean traditions, and argues that his true genealogy stems from an English, Tudor root (as if the Tudors themselves were authentically or unproblematically 'English'). In Carlyle's reading, one unquestioningly discounts Burns's declaration that 'the Scotish Muses were all Jacobites'.[34] Indeed, with reference to two specifically Jacobite songwriting precedents, Carlyle claims that, despite having only 'the rhymes of a Ferguson or Ramsay for his standard of beauty, he sinks not under these impediments: through the fogs and darkness of that obscure region, his lynx eye discerns the true relations of the world'.[35] For Carlyle, the negroid darkness of a Jacobite Scotland does not hinder the penetrating eye of the poet who can burn away such surface illusions to discover the 'true relations of the world'. No doubt, the reason for Burns's pre-eminence in this lies in the fact that, for Carlyle, perversely, he is to be seen as 'a piece of the right Saxon stuff: strong as the Harz-rock, rooted in the depths of the world . . . like the old Norse Thor, the Peasant-god!'[36] In all of this, Carlyle effects an erasure of Scottish ethnicity and political reality, aligning Burns within a specifically British identity devoid of any Celtic content at all – perhaps a surprising manoeuvre for a post-Walter Scott historian writing in the midst of an increasing mania for tartan tourism in its almost venereal condition of Jacobitic nostalgia.

Yet to locate 'Bruce's Address' within the context of such an Anglocentric British nationalism would be to logically imply that the song constitutes a hymn to *civil war*, and therefore the rupture of the presumed political unity of the British imperial state in which Carlyle had invested so much. His realignment of the specific political traces of revolutionary thought in Burns's song can be seen to stem from passages such as the following, where he further invokes the powerful spectre of Andrew Fletcher:

> It is on his Songs, as we believe, that Burns's chief influence as an author will ultimately be found to depend: nor, if our Fletcher's aphorism is true, shall we account this a small influence. 'Let me make the songs of a people,' said he, 'and you shall make its laws.' Surely, if any Poet might have equalled himself with Legislators on this ground, it was Burns.[37]

Carlyle's misquotation here at once invokes and reinscribes the radicality of Fletcher's statement. Fletcher was, of course, directly and famously opposed to the ratification of the 1707 Treaty of Union. In this context, Carlyle's Unionist determination of him as 'our' Fletcher is an odd example of political appropriation to say the least. The precise nature of the misquotation suggests that Fletcher views the roles of the songwriter and the legislator as somehow complementary. However, the passage in question actually reads in full: 'I said, I knew a very wise man so much of Sir Chr—'s sentiment, that he believed if a man were permitted to make all the ballads, he need not care who should make the laws of a nation.'[38] Fletcher's acquaintance's determination of song here suggests more that it potentially makes legislation redundant: song as a political act in itself, and one which has a powerful hold over the minds of a nation. Burns himself echoes this sentiment in his comments on 'political combustion' already quoted above. In both Fletcher's and Burns's statements, we find not that song and law are complementary, as Carlyle's misquotation suggests, but that song is potentially more powerful than law; in short, that cultural power outweighs legislative power, and is capable of usurping its place when legislatures renege on their responsibilities. As with the Radical iconographic investments in 'Bruce's Address', culture becomes the *locus* of 'political combustion', as Burns put it, when a society is deserted by its political institutions.

Yet Carlyle's strange misquotation and appropriation of Fletcher is a mere prelude to the following, even more surreal passage from *Past and Present*:

> A heroic Wallace, quartered on the scaffold, cannot hinder that his Scotland become, one day, a part of England: but he does hinder that it become, on tyrannous unfair terms, a part of it; commands still, as with a god's voice, from his old Valhalla and Temple of the Brave, that there be a just real union as of brother and brother, not a false and merely semblant one as of slave and master. If the union with England be in fact one of Scotland's chief blessings, we thank Wallace withal that it was not the chief curse. Scotland is not Ireland: no, because brave men rose there.[39]

The subsequent historical ironies with respect to the statement concerning Ireland aside, here we find Carlyle asserting a patriotism with respect to the Scotland of the British Union – a 'part of England'. For Carlyle, the Union is 'one of Scotland's chief blessings' precisely because of Wallace's previous, Nordically defined resistance to it – once more, we have the claim of a Germanic authenticity, rather than a Celtic one, at the heart of Scottish culture. Now, not only will it be hard to fit Carlyle's theories of Irish submission into recent history, but the contention that Wallace and Bruce were somehow preparing the ground for the Union appears more than remarkable. Carlyle would seem to be arguing from a position which defines the 1707 Treaty of Union as the logical conclusion of the 1320 Declaration of Arbroath. For Carlyle, *this* political union is the divine message of national *telos* which Wallace 'commands still, as with a god's voice', from Valhalla, and which is *inspired* 'through the soul of Burns' in his composition of 'Bruce's Address'. Freedom is not to be found in Scottish independence here, but within the structure of the UK imperial state, thoroughly bound to the constitutional apparatus of Westminster, and only through this can one escape, in Burns's words, 'Chains and slavery'. In all of this, Carlyle achieves an ideological assimilation of precisely that which overtly opposes his politics. 'Free-man stand, or free-man fa''', indeed.

Yet Carlyle's surreal reading of Wallace, Bruce and Burns as proto-Unionists has further textual resonances which suggest that this mode of reading was less than completely idiosyncratic or singular. In Robert

Archibald Smith's six-volume *The Scotish Minstrel* (1821–1824), edited from within the Radical heartland of Paisley, we find an alternative lyric to 'Bruce's Address', entitled 'Waterloo', written in English by one Captain Skinner, and printed directly beneath the Burns original:⁴⁰

WATERLOO (same air)

Revolving time has brought the day,
That beams with glory's brightest ray,
In hist'ry's page, or poet's lay
    The day of Waterloo!
Each British heart with ardour burns,
As this resplendent day returns,
While humbled France in secret mourns
    The day of Waterloo.

Then lift the brimful goblet high,
While rapture beams in every eye!
Let shouts of triumph rend the sky,
    The toast of Waterloo!
To all who can the honour claim
From Wellington's immortal fame,
To the humblest son of martial fame,
    Who fought at Waterloo!

Fill, fill the wine-cup yet again;
But altered be the joyous strain;
To those, the cup now silent drain,
    Who fell at Waterloo!
Soft sigh, ye breezes, o'er the grave
Where rests the relics of the brave
And sweetest flowers o'er them wave
    Who sleep at Waterloo!

From their ensanguin'd honour'd bed,
The olive rears its peaceful head,
Nurs'd by the sacred blood they shed
    At glorious Waterloo.
In freedom's sacred cause to die!
In victory's embrace to lie!
Who would not breathe his latest sigh,
    Like those at Waterloo!

Significantly, perhaps, this British nationalist version was published by a Paisley weaver, Smith, who one might expect to have had intimate knowledge of the Radical traditions surrounding 'Bruce's Address' and its use within the Paisley Radical community, centred as it was on the weaving industry. Certainly, the songwriting collaborations he had with the Paisley weaver-poet Robert Tannahill were widely sung by the weavers of the time, and on occasion a political content has been read into the figure of Tannahill as, if not an overtly political figure himself, then at the very least a songwriter of the people.⁴¹ Nonetheless, being published in the immediate aftermath of the Scottish Radical insurrections around 1820, the overtly politicised content of this editorial decision is intense to say the least. Further, the redistribution of the Burnsian text within Skinner's is heavily ironic. Just as 'Bruce's Address' deals with a complex series of resonances both historical and contemporary around the Scottish political relationships to France and Britain, Skinner's text overturns the directions in which Burns's alignments are drawn. Here, the Napoleonic legacy of the Revolution itself is deeply contested, and the Battle of Bannockburn is transposed into the Battle of Waterloo, a specifically British victory against the other partner in the Auld Alliance. Moreover, the irony operates intimately within the revolutionary lexis of Burns's original – once more, the language of 'freedom's sacred cause' is invoked, albeit usurped for a British nationalism. In this, no doubt, Skinner overtly activates many of the ideological positions which Carlyle was also perversely attempting to read into Burns's work.

It is also noteworthy that I have found no Radical recompositions of 'Bruce's Address', despite the existence of satirical rewrites of Burns songs such as 'John Anderson, My Jo' (as 'John Henderson My Jo, John') by the Paisley weaver and playwright, Edward Polin.[42] Evidently, Burns's own piece served the Radical agenda perfectly well without any need for modification, while bourgeois British ideologies required the ability to at once invoke the nationalist power of the Burns original while erasing its specific politics.

Perhaps even more ironically surreal, though, is yet another version of the song which appeared more recently in a Glaswegian publication entitled *Orange Standards*, in which the mythos of Wallace is transplanted into a specifically Unionist text calling for a religious war against Catholicism:

Example 11.5. 'Sons Whose Sires with William Bled' from *Orange Standards* (Glasgow, Mozart Allan, n.d.), p. 3.

2.	3.
Loud and high their clamors rise,	Now they whine, as 'bondsmen' poor,
Of pretended miseries;	Now they boast their millions o'er,
The Papist creed is only lies,	And forth the Popish rent they pour-
Which none but fools believe.	For pikes and murder given.
All the generous lion can,	Firm, ye sons of Britain, firm,
That belons of right to man,	Shrink not from the gathering storm,
Britain puts within their span	Let it come in any form;
And they ingrate receive.	Our battle-word is – Heaven

Once more, we find the heavy irony of the lyric turning the Burnsian lexis of revolutionary zeal entirely on its head, claiming that, for the Scots-Irish of Northern Ireland, and presumably their Presbyterian brethren throughout Scotland itself, 'liberty' is to be found not in the Radical anti-Unionist republicanism inspired by 'Bruce's Address' on the streets of nineteenth-century Paisley but in the overthrowing of 'the Papist creed' by violent means if necessary: 'Shrink not from the gathering storm, / Let it come in any form; / Our battle-word is Heaven'. In this, the complex ideology of Orange culture lays its structure bare: in aligning itself with the cause of Scottish nationalist history, Ulsterism expresses its Britishness, yet the Unionism of its position relies on adopting cultural models which are in fact deeply anti-Unionist and which, if applied literally to the situation of the Six Counties, would in fact lead most logically to a new state independent of the UK. Increasingly, in the current climate of civic nationalism which has resulted in the development of another Scottish parliament sitting in Edinburgh, one might imagine that the Scottish references of the Ulster Unionists will become not only increasingly anachronistic and paradoxical, but simply untenable.

'A very fragment business'

No doubt such appropriations of the cornerstone of Scottish cultural nationalism – the very national anthem upon which the *auld sang* of the nation finds its constant refrain – had immense power throughout the nineteenth century and beyond. Not least in this is the process by which they at once invoke the nationalist sentiment of Burns whilst at the same time absorbing that potentially dangerous power and channelling it into over-arching Unionist, British ideologies. In this, the specific 'political combustion' which was Burns's intended outcome of his cultural activism becomes defused, its nationalism domesticated. What we have here is a series of Burnsian forms whose content has been hollowed out, inverted, and almost deconstructively turned against itself.

According to Tom Nairn, this is a recognisable process throughout the encounters of nineteenth-century Scottish culture with the hegemonic structures of the UK state:

> Scots differentness could not be harnessed in the way that the young Burns and other radicals imagined. But it did not disappear, for that reason. It simply became a problem ... The problem of its bourgeoisie therefore became – put in the starkest terms – one of neutralizing or repressing the country's more distinctive and proto-national features ... The new romantic consciousness of the past was, in itself, irresistible. As a matter of fact, from Ossian to Sir Walter himself, Scotland played a large part in generating and diffusing it for the rest of Europe. What mattered in Scotland itself, however, was to render this awareness politically null – to make certain that it would not be felt that contemporary Scotland should be the independent continuation of the auld sang.[43]

In all of the many versions of 'Bruce's Address' which follow on in the nineteenth century, the question which was posed to Thomas Carlyle's reading of the song stands at the centre of the issue: if this song does indeed invoke a national identity, if it is indeed the unofficial national anthem, then the question of which nation it has been forced to serve remains in its full intensity. Ironically, perhaps, as a national anthem, 'Bruce's Address' is a deeply contested text. Not only did Carlyle attempt to read a British agenda into it, but the numerous recompositions which substitute specifically Unionist and imperialist lyrics serve to problematise the legacy of the song even further. The irony here, of course, lies in the fact that, while the intentionality behind a national anthem is directed towards a unifying concept of nationhood, relying on a concept of national identity as an integral whole, 'Bruce's Address' (as, indeed, with many other national anthems) becomes a very fragmented, intertextually charged piece when subjected to analysis. Not only was its initial publication shot through with complexities of relationship between tune and lyrics, but the uses to which it has found itself put – not least in the nineteenth century – have served only to further complicate the situation. As with the widely discredited modernist conception of the nation-state as an ethnically unified construct, we must also recognise the intertextuality of this national anthem and perhaps perceive within it Burns's notion of traditional songwriting as 'a very fragment business'.[44]

Notes and References

1. John Barbour, *The Bruce* (Oxford, 1968), p. 1.
2. Andrew Fletcher, *An Account of a Conversation Concerning a Right Regulation of Governments for the Common Good of Mankind* (1704), in David Daiches (ed.), *Fletcher of Saltoun: Selected Writings* (Edinburgh, 1979), p. 109.
3. Robert Burns, Letter to Alexander Cunningham, 11 March 1791, in G. Ross Roy (ed.), *The Letters of Robert Burns*, Vol. II (Oxford, 1985), p. 82.
4. Paul H. Scott, *Andrew Fletcher and the Treaty of Union* (Edinburgh, 1992), pp. 208–10.
5. Marjory Kennedy-Fraser, *Scots Folk Song* (Glasgow, 1922), p. 17.
6. David Daiches, Robert Burns (London, 1966), pp. 308–9.
7. See Bill Ashcroft et al., *The Empire Writes Back: Theory and Practice in Post-Colonial Literatures* (London, 1994).
8. For a more detailed account of this process see Steve Sweeney-Turner, 'Borderlines: Bilingual Terrain in Scottish Song', in Leyshon, Matless and Revill (eds.), *The Place of Music: Music, Space, and the Production of Place* (London, 1998).
9. Robert Burns, Letter to George Thomson, c.30-8-1793, in *The Letters of Robert Burns*, Vol. II, pp. 235–6.
10. John Purser, *Scotland's Music* (Edinburgh, 1992), p. 63.
11. Burns, Letter to George Thomson, c.8-9-1793, p. 237.
12. Burns, Letter to George Thomson, c.15-9-1793, p. 248.
13. Burns, Letter to George Thomson, c.8-9-1793, p. 237.
14. As can be heard on the Scottish Early Music Consort's recording, *Robert Burns: Songs and Music* (Colchester, CHAN 8636, 1988).
15. James Johnson, *The Scots Musical Museum* (Edinburgh, 1787), Vol. 1, title page.
16. In particular, see David Johnson, *Scottish Fiddle Music in the 18th Century* (Edinburgh, 1984).
17. For a more detailed analysis of the status of art music in Scotland see Steve Sweeney-Turner, 'Reading Scottish Classical Music: A Historiographical Critique', *Journal of Area Studies* 10 (1997).
18. Cedric Thorpe Davie, *Scotland's Music* (Edinburgh, 1980), pp. 15–16.
19. Letter from Straton to Thomson, 28-10-1797, quoted in J. Cuthbert Hadden, *George Thomson, The Friend of Burns: His Life and Correspondence* (London, 1898), pp. 298–9.
20. Christina Bewley, *Muir of Huntershill* (Oxford, 1981), p. 85, and Marilyn Butler, *Romantics, Rebels & Reactionaries: English Literature and its Background, 1760–1830* (Oxford, 1985), p. 37. However, William Donaldson makes the counter claim that it was 'inspired by the Jacobite rebellions', *The Jacobite Song: Political Myth and National Identity* (Aberdeen, 1988), p. 87. Nonetheless, the coincidence of Burns's letter to Thomson and Muir's trial around the same day does lead to an enticing possibility.
21. Peter Berresford Ellis and Seumas Mac a' Ghobhainn, *The Scottish Insurrection of 1820* (London, 1989), p. 123.
22. Ibid., p. 124.
23. Ibid., p. 231. One might also mention at this point the custom at the annual Scottish Proms at the Usher Hall in Edinburgh of a stand-off between those members of the audience (often very few in number) who stand for and sing 'God Save the Queen' and those who stand for and bellow (often in a be-kilted condition) the lyrics of 'Bruce's Address'.
23. Burns, Letter to Peter Millar, c.15-3-1794, in *The Letters of Robert Burns*, pp. 288–9.
25. Alexander Campbell Mackenzie, *A Musician's Narrative* (London, 1927), p. 5.
26. Edward Said, *Orientalism* (New York, 1978).
27. Amy Hale, 'Rethinking Celtic Cornwall: An Ethnographic Approach', in *Cornish Studies*, 5 (Exeter, 1996), p. 94.

28 Friedrich Nietzsche, *The Birth of Tragedy out of the Spirit of Music* (London, 1993), p. 100: 'Tragedy absorbs the highest musical ecstasies, and thus brings music to a state of true perfection. But then it places alongside it the tragic myth and the tragic hero who then, like a mighty Titan, takes the entire Dionysiac world on his back and relieves us of its burden. On the other hand it uses the same tragic myth, in the person of the tragic hero, to deliver us from our eager striving for this existence, and with an admonishing gesture points to another form of being and a higher delight, for which the struggling hero prepares himself by his destruction, not by his triumphs.'
29 Mackenzie, *A Musician's Narrative*, p. 4.
30 Thomas Carlyle, quoted in Thea Holme, *The Carlyles at Home* (Oxford, 1979), p. 182.
31 Thomas Carlyle, 'Burns', in *Critical and Miscellaneous Essays*, Vol. 1 (London, 1887), pp. 252–3.
32 Ibid., p. 257.
33 Ibid., pp. 255–6.
34 Robert Burns, *Notes on Scottish Song*, pp. 4–5.
35 Carlyle, *Lectures on Heroes*, in *Critical and Miscellaneous Essays*, p. 237.
36 Carlyle, *Lectures on Heroes*, pp. 326–7.
37 Carlyle, 'Burns', p. 237.
38 Fletcher, *An Account of a Conversation*, p. 109.
39 Carlyle, *Past and Present*, p. 80.
40 Robert Archibald Smith, *The Scotish Minstrel* (Glasgow, 1821–24), Vol. 4, p. 57.
41 Steve Sweeney-Turner, 'Pagan Airts: Reading Critical Perspectives on the Songs of Burns and Tannahill', in *Scotlands*, 2, 2 (Edinburgh, 1996).
42 Tom Leonard, *Radical Renfrew: Poetry from the French Revolution to the First World War* (Edinburgh, 1990), pp. 160–1 and 164–5.
43 Tom Nairn, 'Old Nationalism and New Nationalism', in Gordon Brown (ed.), *The Red Paper on Scotland* (Edinburgh, 1975), pp. 31 and 33.
44 Burns, Letter to John Skinner, 25-10-1787, in *The Letters of Robert Burns*, Vol. 1, p. 168.

12.
Wagner's Children: Incest and *Bruderzwist*

ROBERT VILAIN

Thematically, stylistically, psychologically, morally and ideologically, the works of Richard Wagner have inspired countless hundreds of novels, poems and plays, many thankfully consigned to oblivion, others load-bearing pillars of what used to be called 'the canon'. Most ring the changes on the themes of incest, *Liebestod*, the fatal attractions of Venice and the decline of great families (what Koppen calls 'Sippendämmerung', or twilight of the clans).[1] Wagnerism is a sub-category of decadence, neo-Romanticism, the *fin de siècle*, even of modernism; the movement known as Symbolism arose, arguably, as a sub-category of Wagnerism. Most of these movements are usually associated with élitism, hermeticism and aesthetic refinement. But another of Wagner's more controversial fields of influence is coarsely public: his political adoption as the cultural standard-bearer of German nationalism, ultimately by Hitler and the Fascists, but much earlier, too, by elements in the Second Reich, and by Kaiser Wilhelm II himself. During the First World War, the Bayreuth circle and the *Bayreuther Blätter* under Hans von Wolzogen helped to mythologise the conflict in Wagnerian terms, anticipating the twilight of the Western gods in the defeat of the French and the British. Richard Sternfeld – one of Wagner's most influential editors – famously published a selection of writings on Wagner and the 'holy German war'.[2]

Historians and musicologists are disentangling Wagner from his Nazi receptors, but this essay is not another contribution to this process.[3] Neither is it a survey, although it may usefully be read in the context of broader-ranging works.[4] It is an inquiry from the perspective of the literary scholar into the relationship between nationalistic and aesthetic elements in the Wagner reception of German and French writers, principally Thomas Mann and Stéphane Mallarmé. Both are Wagner's children, in that some of the defining 'genes' of their work are inherited from Wagner. Mann's overtly politicised responses have a fundamentally aesthetic root, whilst Mallarmé's apparently unworldly attitude has important nationalistic components. By focusing on the question of nationalism, this essay aims to suggest some realignments in the way Franco-German literary Wagnerism is usually perceived and bring out some of the less familiar continuities and discontinuities.

Thomas Mann's obsession with Wagner underwent many changes of emphasis, but never lost either its passion or its ambivalence. In a short essay entitled 'On the Art of Richard Wagner' (1911) Mann writes, 'as a mind, a character, he seemed suspicious to me, but as an artist he was irresistible',[5] and he calls his early attitude to Wagner a 'love without belief':

> It was a relationship that was sceptical, pessimistic, clear-sighted, almost spiteful, but at the same time deeply passionate and giving an indescribable stimulus for life.

The cerebral, literary author loved the erotic qualities of Wagner's music; he both admired and envied someone who seemed to have none of the self-consciousness by which he was himself beset. This did not mean that he did not question Wagner: there was always a voice within him, egged on by Nietzsche (whose critique he had read at nineteen[6]), that wondered whether Wagner's apparently fathomless genius was not in reality a gigantic con trick; this in turn was linked to Mann's own self-doubts concerning his ability and standing as an artist.

The self-referential aspect of this relationship is brought out in the work that perhaps more than any other served as a laboratory for Mann's own artistic problems using a fictional mask, *Der Tod in Venedig* (Death in Venice). Wagner died in Venice in 1883 and his autobiography, *Mein Leben* (My Life), appeared in 1911, just as Mann was writing his novella, and it has been plausibly suggested that Mann consciously echoes the autobiography at several points. When Mann's alter ego Aschenbach disembarks from his ship, he is reminded by the black gondolas of coffins, of 'death itself, the bier, the dark obsequies, the last silent journey'.[7] The image of the coffin-gondola is found elsewhere – in Goethe, Platen, Byron, Werfel and Rilke, for example – but Wagner specifically has 'the impression of an earlier cholera scare that had been withstood'; he feels he is 'to take part in a procession of corpses in a time of plague'.[8] It is of course cholera that kills Aschenbach. Mann's essay 'On the Art of Richard Wagner' was partly written on the notepaper of the Grand Hotel des Bains in May 1911.[9]

Many of Mann's early stories involve a Wagner opera at their turning-point or are ironically counter-modelled on a Wagnerian plot; and the technique of using the leitmotif symbolically, to relay an emotional point or for structural purposes, is almost a constant.[10] With the leitmotif, Mann's aim is often satirical: the shop girls in 'Gladius Dei' have 'plaited hair and rather too large feet'; Pastorin Höhlenrauch in 'Tristan' is always the lady 'who has had nineteen children and is now totally incapable of thought'.

But on a much larger scale, in *Buddenbrooks,* leitmotifs are used in a manner that Hans-Rudolf Vaget argues is imitated directly from Wagner's *Ring*,[11] and they are central to Mann's articulation of how the two themes of the decline of the family and its refinement are simultaneous and inseparable.[12]

Technically, then, the leitmotif is used to combine the apparently incompatible. Thematically, too, Mann uses Wagner for celebration and irony. The short story 'Tristan' is modelled both for and, ironically, against Wagner: the vitalistic Klöterjahn corresponds to ageing King Mark, the aesthete Spinell to the heroic Tristan, and the debilitated Gabriele to sensuous Isolde. Gabriele and Spinell remain behind whilst the other inhabitants of the sanatorium go sleighing – in *Tristan und Isolde* the lovers are left alone during a hunting party – and Spinell induces her to play from the vocal score the Prelude, love-duet and *Liebestod* of the opera. The resulting emotional disturbance leads directly to her own death. Until this point the story has been a virtuosic display of Mann's ironic gifts; Spinell has been lampooned (with the help of Wagnerian leitmotifs that emphasise his oddity), Gabriele has been almost deified and her husband demonised or ridiculed. But as the music is played the irony is left behind and Mann's hymnic prose conflates the scenario in the sanatorium with that conjured up by the music:

> The sound of horns dying away in the distance . . . or was it the wind in the leaves? The soft murmuring of the stream? . . . Delivered from the tormenting illusion, set free from the bondage of space and time, self and not-self blissfully mingling, 'thine' and 'mine' mystically made one! . . . Oh sink down, night of love, upon them; give them that forgetfulness they long for . . . And then, as the shining phantasm fades and my eyes fail with passion: then this world from which the falsehood of day debarred me, which to my unquenchable torment it held out before me as the object of my desire – then I myself, oh wonder of wishes granted! then I *myself* am the world.[13]

If the setting and characters are satirised, these quotations and paraphrases of the *Tristan und Isolde* libretto dignify them again and wrench the critique of Spinell back into balance: 'Nowhere is the secret identification of Mann with Spinell more evident than in the scene in which this extraordinary Wagnerian seduction is carried out.'[14] The entire story is another of Thomas Mann's distanced self-appraisals.

'Wälsungenblut' ('Blood of the Volsungs') is a similar counterfacture of Wagner; its title is from Siegfried's last words in Act I of *Die Walküre*. The twins Siegmund and Sieglinde Aarenhold consummate their incestuous love on a polar-bear skin after returning from a production of that very opera. The sublime action on stage is mirrored in the decadence on the page; Hunding has his ironic counterpart in the bourgeois philistine von Beckerath, called by the twins 'der Germane' (roughly 'the Hun'). Whilst there are certainly elements of parody, Wagner is not fatally wounded, and it is enfeebled decadence that suffers. Nonetheless, the decadent Siegmund is stirred to his only real *action* by Wagner, by a vision of life not in the bourgeois world outside but on the stage. His quiet reflections during Act II contrast with the condescending banter with Sieglinde about chocolates and the quality of the production during Act I:

> it came to him in a yearning vision that creation was born of passion, and was reshaped anew as passion . . . He saw his own life, and knew its contradictions, its clear understanding and spoilt voluptuousness, its splendid security and idle spite, its weakness and wittiness, its languid contempt; his life, so full of words, so void of acts, so full of cleverness, so empty of emotion and he felt again the burning, the searing anguish which yet was sweet – whither, and to what end? Creation? Experience? Passion?[15]

However perverted the act, it is less vapidly decadent than the sybaritic inactivity previously characteristic of Siegmund's existence. Mann's celebratory, hymnic style at key points shows how completely fused are his admiration and disapproval. The simultaneous co-presence of these attitudes (as opposed to an oscillation between them) is fundamentally characteristic of Mann's work.[16] Mann has not succumbed uncritically like the National Socialists; nor could his work be further from a true satirical attack such as, say, Charlie Chaplin's satirical dance with the globe to the music of *Lohengrin* in *The Great Dictator*.

It could not be further from that of Heinrich Mann either. On the face of it Thomas Mann's is a purely aesthetic response, but its political implications emerge when his elder brother's work is seen alongside it. Consonant with his later role as an apologist for Romance culture, Heinrich's early enthusiasms were for the sensuousness of Italian opera, especially Puccini, 'consummate at representing the passionate feeling for life of those days: lustre, exhilaration, longing for death'.[17] This is reflected in his novels *Die Jagd nach Liebe* (The Hunt for Love, 1903) and *Zwischen den Rassen* (Between the Races, 1907). But Diederich Heßling in *Der Untertan* (Man of Straw) is drawn to Wagner.[18] In a scene that reads like a parody of Thomas Mann's 'Wälsungenblut', he takes his fiancée to see *Lohengrin*. Like Thomas's twins, Diederich and Guste sit in their box munching chocolates, although Guste's remarks are much coarser than Sieglinde's as she wonders which of the women on stage is 'doing it' with the king under the oak tree. Diederich snobbishly pays most attention to King Heinrich:

> He did not look particularly dashing . . . but what he had to say was to be applauded, from the nationalist standpoint. 'To defend the honour of the Reich, East or West'. Bravo! Every time he sang the word 'German' he stretched his arm upwards and the music lent its support. It also emphasised trenchantly what one ought to be listening to. Trenchantly, that

was the word. Diederich wished he had had such music for his speech in the drainage debate.[19]

The whole scenario – 'shields and swords, much jingling of armour, imperialist atmosphere, Ha! and Heil!'[20] – satisfies Diederich's shallow sense of the dignity and grandeur of Germany's medieval past. Mann further incriminates Heßling by having him parade his anti-Semitism in his response to the performance. The couple's reaction to the opera is presented with ironic disdain, and Mann treats the spectacular events themselves in a tone designed to offend Wagnerolaters, composed of a mixture of boredom, matter-of-factness and gossipy camp:

> Lohengrin came, sparkled, sent the magic swan away, sparkled even more bewitchingly ... Elsa knew perfectly well why she fell plop onto her knees in front of him ... Telramund was behaving quite impossibly.[21]

Heßling is the vehicle for Mann's critique of the nationalistic politics and social structures of Wilhelm II's Germany, and Wagner is unmistakably implicated in the attack. Thomas was in no doubt about this, complaining in his diary of Heinrich's 'disgusting anti-Wagnerian political chattering'.[22] Heinrich himself made it yet more explicit in his 1919 essay 'Kaiserreich und Republik' ('Empire and Republic'), associating him with the worst forms of Wilhelmine corruption and claiming, 'it would not have become so immeasurably awful without Wagner's heroes.'[23] Wagner is criticised for betraying the 1848 revolution and defecting to the side of power:

> How does he see the power that is sacred to him? In the form of sorcerers with swan-helmets. How does he see the people? In the ranks of a chorus dazzled by the splendour of its masters, perpetually surprised by events. How does he see the Germans? As the ruthless boor Siegfried. How does he see himself, the plebeian? With the features of a haughty blond-haired nobleman.[24]

In Wagner's hands, opera has become a coarse, materialised personal industry.[25] When he went to see *Lohengrin* in Augsburg, for reasons of research, he wrote to his future wife, 'I have just seen Lohengrin: it was fantastically beautiful. Diederich and Guste were swimming in delight'; and then, 'Lohengrin in Augsburg was melancholy and odd ... I made observations from Diederich's and Guste's point of view ... What stupidity in a Wagner hero like that, in the chorus, in everything!'[26]

Carl Sternheim parodies *Die Meistersinger* in his 1913 play *Bürger Schippel* (*Paul Schippel, Esq*) to make similar social points:

> Wagner brought the public good old Valhalla and its inhabitants again, easy-going creatures to judge by their clothing and other considerations, but in whose heavenly halls life was so scandalous and petty-bourgeois as to convince the ordinary mortal-in-the-street that if the lives of the

gods were so miserably restricted and dependent, he could be quite satisfied with his Prussian-Berlin brand of freedom.²⁷

Sternheim began by admiring Wagner, counting *Die Meistersinger* in 1906 amongst 'the eternal masterpieces'.²⁸ His satire began with attacks on the foolish response of the Wilhelmine public, but it grew to encompass the works themselves, and he never retrieved, even temporarily, his original love of Wagner.

The nobility and passion that Thomas Mann found in Wagner fed directly into his justification of the German position in the First World War and into the essays that form the *Betrachtungen eines Unpolitischen* (Observations of a Non-Political Man, 1918). This book is an episode in the Manns' 'Bruderzwist'²⁹ (and is partly a response to a thinly veiled personal attack on Thomas by Heinrich in a 1915 essay entitled 'Zola'), directly attacking Heinrich, who is caricatured as the Francophile *Zivilisationsliterat*. 'Civilisation' is in opposition to 'culture', where true value is to be found; and progressive, analytical 'literariness', in alliance with politics, is in opposition to music and philosophy, in alliance with an anti-political, anti-literary, conservative, ironic form of aestheticism. It is also a nationalistic defence of the war and an onslaught on the ideals of Western democracy, which he compares unfavourably with the profundity of the German spirit and the culture of authority and service that Germany represents. There are elements in the objects of Mann's attack – detachment, critical distance, intellectualism – that actually characterised his own work before 1914, but these had always been in tension with the Romantic values represented in part by Wagner and which now came to be seen as pre-eminently German and uniquely defensible.³⁰ Notes begun in 1909 for an uncompleted essay called 'Geist und Kunst' ('Mind and Art') suggest that Mann's view of Wagner was becoming increasingly sceptical before the war.³¹ But in 1918 the *Betrachtungen* enlisted him, now wholly free from criticism, in a nationalistic defence of Germanness, under circumstances that did Mann little credit. I shall return briefly to this after considering how Wagner was the catalyst for Mann's exile from Hitler's Germany.

On the fiftieth anniversary of Wagner's death, 10 February 1933, Mann gave a speech entitled 'Leiden und Größe Richard Wagners' ('The Sorrows and Grandeur of Richard Wagner') in the *Auditorium maximum* of Munich University (the very hall in which Hugo von Hofmannsthal had delivered his own much-debated reflections on the relationship between art and nation six years previously). Mann's speech was a wide-ranging reflection on Wagner's achievements and shortcomings alike, set in their cultural and intellectual contexts. Mann carefully weighs up the influence on him of Schopenhauer and the German Romantics, seeing in Wagner an intuitive consonance with Freud, acknowledging and building upon Nietzsche's critique, yet arguing powerfully for the recognition of his genius.

Mann takes up the issue of Wagner's nationalism, acknowledging his 'celebration and glorification of Germanness'. He claims, however, that,

> it is quite inadmissible to attribute to Wagner's nationalistic gestures and speeches a contemporary sense – the sense they would have today. That is to falsify and misuse them, to besmirch their romantic purity.[32]

Much of the remainder of the essay is devoted to a carefully managed defence of this assertion. Wagner the politician was 'more a socialist and cultural utopian working for a classless ... society, founded on love, ... than a patriot believing in an authoritarian state'.[33] Wagner's nationalistic outcries from the 1850s and 1860s are seen as motivated by the spiritual trials of his exile, and balanced against the resentment Wagner voiced when his work was not received enthusiastically upon his return.[34] Similarly, Wagner's support for German unification is attributed to opportunism:

> Wagner was enough of a politician to link his own cause with that of Bismarck's Reich: he saw an incomparable success and harnessed his own to it ... Wagner's work was installed as a national institution, had the official stamp of the Reich and has in a sense remained associated with the imperial colours – *little though it has to do, in its innermost essence or in the manner of its Germanness, with any form of authoritarian or militaristic empire*.[35]

Mann then moves from this trenchant, anti-nationalistic assertion to establish Wagner's European credentials, for a deep-rooted association with Germany in no wise prevents his work from being European and international.[36] Of Wagner's operas Mann insists:

> their Germanness is profound, powerful and indubitable ... but despite all this is true to the whole world, accessible to the whole world in a way that no German art of this calibre has ever had the privilege to be.[37]

Quoting the Swedish critic Wilhelm Peterson-Berger, Mann asserts that, whilst Wagner may sometimes strike a German 'Volkston' for purposes of characterisation, this is never the spring from which his music spontaneously wells up, as it was for Schumann, Schubert and Brahms. A distinction must be made between 'Volkskunst' and 'nationale Kunst': the former, folk art, aims inwardly, the latter – Wagner's type of national art – outwardly. Whilst a *foreigner* will therefore see it as quintessentially German, it nonetheless has an unmistakably cosmopolitan cachet. 'Wagner is German, is national in an exemplary, perhaps too exemplary manner',[38] but at the same time he displays Germanness theatrically, even thematises it. He is, so to speak, a 'professional German'. However,

> this Germanness, genuine and powerful though it is, is cracked and fragmented in the modern way, decorative, analytical, intellectual, and from

> this derives the fascination exercised by his innate ability for a cosmopolitan, planetary effect.[39]

Wagner is thus both *urdeutsch* and modern.

Mann concludes this section thus:

> Wagner's art is the most sensational self-portrayal and self-critique of things German imaginable, it is aimed at making Germanness interesting even to an ass of a foreigner, and a passionate involvement with this art is always at the same time a passionate involvement with the very Germanness that it glorifies critically and decoratively. In this lies its nationalism, but this nationalism is steeped in European artistry to a degree that makes it profoundly unsusceptible to any kind of simplification [zu irgendwelcher Simplifizierung, auf deutsch: Versimpelung].[40]

The increasingly charged language is a cover for the sober calculation with which Mann aims both to have his cake and eat it. The sideswipe at asinine foreigners establishes his credentials as an instinctive patriot; rhetorical devices such as repetition confirm his commitment to Germany; in one gesture he offers his nationalist listeners what they want to hear, namely that Wagner is nationalist too, but in the next he quickly redefines the term so that his own intellectual honesty is not compromised. The fact that this redefinition of nationalism as internationalism has been achieved from an external vantage point, with the help of a Swede, suggests a degree of objectivity. Finally, Mann ties together the complex of native and foreign with a linguistic trick: when he protests against a reductive understanding, he uses first the French- or Latin-sounding word 'Simplifizierung', which he then translates into 'real' German as 'Versimpelung' so that not even the Fascists can claim to have misunderstood.

Two months later, on 16 April, the *Münchner Neueste Nachrichten* printed a letter of protest, the 'Protest der Richard-Wagner-Stadt München', signed by 45 notable figures including Pfitzner, Strauss and Knappertsbusch. Mann and his wife had left for a pre-arranged lecture tour the day after the Wagner speech was delivered, and, to cut a long story short, the hate-campaign that ensued in the press and on the radio persuaded Mann not to return. Indeed, had he done so, he would almost certainly have been interned in Dachau.

It is a bitter irony that Mann was driven into exile from a nationalist regime by a speech made up in part from verbatim quotations of his *Betrachtungen eines Unpolitischen*, a work that earned him such opprobrium for his nationalist sympathies. The last two quotations above ('This Germanness . . .' and 'Wagner's Art . . .'), the quotations from Peterson-Berger and the point about Wagner's Germanness being thematised in his works, all these are also substantial, nearly word-for-word extracts from the 1918 text. Slight changes were made (the imagined cry of the foreigner, 'Ah, ça c'est bien allemand par exemple!', is attributed to an '*Entente* audience' in 1918 and to an 'international audience' in 1933) but the point is the same. The intentions have changed radically, but Mann's analysis of Wagner's nationalism as *inter*nationalism remains.

Mann's views changed with time. In a letter to Emil Preetorious of 1949 he gives way to peevishness:

> Act II of *Tristan*, with its metaphysical web of bliss is, I now find, more something for young people, who don't know where to begin with their sexuality.[41]

Mann's youthful concern with Wagner's eroticism is still present in modulated form, but historical and cultural events have also had an effect:

> There is in Wagner's bombast, eternal sermonising, wanting to be the centre of attention and wanting to have a view on everything, there is an ineffable lack of modesty that prefigures Hitler – certainly, there is plenty of Hitler in Wagner.[42]

But in another letter, written in 1951, Mann writes of the 'enthusiastic ambivalence which determines [his] relationship to Wagner and which one could simply call passion'.[43] Mann's relationship with this particular artistic 'parent' has been through adulation and imitation, rejection, embarrassment, distaste and back again to a passion that, given the extent to which he used Wagner as a lens for self-contemplation, can fairly be called incestuous.

It has often been noted that French Wagnerism 'was scarcely affected by the increasingly passionate political and military differences between France and Germany' and showed 'no appreciable reaction to the national and nationalistic exploitation of Wagner that was rife in Germany from the 1870s on'.[44] The French saw Wagner less as an object of study than as a catalyst for their own writing – and, like a true catalyst, Wagner is untouched by the reaction. What changes is nothing less than poetry, not thematically but stylistically, technically, and in the very understanding of what poetry *is*.

The alliance of Wagner and French Symbolism was effectively sealed by Edouard Dujardin and Théodor de Wyzéwa in *La Revue wagnérienne* which ran from 1885 to 1888. Although the review was originally designed to perpetuate the cult of the Master and to develop a true Wagnerian aesthetic, the French Wagnerians, unlike those of the *Bayreuther Blätter*, were more concerned with the emergence of their own, predominantly Symbolist aesthetic, than with the explication of the works and teachings of Wagner himself. Such was the blinkered enthusiasm of the minor Symbolists for Wagnerian themes – verse enriched with 'musicality' (dense sound-patternings), and heightened dream-states or evocations of spiritual purity – that much of it slips unconsciously into parody.

Deliberate parody of a quite different order is offered by Jules Laforgue in his hilarious 'Lohengrin, fils de Parsifal' ('Lohengrin, son of Parsifal').

Wagner's lofty ideals are pitilessly punctured; Laforgue's elaborate language is full of neologisms and is brilliantly self-conscious; the characters are *déclassé* and chatty, and speak as if looking over their shoulders at their 'serious' models. Lohengrin announces himself thus:

> I have come straight here from Grail. Parsifal is my father: I never knew my mother. I am Lohengrin, the knight-errant, lily of future crusades for the emancipation of Womankind. But whilst I was waiting I was just too miserable working in my father's office.[45]

As they take communion, Elsa and Lohengrin whisper to each other:

> 'You'll see how nice I am,' she assures him under her breath. 'What? Your teeth are chattering! But don't take all this so seriously! *I* don't believe a word of it all, I swear it, I think of their Moon as a wicked step-mother, a bald idol for old people.' 'But you see it's the organ . . .' 'Ah! You know, me, I just *love* music.'[46]

Wagner is not a victim here and the comedy is in a perpetually implied bathos, as if Thomas Mann's admiration were being communicated by Heinrich Mann's satirical means. Laforgue was a fervent admirer of Wagner, linking his music to Impressionist painting and Hartmann's view of the 'Unconscious' as the law underlying the universe:

> [There are] no more isolated melodies, the whole is a symphony, vital and varying life itself, like 'the voices of the forest' of Wagner's theory in vibrant competition for the *great* voice of the forest, as the Unconscious, the law of the world, is the great melodic voice that results from the symphony of consciousnesses of races and individuals.[47]

This, he goes on to say, is the same principle that has been adopted by poets and novelists. In the novel, it was Laforgue's friend Dujardin who invented the interior monologue and the stream-of-consciousness technique in *Les Lauriers sont coupés* (The Laurels have been Cut, 1887). Dujardin later claimed that this was an attempt to transpose Wagnerian techniques into literature; he was in turn a direct inspiration for James Joyce's revolutionary prose.[48] Laforgue's own complex use of recurrent images to structure his poetry, especially in the *Derniers vers* (Last Poems), is akin to the leitmotif technique on a small scale, and was again a deliberate attempt to transpose the insights prompted by Wagner into literature.[49]

But this and the self-indulgent effusions of the lesser Symbolists were not what the financial backers of the *Revue* had in mind. Agénor Boissier withdrew his support, forcing *La Revue* to close.[50] The Symbolists wrote for an élite, those few supposedly with sufficient aesthetic refinement to appreciate Wagner's genius. For contributors such as Huysmans and Villiers de l'Isle Adam it was axiomatic that such an audience would be small; they wrote in a highly stylised, often overtly condescending manner at odds with Wagner's own ambitions for wider popular effect. The élitist view of Wagner was effectively enshrined in the review's editorial policy, for in a four-part exposition entitled 'Wagner's Art' Wyzéwa presented it as solipsist, aiming to appeal only to a limited number of intellectuals – a gross distortion of Wagner's own insistence on the socially regenerative power of his work and the crucial role of 'das Volk' in his thinking.

A. G. Lehmann gives a concise summary of Wyzéwa's other misreadings and inventions.[51] He and others have suggested that the general trend of *La Revue wagnérienne* was to force Wagner into the mould of Mallarmé, the very guardian of the keys to the Symbolists' ivory tower. The aim was plausible, and Wagner's 'Zukunftsmusik', for example, contains much that was cognate with Mallarmé's concerns for art:

> the relationship between art, silence, and the contemplation of nature ... the state of receptivity necessary to appreciate theatrical art; the universally human nature of the matter of art; the importance of the audience, of communion, in the performance; the rôle of coherent structure in the work of art; the notion that art should show its universally human (rather than contingent) reference by making it clear to the audience that they are not simply looking at a representation of common reality; the conception of human truth as a set, not of reasonings or revelations, but of distant myths; and the close relationship between the proper constitution of a people, and its possession of a public art.[52]

They both also shared the dubious distinction of being cult figures for their contemporaries. Yet ironically Mallarmé kept his distance from the review. More ironically, the sonnet 'Hommage' and the essay 'Richard Wagner: Rêverie d'un poëte français' that Mallarmé eventually contributed both register the explosive effect of Wagner on Mallarmé's own aesthetics. The sonnet is arguably a nostalgic contemplation of the rubble of an out-of-date ivory tower.

The context for both poem and essay is quite specifically *French*: the emergence in France of *vers libre* or free verse, which Mallarmé experienced as an 'exquisite fundamental crisis' of literature.[53] Victor Hugo, the venerable guardian of the French poetic and prosodic tradition died in 1885 (on 22 May, Wagner's birthday); in 1886 *La Vogue* opened the floodgates for *vers libre*, publishing revolutionary works by Rimbaud, Laforgue, Gustave Kahn, Moréas and others.[54] Mallarmé's verse had previously been characterised by the imaginative and flexible use of standard metres and fixed forms, but he now felt that a watershed had been reached and offered a measured welcome to the new style. Later, in the mid-1890s, he was to distance himself from it; later still, however, he pushes the freedom of verse to even further extremes than the *verslibristes*. Mallarmé's most ambitious work ('Un coup de Dés jamais n'abolira le Hasard' or 'A Throw of the Die Will Never Abolish Chance') is the most extreme example of the abandonment of tradition, the decomposition of hitherto accepted typographical, spatial, syntactic, rhythmic and prosodic conventions. The 'radically new "versification"' of Mallarmé's *least* metrically formal work is also an attempt 'to create order out of the prosodic chaos caused by the abandonment of traditional versification'.[55] Both this and Mallarmé's dissatisfaction with the liberation offered by *vers libre* are determined by how he understood the relationship between words and music. In fact, as Mallarmé was to realise, 'the real crisis facing poetry derive[d] not so much from the efforts of the *verslibristes* as from its new rivalry with music',[56] and Mallarmé's thinking on this relationship was in considerable part the product of his assessment of the implications of Wagner for French poetry. Wagner came in a sense to *define* poetry, as is suggested by a phrase in 'Crise de vers': 'Music joins Verse to form, since Wagner, Poetry'.[57] Mallarmé's most intense involvement with Wagner was expressed at exactly the same time as the *vers libre* crisis: the 'Rêverie' was published in *La Revue wagnérienne* on 8 August 1885, and the sonnet 'Hommage (à Wagner)' on 8 January 1886.

Mallarmé's essay is shot through with the consciousness that he is 'cet étranger',[58] a foreigner in the sense of being both non-French and non-Poet. Nonetheless, Wagner's concept of the *Gesamtkunstwerk* is a challenge that cannot be ignored:

> It is a singular challenge that Richard Wagner issues to the poets whose task he is usurping with the most candid and splendid bravura![59]

By allying music with drama, Wagner has overturned traditional mimetic dramaturgy and made the action allegorical. The audience is emotionally drawn into the allegory by the music, without which 'the action would at once remain frozen'. His achievement is to have married 'two elements of beauty that are mutually exclusive and ignorant of each other', namely personal drama and ideal music.

Here the tone changes and Wagner is repudiated. Legend has been used to represent for the public, 'first Hellenic, now Germanic',[60] the secret of its origins; but in Wagner these are still particular legends, not 'Fable, pure of everything, of place, time and known persons'.[61] This 'Fable' is the absolute, inscribed on the pages of the heavens, something of which history itself is only a futile interpretation, 'a Poem, the Ode'.[62] Mallarmé renames this absolute 'Myth' in the sense of a universal rather than a particular legend. In it is contained the essence of human experience, and, despite his achievements, Wagner has merely juxtaposed music with a particular narrative, not fused them to form the higher art. Wagner's art, in Mallarmé's image, is a temple only halfway up the holy mountain,[63] and Mallarmé gazes further ahead at 'the threatening pinnacle of the absolute'.[64] Wagner is 'saying too much ... being too narratively particular'.[65]

At the very end of the essay Mallarmé describes Wagner's art as a 'convivial fountain'[66] but at the end of the preface to 'Un coup de Dés' poetry is defined as the 'unique source' or 'single well-spring'.[67] Wagner's insufficiency is ultimately due to his failure to insist on the primacy of poetry in the *Gesamtkunstwerk*. For Mallarmé, music shares an ambition with language, namely the expression of the Idea. But, whilst language can embrace the rhythms that constitute true music, music cannot do what language does, which is to name things. Music, in its true sense, has little to do with orchestral performance and instrumentation; Mallarmé understands it 'in the Greek sense, at root signifying Idea or rhythm between relationships' ('rhythme entre des rapports').[68] In other words, music is structural, a system of relationships that Mallarmé calls 'rhythm'. This kind of music reaches its peak not in the orchestra or the human voice but in poetry:

> it is not from elemental sounds made by brass, strings and woodwind that Music – in the sense of the totality of the relations existing between all things – must result in manifest fullness, but undeniably from the intelligible word at its pinnacle.[69]

However, in placing music above words, Wagner has vitiated his attempts to achieve the *Gesamtkunstwerk*. The ambition as such is perfectly acceptable, and Mallarmé shared it, although for him this could only take the form of a book: 'The world was made to culminate in a beautiful book,' he said to Jules Huret in 1891.[70] 'Un coup de Dés' is generally accepted as the nearest he was to get to this ambition. For Mallarmé the book takes priority over music because it includes and subsumes music in Mallarmé's understanding of the term. This understanding of music was reached in the context of French verse – Mallarmé had little or no appreciation of German versification, which is fundamentally different – and, as Pearson notes, 'Mallarmé's attempts to repulse the colonising ambition of (Wagnerian) music by asserting the priority of poetry is consciously presented in nationalistic terms as an ironic imitation of the contemporary Franco-German power struggle'.[71] Mallarmé's turning away in the 'Rêverie' from Wagner's use of legend is couched in specifically nationalist terms: 'the French spirit, strictly imaginative and abstract and thus poetic . . . rejects Legend'.[72] The Germanic subject matter has also been implicated in Mallarmé's repolarisation of the two constitutive arts of opera.

Mallarmé's sonnet shares some of this ambivalence.

> Le silence déjà funèbre d'une moire
> Dispose plus qu'un pli seul sur le mobilier
> Que doit un tassement du principal pilier
> Précipiter avec le manque de mémoire.
>
> Notre si vieil ébat triomphal du grimoire,
> Hiéroglyphes dont s'exalte le millier
> A propager de l'aile un frisson familier!
> Enfouissez-le-moi plutôt dans une armoire.

> Du souriant fracas originel haï
> Entre elles de clartés maîtresses a jailli
> Jusque vers un parvis né pour leur simulacre,
>
> Trompettes tout haut d'or pâmé sur les vélins,
> Le dieu Richard Wagner irradiant un sacre
> Mal tu par l'encre même en sanglots sibyllins.

[The already funeral silence of a shroud lays more than a single fold over the furniture that a collapse of the principal pillar must send flying with the absence of memory. Our so old triumphant caper with the magic book, hieroglyphs with which the crowd excites itself to send out with its wing a familiar thrill! Stuff it into a cupboard for me now.

Hated by the original smiling noise, there has burst out from sovereign brightness towards a stage born for their performance, loud golden trumpets fainted on vellum, the god Richard Wagner illuminating a rite ill-silenced by the very ink in sibylline sobs.][73]

Mallarmé wrote of the poem that its theme is 'the melancholy of a poet who sees the old challenge of poetry collapsing and the luxury of words paling away before the sunrise of contemporary Music, whose latest god is Wagner'.[74] In this light a simple reading of the poem might run thus: The furniture shrouded in silence is traditional French verse, which will be ruined when the principal pillar, or rigid prosody, collapses – which is what the advent of *vers libre* meant, implying too a 'lack of memory', an abandonment of the past-consciousness that defines what it means to belong to a tradition. 'Our old triumphant caper' is the traditional activity of 'us poets', more specifically, of 'us *French* poets' – and 'vieil' here might indicate old-and-decrepit, or old-and-venerable. Likewise the magic book and the hieroglyphs, both representing poetry, may be read as mysterious-and-obscure, or mysterious-and-sacred. The poet might be expected to prefer the second alternative, but Mallarmé seems cynical, for the last line of the second quatrain is deliberately coarse. The rhyme 'grimoire / armoire' is blatantly contrived – it is itself a 'frisson familier' ('frisson' is often used by Mallarmé to indicate rhyme or the musicality of poetry), where familiar might be reassuring or boring. The first part of the sonnet therefore encapsulates both the dignity of the tradition and the way in which this dignity may at the same time be noble and stuffy; the deliberate *Stilbruch* of line eight points up the clash.

In the tercets Wagner's brilliance illuminates the sombre scene, and his golden trumpets and sibylline sobs break the silence left by poetry. The 'fracas' of the forced rhyme hates Music because Music, in Wagner, has tried to usurp the primacy of 'original' language. But language still smiles whilst music weeps; the ritual that it enacted has only been 'ill-silenced' and that was done 'by the ink itself', by the written word, perhaps by the advent of *vers libre*. Wagner is after all a foreign god, foreign to poetry and foreign to France, and the tercets of Mallarmé's sonnet, ostensibly capitulating to music as his self-interpretation suggested, maintain the ambivalence of the quatrains.

There is no doubt that Mallarmé's rejection of Wagner's priorities was motivated in part by the need to repel the 'invasion' of the German. There is admiration, too, for an immense achievement, but this does not suppress the element of the younger generation's wish to revise, supersede and recreate. Without wishing to push the 'parent/child' conceit too far, this is in a sense an Oedipal impulse, accompanied in both Wagner and Mallarmé by the rivalry of siblings, words and music. For Mallarmé, music is so intimately implicated in language that the relationship is virtually an incestuous one.

Notes and References

1 See Chapter B4 of Erwin Koppen, *Dekadenter Wagnerismus. Studien zur europäischen Literatur des Fin de siècle* (Berlin and New York, 1973).
2 Richard Sternfeld, 'Vorwort' to *Richard Wagner: Was ist deutsch? Schriften und Dichtungen des Meisters für die Zeit des heiligen deutschen Krieges* (Leipzig, 1915).
3 For a careful analysis, see Thomas Koebner, 'Richard Wagner und der deutsche Nationalismus. Ein Versuch', in Gerhard Heldt (ed.), *Richard Wagner: Mittler zwischen Zeiten* (Anif/Salzburg, 1990), pp. 159-81.
4 Besides Koppen, the most relevant are: Hans-Joachim Bauer, *Richard-Wagner-Lexikon* (Lubbe, 1988); Raymond Furness, *Wagner and Literature* (Manchester, 1982); Elwood Hartmann, *French Literary Wagnerism* (New York and London, 1988); Barry Millington (ed.), *The Wagner Compendium: A Guide to Wagner's Life and Music* (London, 1992); Ulrich Müller and Peter Wapnewski (eds.), *Wagner Handbook* (Cambridge, MA, & London, 1992).
5 Thomas Mann is quoted from *Gesammelte Werke in zwölf Bänden* (Frankfurt/M, 1960), here Vol. X, *Reden und Aufsätze 2*, p. 841 (henceforth abbreviated as *GW, X*, p. 841, etc.). All translations are my own except for those from Mann's fiction where I have preferred to use the excellent published versions.
6 See T. J. Reed, *Thomas Mann: The Uses of Tradition* (Oxford, 1974), p. 77, and his entry in Helmut Koopmann (ed.), *Thomas-Mann-Handbuch* (Stuttgart, 1990), esp. pp. 122-4.
7 Thomas Mann, *Selected Stories*, trans. David Luke (Harmondsworth, 1993), p. 214.
8 Richard Wagner, *Mein Leben* (Munich,1963), p. 665. For details see Koppen, *Dekadenter Wagnerismus*, pp. 228-32; Furness, *Wagner and Literature*, pp. 47-8; Werner Vordtriede, 'Richard Wagners Tod in Venedig', *Euphorion*, 52 (1958), pp. 378-96; and Koppen, 'Wagner und Venedig', in Heldt (ed.), *Richard Wagner: Mittler zwischen Zeiten*, pp. 105-25.
9 See Herbert Lehnert, *Thomas Mann: Fiktion, Mythos, Religion* (Stuttgart, 1965), pp. 99-108, for details and the suggestion that this essay corresponds in some respects to the 'page and a half of exquisite prose' on which Aschenbach is engaged just before his death.
10 Reed (*Thomas Mann*, p. 74) points out that Mann did not regard Wagner's use of it as new, and that he considered it as profoundly epic, not dramatic. See *GW, X*, p. 27, and, for a sceptical view of this opinion, Hilda Meldrum Brown, *Leitmotiv and Drama: Wagner, Brecht and the Limits of 'Epic' Theatre* (Oxford, 1991), pp. 43-61. Nonetheless, it seems certain not only that Mann was aware of parallels between

Wagner's use of the technique and his own, but that his extensive use of the leitmotif is self-consciously Wagnerian.

11 Hans-Rudolf Vaget, 'Thomas Mann und Wagner: Zur Funktion des Leitmotivs', in Steven Paul Scher (ed.), 'Der Ring des Nibelungen und Buddenbrooks', in *Literatur und Musik: Ein Handbuch zur Theorie und Praxis eines komparatistischen Grenzgebiets* (Berlin, 1984), pp. 326-47.
12 Vaget points out numerous parallels between the works – the opposition of Volsungs and Nibelungs, for example, reflected in that of the Buddenbrooks and their carefully named business rivals, the *Hagen*ströms – and outlines how Mann was aware that the genesis of *Buddenbrooks* parallels that of *Der Ring*.
13 Mann, *Selected Stories*, p. 118.
14 Luke, introduction to Mann, *Selected Stories*, p. xxv.
15 Quoted from the translation by Ray Furness in *The Dedalus Book of German Decadence: Voices of the Abyss*, ed. Ray Furness (Sawtry, 1994), p. 276.
16 Koppen neglects the critical dimension of Mann's response when he writes that 'Mann was doing nothing more than joining in with the original judgement of European *fin-de-siècle* literature on Wagner the *décadent*' ('Vom Décadent zum Proto-Hitler: Wagner-Bilder Thomas Manns', in Peter Pütz (ed.), *Thomas Mann und die Tradition* [Frankfurt/M, 1971], p. 208). Equally, to write (of *Buddenbrooks*) that 'the composer's music is described as having an erotic effect or else as inspiring a death wish in its listeners' is reductively negative (Ulrich Müller, 'Wagner in Literature and Film', in *Wagner Handbook*, p. 384).
17 Heinrich Mann, *Gesammelte Werke in Einzelausgaben*, 14 Vols. (Hamburg, 195 ff.), Vol. 13, *Ein Zeitalter wird besichtigt*, p. 284.
18 Written 1906-1914, published 1918. The title literally means 'The Subordinate'.
19 Heinrich Mann, *Gesammelte Werke*, Vol. 1, *Der Untertan*, p. 361.
20 Ibid., p. 362.
21 Ibid., p. 363.
22 29 June 1919 and 29 April 1920, quoted by Raymond Furness, 'The Unsuccessful Exorcism: Thomas Mann and Richard Wagner', *Publications of the English Goethe Society*, 62 (1991-92), p. 69.
23 Heinrich Mann, *Gesammelte Werke*, Vol. 4, Essays, p. 410.
24 Ibid., p. 410.
25 Ibid., p. 411.
26 Deutsche Akademie der Künste (ed.), *Heinrich Mann 1871-1950. Werk und Leben in Dokumenten und Bildern* (Berlin and Weimar, 1971), p. 129. By omitting parts of these quotations, Willi Jasper misleadingly interprets Mann's response as enthusiasm: *Der Bruder. Heinrich Mann. Eine Biographie* (Munich, 1992), p. 63.
27 Carl Sternheim, *Das Gesamtwerk*, ed. Wilhelm Emrich (Neuwied and Darmstadt, 1963-76), Vol. 6, pp. 129-30. See also Manfred Linke, 'Sternheim und die Musik', in Andreas Rogal and Dugald Sturges (eds.), *Carl Sternheim 1878-1942* (Stuttgart, 1995), pp. 43-61.
28 Letter to Thea Bauer of 22 June 1906, quoted by Linke, in 'Sternheim und die Musik', p. 49.
29 'Bruderzwist' is the standard German term for sibling conflict on a grand scale (see Grillparzer's play, *Ein Bruderzwist in Habsburg*, concerning rivalry in the Austrian imperial house). Heinrich was to thematise this rivalry in *Der Kopf* (The Head, 1918-1924), the last of the trilogy that begins with *Der Untertan*, in which Terra/Heinrich turns against Wilhelmine society, and Mangolf/Thomas accepts it; both commit suicide.
30 This is not the place for an investigation of the consistencies and inconsistencies in Mann's positions before, during and after the war, but consulting Reed's account in

>   *Thomas Mann*, pp. 179-225, will reveal parallels with the twentieth century's conflicting readings of Wagner.
31 The relevant notes are collected in English in Thomas Mann, *Pro and Contra Wagner*, trans. Allan Blunden (London, 1985), pp. 37-44.
32 Thomas Mann, *GW*, IX, p. 417.
33 Ibid., p. 418.
34 Ibid., p. 419.
35 Ibid., p. 420, my italics.
36 Ibid., p. 421.
37 Ibid., p. 421.
38 Ibid., p. 422.
39 Ibid., p. 422.
40 Ibid., pp. 422-3.
41 Ibid., p. 926.
42 Ibid., p. 926.
43 Thomas Mann, *GW*, X, p. 928.
44 Müller, 'Wagner in Literature and Film', p. 376.
45 Jules Laforgue, *Moralités légendaires*, ed. Pascal Pia (Paris, 1977), p. 98. The French for 'Holy Grail' is 'la Sainte Graal'; here 'Saint-Graal' is a deliberate deformation that makes it sound like a country estate or a railway station.
46 Laforgue, *Moralités légendaires*, p. 100.
47 Laforgue, *Mélanges posthumes*, ed. Philippe Bonnefis (Paris and Geneva, 1979), pp. 137-8.
48 See Anne Holmes, *Jules Laforgue and Poetic Innovation* (Oxford, 1993), pp. 145-51.
49 See Holmes, *Jules Laforgue and Poetic Innovation*, p. 148, writing of 'Solo de lune': 'Each motif develops through the poem – that is, follows a modulated sequence. While the motifs are contrasted with each other, they also interrelate, introducing or provoking one another.'
50 See David C. Large and William Weber (eds.), *Wagnerism in European Culture and Politics* (Ithaca and London, 1984), p. 282 and p. 351, n. 2. (Koppen, *Dekadenter Wagnerismus*, p. 76, names Comte Robert de Bonnières de Wierre as the financier who pulled out).
51 A. G. Lehmann, *The Symbolist Aesthetic in France 1885-1895* (Oxford, 1968), pp. 194-206, here p. 204. Wyzéwa was perhaps never the perfect Wagnerian; his most durable musical work is a book on Mozart.
52 Peter Dayan, *Mallarmé's 'Divine Transposition': Real and Apparent Sources of Literary Value* (Oxford, 1986), p. 96.
53 Mallarmé is quoted from *Œuvres complètes*, ed. Henri Mondor and G. Jean-Aubry (Bibliothèque de la Pléiade, Paris, 1945), abbreviated *OC*. Here *OC*, p. 360.
54 See Clive Scott, *Vers libre: The Emergence of Free Verse in France 1886-1914* (Oxford, 1990), esp. pp. 54-74.
55 Roger Pearson, *Unfolding Mallarmé: The Development of a Poetic Art* (Oxford, 1996), p. 233. In what follows I am much indebted to Professor Pearson's argument.
56 Ibid., p. 238.
57 Mallarmé, *OC*, p. 365.
58 Ibid., p. 542.
59 Ibid., p. 541.
60 Ibid., p. 544.
61 Ibid., p. 544.
62 Ibid., p. 545.
63 Ibid., p. 546.
64 Ibid., p. 546.

65 Pearson, *Unfolding Mallarmé*, p. 241.
66 Mallarmé, *OC*, p. 546.
67 Ibid., p. 456.
68 Letter to Edmund Gosse, January 1893, quoted by Pearson, in *Unfolding Mallarmé*, p. 239.
69 Mallarmé, *OC*, p. 368.
70 Ibid., p. 872.
71 Pearson, *Unfolding Mallarmé*, p. 240, n. 32.
72 Mallarmé, *OC*, p. 544.
73 Ibid., p. 71. The 'translation' is a bare paraphrase only, of necessity hiding many alternative constructions of the imagery.
74 Letter to Colonel Mathieu, 17 February 1886, quoted by Graham Robb, in *Unlocking Mallarmé* (New Haven and London, 1996), p. 111. For a much more detailed reading along the same lines as mine, see Robb, *Unlocking Mallarmé*, pp. 110-22. Turbow's reading (p. 162) finds no support in the text: 'In implying that realism and naturalism would be replaced by the deeper truth of symbolism as revealed by "the god Richard Wagner", the poem displayed its author's characteristic intellectual arrogance.'

13.
Nationalism, Colonialism and the Cultural Stasis of Music in Ireland

HARRY WHITE

I

> So at the opening of the first piece, it was hard not to smile on seeing around the hall the fine-looking women of the Gaelic League chattering in abominable Irish to some of the young clerks and shop assistants who were quite pale with enthusiasm. But it happened that during an interval of *Diarmuid and Grainne*, as was the custom in the theatre, the people in the Gallery began to sing some of the old popular songs. Until that moment, these songs had never been so heard, sung by so many people together to the old, lingering Irish words. The whole auditorium shook. It was as if one could hear in these long-drawn-out notes, with their inexpressible melancholy, the death-rattle of a nation. First one head, then another, was seen to bend over the programme notes. People were crying.
>
> Then the curtain went up. The play restarted in a deeply emotional atmosphere. For an instant, we had glimpsed, hovering in that hall, the soul of a nation.[1]

It is characteristic of the condition of music in Irish cultural history that music itself should register in a definitive way 'the soul of a nation'. John Millington Synge's account of what happened during the first performance of Douglas Hyde's *Casadh an tsugáin* ('The Twisting of the Rope') in 1902 is justly famous for its acute perception of cultural transition. The disappearance of Gaelic culture and its brilliant afterlife in the Literary Revival were marked by that transitory moment, even if the integrity of Gaelic revivalism (mocked here by Synge, but no less understood) endured for long afterwards. But the passage is interesting for another reason: it explicitly identifies music and the 'old, lingering Irish words' associated with it as the absolute expression of nationalist feeling, aesthetics and culture. By 1902, of course, this sense of identification had long since attained conventional status in the cultural history of Irish music. How this should have come to be so, and the implications therein for music itself, are central questions in what follows here.

The problem in tracing the history of an idea about music in Ireland is that the metaphorical status of 'Irish music' almost always eclipses the actual condition of the music itself. This metaphorical status extends to two fields of semantic and political meaning: it enables music to function as an emblem of the literary imagination (an idea which originates in Thomas Moore), and it imposes on the music itself, and above all on the corpus of ethnic melody, an irreducibly nationalist aesthetic (an idea which is consolidated in Thomas Davis).

In Ireland, it is music which tends to stimulate political thought, rather than the other way around. As the book to which this essay belongs is entitled *Musical Constructions of Nationalism* (in Europe), so it could almost be said that the proper perspective for this essay might nevertheless be formulated as 'Nationalist Constructions of Music in Ireland'. The association between nationalism and music is so strong in Ireland that it can become an obstructive *donné* in almost any consideration of the history and development of musical thought. Carl Dahlhaus's remark that 'the national aspect of music is not a property attached to a musical creation from its origins, but one which emerges in a historical process' alerts us to the complex of ideas ('political, social, aesthetic and compositional') which produces the idea of musical nationalism itself.[2] When this idea attains a life of its own, so that the compositional process is severely undermined by it, we confront a problem rather than a phenomenon. In Ireland, the pervasive nature of this problem has produced an acute crisis of meaning as to the composition and reception of music. In short, the problem of nationalism in Irish music cannot simply be regarded as a subset of European musical nationalism. Although there is much in common between Ireland and other European countries in this respect, particularly with respect to the tension between 'ethnomusical substance' and 'the negligible effect of adopting folk music' (or more generally between art music and the indigenous traditions of any given region), the fragile condition of a central European aesthetic of art music in Ireland, constantly endangered by the ideology of colonialism, prohibits too close a comparison between Ireland and other European states.[3] When nationalism arises in European music – above all, perhaps, in opera, but also notably in the keyboard and symphonic repertoire – it does so in response to political circumstances which sometimes bear comparison with those in Ireland. But the question of European musical nationalism can be seen in the context of a strong, central art tradition. In fact the consciousness of such a tradition, particularly with regard to German music in the nineteenth century, provides a (natural?) means of absorption by which the nationalist impulse is both identified and emancipated from the circumstances of socio-political ferment. In very general terms, the fundamental tension in European art music of the nineteenth century can usefully be characterised as that between the claims of Italian opera on one side and of the German instrumental tradition on the other, a tension resolved in the music dramas of Richard Wagner (thus Carl Dahlhaus's argument). However deeply imbued this struggle is with nationalist feeling, these rival claims are first and last musical. The musical tradition remains an end in itself. And it is received into the European cultural matrix not simply as an expression of political or cultural identity, but as a self-contained and immanent presence. In fact, as Lydia Goehr has argued, the distinguishing feature of European art music in the nineteenth century is that the musical work itself becomes an autonomous object, a self-subsisting idea which is independent of the circumstances which bring it into being.[4] And a tradition which comprises a succession of such autonomous works (or, more laconically, an 'imaginary museum of musical works') is at least able to withstand the pressures of ideology, as these bear upon the nature of the tradition, particularly with regard to nationalism.

As I have argued elsewhere, the absence of such a tradition in Ireland (except as a tentative and polarised manifestation of colonial difference), together with the corresponding presence of a verbally-dominated culture, radically delimits the question of nationalism in Irish music.[5] George Steiner's observation that 'in a society made inert by repressive authority, the work of art becomes the quintessential deed', is a remark underwritten by the proper existence of an art-work tradition.[6] Where this is not allowed to arise, the concept of a 'work of art' is necessarily diminished. In Ireland, the status of music in the nineteenth century was such that it could not survive as an independent entity, so deeply indentured was it to political and cultural propaganda. The projection of Irish music either as a textual adjunct in the service of Romantic nationalism or as the symbol of a sectarian ideology of culture tended to eclipse the possibility of a music sufficiently emancipated from these burdens to develop freely of them. This possibility lay in the art tradition, but so vulnerable was this tradition to the claims and counterclaims of nationalism and colonialism, respectively, that it collapsed inwards under the weight of ideological pressure from both sides.

To press home this argument, it is instructive to compare the state of music in Ireland in the nineteenth century with Poland, a country that shares something of the same pattern of revolution and parliamentary reform in the quest for national independence. The parallels between Irish and Polish history are not hard to discover: both Ireland and Poland were colonised countries in the nineteenth century; both countries endured the crushing aftermath of insurrection (Poland in 1794, 1831 and 1863; Ireland in 1798, 1803 and 1848); and in both countries the cult of Romantic nationalism flourished under similar conditions of political deprivation. The cultivation of a nationalistic aesthetic in Polish literature, moreover, particularly in the verse of Adam Mickiewicz, was partly indebted to the precedent of Thomas Moore, whose writings Mickiewicz both translated and imitated.

But the parallels begin to break down when we address the sphere of music. In Ireland, Moore's verse – together with the ethnic melodies which he set – influenced not a musical genre but the perpetuation of a literary one (with an admittedly subservient reliance on melody): namely, the ballads of Thomas Davis. In Poland, the narratology of cultural nationalism expressed itself not only in literature but also in music, so that we find ourselves at mid-century facing an essentially untenable comparison between the ballads of Thomas Davis and the *ballades* of his close contemporary, Frédéric Chopin. If Chopin's music 'came to symbolise the national struggle, helping to cement the Polish spirit at a time when the country was without political status',[7] the nature of Chopin's achievement – its substantive presence in the tradition of keyboard music which it both redefined and enlarged – was not dependent on this narrative or symbolic function. It is self-evident that, without the means of infrastructure (the Warsaw Conservatory) and exposure (the concerts in Munich, Stuttgart, Vienna, Paris, London) which Chopin's birthright provided, his natural genius would have floundered. But the crucial factor by which his music at once retained its cultural integrity and yet was wholly integrated in terms of the European aesthetic was exile. Chopin's years in Paris provided him with a vital disengagement from the immediacy of political struggle in Poland. The enclave of which he was a part opened up a space (actual, imaginative) in which his synthesis of art and ethnic traditions was subsumed under a freedom to 'work in the world at large', as Jim Samson describes it.[8] And to 'work in the world at large' for Chopin was to partake of a cultural nationalism at once more productive and less politically engaged than that which confined the imaginative space of those who remained at home.

The integrity of Chopin's nationalism endured in the minds of his Polish contemporaries (even if this was only a matter of 'minor interest' to Schumann)[9] precisely because of its substantive existence in the music itself. If nationalism 'inspired' some of Chopin's music, it was nevertheless the musical work which finally mattered. In Warsaw, no less than in Paris, the narrative power of Chopin's art supervened its nationalistic origins. The reality, the sheer existence of his piano music, did not remain contingent upon the production of verbal or expressly political thought.[10]

In Ireland, by contrast, the failure of art music to emancipate itself from the political ideology of nationalism (which it helped to foster) was also to endure. By 1902, when the fleeting ghost of Gaelic culture manifested itself between the acts of Hyde's play, it did so in song. This means that music in Ireland functioned in a vitally different way to music elsewhere. It functioned primarily as an idea of something other than itself.

II

> It has often been remarked, and still oftener felt, that in our music is found the truest of all comments upon our history. The tone of defiance, succeeded by the languor of despondency – a burst of turbulence dying away into softness – the sorrows of one moment lost in the levity of the next – and all that Romantic mixture of mirth and sadness, which is naturally produced by the efforts of a lively temperament to shake off, or forget, the wrongs which lie upon it. Such are the features of our history and character, which we find strongly and faithfully reproduced in our music; and there are even many airs, which it is difficult to listen to, without recalling some period or event to which their expression seems applicable.[11]

Thomas Moore has become the whipping boy of Irish nationalism. In the postmodernist turn which attends certain aspects of Irish literary criticism, the appeal of this image is so strong as to be irresistible: Terry Eagleton detects a strain of masochism in Moore's verse, so that his image of Ireland reinforces a passive strain of complaint which is received into the canon at large as a trope for Ireland's disgraced condition.[12] The trappings of a ruined civilisation – the iconic and verbal shibboleths of decay – which dominate the landscape (real as well as imagined) find their literary correlative in Moore's tentative address upon the exacerbated condition of colonial enslavement. Thus goes the general argument. Looking at Moore's prefatory letters to the *Irish Melodies*, however, and especially with regard to his initially suppressed address to Lady Donegal, one finds good grounds for disagreement with this point of view. It is not only that Gavan Duffy and Young Ireland found much to commend in Moore's vision of a disgraced history from which a culture of nationalist (if sectarian) integrity might emancipate Ireland, it is also that Moore's realism with regard to Irish music – in particular, his insistence on the recent provenance of the greater number of melodies which he set and his frankly bourgeois representation of them – does not smack of masochism but of Romantic historicism. The author of *Captain Rock* and of numerous satirical indictments of slavery and torture did not disdain a softer address in his Irish verses, but the tone of indictment is unmistakable nevertheless. And at the very least, we must allow that Moore's explicit association between Irish music and verbal feeling connotes not simply a characteristically Romantic alignment between tone and word, but more specifically a relationship between the 'sad, degrading truths' of Irish history and the representational power of the music itself. If Moore, as in the passage quoted here from the letter to Lady Donegal, clearly believed that Irish music entailed a narratology of character and a psychological disposition born of its dysfunctional origins, this belief is not to be misconstrued either as a mere trope of literary Romanticism or as a means of aggrandising the melodies themselves. In any case, we need not impugn the sincerity of Moore's understanding of

'Irish music' in order to distance ourselves from it in the aftermath of modern commentary and scholarship.

Nor should we overlook the sheer anxiety of influence which Moore's conception of Irish music exerted on those ideologues of nationalism who came after him. It is all very well to have some fun at Moore's expense, to repudiate sardonically the *Irish Melodies* as a product designed for domestic consumption among those sufficiently well-placed to possess both a drawing-room and a pianoforte. But this is beside the point, except that Moore himself was realistic enough to realise that both his talent and its dissemination depended upon a contractual reciprocity between his vision and its reception. That reciprocity lay not in the fraught circumstances of armed rebellion or the seditious harangues of the broadsheet, but in the calmer arena of middle-class recreation. The aesthetic appeal, the sheer popularity of the *Melodies*, did not attenuate their political currency: on the contrary, Moore's reputation as a 'castle Catholic' did not redeem his verse from the charge of irresponsibility, especially in the reception of his work in the 1830s.[13] But we must distinguish between Moore's claims for the inherently political condition of Irish music (especially if we dismiss these as fanciful) and the reception history which attend these claims throughout the nineteenth century. Moore himself inherited from Bunting and thereby from Joseph Cooper Walker the conventional (if overly Romanticised) understanding of Irish music as a barely redeemed shibboleth of culture which spoke of a dislocated and ruined civilisation. He refined this understanding, to the extent that he refined the melodies, set new verses to them and had them decked out in the modern apparatus of pianoforte accompaniment. Nevertheless, he also ensured the currency of Irish music beyond the confines of antiquarian scholarship and pedantic debate which so clearly contextualise Bunting's own efforts in the preservation of Irish music. Moore's impulse was not to preserve, even if that motivation remained the ostensible one for those collectors who followed him. Instead, he claimed for the *Melodies* a vital role in the modernisation of Irish culture, a role which would not compromise the integrity of its political discourse. This is why he take pains to defend Sir John Stevenson in the third number of the *Melodies* from the charge of rash interference with the natural purity of Irish music. In aligning Stevenson's 'musical science' with Haydn's, Moore was conscious of an impeccable precedent for his own drive to make Irish music intelligible in terms of a European aesthetic of art music. This impulse, too, was not inconsistent with his essentially verbal understanding of Irish music and its narrative and psychological functions.[14]

But what is of even greater account than Moore's own understanding of Irish music as an adjunct to verbal feeling is the development of this idea as a conventional and exclusive resource in the rehabilitation of nationalist culture in Ireland throughout the nineteenth century. Moore took the intimacy between politics and music in Ireland virtually as a *donné*; those who followed him took it to be a requirement.

Thomas Davis was foremost in this enterprise: his explicit prescriptions for Irish music in *The Nation* newspaper, together with the ballads he published in *The Spirit of the Nation*, radically advanced the notion that Irish music was a static resource to be enlisted in the service of a cultural nationalism which Young Ireland helped to foster. It is not simply that Davis disavowed the idea of musical composition as a phenomenon worthy of independent development ('it is not needful for a writer of our songs to be a musician') but rather that music must be a means to political stimulus rather than an end in itself.[15]

But we must also take note of Davis's programmatic intent for Irish music, namely that it become emblematic of the cultural programme which was Young Ireland's *raison d'être*. In the case of music, 'cultural programme' meant the writing of ballads in order to create a political and cultural resource which would instigate change. He understood the reception of Irish music in his own day to be a matter of progressive understanding which derived from the antiquarianism of Walker, through the researches of Bunting and the identification of Moore's poetry with a nationalist vision of Ireland. He read the native repertory as a kind of programme music (even more explicitly than Moore had done), and he claimed for it the kind of psychological insight and literal representation ('moan of penal days') which Moore so readily identified in his prefatory remarks to the *Irish Melodies*.[16] If music required to be written, it was to repair a weakness in the despondent tone of Irish political songs to date and to circumvent the debilitating influence of the European aesthetic, manifested in those 'paltry, scented things from Italy' which passed for music among other nations. His condemnation of Balfe and Rooke and those who disdained the writing of 'Irish-like' music was justified on the grounds of their irrelevance to the cultural nationalism which he so vigorously (and sometimes simplistically) espoused.[17]

In Davis, too, we find the subordinate condition of music firmly associated with the corpus of traditional melody; the corpus of Irish airs existed for him in the same way that the mountains and valleys existed: they were part of Ireland's cultural topography, to be pressed into service but inherently incapable of development. Thus a new idea of Irish music, and a negative one, emerges as a by-product of Davis's strictly utilitarian conceptualism: not only is music *per se* to be regarded as an adjunct to verbal feeling, but it also partakes of a condition of absolute cultural stasis. Davis was impatient of Moore's understanding of Irish music because it conventionalised 'the wail of a lost cause'; furthermore, he offered three categories of Irish music ('the lyrics of Moore', 'Songs of the Irish-speaking people…' and 'Ballads'), each of which he found deficient in one overriding respect. For Davis, the purpose of song was to bring 'Love, Courage and Patriotism' to every heart and in every department of life: 'Fair and Theatre, Concert and Drawing-room, Road and Shop'. These prescriptions assume that the condition of the music itself is inherently of the past, the 'great heritage of national music'. The method of songwriting proposed by Davis – 'to learn an air for the purpose of writing words to it' – supposes that music exists as a resource for the propagation of political ideology, a prior resource which is incapable of any other function or independent growth. Davis, in short, could not conceive of a music which is not subordinate to ideology and which is removed from the 'heritage' of Bunting and Moore.

Davis's ignorance of, or contempt for, the European art tradition would not have been of much moment were it not for the decisive nature of his influence in the formation of modern Ireland. Nevertheless, the cultural nationalism which he espoused (above all with regard to music) was not of exclusive significance. Two other elements were required to confirm the stasis of music as an independent mode of thought in Ireland's verbally dominated cultural matrix. One of these was the regeneration of antiquarian research after the Famine and the other was the projection of music as a form of cultural absolutism which we associate with the Gaelic League. The ultimate condition of music in Ireland would only become clear with its failure to function within the otherwise abundantly fertile terms of the Celtic Revival except as a powerful symbol of renascent Irish culture. In the meantime, i.e. between the 1840s and the 1890s, the impact of Davis's ideas was such that the growth of music itself became secondary to the static conception of 'Irish music' as a cultural resource.

If, in Seamus Deane's phrase, the mutation from 'Celtic to the Gaelic Revival is quick, subtle, and in the end sectarian', it is partly because the role of music in this mutation was so symbolically effective.[18] Long before the widespread revival of the Irish language late in the century, Irish music continued to function as a vigorous intelligencer of cultural separatism. Samuel Ferguson's famous review of Hardiman's *Irish Minstrelsy* – in which he took Moore to task for his overly politicised reading of Irish music – is a marker in the development which is contemporaneous with Davis: it appeared in 1834 and it confirmed an awareness of music in Ireland as a political force, or at least potentially so. If Ferguson believed that literature was a part of his own conception of modern Ireland in terms of a cultural nationalism which was pro-Unionist and politically conservative (just as Davis's was anti-Union and politically separatist), he also relied on music in his meditations on Irish culture as a symbol of creative rehabilitation. The essential metaphor which recurs in these meditations is song. The song as an expression of Gaelic civilisation, as the source of cultural regeneration in Ireland, attains to such symbolic strength that the music itself is taken for granted, once more as a static fact rather than a living, regenerative force, to be adapted or pragmatically emulated at will. Music in Ferguson, as in Davis (however, differently), lives in the shadow of its own symbolic brilliance.[19]

But this symbolic force was not limited to ideologues of culture: it gained currency also among those engaged with the collection and preservation of Irish music, particularly after the Famine. The devastations of that genocidal episode cannot be reduced to an event in Irish cultural history, but there can be little doubt but that it was the Famine which inspired George Petrie in particular to recover, before it was too late, what remained of Irish music in its dreadful wake. In Petrie, and especially in his preface to the *Ancient Music of Ireland* (1855), the consolidation of music as a fundamental constituent of sectarian culture is almost complete. Unlike his predecessor Bunting, Petrie belonged to an Ireland in which antiquarianism had become so imbued with political resonance that the recovery of the (musical) past could not but signify immediate implications for the present. And in a present determined by the aftermath of famine, by violent struggle and by land reform, the Petrie Collection argued the existence of a cultural discourse radically at odds with the Union and conversely at one with the more widespread claims of an indigenous civilisation. Such claims were not slow to accumulate in the latter part of the nineteenth century, although there is nothing in Petrie's work which expressly advocates a challenge to the political *status quo*. His own sense of cultural revival, and of the role of the collector therein, nevertheless embraced a critique of the political constituency of which he himself was a part:

> Could music penetrate their stony hearts, the melodies of Ireland would make them weep for the ills they were the means of perpetrating on this unhappy land, and they would embrace the ill-treated people with a generous affection, anxious to make reparation for past injuries.[20]

Here it is Moore's reading of Irish music rather than Bunting's which endures, and the understanding of this music as an agent of social (if not political) redress is one which achieves conventional status in Petrie's work. The equation between musical preservation and social well-being which the collectors who followed Petrie repeatedly drew was to become virtually an axiom of Irish musical thought. The equivalence, moreover, which Petrie's work established between 'Irish music' and the traditional repertory was now to be more firmly voiced as an equivalence between traditional music and Gaelic culture.[21] This conventional understanding, firmly wedded to the reception of Irish music as a symbolic resource and – underlying these ideas – as an adjunct to verbal discourse, was profoundly to inhibit the emancipation of music as an independent art in Ireland.

The transcendence of Gaelic culture achieved by the Literary Revival helped to consign music to this limbo of cultural stasis. In terms of the Gaelic Revival itself, of course, the progression from preservation as a form of collection to preservation as a form of cultural isolationism was swift and all but impossible to arrest. Douglas Hyde's famous appeal to 'de-Anglicise' Ireland, delivered less than a year before the founding of the Gaelic League in 1893, apostrophised this new reading of Irish music as a safeguard of cultural identity:

> Our music too, has become Anglicised to an alarming extent. Not only has the national instrument, the harp . . . become extinct, but even the Irish pipes are threatened with the same fate . . . If Ireland loses her music, she loses, what is, after the Gaelic language and literature, her most valuable and most characteristic expression. And she is rapidly losing it.[22]

However powerful the appeal of Hyde's cultural protectionism, it deepened the divisions between art music and the ethnic repertory in Ireland to a point of irreconcilability. Hyde's separatism was intimately connected to a political movement for autonomy which self-evidently gained force as the century drew to a close. But the consequences of this separatism for music were to prove almost lethal. As the ethnic repertory continued to function more and more stridently as an emblem of nationalism (and thereby of political independence), the condition of music itself as a generative force all but disappeared. It would be absurd to deny the revivalist impact of the Gaelic League upon the performance of traditional music, even if the division between 'Sinn Féiner' and 'West Briton' was sometimes a matter of inadvertent humour, as it was for Synge and James Joyce. Nevertheless, it is fair to say that those most closely involved with the music revival at the turn of the century trenchantly endorsed Hyde's static conception of music as a badge of cultural identity and purity. Charlotte Milligan Fox, Alfred Perceval Graves and even Richard Henebry (among the most strident 'Irish Irelanders' in music) firmly repudiated the usefulness or desirability of any kind of musical cross-fertilisation between ethnic and European ideologies of music. 'The more we foster modern music the more we help to silence our own' was Henebry's uncompromising expression of this point of view, but even those less committed to the wholesale appropriation of 'Irish music' as a weapon in the propaganda war could not supervene the cultural (and thereby political) divisions which so radically inhibited the reception of music into the Irish mind.[23]

The supreme irony of this failure is that the idea of Irish music should have shown itself so fertile both as a symbol of cultural autonomy and of imaginative regeneration, above all in the Literary Revival. That Yeats should have shown himself so hostile (at best indifferent) to actual music, especially to music of the European tradition, while at the same time saturating his poetry and plays with musical symbolism is the best-known expression of the radical duplicity. Synge's own abandonment of music for drama is expressive of a slightly different but not unrelated quandary: he became aware of the European tradition by studying music in Germany, but he could not resist Yeats's appeal to give up music for a part in the Revival, especially given his acutely painful awareness of the depleted condition of art music in his native country. Meanwhile, the cultural chauvinism preached by Hyde in the service of nationalism came to depend so heavily on music that 'Irish music' – in effect the performance of a small repertory of native airs, intermixed with Moore and the more or less reliable publication of thousands of arrangements – became synonymous with music of *any* kind in the minds of those who determined Ireland's cultural sense of itself.

How one-sided this cultural stasis was is difficult but not impossible to determine. The reception of the ethnic repertory into the history of Irish ideas offers at least a clear path from antiquarian zeal, through Romantic appropriation and political association to full-blown nationalist ideology and the service of a fundamentally verbal culture. But what of music in the art tradition? Is it fair to consign its long and uncertain history in Ireland to the limbo of colonial pleasure and expression of ascendancy values largely irrelevant to Ireland and the Irish, except by way of antagonism and hostility? Two facts of Irish cultural history consign this reading in turn to irrelevance. The first is that the art tradition maintained a frail but unbroken presence in Ireland in spite of the hostile division (between colonial and ethnic ideologies of culture) which plagued its existence. By mid-century at the latest, notably in the foundation of an Irish (later Royal Irish) Academy of Music, a tentative but unmistakable recognition of music as an art first, and as an expression of ideology second, had taken hold in Ireland, even if the Academy itself for many years afterwards upheld (consciously or otherwise) the cultural divisions which so starkly characterised the pursuit of music in Ireland.[24] This recognition, entirely unrelated to the success of individual composers (such as Michael Balfe) who happened to be Irish but who attained success independently of music in this country, did in turn foster attempts to bridge the daunting gap that lay between 'Irish music' and the possibility of original composition in Ireland. However unsuccessful these attempts were to remain, they provided the impetus for later developments which could scarcely have survived without these initial efforts. Secondly, the emancipation of certain genres (above all other, opera) from the stranglehold of 'ascendancy culture' in Irish urban life towards the last quarter of the nineteenth century signified a wider consciousness of the European aesthetic, however depleted and inadequate its presence in Ireland by comparison with other countries. One might say that, beneath the surface level of nationalist ideologies of culture in Ireland, a certain amount in the service of the European aesthetic was being achieved. Nevertheless, the fact of irrelevance to that culture obstinately remains. Even after the turn of the century, Arnold Bax's sojourn in Ireland was marked by a curious double-life: as an aspiring composer, he was stimulated by Yeats and the Literary Revival to create in musical terms an image of Ireland consonant with the Revival itself, but, as a resident of Dublin, he turned pragmatically (albeit briefly) to fiction and drama, because the Revival simply could not accommodate within its terms of reference a 'composer' in the ordinarily understood sense of that term. Meanwhile, those who *did* compose sought refuge in Britain or proclaimed their distance from the Revival in exotic (and sometimes risible) appropriations of the native repertory which underlined the ethnic-colonial division of musical culture ever more emphatically. Stanford's 'Irish' music is a case in point, and one which adumbrated a recurring problem for Irish composers generally in the new Free State: how to circumvent the ethnic repertory, in order to liberate art music in Ireland from the dutiful arrangement of traditional melodies? In this sense too, the cultural stasis of a pre-existent repertoire was to prove an insuperable burden.

III

> It is difficult to understand upon what ground such a view can be maintained as that Irish music in particular should not be developed in any of the modern forms in which the musician ... so delights. To accept such doctrine would be to condemn to barrenness and ultimately to death the most expressive monument of our ancient national character and civilization, to roll back the tide of progress in art to stop inventiveness and originality in our artists; in short, it would be to condemn ourselves to a backwardness and stagnation which nothing in the past history of our country and nothing in the present condition of the art could excuse or palliate.[25]

The emancipation of music in Ireland from the burdens of nationalist ideology was undoubtedly complicated by the burden of the ethnic tradition itself in the matter of original composition. As composers such as Michele Esposito and Hamilton Harty struggled to find a musical voice answerable to the myths of the Literary Revival, it soon became clear that the prestige of nationalism was all but synonymous with the presence of an Irish air. Whereas the Literary Revival had brilliantly rehoused the myths of Gaelic civilisation in English, no such easy passage was available to music. While music continued to flourish as an idea of cultural integrity, the corpus of melody itself appeared to inhibit the Irish musical imagination in its tentative and painful journey away from its chronic dependence on a very small stock of pre-existent material. This problem was undoubtedly aggravated by the indifference shown by the new Free State to art music, an indifference notably redeemed by the prominence of music in broadcasting services from the mid 1920s onwards. But those vital structures of European music, so long neglected in Ireland and so necessary to the reception and development of music, not as a symbolic or ideological resource but simply for its own sake, were all but impossible to attain in a country struggling with economic, cultural and of course political problems which all but occluded the claims of a peripheral art. If it can be said that the Irish mind took brilliant refuge instead in language, it can be equally maintained that the long silence of music in Ireland, and especially of art music, was expressive of something other than incapacity or indifference. It was expressive, too, of the vulnerable condition of music in an essentially verbal culture which had overtaken the symbolic properties of music at the expense of music itself. The dominant claims of nationalism, especially, decisively eclipsed the cultivation of music for its own sake. In turn, the weak and increasingly untenable foundations of colonial thought made of the European aesthetic a second-hand experience, mediated through the harsh tonalities of foreign occupation and social dysfunction. In this strange climate, and in this strange country, music itself fell silent.

Notes and References

1 John Millington Synge, 'Le Mouvement Intellectuel Irlandais', in *L'Européen* of 31 May 1902, reproduced in Synge, *Collected Works*, Vol. 2, ed. Robin Skelton (London, 1966), pp. 381–2; cited and translated by Seamus Deane in *Celtic Revivals* (London, 1985), pp. 61–2.
2 Carl Dahlhaus, *Nineteenth-Century Music*, trans. J. B. Robinson (Berkeley, 1989), pp. 38–9.
3 Dahlhaus's reading of nationalism (note 2 above) in music appears to take (reasonably) for granted that the emergence of nationalism as a phenomenon of European art music occurs nevertheless against a strong tradition of art music, whatever the regional, political or socio-cultural motivations which stimulate the perception of this music as 'nationalist'. Such an assumption, however, cannot be made of music in Ireland, where the marginal condition of art music, imbued as it was with the ethos of colonialism, rendered it powerless to absorb the forces of nationalist ideology.
4 See Lydia Goehr, *The Imaginary Museum of Musical Works* (Oxford, 1994).
5 See Harry White, *The Keeper's Recital: Music and Cultural History in Ireland, 1770–1970* (Cork & Indiana, 1998), *passim*.
6 George Steiner, *In Bluebeard's Castle* (London, 1971), p. 27.
7 Jim Samson, 'A Biographical Introduction', in *The Cambridge Companion to Chopin* (Cambridge, 1992), p. 7.
8 Ibid., p. 6.
9 Schumann in 1835 on Chopin, as cited by Dahlhaus, *Nineteenth-Century Music*, p. 37: 'The minor interest attaching to the patch of earth on which he was born was destined to be sacrificed to the Universal [*Weltbürgerlich*]; and true enough, his recent works have shed their excessively specific Sarmatic physiognomy'.
10 I have pursued this argument at greater length in *The Keeper's Recital*, pp. 70–3.
11 Thomas Moore, 'Letter to the Marchioness Dowager of Donegal', reproduced in *The Poetical Works of Thomas Moore* (London, 1865), p. 221. This letter originally appeared as a preface to the third number of the *Irish Melodies* in 1810.
12 See Terry Eagleton, 'The Masochism of Thomas Moore', in *Crazy John and the Bishop* (Cork and Indiana, 1998), pp. 140–58.
13 See, for example, Samuel Ferguson's remarks on Moore in the course of his lengthy review of Hardiman's *Irish Minstrelsy* which appeared in *The Dublin University Magazine*, 4 (July–December, 1834): 'Mr Moore's idea that the point of honor and its effects were done away with by the Relief Bill is utterly fallacious. Mr Hardiman's book is a striking illustration of the truth of our assertion. He had written the greater

part of his notes and comments previous to Catholic Emancipation [1829], and in them, he freely indulged in what those who agree with Mr Moore would denominate natural indignation against England and the English. The work, however, is not published till 1831, two years after all cause for that obstinate hatred in which Mr Moore thought himself justifiable, had been removed.' (p. 464). It is interesting to note that Ferguson's response to Moore ('obstinate hatred') contrasts sharply with the later reception of Moore's work as a politically ineffectual gloss on Irish history. In any case, the reading of Moore offered by Ferguson can scarcely connote the 'masochism' which Eagleton discerns in his work.

14 For a more comprehensive discussion of Moore's verbal understanding of Irish music, see White, *The Keeper's Recital*, pp. 42–52. In an undated letter to Stevenson, Moore clarifies his explicitly political reading of Irish music in the following terms: 'Our National Music has never been properly collected, and while the composers of the Continent have enriched their operas and sonatas with melodies borrowed from Ireland . . . we have left these treasures in a great degree unreclaimed and fugitive. But we are come, I hope, to a better period of both politics and music; and how much they are connected in Ireland at least, appears too plainly in the tone of sorrow and depression which characterises most of our early songs'; see Wilfred S. Dowden (ed.), *The Letters of Thomas Moore* (Oxford, 1964), Vol. 1, pp. 116–17. Moore's awareness of the European tradition in respect of Irish music (as in his comparison between Haydn and Stevenson in the third number of the *Melodies*) is here advanced by striking contrast with the impoverished condition of art music in Ireland. See also Barry Cooper, 'Beethoven's Folksong Settings as Sources of Irish Folk Music', in Patrick F. Devine and Harry White (eds.), *The Maynooth International Musicological Conference: Part Two* (Dublin, 1996), pp. 65–81.

15 For Davis's view on music, see D. J. O'Donoghue (ed.), *Essays Literary and Historical by Thomas Davis* (Dundalk, 1914). Many of these pieces originally appeared in *The Nation* newspaper.

16 Three essays from *The Nation*, 'Irish Music and Poetry', 'A Ballad History of Ireland' and 'Irish Songs', offer a conspectus of Davis's musical thought which clarifies his remarkable sense of music not merely as a textual adjunct but as an instigator of political change.

17 See Davis, *Essays*, pp. 160–1. It is interesting to note that Davis deplores the performance of arrangements of Italian and English Opera (Rossini and Balfe) by the temperance bands which formed an important element in the mass repeal meetings held by O'Connell after Catholic Emancipation.

18 Deane, *Celtic Revivals*, p. 25.

19 The difference between Ferguson and Davis with respect to Irish music is indicated by a comparison of Ferguson's censure of Moore's pro-Catholic agitations as these are expressed in the *Melodies*, and Davis's complaint that Moore was 'deficient in vehemence'. The striking similarity between them is that Davis and Ferguson both conceived of music as secondary to verbal nuance and meaning.

20 From an entry in Petrie's journals, cited in William Stokes, *The Life of George Petrie* (London, 1868), p. 317.

21 Petrie's motivation for the collection of Irish music is explicitly stated in the preface to his collection: he wanted to redeem Irish music from that 'awful, unwonted silence' which had been visited upon Ireland in the wake of the Famine. He continues: 'I felt that the new generations, unlinked as they must be with those of the past . . . will necessarily have lost very many of those peculiar characteristics which so long had given them a marked individuality; and, more particularly, that among the changes sure to follow, the total extinction of their ancient language would be inevitably, accompanied by the loss of all that as yet unsaved portion of their ancient

music which had been identified with it' preface to *The Ancient Music of Ireland* [Dublin, 1855], pp. xii–xiii. It is worth adding that it is the influence of Petrie's collection, rather than any self-conscious programme on his behalf, which validates the argument advanced here. The tradition of similar collections which it established (by Patrick Weston Joyce and Francis O'Neill in particular) consolidated a projection of the collected melodies as the *exclusive* repository of Irish music: this exclusivity was almost exactly analogous to the inherent exclusivity of one language (Gaelic/Irish) as against another (English).

22   See Douglas Hyde,'The Necessity for De-Anglicising Ireland' (1892) reproduced in Breandán Ó Conaire (ed.), *Douglas Hyde: Language, Lore and Lyrics* (Dublin, 1896), p. 167.
23   See Richard Henebry, *Irish Music* (Dublin, n.d. [1903?]), p. 14. Until further research has been undertaken into the question of music within the Gaelic League, it is not possible to determine how widespread was Hyde's repudiation of the European aesthetic. For a discussion of attempts to incorporate art music into Gaelic League festivals and the role of the Feis Ceoil in fostering an art music based on Irish idioms, see *The Keeper's Recital*, pp. 11–17.
24   See Charles Acton and Richard Pine (eds.), *To Talent Alone: A History of the Royal Irish Academy of Music, 1848–1998* (Dublin, 1998). For an assessment of the art tradition in Ireland which considers this tradition in the context of the Literary Revival, see *The Keeper's Recital*, pp. 94–124.
25   Brendan Rogers,'An Irish School of Music', *New Ireland Review*, 13 (1900), p. 151.

Bibliography

Theories of political and cultural nationalism

Anderson, Benedict, *Imagined Communities: Reflections on the Origin and Spread of Nationalism* (London, 1983)
Dahbour, O. and Ishay, M. R. (eds.), *The Nationalism Reader* (New Jersey, 1995)
Gellner, Ernest, *Nations and Nationalism* (Oxford, 1983)
Greenfeld, Liah, *Nationalism: Five Roads to Modernity* (Cambridge Ma., 1992)
Hobsbawm, E. J., *Nations and Nationalism since 1780: Programme, Myth, Reality* (Cambridge, 1990)
Hutchinson, John, *The Dynamics of Cultural Nationalism* (London, 1987)
Hutchinson, John and Smith, Anthony D. (eds.), *Nationalism: A Reader* (Oxford, 1994)
Kedourie, Elie, *Nationalism* (London, 1960 [reprinted 1985])
Kohn, Hans, *The Idea of Nationalism* (New York, 1945)
Pearson, R., *The Longman Companion to European Nationalism* (Harlow, 1994)
Smith, Anthony, *National Identity* (London, 1991)

Music-specific texts on nationalism

Applegate, Celia, 'How German is it? Nationalism and the Idea of Serious Music in the Early Nineteenth Century', *19th-Century Music* XXI/3 (Spring 1998), pp. 274–96.
Dahlhaus, Carl, 'Nationalism and Music', *Between Romanticism and Modernism: Four Studies in the Music of the Later Nineteenth Century* trans. Mary Whittall (California, 1980)
Forsyth, Cecil, *Music and Nationalism* (London, 1911)
Frigyesi, J., 'Béla Bartók and the concept of nation and volk in modern Hungary', *The Musical Quarterly*, 78/2 (Summer 1994), pp. 255–87
Gossett, P., 'Becoming a Citizen: the Chorus in "Risorgimento" Opera', *Cambridge Opera Journal*, Vol. 2 (1992), pp. 41–64
Hepokoski, James 'The Dahlhaus Project and Its Extra-Musicological Sources', *19th-Century Music*, XIV/3 (Spring, 1991), pp. 221–46
Kallberg, Jeffrey, 'The Rhetoric of Genre: Chopin's Nocturne in G minor', *19th-Century Music*, XI/3, (Spring 1988), pp. 238–61
Large, D. C. and Weber, W. (eds.), *Wagnerism in European Culture and Politics* (Ithaca, 1984)
Pederson, Sanna, 'A. B. Marx, Berlin Concert Life, and German National Identity', *19th Century Music* XVIII/2 Fall (California, 1994), pp. 87–107
Potter, Pamela M., 'Musicology Under Hitler: New Sources In Context', *Journal of the American Musicological Society*, Vol. XLIX/1, Spring (1996), pp. 70–113

Rumph, Stephen, 'A Kingdom Not of This World: The Political Context of E. T. A. Hoffmann's Beethoven Criticism', *19th Century Music* XIX/1 Summer (California, 1995), pp. 50–67

Stradling, R. and Hughes, M., *The English Musical Renaissance 1860–1940: Construction and Deconstruction* (London, 1993)

Taruskin, Richard, *Defining Russia Musically* (Princeton, 1997)

Taruskin, Richard, 'Nationalism', Stanley Sadie (ed.), *The New Grove Dictionary of Music and Musicians* 2nd Edition. (London, 2001).

Index

Abraham, Gerald, 117, 118
Adler, Guido, 6
Adorno, Theodor, 16, 25, 126, 198–9
Ady, Endre, 19
Agulhon, Maurice, 77
Aleksander II (Czar of Russia), 168
Allen, Warren Dwight, 7–8
Alter, Peter, 4, 125
Andersen, Hans Christian, 135
Anderson, Benedict, 125
Applegate, Celia, 9–10
Aristotle, 77, 79
Arnold, Matthew, 36
Arnold, Samuel, 39
Ashcroft, B., 27–8
Attey, John, 39
Auber, Daniel, 171
Austro-German musical tradition, 6, 26, 28, 34–5, 44, 123, 182
Ayrton, William, 37

Babbit, Milton, 209
Bach, C.P.E., 193
Bach, Johann Sebastian, 8, 44
Bacon, Richard, 37
Balakirev, Mily, 108, 109, 112, 118, 120
   First Symphony, 109–10, 113–15, 117
   influence of Schumann, 115–16
Balázs, Béla, 22, 32n
Balfe, Michael, 33, 263, 267
Barbier, Jules, 75–6
Barrès, Maurice, 74
Bartók, Béla, 11, 142, 156
   disdain of experimental compositions, 26, 27
   essay on Nazi anti-Semitism, 23
   First Piano Concerto reviewed, 26
   Kossuth, 18
   musical nationalism, 24–7, 28–9
   notation of scores, 25
   and peasant music, 16, 18–20, 21–2, 23–5, 26–7, 28, 207–8
   rejects Gypsy music, 16, 18–20, 21–2, 26
   socialist policies, 22
   works performed in Nazi Germany, 23
Bateson, Thomas, 39
Bax, Arnold, 206, 267–8
Bayreuther Blätter, 239, 247
Beethoven, Ludwig van, 43, 46, 74, 89, 90, 110, 113, 117, 118, 191, 220
   symphonic paradigm, 119–20
Belfast Harpers' Festival (1792), 201
Bellaigue, Camille, 87
Bellini, Vincenzo, 185
   Norma, 184–5, 188, 189–90
Bentham, Jeremy, 34
Berend, I.T., 17
Beringer, Oscar, 35
Berresford Ellis, Peter, 222–3
Bertrand, Gustave, 72, 74, 87
Berwald, Franz, 135
Bethlen, Count István, 18, 29n
Bewley, Christina, 222
Biblioteka Warszawska, 168
Biedermeier, 134
Boieldieu, François-Arien, 84
Boissier, Agénor, 248
Boito, Arrigo, 192
Bordes, Charles, 85
Borodin, Aleksandr, 109–10, 117, 118, 119, 120
   First Symphony, 109–13, 115, 117–18
   influence of Schumann, 111–12
Botstein, L., 27
Boulanger, General, 80
Bourcault-Ducoudray, Louis-Albert, 77–8, 85
Boyce, William, 39
Brahms, Johannes, 28, 74, 90, 119, 205, 245

Brandes, Georg, 126, 136
Bremnor, Robert, 39
Breuer, János, 23
Britain, see also Dictionary of Music and Musicians
  anti-German feelings, 33–4
  Crystal Palace Concerts, 38, 40
  folksong, 34
  Great Exhibition (1851), 34, 38
  inferiority to German music tradition, 34–5, 43, 46
  masculinisation of music, 91
  musical nationalism, 33–5, 38, 43, 46
  musicology, 35–6
  opera, failure to take root in, 33–4, 39
Brod, Max, 136
Bronsart, Hans von Schellendorf, 45
Brown, David, 119
Bruch, Max, 35
Bruckner, Anton, 119–20
Bülow, Hans von, 45, 171, 172–3
Bunting's *Antient Irish Music*, 204, 262, 263, 264, 265
Burney, Charles, 182
Burns, Robert
  Anglicised stanzas, 215–16
  'Auld Lang Syne', 213
  'Bruce's Address', 213–16, 218–19, 221, 222–3, 224, 230, 231, 232
  alternative versions of, 225–7, 233–5, 236
  'Hey Tuttie Taitie', 216–18, 221, 222, 227
  nationalism, 212, 213, 216, 222, 223–4, 225, 227, 229–31, 232, 236
  popular image of, 229–30
  'Scots, Wha Hae wi' Wallace Bled', 213–16, see also Burns, 'Bruce's Address'
Buşiţia, János, 19
Butler, Marilyn, 222
Byrd, William, 39

Callcott, Dr, 37
Caponi, Jacopo 'Folchetto', 184
Carlyle, Thomas, 229–32, 233, 236
Carte, Richard D'Oyly, 33
Chaplin, Charles, 242
Chappell, William, 39, 40
Chausson, Ernest, 88

Chebroux, Ernest, 80
Chopin, Frédéric, 63, 74, 126, 174, 175, 176, 177
  nationalism, 260
choral singing, 77–9
Choron and Fayelle, 37, 85
Chouquet, M. Gustave, 38, 42, 44
Chybiński, Adolf, 176
Chylińska, Andrzej, 64
Claussen, Sophus, 126
Cole, Henry, 38, 40
Coleridge, Arthur Duke, 42
Colles, Frederick, 44, 47
Collin, Laure, 90
Combarieu, Jules, 78
Comte, Auguste, 88
Conservatoire de Musique de Paris, 38, 42, 88
Cooper, Martin, 119
Corder, Frederick, 46
Coulanges, Fustel de, 73
Cousin, Victor, 83, 88
Cowen, Frederick, 34, 46
Cronin, Anthony, 204
Cui, César, 116, 120
Cummings, William, 40

Dahlhaus, Carl, 8–9, 10, 12, 101n, 124–5, 170, 177, 258, 259
Daiches, David, 215, 216
Dallapiccola, Luigi, 193
Dannreuther, Edward, 35, 45–6
D'Annunzio, Gabriele, 193
d'Arc, Jeanne, 75–7, 83, 217
d'Arcais, Francesco, 192
David, Ferdinand, 44
David, J.P. Paul, 44
Davis, Thomas, 201–2, 208, 258, 260, 263–4
de' Calzabigi, Ranieri, 183
de Paor, Liam, 204, 207
Deák, I., 17
Deane, Seamus, 202, 203, 264
Debussy, Claude, 89, 90, 142
  Etudes, 143–4
  influence on Monrad Johansen, 143–4, 156, 157, 158, 159
Dembowski, Edward, 165, 168, 169–70, 171, 173

Denmark
- art and national identity, 132–4
- elementalisation in music, 128–9, 131–2, 134, 139
- flattened sevenths in music, 129–30, 139
- folk music, 129
- horn calls, 128, 129, 131–2, 134, 139
- literature, 126
- music peripheralised, 123–4, 125–6
- musical nationalism, 124–6, 134–5, 139
- Romanticism, 126, 129, 131–2

d'Espiard, l'abbé, 82
Dictionary of Music and Musicians, 10
- aims of, 38–9, 46
- articles in, 39–43, 44–6
- conception of, 37–8, 40
- contribution of Parry, 42–4

d'Indy, Vincent, 85, 88, 89–90
Dmowski, Roman, 51–2
Dohnányi, Ernö, 22
Dollimore, Jonathan, 56
Donizetti, Gaetano, 185, 190
Dósa, Lidi, 18
Dreyfus, Alfred, 73
Duffy, Gavan, 261
Dujardin, Edouard, 247, 248
Duparc, Henri, 87
Dvořák, Antonín, 24

Eagleton, Terry, 261
Eichendorff, Joseph, 131
Einstein, Albert, 65
Einstein, Alfred, 7–8
Elgar, Edward, 34, 44, 140n
Eliot, T.S., 158
Ellis, A.J., 41
Ellis, Havelock, 57
Elsner, Józef, 165–6
Engel, Carl, 35, 36–7, 38
Espagne, Michel, 90
Esposito, Michele, 268
ethnicity, 1, 5–6
- Germany, 4
- Hungary, 16–18, 19, 26
- Poland, 164

Expert, Henry, 85–6

Fanning, David, 135, 139

Fanon, Frantz, 203, 207
Farrenc, Aristide, 85
Fascism, 7, 18, 246
- adoption of Wagner, 239, 247
Fauré, Gabriel, 85
Ferguson, Samuel, 202, 203, 204, 264, 269–70n
Ferry, Jules, 73
Fétis, François-Joseph, 88
Finkielkraut, Alain, 73
Fletcher, Andrew, 212, 231–2
folk music, 5
- Britain, 34
- Denmark, 129
- France, 80–5, 90
- Germany, 3, 245
- Hungary, 16, 18–20, 21–2, 23–5, 26–7, 28
- Ireland, 205, 207–8, 258
- Italy, 182, 193
- Norway, 156–8, 159, 162
- Poland, 58–9, 62, 166, 171, 176
- Russia, 26, 106, 108, 119
Forsyth, Cecil, 33–4
Foscolo, Ugo, 183
Foucault, Michel, 61
Fox, Charlotte Milligan, 266
France
- *chanson populaire*, 80–5, 86
- choral singing instils patriotism, 77–9
- cultural progression, 81–3
- folksong movement, 80–5, 90
- legacy of Franco-Prussian war, 72, 73
- masculinisation of music, 74–7, 81, 83, 85, 87, 90, 91
- music education, 75, 76–80
- musical heritage, 85–91
- musical nationalism, 72–3, 75–6
  - in education, 77–9
  - 'La Française', 75
  - 'Marseillaise', 73
- musical rivalry with Germany, 72, 75, 77–8, 80, 81, 83, 84–5, 89–90
- nationalism, 2, 3, 4, 73–5
- *opéra comique*, 72, 74, 84, 85, 87
- orchestral song, 87–8
- Renaissance music, 85–6
- Romanticism, 83

Symbolist movement and Wagner, 239–40, 247–9, 251
Franck, César, 87, 89–90
François I, King of France, 75, 82
Fraser, John, 223
Frederick Bridge, J., 42
Freud, Sigmund, 53–5, 59–60, 64, 65–6, 244
Frigyesi, Judit, 20, 22
Fuller Maitland, J.A., 40, 42, 47
Fyffe, C.A., 42

Gail, Sophie, 87
Garborg, Arne, 160–2
Gauntlett, H.J., 39
Gehring, Franz, 44
Gellner, Ernest, 4–5, 9, 125, 181, 202–3
Geoffroy, Julien Louis, 81
George Boyce, D., 202
Germany, see also Austro-German musical tradition
　character of national music, 104, 105, 107
　choral singing, 79
　citizenship, qualification for, 205–6
　ethnic groups, 4
　folk music, 3, 245
　masculinisation of music, 91
　music education, 77–8
　musical tradition, 34–5, 43, 44, 89–90, 131, 161, 258–9
　prejudice against in Italy, 182, 192–3
　musicology, 7–8, 35
　nationalism, 3–4, 7–8, 9–10, 239
　Nazism, 7, 23
　adoption of Wagner, 239, 247
　Reichsmusikkammer, 208
　Romanticism, 3, 8, 9, 26, 80, 244
　Weltanschauung, 44, 87
Gesellschaft der Musikfreunde (Vienna), 38, 42
Gibbons, Orlando, 39
Gilbert, W.S. and Sullivan, Arthur, 39
Gillies, M., 22
Gioberti, Vincenzo, 184
Giusti, Giuseppe, 190–1
Glazunov, Aleksander, 108, 109, 116, 118, 119, 120
Glinka, Mikhail, 104–5, 106, 176
　Kamarinskaya, 108–9, 118, 119, 120

Gluck, Christoph, 183
Gnesin, Mikhail, 116–17
Goehr, Lydia, 259
Goldschmidt, Otto, 35
Gömbös, Gyula, 18
Goncharov, Ivan, 119
Gounod, Charles, 75–7
Graves, Alfred Perceval, 266
Gray, Cecil, 7
Gregorian modes, 41, 84
Grétry, Lucile, 87
Grévy, François, 73
Grieg, Edvard, 24, 45, 136
　connections with Monrad Johansen, 143, 159
　German attitude towards music of, 161
　extended tonality in music, 142–3
　Slåtter Op.72, 142, 143
Grove, George, 37–47, see also *Dictionary of Music and Musicians*

Hába, Alois, 26
Hale, Amy, 228
Halévy, Fromenthal, 171
Halle, Adam de la, 84
Hallé, Charles, 35
Hamilton's *Dictionary of 1,000 Musical Terms*, 37
Hammershøi, Vilhelm, 132–3, 135
Hamsun, Knut, 157
Handel, George Frederick, 34
Hardiman, James, 202, 264
Harrison, William, 33
Harty, Hamilton, 268
Haydn, Franz Joseph, 8, 46, 193, 205, 262
　arrangements of Scots material, 218, 220, 221
Heap, Charles Swinnerton 46
Hegel, G.W.F., 3
Heine, Heinrich, 131
Helmore, Thomas, 41
Henebry, Richard, 266
Herder, Johann von, 3, 5
Hérold, Ferdinand, 72
Heugel, Henri, 75
Hipkins, A.J., 41
Hitler, Adolf, 239, 244, 247
Hobsbawm, Eric, 1

Hoffmann, E.T.A., 9
Hofmannsthal, Hugo von, 244
Hopkins, Edward John, 42
Horthy, Admiral Miklós, 17, 22–3
Hughes, M., 33, 35
Hugo, Victor, 249
Hullah, John, 41
Hungary
  anti-Semitism in, 17, 18, 20, 21, 22–3, 29–30n
  Arrow-Cross Party, 18
  demography, 16–17
  ethnic assimilation, 16–18, 19, 26
  folk music development, 23–4, 28–9
  Gypsy music, 16, 18–21, 26
  musical nationalism, 23–7, 28–9
  musicology, 19
  nationalism, 16–17, 28
  peasant music, 16, 18–20, 21–2, 23–5, 26–7, 28–9
Huret, Jules, 251
Hurum, Alf, 143
Husk, William, 39, 42
Hutchinson, John, 1, 4, 12, 125–6
Huysmans, Joris, 248–9
Hyde, Douglas, 257, 260, 265–6, 267

International Institute of Intellectual Co-operation, 65
Ireland
  ballads, 202
  bicentenary of 1798 rebellion, 199, 200–1
  colonialism, 258, 259, 261, 267, 269
  comparison with Poland, 5, 259–60
  Famine, 264, 265
  folk music, 205, 207–8, 258
  Gaelic League, 257, 264, 265–6
  Gaelic revival, 257, 264, 265–7, 268
  music preservation, 264, 265
  musical nationalism, 201–9, 257–8, 259–60, 261–9
  musical tradition divided, 207–9, 259, 267
  nationalism, 5, 199–201, 202–3
  'Orange and Green Will Carry the Day', 202
  revisionism, 200–2, 204–5
  Ulster Unionism, 235

Young Ireland, 201, 261, 263
Irish (Royal) Academy of Music, 267
Italy, 90
  censorship, 186–8
  folk music, 182, 193
  geography, pre-unification, 181–2
  and German symphonism, 182, 192–3
  military bands, 189–90
  nationalism, 181–4
  Northern League, 188
  opera and nationalism, 181, 182–9, 191, 192–3
  Risorgimento, 4, 185–6, 189, 192
Iwaszkiewicz, Jarosław, 58

Jacobsen, Jens Peter, 126–7, 129
Jaeger, Augustus, 35
Janáček, Leoš, 25, 152
Jeanne d'Arc, 75–7
Jensen, Johannes V., 126
Jensen, Jørgen I., 134–5
Jeszensky, G., 16
Joachim, Joseph, 35
Johansen, David Monrad, 11
  influence of Debussy, 143–4, 156, 157, 158, 159
  influence of Grieg, 143, 159
  interest in folk music, 156–8, 159, 162
  juxtaposition of complementary sonorities, 144–56
  musical nationalism, 159–60, 161–2
  Nordlandsbilleder, 143–57
    Den lille Stengud, 144–8, 155
    Kvinneprofil, 148, 153–6
    Rensdyr, 149–53, 155–6
  Syv sanger, 157
  use of melody, 158–9
  Voluspaa, 160
Johnson, James
  Scots Musical Museum, 217–18, 219–20, 221, 222, 224, 227
Journal des débats, 81
Joyce, James, 206, 248, 266
Jurkovics, Irmy, 18

Kahn, Gustave, 249
Kallberg, Jeffrey, 174
Kant, Immanuel, 4
Karłowicz, Mieczysław, 176

Kątksi, Apolinary, 175
Kavanagh, Patrick, 208
Kedourie, Elie, 4
Kennedy, David, 213
Kennedy-Fraser, Marjory, 213
Kerman, Joseph, 1, 198, 209
Kiberd, Declan, 200
Kireyevsky, Ivan, 107–8
Klindworth, Karl, 45
Knappertsbusch, Hans, 246
Købke, Christen, 132
Kodály, Zoltán, 18, 22, 24
Kohn, Hans, 3, 4, 125
Kolberg, Oskar, 174
Koppen, Erwin, 239
Kozeluch, Johann, 218, 220
Krafft-Ebing, Richard von, 57
Krasiński, Zygmunt, 170
Kraszewski, Józef Ignacy, 167, 174–5, 177
Krøyer, Peder Severin, 132–3
Kun, Béla, 22

La Borde, Jean-Benjamin De, 88
Laforgue, Jules, 247–8, 249
Lalo, Pierre, 85, 192
Landstad's *Norske Folkeviser*, 157–8
Lang, Paul Henry, 7
L'Art musical, 78
Lavignac, Albert, 86
Lavoix, H., 90
Le Bon, Gustave, 55
Leclerc, Jean Bapiste, 206–7
Lee, Joe, 207
Lehmann, A.G., 249
Lelewel, Joachim, 165
Lendvai, E., 27
Leoncavallo, Ruggero, 191
Leopardi, Giacomo, 184
Lévi-Strauss, Claude, 57
l'Isle Adam, Villiers de, 248–9
Liszt, Franz, 20–1, 28, 45, 110
Lithuania, 176
Lucas, Stanley, 40
Luther, Martin, 78

Mac a'Ghobhainn, 222–3
MacCunn, Hamish, 213–15
Macfarren, George, 41

Mackenzie, Alexander, 34, 46, 224–5, 229
Mackeson, Charles, 40
Macmillan's Magazine, 38
Maczewski, A., 38, 44
Mahler, Gustav, 120, 131–2, 140n
Maistre, Joseph de, 73
Malczewski, Antoni, 167
Malinowski, Bronisław, 53, 66
Malipiero, Gianfrancesco, 193
Mallarmé, Stéphane, 11, 158
  influence of Wagner, 239, 249–53
Mann, Heinrich, 242–3, 244, 248
Mann, Thomas, 11
  Der Tod in Venedig, 240
  exiled following Wagner speech, 246–7
  influence of Wagner, 239, 240–3, 244–7, 248
  'Leiden und Größe Richard Wagners', 244–6
Manns, August, 35
Manzoni, Alessandro, 184
Mapleson, James, 33
'Marseillaise', 73
Marx, A.B., 9, 110
Massenet, Jules, 192
Mazzini, Giuseppe, 182, 184, 186, 190, 201
Mazzucato, Gian Andrea, 44
Meinecke, Friedrich, 3
Mendelssohn, Felix, 34, 46
Ménestrel, Le, 72, 88
Metastasio, Pietro, 188, 189
Metternich, Klemens, 169
Meyerbeer, Giacomo, 174, 191
Mhac an tSaoi, Maire, 202
Michelet, Jules, 75
Mickiewicz, Adam, 53, 167, 169, 174, 259
Milan Conservatory, 44
Mill, John Stuart, 34, 43
Miller, Mina F., 123–4
Miłosz, Czesław, 59
Mistral, Frédéric, 85
Mochnacki, Maurycy, 163, 165, 168, 171
Moeran, Ernest, 206
Moffat, Alfred, 226–7
Monaldi, Gino, 184
Mondrian, Piet, 26

Moniuszko, Stanisław
  career, 166
  Halka, 163, 165, 167–73
  and national school, 173–5
  nationalism, 163, 170–7
  Śpiewnik domowy, 166–7
Monteverdi, Claudio, 193
Moore, Thomas, 204–5, 208, 209n, 264, 265, 267
  Irish Melodies, 261, 262, 263
  and Irish nationalism, 258, 259–60, 261–3
Moréas, Papadiamantopoulos, 249
Morley, John, 42
Morley, Thomas, 39
Mosse, George L., 57, 60
Mozart, Wolfgang Amadeus, 46, 189, 193
  Ein musikalischer Spaß, 143
Muir, Thomas, 222
Münchner Neueste Nachrichten, 246
Music and Society: The Politics of Composition, Performance, and Reception, 197–8
Musica, 88
Musical Antiquarian Society, 39
musical dictionaries, 37–8, *see also Dictionary of Music and Musicians*
musical nationalism, 1–2, 8, 10, 12–13, 124–5, 258–9
  analysis of (Leclerc), 206–7
  and choral singing, 77–9
  masculinisation of music, 59–61, 74–7, 81, 83, 85, 87, 90, 91, 183
musicology, *see also Dictionary of Music and Musicians*
  critical approach to, 197–9
  and evolutionary theory, 43
  methodology, 6–7, 8–9, 35
  and nationalism, 6–10
Mussorgsky, Modest Petrovich, 104, 106–7, 110, 117

Nairn, Tom, 236
Nairne, Caroline, 227, 228, 229
  'The Land o' the Leal', 225–7
Nation, The, 263
National Training School of Music, 38, 40, 47n

nationalism
  cultural, 3, 4–5, 6, 12–13
  definitions of, 181
  and ethnicity, 1, 5–6
  and musical culture, 1–2, 12–13
  and musicology, 6–10
  and national frontiers, 17, 51–2, 56–8, 64, 65
  political, 1, 3–4, 6, 8, 12–13, 73, 91, 125
  and statehood, 5
  theories of, 2–6
Nationalist Socialist Hungarian Workers' Party, 18
Nerval, Gérard de, 80
New Grove Dictionary of Music and Musicians, 1
Nicolodi, Fiamma, 85
Nielsen, Carl
  association with poetry, 126–7, 129
  attachment to soil, 134–5
  comparison with Hammershøi, 132–4
  elementalisation, 128–9, 131–2, 134, 139
  Genrebillede, 129–32, 134, 139
  Har Dagen sanket al sin Sorg, 126–9, 131, 132, 139
  Min fynske barndom, 134–5
  music neglected, 123–4, 125–6
  Sinfonia Espansiva, 135–9
Nietzsche, Friedrich, 62, 63, 74, 228, 240, 244
Nisard, Charles, 80
Norway
  folk music, 156–8, 159, 162
  language, 160–2
  music peripheralised, 123, 125–6
  musical nationalism, 159–62
Noskowski, Zygmunt, 174
Nowaczyński, Tadeusz, 166

Oakely, Herbert, 41
O'Brien, Conor Cruise, 200, 201
Odyniec, Antoni Edward, 167
Oehlenschläger, Adam, 134
opera, 258
  in British musical tradition, 33–4
  and Italian nationalism, 181, 182–9, 191, 192–3, 258–9
  opéra comique, 72, 74, 84, 85, 87
  Wagner's reform of, 45–6, 243, 245

Orange Standards, 234
Ouseley, Frederick, 35, 41

Pacini, Giovanni, 185
Paris, Gaston, 81, 83
Parry, Hubert, 35, 42–4, 45, 46
Pater, Walter, 60, 61, 62
Pater, William, 35–6
Pauer, David, 44
Pauer, Ernst, 35, 44
Pearse, Padraic, 201
Pearson, Roger, 251
Pederson, Sanna, 9
Péladin, Joséphin, 74
Peterson-Berger, Wilhelm, 245, 246
Petrie, George, 203–4, 265
Pfitzner, Hans, 246
Philosophies of Music History, 7–8
Piłsudski, Józef, 51–2
Pius IX, Pope, 184, 188
Planard, Eugène de, 72
Plato, 53, 54, 59–60, 61, 65, 77, 79
Platti, Giovanni, 193
Pohl, Ferdinand, 38, 42, 44, 46
Pol, Wincenty, 167
Poland
    art modernism, 53
    comparison with Ireland, 5, 259–60
    ethnicity, 164
    folk culture, 58–9, 62, 166, 171, 176
    Galicia uprising, 164, 169–70
    German influence on music, 165
    literature, 163, 167, 168, 259–60
    Messianism, 171–2, 173, 174
    national frontiers, 51–2, 56–8, 64, 65
    national school, 173–5
    national style, 165–6, 167
    nationalism, 5, 51–2, 56, 61, 63–5, 66, 163–4, 170–7
    typology of, 164–5
    peasant culture, 163, 164–5, 168, 169–70, 172, 173
    Romanticism, 163, 164, 166–7, 170
    Young Poland, 163, 175–7
Pole, William, 41
Poliński, Aleksander, 176
Poole, Mary Ellen, 80
Potter, Pamela M., 7–8
Prout, Ebenezer, 41

Przegląd Naukowy, 168
Przybyszewski, Stanisław, 57
Puccini, Giacomo, 193, 242
Purcell, Henry, 39
Pushkin, Aleksander, 106
Pyne, Louisa (Fanny), 33

Rákóczi March, 29
Ránki, G., 17
Rask, Rasmus, 135
Renan, Ernest, 4, 73, 75, 77, 86, 181
Revue wagnérienne, La, 247, 248–9, 250
Reynolds, Anne-Marie, 126, 131
Richter, Hans, 35
Riemann, Hugo, 7
Rimbaud, Arthur, 249
Rimbault, Edward Francis, 39
Rimsky-Korsakov, Nikolai, 107, 108–9, 110, 116, 120
Rockstro, William, 41, 42, 46–7, 48n
Roesner, Linda, 112
Romania, 17, 19
Rooke, William, 263
Ropartz, Joseph, 88
Rosa, Carl, 33, 39
Rossini, Gioacchino, 185, 187, 189, 190
Rostovtzeff, Mikhail, 57
Rousseau, Jean Jacques, 5, 80–1, 86, 89
Royal Academy of Music, 40
Royal College of Music, 40, 44, 47n
Royal Society of Arts, 38
Rudziński, Witold, 169
Rumph, Stephen, 9
Rushdie, Salman, 64
Ruskin, John, 36, 43
Russell, J.S., 38
Russia, 90
    Bolshevik revolution, 17, 51, 52
    character of national music, 104, 105, 107, 109, 117, 118–19, 120–1
    cultural nationalism, 105–6
    folk music, 26, 106, 108, 119
    language and nationalism, 105–7
    literature and nationalism, 104, 105–6, 107
    musical nationalism, 104–5, 106, 117–21
    national identity, 58, 107–8
    symphonic development, 104, 105, 106, 108–9, 115–18

influence of Schumann, 111–12, 118, 120
and Western values, 107–8
Rutini, G.M., 193

Sacred Harmonic Society, 39, 40
Said, Edward, 225
Sainsbury's *Dictionary of Musicians*, 37
St Mark's College, Chelsea, 41
Saint-Saëns, Camille, 86, 87–8
Saintsbury, George, 204
Samson, Jim, 172, 260
Sandvik, Ole, 157
Sayn Wittgenstein, Princess Carolyne von, 21
Schneider, Louis, 85
Schoenberg, Arnold, 23, 25–6, 27, 126, 128
Schola Cantorum, 84, 85
Scopenhauer, Arthur, 244
Schubert, Franz, 38, 46, 245
Schumann, Clara, 38
Schumann, Robert, 46, 90, 110, 113, 131, 245, 260
  influence on Russian composers, 111–12, 118, 120
  musical themes, 111–12, 118
Schünemann, Georg, 9
Schuré, Edouard, 85
Scotland
  Anglicisation of culture, 215–16
  Battle of Bannockburn, 216–17, 233
  'Bruce's Address', 213–16, 218–19, 221, 222–3, 224, 230, 231, 232
    alternative versions of, 225–7, 233–5, 236
  Chartism, 222, 223
  Jacobitism, 222, 224, 230–1
  Highland Clearances, 222, 225
  musical nationalism, 212–13, 222–4, 235–6, *see also* 'Bruce's Address'
  musical tradition and Viennese style, 220–1
  national song, 213–21, 223, 235–6, *see also* 'Bruce's Address'
  Orangeism, 234–5
  Radicalism, 222, 223, 224, 228, 233, 234
  Romanticism, 224–9
  union with Britain, 212, 231, 232

Scott, Sir Walter, 224–5, 228
Scottish Friends of the People, 222
Scruton, Roger, 60
Seafield, Earl of, 212
Serpette, Gaston, 75
sexuality in music, 52–4, 56, 57, 59–61, 68n, 240, 247
Shaw, George Bernard, 199, 201
Sheehan, James J., 9
Showalter, Elaine, 56–7
Sibelius, Jean, 124, 126, 135, 136, 140n
Sieyès, Abbé, 73
Sikorski, Józef, 175
Skinner, Captain, 233
Słowacki, Juliusz, 170
Smetana, Bedřich, 25, 176
Smith, Anthony, 1, 2, 3, 5–6
Smith, Robert Archibald, 232–3
Smith, William, 38
Société Nationale de Musique, 72
Society for the Preservation and Publication of the Melodies of Ireland, 204
Solera, Temistocle, 187
'Sons Whose Sires with William Bled', 234–5
Soubies, Albert, 89, 90
Spencer, Herbert, 43
Spiess, Stefan, 53
Spitta, Philip, 44, 46
Squire, William Barclay, 40, 42
Staël, Madame de, 73
Stainer, John, 41
Stainer and Barrett's *A Dictionary of Musical Terms*, 37
Stanford, Sir Charles, 33, 34, 35, 42, 44, 46, 205, 268
Stanley, Dean, 38
Stein, Heinrich, 9
Steiner, George, 259
Stendhal, 81, 90
Stephen, Leslie, 42
Sterndale Bennett, James R., 41–2
Sterndale Bennett, William, 35, 40, 41
Sternheim, Carl, 243–4
Stevens, Denis, 198
Stevenson, Sir John, 205, 262
Stewart, Robert Prescott, 41, 204
Stoker, Bram, 68n
Stone, William, 42

Stradling, R., 33, 35
Strauß, Ludwig, 35
Strauss, Richard, 28, 176, 246
Stravinsky, Igor, 26, 31n, 71n, 140n, 142, 152
Sturlason, Snorri, 134
Subotnik, Rose Rosengard, 198
Sullivan, Sir Arthur, 38, 39, 41, 46
Synge, John Millington, 257, 266–7
Syrokomia, Władysław, 167
Szálasi, Ferenc, 18
Szymanowski, Karol, 11, 176
  constructive power of music, 64–5
  'Efebos', 52–4, 55–6, 58, 59, 62, 64, 66
  King Roger, 58–61, 62, 66
  and nationalism, 61–6
  paneuropeanism, 56, 59, 62–6
  sexuality in compositions, 52–4, 56, 57, 59–61, 68n
  Songs of a Mad Muezzin, 58
  'Symposium', 53, 55
  and Ukrainian culture, 52, 57–8

Tacitus, 82–3
Taneyev, S.I., 116, 118
Tannahill, Robert, 233
Taruskin, Richard, 58, 107
Taylor, Franklin, 42
Taylor, Wanda, 164–5
Tchaikovsky, Pyotr, 25, 45, 116, 117
  Pathétique, 119–20
Thayer, Alexander, 38
Thomas, Ambrose, 84, 192
Thompson's *A Dictionary of Music*, 37
Thomson, George
  A Select Collection of Scottish Airs, 216, 217, 218, 220–1, 224, 229
Thorpe Davie, Cedric, 220
Tiersot, Julien, 80, 81–5, 89
Tone, Theobald Wolfe, 201, 202
Torrefranca, Fausto, 193
Transylvania, 17, 19, 68n
Treitler, Leo, 6
Tuwim, Julian, 58

Ukraine, 51, 52–3, 57–8, 105
United States, 3, 7–8, 91

Vaget, Hans-Rudolf, 241
Valen, Fartein, 159–60

Vaughan Williams, Ralph, 44, 205, 206
Verdi, Giuseppe
  Attila, 187–8, 189
  choruses, 188–9, 191
  early operas, 187–9
  La battaglia di Legnano, 186, 191
  nationalism, 184, 185–9, 190–1
  views on German symphonism, 192
Viardot, Pauline, 75
Victor Emmanuel II, King of Piedmont, 186
Vigoureux, Elise, 90
Viollet-le-Duc, 83
Vogue, La, 249

Wagner, Richard, 11, 28, 77, 80, 84–5, 89, 90, 176, 190, 191
  adoption by Nazis, 239, 247
  Die Meistersinger, 243–4
  Die Walküre, 87, 241–2
  Der Ring des Nibelungen, 45, 241
  eroticism of music, 240, 247
  essays, 46
  Festival in London, 45
  Germanness of, 245–6
  Gesamtkunstwerk, 250, 251
  influence on Mallarmé, 239, 249, 250–3
  influence on Mann, 239, 240–3, 244–7, 248
  leitmotif, 240–1, 248
  masculinity of work, 74
  Mein Leben, 240
  nationalism of, 244, 245–6, 259
  Oper und Drama, 84
  Parsifal, 45
  prejudice against in Italy, 192–3
  reform of opera, 45–6, 243, 245
  Revue wagnérienne, La, 247, 248–9, 250
  and Symbolist movement, 239–40, 247–9, 251
  Tristan und Isolde, 240, 241
Walicki, Aleksander, 175
Walicki, Andrzej, 164, 171
Walker, Joseph Cooper, 262, 263
Wallace, Sir William, 223, 229, 232, 234
Warsaw Philarmonic Hall, 175
'Waterloo', 233
Weber, Carl Maria von, 8, 46, 220
Weber, Max, 124

Weber, William, 9
Weckerlin, Jean-Baptiste, 80, 81, 83, 85
Weisshaus, Imre, 26
Werner, Zacharias, 187
Wilde, Oscar, 55
Wilhelm II, Kaiser, 239, 243
Winckelmann, Johann, 60
Winkler, Heinrich August, 3
Witkiewicz, Stanisław, 53–4, 66
Witwicki, Stefan, 167
Wolff, Janet, 198

Wolski, Włodzimierz, 168, 172, 173
Wolzogen, Hans von, 239
Wuiet, Caroline, 87
Wyzéwa, Théodor de, 247, 249

Xenephon, 61

Yeats, W.B., 203, 266, 267

Żeleński, Władysław, 174
Zelter, Carl, 9, 10